AF504002

Expanded Animation

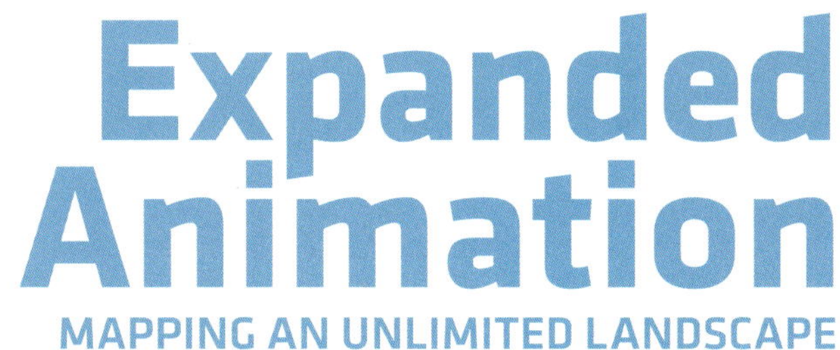

MAPPING AN UNLIMITED LANDSCAPE

Edited by Juergen Hagler / Michael Lankes / Alexander Wilhelm

Expanded Animation Anthology
Mapping an Unlimited Landscape

Editors: Juergen Hagler, Michael Lankes, Alexander Wilhelm

Editing: University of Applied Sciences Upper Austria, Ars Electronica

Translations: Laura Freeburn

Copyediting: Aimee Levitt, Laura Freeburn, Wolfgang Hochleitner

Graphic design and production: Elmar Glaubauf

Cover illustration: Alexander Wilhelm, Martina Stiftinger

Typeface: Klavika

Printed by: Gutenberg-Werbering Gesellschaft m.b.H, Linz

Paper: Magno Volume 1,1 Vol., 115 g/m², 300 g/m²

Published by
Hatje Cantz Verlag GmbH
Mommsenstrasse 27
10629 Berlin
Germany
Tel. +49 30 3464678-00
Fax +49 30 3464678-29
www.hatjecantz.com
A Ganske Publishing Group company

Hatje Cantz books are available internationally at selected bookstores. For more information
about our distribution partners please visit our homepage at www.hatjecantz.com

ISBN 978-3-7757-4525-3

Printed in Austria

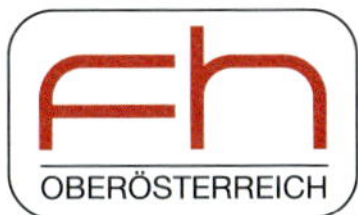

ARS ELECTRONICA

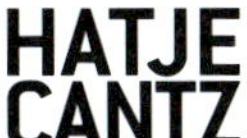

HATJE
CANTZ

Gerfried Stocker (AT)

Preface

When the first Ars Electronica Festival for art, technology and society took place 40 years ago, the scientist and computer artist Herbert W. Franke played a leading role. He was an early pioneer of computer graphics in Europe and a visionary thinker about the profound and, as we say nowadays, disruptive changes that would come about through the spread of computers in our culture.

In his introductory text for the catalog of the first Ars Electronica Festival, he writes in depth about "visual computer art," its beginnings in the 1960s, and the first computer films by James Whitney and Jack Citron; he dedicates an interesting section to "graphic music" and makes some very informative and cutting-edge connections to kinetic art. However, in the course of many pages he uses the term "computer animation" itself only once. There he writes:

Finally, the successes achieved by the Americans in "computer animation" are astonishing. Today, programs are available that make it possible to render every conceivable object – even one that does not actually exist – as a realistic represen-

tation. All that is needed is a description of the shape, e.g. by entering spatial coordinates; then it appears on the screen, three-dimensional, with correct perspective, from any angle and in any kind of motion. There is also a choice of different surface forms, such as smooth, corrugated, or transparent; even reflections of an assumed environment and the phenomena of optical refraction are automatically calculated with transparency and represented according to the underlying form of the object. This is also a step towards perfection of the technology of illusion, with which non-existent fantasy worlds can be fabricated for the public.

In making his connections to kinetic art, the "moving works of art," he pursues an idea that was to become (although only much later) perhaps one of the most important aspects of computer art—interactivity—and expresses regret that the *viewer must be satisfied with recording the processes that are presented and has no opportunity to intervene* and continues by introducing great expectations for future computer art:

Information technology and cybernetics are creating a whole new state of affairs here: works of art can be conceived as automata that evolve their own activity or react to actions by the audience. Objects of this kind are considered "cybernetic art."

And vaguely (in accordance with the state of development in the 1970s) but convincingly, he predicts that it will be the expansion and connection of these two aspects—the completely new possibilities for visual simulation and animation and the "bidirectional communication" between work and observer—that represent the great potential for the future. How right he was. As in all other areas where digital technologies are used, the field of "visual computer art" is exploding. It has branched off in many independent and heterogenous directions and become inextricably intertwined with music, sound and interaction. It is algorithmic, auto-generative and now learns on its own. Add to this the easy availability of inexpensive soft and hardware and a still growing number of educational institutions that are revealing multitudes of talented young people.

Today, 40 years later, we might ask how many young people even think of the good old hand-drawn animated films from Walt Disney or Hanna-Barbera Studios when they hear the word animation, with computer-generated imagery having become a ubiquitous matter of course. Meanwhile, the expected "perfection of illusion technology" has become the actual impossibility of recognizing digital simulations or manipulations with the naked eye.

From the little animations designed to help us pass the time while booting up or downloading to the gigantic technological battles of modern movies, from elaborate data visualizations, to epic computer games, to breathtaking imaging methods in medical technology, digital images are expanded, boundless, and omnipresent.

To return to the first Ars Electronica Festival, it is interesting that the passage quoted above remains the only instance of the term "computer animation," which later became so popular, in the many pages of the first Ars c atalog, although the catalog contains a comprehensive discussion of the contingency of the new electronic and digital forms of imaging and image generation. The explanation may be that, as so often happens with technological developments, the time before they can be practically applied is always a phase of far-reaching visions that are then captured and narrowed by the commercial reality of consumer markets. This broad spectrum and potentiality of new possibilities must be rediscovered and redeveloped now that digital image production has been established even in the mainstream film, entertainment, and advertising industry. It is only in this expansion, which does not merely explore new possibilities but also lays claim to an elevated artistic interpretation of the possibilities of a new medium and its forms of expression, that we will find the true core of a new medium or a new form of art.

This book is therefore fully consistent with the tradition of Ars Electronica and the early thought leaders of a "computer culture."

As the result of a successful collaboration between Ars Electronica and the University of Applied Science Upper Austria, Hagenberg Campus and many international experts from the arts and sciences, the book is, to all intents and purposes, the essence of the Expanded Animation symposia that have been taking place since 2013. A series of events which, as the discursive center of the Ars Electronica Animation Festival, have made it their goal to explore the far-reaching potential of technological and artistic development of computer animation and digital film, to think ahead from the status quo and to add artistic and content-related visions to its commercial applications.

The range and expertise of the artists gathered here, along with the fascinating examples of artistic practice, represent an outstanding bridge between the power of storytelling with moving images and the still-expansive horizons of computer culture.

For the foreseeable future, we will be part of a culture completely dominated by images and visual communication. The artistic practices described in this book will be an essential foundation for the cultural inheritance and remembrance of our time.

Contents

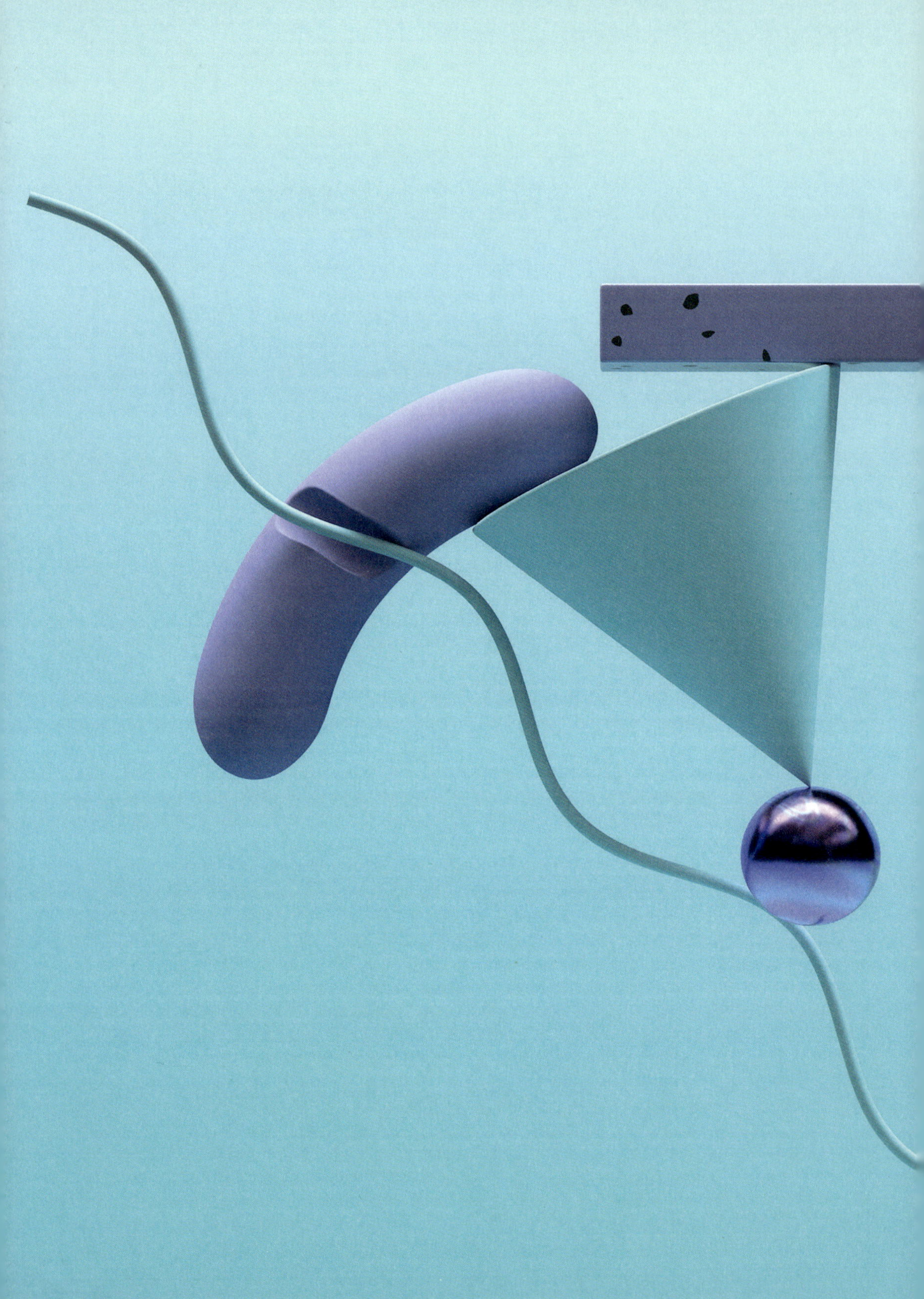

Introduction:
Expanded Animation

Mapping an Unlimited Landscape

Juergen Hagler (AT) | Michael Lankes (AT) | Alexander Wilhelm (AT)

Introduction

Animation has become a pervasive element in contemporary moving image culture[1] and in our daily lives, at times visibly recognizable as a simulation and at others almost indistinguishable from real-world content. Since the digital shift, the manifestations of animation have expanded and the definitions have become unstable.[2] Meanwhile, moving pictures created with computer technology constitute a very diverse spectrum, particularly in hybrid forms, and are products of highly interdisciplinary collaborative activities of individuals from the worlds of industry, research, art, and science. In this unlimited domain, animation is ubiquitous and yet simultaneously undifferentiated. Any attempt to develop a concept of computer animation requires close examination of this dynamic and constantly expanding field.

Over the last 40 years, Ars Electronica has tackled this issue and discussed animation in the context of media arts. Since 2013, the University of Applied Sciences Upper Austria, Hagenberg Campus and Ars Electronica have organized the symposium "Expanded Animation," which aims to address the traversal of borders, hybrid forms, and fringe areas within the field of computer animation. Based on various approaches to that topic, this book contributes to the discussion, focusing on current positions of Expanded Animation in media arts. The book summarizes the examinations presented in the six symposium editions from 2013 to 2018, including theoretical and artist perspectives. It also features a selection of current artworks.

The first chapter reviews and discusses the six editions of the symposium *Expanded Animation*. This recap is preceded by an introduction to the concept of Expanded Animation and its roots in Expanded Cinema as well as the discussions on that topic at Ars Electronica. The following section provides a selection of six theoretical perspectives. In *Stan VanDerBeek: From Collage Film to Cybernetic Cinema* Ulrich Wegenast introduces the reader to the complex work of the American artist VanDerBeek, who developed a multitude of concepts ranging from subversive underground film, immersive dome cinemas and global networks to media performances and computer films. In *Paracinema and the Dematerialization of Animation* Birgitta

---

1 Suzanne Buchan, "introduction. pervasive animation," in *Pervasive Animation*, edited by Suzanne Buchan (New York and London, 2013), pp. 1–21.
2 Chris Gehman and Steve Reinke, "Introduction," in *The Sharpest Point: Animation at the End of Cinema*, edited by Chris Gehman and Steve Reinke (Toronto, 2005), p. 7.

Hosea reflects on one strand of expanded cinema—the concept of paracinema coined by film theorist Jonathan Walley—by considering the expanded work of VALIE EXPORT and Anthony McCall. Juergen Hagler writes in *Anomalies at the Intersection of Animation, Media Art and Technology* about how to distinguish different types of animation anomalies, ranging from deconstruction, self-critical reflection, to stereoscopy, virtual reality (VR) or artificial intelligence (AI). These anomalies at the interface of animation, media art, and technology could offer novel qualities that can foster developments in science, art and economy. The aim of Franziska Bruckner's paper: *Virtual Hybrid Image, Virtual Hybrid Montage: Notes on the Hybridization of Live Action and Animation within Virtual Reality Environments* is to identify potentials and challenges of animated content in virtual reality environments via a method of film analysis designed for animation-film studies.

Rupturing Visions: Towards an Expanded Stereoscopy by Max Hattler investigates the potential of stereoscopic imagery to create experiences for the audience that go beyond the mere re-creation of three-dimensional space, creating visual ruptures as well as confusion in spatial perception. *Radical Action and Pure Joy: David OReilly's Video Game Everything in the Context of Game Art, Art History, and a new Gamic Avant-garde* by Stephan Schwingeler discusses OReilly's *Everything* from different perspectives and situates it in art history. The game serves as an example for a new form of radical gameplay, being one of the first games to embrace the potentialities of videogames as artistic and hybrid material. Diana Arellano describes in her article *The Other Face of Animation* the work that she and her colleagues have done in the field of facial character animation at the Animationsinstitut, Filmakademie Baden-Württemberg.

The next section features six artist perspectives that are traversing the borders of art, science, and play. From the perspective of a visual artist, Markos Kay explores the intersection of art and science in his work *Simulating Scientific Observation* in order to create public engagement with scientific theory through a visual communication approach. Abigail Addison presents the project *Silent Signal*, six experimental animated artworks that explore novel approaches to thinking about the human body and the signals that enable the bodies to operate and to adapt in order to fight disease. The contribution *Bringing Art to Everyday: Media Art Nexus NTU Singapore in Review 2016–18*, written by Ina Conradi and Mark Chavez looks at the emergence of the *Art on Campus* initiative at

Nanyang Technological University Singapore and at the roles of the artists who led the urban media platform, also known as the Media Art Nexus (MAN). The article *gold extra: Endeavors in Artistic Diversity* by Reinhold Bidner, Sonja Prlic and Karl Zechenter details their work in the artist group gold extra by describing the group's use of animation and the role it plays in a collaborative artistic process. In the contribution *Now You Touch it, Now You Don't: Experiments in Virtual Interfaces,* Anezka Sebek presents a variety of interface experiments made by her graduate students. Their experiments raise several questions, such as how an interface is felt or how people experience the stories embedded in VR. In I*mages between Digital Realism and Analog Believability* Virgil Widrich addresses the combination of analog and digital film techniques, which he sees as an unexplored treasure to create entirely different images that make no pretense at realism, but become precise through their abstraction. The last section, *Expanded Animation: Selection of Ars Electronica 2011–2018* features a compilation of 41 projects that illustrate current positions. All selected projects were presented at the Ars Electronica Festival, for instance exhibited at Ars Electronica Center or at the CyberArts exhibition, screened at the Ars Electronica Animation Festival or featured at the Deep Space 8K. Of these, about two thirds were male artists, and one third consisted of female artists and groups of male and female artists. The selection also includes 7 Golden Nica winners, 7 Award of Distinction winners, and 19 Honorary Mentions. In total, 28 artists were invited as speakers at the Expanded Animation symposium. The selection comprises a wide range of experimental contributions in an interdisciplinary field at the nexus of art, industry, R&D, and science, including hybrid-blending elements of animation, computer gaming, theater and performance, projection mappings, media façades, site-specific installations, trans-media projects, interactive and reactive works, or VR experiences.

In spite of the vast spectrum, some evolving trends can be noted: first, many works follow the main idea of expanded cinema that regards moving images as an art form in the context of media art or contemporary art. Many of these are exhibits presented in galleries and museums, in site-specific installations or in performances commissioned by art festivals, concerts or public events. This is not a new trend, as these tendencies have been significantly evident in the Prix category Computer Animation in the last two decades. The first example in the presented selection is the video installation *Flux* (2011) by Candaş Şişman, commissioned by Plato Art Space, given an Honorary Mention in 2011. In the following years, four installations were awarded with a Golden Nica: *Rear Window Loop* (2012) by Jeff Desom, a multichannel installation showing a found footage collage of Alfred Hitchcock's classic film Rear Window, *Forms* (2013) by Quayola & Memo Akten, an abstract motion sculpture, *Walking City* (2014) by Universal Everything, a museum installation that formally scrutinizes the human walk cycle, and *Idle Times / Temps Mort* (2015), by Alex Verhaest. The last-mentioned artwork consists of multiple interactive screens and can be considered a prime example for interactive artworks in the context of animation. The selection presents various forms of works on the blurring border between computer animation, playful installations, and interactive art like *Augmented Hand Series* (2015), by Golan Levin and his team, or the game *Everything* (2017) by David OReilly. In the realm of expanded cinema, various new presentation forms that go beyond the conventional screens, such as projection mappings, media façades, or experimental devices like *Light Barrier 3rd Edition* (2017) by Kimchi and Chips, are among the selection.

Furthermore, there are various examples of hybrids between the analog and digital world, ranging from experimental approaches like *Rediscovery of Anima* (2018) by Akinori Goto without any digital technology, to common hybrids between traditional and digital technologies (e.g., impressively demonstrated by Boris Labbé's recent animated short movies). Beyond that, various experimental works are exhibited that utilize new digital technologies like drones, VR, AI, or real-time technologies. The selected VR works in animation show a broad range of application, from 360° videos to interactive installations, like James Paterson's animation software *Norman* (2018).

This selection explores the fringes of computer animation and of course, the question arises of whether some of these artworks can be considered part of the expanded field of animation or whether the artists themselves would place their work in that category. Many artworks defy categorization and comparison and are unique in their kind. However, as the evolution of Prix Ars Electronica illustrates, boundaries within computer animation, interactive art, sound art, and hybrid art are blurring. For instance, the oeuvre of Irish artist John Gerrard is primarily a work of contemporary art. As the artist utilizes new animation technology for his creations, like motion capture, real-time technology or simulation software, several of his installations, such as *Western Flag* (2018), are prime examples for expanded digital animation. Another vivid example is Golan Levin, who won awards in the Prix Ars Electronica category Computer Animation as well in Hybrid Art, Interactive Art and Net Vision / Net Excellence.

Many of the works presented here serve as a basis for the articles in the previous sections.

Franziska Bruckner analyzes the VR experiences *Out of Exile* (2017) and *Zero Days VR* (2017). Juergen Hagler's analysis of artistic anomalies is based on many of the presented works and further examples from Prix Ars Electronica's category Computer Animation. Max Hattler's article discusses the experimental and expanded stereoscopy found in many artworks that were exhibited at Ars Electronica (e.g., *The Chimera of M.* (2013) by Sebastian Buerkner or *Shadowland* (2014) by Kazuhiro Goshima). Markos Kay gives an insight into his artistic work and Stephan Schwingeler's article centers on the game *Everything* by David OReilly. The selection offered here fits in perfectly as a supplement to the theoretical and artistic perspectives.

Juergen Hagler (AT) | Michael Lankes (AT) | Alexander Wilhelm (AT)

6 Years of Expanded Animation Symposium

Mapping an Unlimited Landscape

The point of departure for exploring the unlimited landscape of expanded animation was the idea to invite international experts to the University of Applied Science Upper Austria, Hagenberg Campus[1] to provide an inspiring program about current trends in digital animation in an interdisciplinary context for students in the Department of Digital Media. In a further step, a more international scientific exchange on animation at the university was established. Taking into account the ongoing and vibrant discussion on animation after the digital shift at the media festival Ars Electronica Linz,[2] the core topic "Expanded Digital Animation" was introduced. Since computer animation has been an important part of the media festival since it began, it was therefore an obvious choice to get Gerfried Stocker, artistic director of Ars Electronica, on board. With his input the idea was born, to host a symposium on the expanded field of computer animation, closely connected to Prix Ars Electronica's category Computer Animation.[3] The symposium should broach the issue of transcending borders, hybrid forms and fringe areas within the field of computer animation and should feature theoretical and artistic views in equal measure. In a series of panels, filmmakers, artists, researchers, and curators addressed current positions regarding the crossing of boundaries in the field of animation. The symposium is open to all artists, producers, academics, students, and pioneers who are interested in navigating the unknown terrain of computer animation. Due to its scheduling in conjunction with the Ars Electronica festival, it aims to offer a highly relevant setting and an excellent foundation for profound reflections on potential approaches to this expanding field.

Context Expanded Animation

A wide range of strategies originates from the term "expanded" in the context of animation. Within the discussion on animation studies, various scholars portray animation as part of an extended field. Alan Cholodenko, for instance, classified a limited and an

---

1 University of Applied Science Upper Austria, Hagenberg Campus, https://www.fh-ooe.at/campus-hagenberg/ (accessed April 10, 2019).

2 Ars Electronica, https://ars.electronica.art/news/ (accessed April 10, 2019).

3 In 1987 the category started with the title *Computer Animation*. From 1998–2006 the category was entitled *Computer Animation / Visual Effects* and form 2007–2017 *Computer Animation / Film / Visual Effects*. Since 2018 the category's name is again *Computer Animation*.

expanded field in the anthology *The Illusion of Life 2: More Essays on Animation*.[4] The latter focuses more on computer-generated images (CGI), video games, flight simulation, and animation within a broader interdisciplinary perspective. In recent years, the term "expanded animation" has been used by several researchers and artists: Birgitta Hosea operates a blog "Expanded Animation"[5] dealing with many intersections, such as art and performance. Siegfried Zielinski introduces a generalized notion of the term to examine an expanded concept of animation, ranging from philosophy and religion to science and art.[6] In 2018, Vicky Smith and Nicky Hamlyn published the Anthology *Experimental and Expanded Animation*,[7] which can be considered a new edition of Robert Russett's and Cecile Starr's book *Experimental Animation*[8] from 1976. The concept of expanded animation primarily refers to expanded cinema, which was developed in the late 1960s by researchers and artists like Sheldon Renan[9] or Stan VanderBeek,[10] as well as Austrian protagonists VALIE EXPORT, Peter Weibel, or Hans Scheugel and Ernst Schmidt.[11]

"Erweitertes Kino" ist alles was über die kino-übliche Filmprojektion hinausgeht, reicht also von der Mehrfachprojektion bis zur Utopie von Pillenfilmen und Wolkenprojektionen ... sowie von der Verbindung mit anderen Medien ... bis zum filmischen Environment. Expanded Cinema ist der Versuch, die Grenzen der Filmleinwand zu sprengen ....[12]

---

4 Alan Cholodenko, *The Illusion of Life 2: More Essays on Animation* (Sydney, 2007).

5 "Expanded Animation. Expanding ideas about animation," (blog) https://expandedanimation.net (accessed April 10, 2019).

6 Siegfried Zielinski, "Expanded Animation – A Short Genealogy in Words and Images." in *Pervasive Animation*, edited by Suzanne Buchan (New York and London, 2013), pp. 25–51.

7 Vicky Smith and Nicky Hamlyn, eds., *Experimental and Expanded Animation: Origins of a New Art* (New York, 1976).

8 Cf. Robert Russett and Cecil Starr, *Experimental Animation: An Illustrated Anthology* (New York, 1976). Hans Scheugl and Ernst Schmidt, *Eine Subgeschichte des Films. Lexikon des Avantgarde-, Experimental- und Undergroundfilms* (Frankfurt a. M.:, 1974).

9 Sheldon Renan, *An introduction to the American underground film* (New York, 1967).

10 Mark Bartlett, "Socialimagestics and the Visual Acupuncture of Stan Vanberbeek's Expanded Cinema," in *Expanded Cinema: Art, Performance, Film*, edited by A.L. Rees, at al. (London, 2011), p. 50.

11 Hans Scheugl and Ernst Schmidt, *Eine Subgeschichte des Films. Lexikon des Avantgarde-, Experimental- und Undergroundfilms* (Frankfurt a. M.:, 1974).

12 Ibid. p. 253.

"Extended Cinema" is everything that goes beyond conventional movie projection, and therefore ranges from multiple projections to the utopia of pill films and cloud projections … as well as from connection with other media … to the cinematic environment. Expanded Cinema is an attempt to push the boundaries of the movie screen.

Following its initial formulation as a conceptual expansion for what is generally understood as cinema, Gene Youngblood developed a comprehensive concept that was refined and introduced in his book *Expanded Cinema*.[13] Youngblood discusses moving images in media art, including various forms ranging from "computer films" to multi-media environments. Based on these ideas, Robert Russett coined the term "hyperanimation"[14] to address extended manifestations of animation utilizing advanced digital technologies. Russett introduces a variety of artists in the expanded field of animation, including pioneers in computer animation, media art, and VR, like Rebecca Allen, Karl Sims, Jeffrey Shaw, or Roy Ascott. Whereas Russet's examination covers pioneering works of the 80s and 90s, this book features, in particular, current artistic and theoretical perspectives derived from the last ten years of the media art festival Ars Electronica.

Context: Ars Electronica / Computer Animation/ Expanded Cinema

Ars Electronica Linz started hosting conferences, exhibitions, and screenings on media arts including computer animation, graphics and music in 1979. From the beginning, Ars Electronica served as a platform for theory—from humanities to applied sciences—and practice in the field of media arts, based on strong roots in the classical art forms of music, visual arts and film. The first symposia on computer animation in the context of media art took place at the 3rd session of Ars Electronica in 1982.[15] Speakers were well-known media artists like Nam June Paik, Charlotte Moorman or experimental animator and filmmaker Stan Van-

DerBeek. At the same session Herbert Werner Franke, science fiction author and co-founder of Ars Electronica, hosted the "Science Fiction Conference." One panel, entitled SCIENCE FICTION IN PRACTICE: Film, Video, Comics, Music, featured computer animation experts like David Di Francesco and Alvy Ray Smith, both of whom were working at Lucasfilm at that time. In the following years more conferences, workshops and activities on video art and digital filmmaking followed. Among the experts who spoke at the festivals were Peter Weibel, Gene Youngblood, Charles Csuri, VALIE EXPORT or Bazon Brock. Two years later, Weibel and Youngblood underlined the blurring boundaries between video art and artistic computer animation as well as the vivid interfaces to other disciplines like sound art, theatre or interactive art. Weibel outlined the history and aesthetic of digital generated images as well of moving images in the supplement to the 1984 festival catalogue.[16] Gene Youngblood discussed the evolution and future development of digital art and explored the potential of computer generated images in the context of video art.

Combining the apparent objectivity of the photograph, the interpretive subjectivity of the painting and the unrestricted motion of hand animation, three-dimensional computer animation or "digital scene simulation" is by far the most awesome and profound development in the history of symbolic discourse.[17]

In 1987, the festival established the Prix Ars Electronica, a yearly competition in several categories, and started with three disciplines: computer music, graphics, and animation. Since then, the festival has honored excellent works in the field of media arts. The category Computer Animation is one of the oldest ones and therefore offers an excellent archive of artistic computer animation over 30 years.[18] In the last decade, a paradigm shift towards a more artistic and expanded examination of digital animation has taken place.[19]

---

13 Cf. Gene Youngblood, *Expanded Cinema* (New York, 1970).

14 Robert Russett, *Hyperanimation: Digital Images and Virtual Worlds* (United Kingdom, 2009).

15 Otto Piene, "Sky Art Conference," in *ARS ELECTRONICA 82 im Rahmen des Internationalen Brucknerfestes Linz*, edited by LIVA (Linz, 1982).

16 Peter Weibel, *Zur Geschichte und Ästhetik der digitalen Kunst. Supplement zum Katalog Ars Electronica 84* (Linz, 1984).

17 Gene Youngblood, "The Digital Art: A Medium Matures: Video and the Cinematic Enterprise," in *Ars Electronica 84 im Rahmen des Internationalen Brucknerfestes Linz* (Linz, 1984).

18 Ars Electronica Archive, https://archive.aec.at/prix/ (accessed April 10, 2019).

19 Juergen Hagler, "Animation, Kunst und Technologie. Evolution und Expansion am Beispiel Prix Ars Electronica," in *Im Wandel … Metamorphosen der Animation*, edited by Julia Eckel, et al. (Wiesbaden, 2017), pp. 171–185.

2013: Mapping an Unlimited Landscape

In keeping with the motto *Mapping an Unlimited Landscape,* the symposium Expanded Animation was established to reflect on the traversal of borders, hybrid forms, and fringe areas of computer animation. The first symposium took place in 2013 at the art museum LENTOS Linz on the first day of the Ars Electronica Festival. The prelude to this ambitious project was the attempt to map the unlimited landscape of digital animation. That computer animation is expanding and merging with other disciplines is unmistakable. On the one hand, there is an apparent danger for this field to develop into an interdisciplinary fringe domain. On the other, the very fact that it has continually expanded offers substantial potential for a new orientation. What used to be clearly defined boundaries, separating the various types and genres of digital animation, have become blurred.

In the opening speech, Gerfried Stocker emphasized the distinct role of computer animation for Ars Electronica, in particular for the international competition Prix Ars Electronica, and endorsed the initiative as a kind of re-animation of the discourse in the early 1980s. Since 1987, the category *Computer Animation* has discussed animation in media art and, according to Stocker, computer animation as an artistic form that has always been looking for new directions.

The first panel was entitled "Mapping the Landscape: Theory and Art." Suzanne Buchan's keynote was the starting point of the journey into the unlimited frontier. She introduced the recent published book *Pervasive Animation*[20] and opened up the countless possibilities for discussion. A further facet was contributed by artistic positions: Austrian filmmaker and media artist Virgil Widrich talked about moving images between digital realism and analog believability based on his own artistic works at the intersection of experimental film and animation. Referring to his recent work *Exercise*, Irish artist John Gerrard introduced his approach to the spaces of simulation and expanded animation within mainstream contemporary art. The second panel dealt with the collapsing boundaries within performance, interaction, and data narration. Karin Wehn highlighted different ways in which animation is moving in new directions at the intersection between film, games, performance, architecture, media art, comic books, and information visualization. Three further practitioners elucidated specific interfaces: media art-

ist Friedrich Kirschner focused on computer animation in the context of performance, media artist Joreg on real time animation, and Benjamin Wiederkehr on information visualization. The final panel featured current artistic positions addressing the question of how data like human locomotion or scientific data can serve experimental approaches within animation: media artists Memo Akten and Quayola presented their collaborative project *Forms*, Golden Nica winner 2013 in the category Computer Animation. Semiconductors, i.e. the artist duo Ruth Jarman and Joe Gerhardt, gave an insight into their generative works and collaboration with scientists.

Speakers Expanded Animation 2013

Memo Akten (TR) | Suzanne Buchan (CH/GB) | John Gerrard (IE) | Joreg (AT/DE) | Friedrich Kirschner (DE) | Quayola (IT) | Semiconductor – Joe Gerhardt (GB), Ruth Jarman (GB) | Karin Wehn (DE) | Virgil Widrich (AT) | Benjamin Wiederkehr (CH)

2014: Exploring the Vastness of Art, Theory and Play

A distinctive attribute differentiates the winners of the Golden Nica grand prize in the Prix Ars Electronica's Computer Animation category in the last three years from those singled out for recognition prior to that. These three works are not animated films meant to run in a cinema, but rather installations intended for a museum setting where they are screened in a loop. *Rear Window Loop* (Golden Nica 2012) by Jeff Desom is a multichannel installation—a deconstruction of Alfred Hitchcock's classic film *Rear Window*—condensed down to a few minutes of footage. *Forms* (Golden Nica 2013) by Quayola & Memo Akten was commissioned by the National Media Museum for an exhibition entitled *In the Blink of an Eye*. It is an installation consisting of a projection with an additional screen that displays a sort of "making-of" the projected movement studies. *Walking City* (Golden Nica 2014) by Universal Everything is likewise a museum installation that formally scrutinizes the human walk cycle—the foundation of any character animation.

These three works are indicative of a trend in the *Computer Animation* category in particular and in the field of computer animation in general. In addition to classic forms, new varieties have become established—so-called expanded animation that takes

---

20 Suzanne Buchan, "introduction. pervasive animation," in *Pervasive Animation* (New York and London, 2013), pp. 1–21.

leave of the cinema's "black box" for settings such as public squares, museums, and virtual spaces. These animated realms are projection mappings, installations, trans-media projects, interactive and reactive works, media façades, and diverse hybrids blending elements of animation, computer gaming, theater and performance.

The 2nd Expanded Animation symposium continued the examination of the blurring boundaries, leading-edge zones, and hybridization in computer animation. This was once again an effort to shed light on what is happening in the vastness of art, theory, and play.

The first panel was dedicated to current theoretical approaches: Ulrich Wegenast elaborated on areas of tension and interplay among animation, architecture, and game art. Franziska Bruckner introduced film analytical parameters of hybrids of animated filmmaking. The second panel kicks things off on the theoretical side with consideration of diverse artistic positions. While filmmaker Robert Seidel focused on experimental animation, the animation studio Polynoid talked about the synergies and struggles of working as an independent art collective and as a studio for the industry. The collective was honored with a Golden Nica in the category *Computer Animation* in 2006 for the animated short movie *458NM*. Since then, the collective has produced independent animated shorts as well as commissioned work. The third panel addressed the subject of animation at the interface of gaming. The issues under consideration were participation, the transmission of players' actions, and the transference of their personalities into a virtual space, as well as new forms of narration via interaction, presented by game designer Paolo Pedercini and Mario von Rickenbach.

Speakers Expanded Animation 2014

Franziska Bruckner (AT) | Paolo Pedercini (IT) | Polynoid – Csaba Letay (DE), Fabian Pross (DE), Tom Weber (DE) | Mario von Rickenbach (CH) | Robert Seidel (DE) | Ulrich Wegenast (DE)

2015: Deviations and Anomalies at the Intersection of Art and Technology

Expanded Animation has become an important feature within the Ars Electronica Animation Festival lineup and a mainstay of the Ars Electronica Festival as a whole. As an intensive encounter with ongoing technical and aesthetic developments in the digital animation genre, it is therefore an ideal complement to the Prix Forum. After two sessions, the symposium was first hosted under the umbrella of Ars Electronica Animation Festival and expanded to a two-day event. Since then, the new venue CENTRAL Linz, a former movie theater, has served as the hub for all activities connected to computer animation during the Ars Electronica festival. In particular, the third edition focused on what is happening beyond the mainstream: fascinating anomalies and deviations. The subversive use of technology in computer animation has been a prevalent theme ever since, relying on deviations, anomalies, and a deliberate exploitation of flaws. The forms of play and experimentation with animation and technology can be quite diverse.

The Prix Forum provided the prelude to this topic. Together with two top-prize winners, jury member Erick Oh discussed current trends, future developments, and the fringes of digital filmmaking by means of submissions at Prix Ars Electronica. Alex Verhaest presented *Temps Mort / Idle Times*, an interactive installation consisting of various animated portraits that was awarded the Golden Nica. Pascal Floerks gave an insight into his animated short *Bär*, a personal journey into the past of his grandfather. Floerks used found images and replaced his grandfather with a digital bear. At the beginning, the movie is very amusing, but it develops over time into a very emotional retrospective. In the subsequent panel, Roman Tardy presented his views on expanded animation and the poetics of scale. Anezka Sebak showcased current experiments in virtual interfaces at Parsons School of Design, New York. On the second day, Erick Oh showed how he has been using animation as a form of artistic expression and shared his general filmmaking process. Media artist Ina Conradi talked about her artistic work, in particular post-digital paintings that merge the areas of expanded and new cinematic forms, animation, and traditional painting methods for purely artistic expressions. Mark Chavez gave an insight into current research on virtual representation and pseudo-intelligence in virtual characterization. The last panel was dedicated to the main topic: media artist Johannes Poell and Devine lu Linvega explored artistic examinations of real time animation software and experiments on procedural art and its implication for the design and the transformation of the creator. Filmmaker Sebastian Buerkner discussed opportunities, limitations, and strategies of stereoscopic film by means of historical examples as well as of his experimental stereoscopic film *The Chimera of M*.

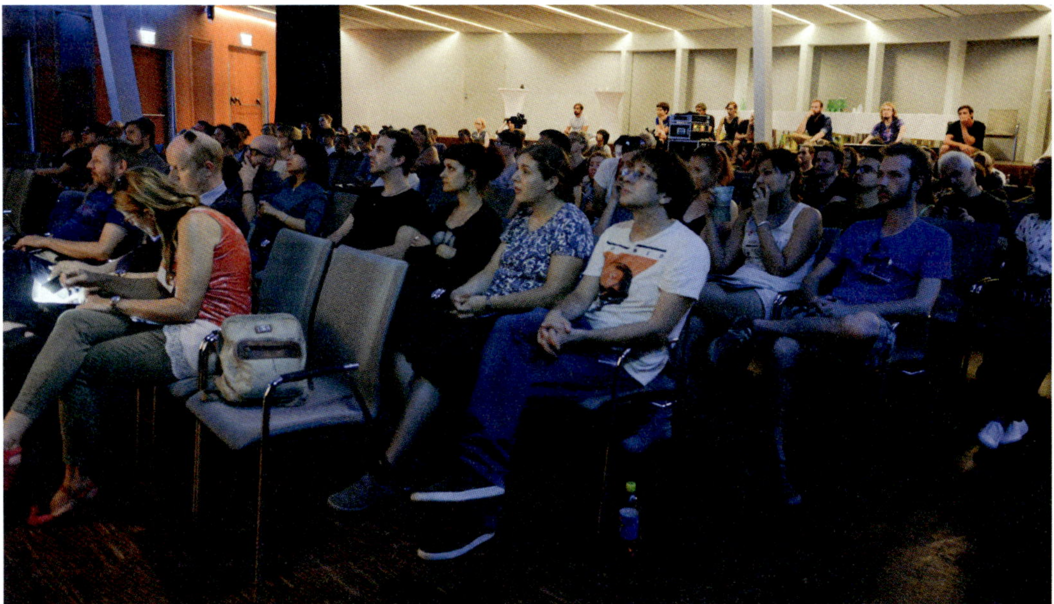

Figure 1: Expanded Animation 2016, Panel: "Art and Industry".

Speakers Expanded Animation 2015

Sebastian Buerkner (DE/GB) | Mark Chavez (US) | Ina Conradi (US/SG) | Pascal Floerks (DE) – Award of Distinction 2015 | Devine Lu Linvega (CA) | Erick Oh (KR) – Juror 2015 | Johannes Poell (AT) | Anezka Sebek (ID/US) | Romain Tardy (FR) | Alex Verhaest (BE) – Golden Nica 2015

2016: The Alchemy of Animation

The fourth symposium was entitled *The Alchemy of Animation* in keeping with the 2016 Festival theme, RADICAL ATOMS and the alchemists of our time. The focus was once again on the fringes of the computer animation field as well as on the reciprocal interaction of animation and technology. The main topics were science, society and industry, which were discussed from a variety of perspectives by three panels made up of animation filmmakers, curators, scientists, and VFX artists. In the beginning, the prizewinners in the Prix Ars Electronica's Computer Animation category, Boris Labbé (Golden Nica) and Yuya Hanai (Award of Distinction) presented their body of work and jury members Marie Liis Rebane and Johannes Friedrich Schiehsl gave an insight into the jury process. The subsequent panel "Art & Science" scrutinized various areas at which animation, art, and science intersect and overlap. Producer and curator Abigail Addison presented *Silent Signal*, a collaborative project by six animation filmmakers and six scientists in the field of biomedicine. This form of cooperation gave rise to experimental works that explored questions concerning new ways of thinking about the human body. Animated visualizations in science and fiction were treated by Erwin Feyersinger, a scholar of film and media. Scholar and software developer Diana Arellano presented interdisciplinary research projects carried out at the Baden-Württemberg Film Academy's Institute of Animation—among them, *The Muses of Poetry* and *SARA—Stylized Animation for Research in Autism*. Markos Kay, an animation filmmaker known for abstract experiments on scientific data, provided an artistic take on the subject of art and science. Three artistic positions occupied the focal point of the "Art & Society" panel. Mihai Grecu, who was honored with an Award of Distinction in the Computer Animation category 2014 for *The Reflection of Power*, an animated short film with a political theme, offered insights into his surreal, metaphorical imagery and personally presided over a screening of some of his recent work. His fellow panelists include experimental filmmaker and media artist Reinhold Bidner as well as the designer and artist Jonas Hansen, who went into interactive installations and experimental games. The "Art & Industry" panel demonstrated how art and industry can influence and inspire one another. Representatives of a London-based studio named ManvsMachine and Aixsponza, a 3D motion design studio based in Munich, presented their latest artistic and commercial work.

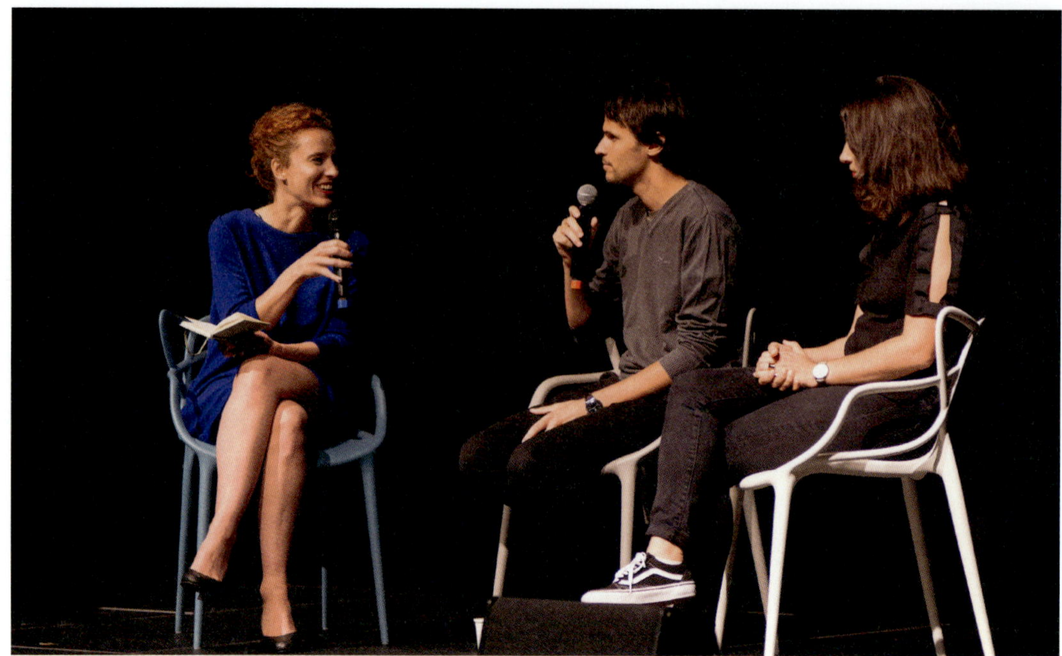

Figure 2: Prix Forum 2018: Alex Verhaest (Juror), Boris Labbé (Award of Distinction), Mathilde Lavenne (Golden Nica).

Speakers Expanded Animation 2016

Aixsponza – Manuel Casasola Merkle (DE), Moritz Schwind (DE) | Abigail Addison (GB) | Diana Arellano (DE/ES) | Reinhold Bidner (AT) | Erwin Feyersinger (AT/DE) | Mihai Grecu (RO) | Yuya Hanai (JP) – Award of Distinction 2016 | Jonas Hansen (DE) | Markos Kay (GB) | Boris Labbé (FR) – Golden Nica 2016 | Marie Liis Rebane (EE) – Juror 2016 | ManvsMachine – Matthias Winckelmann (DE) | Johannes Friedrich Schiehsl (AT) – Juror 2016

2017: Daydreams and Nightmares: Amalgams of Technology and Aesthetics in Animation

The fifth edition symposium endeavored to investigate the utilization of hybrid techniques and technologies and the effects of such usage on animation production. One essential quality of the medium of animation is the sheer diversity in its appearance, which can be seen in the vast number of animation techniques and aesthetics. The use of computers in creating animations has greatly expanded the available visual means of representation.

In recent years, a recognizable trend in computer animation can be seen in the use of unconventional approaches, such as drones, robots, 3D printers, game engines, lasers, and many other technologies, to facilitate new methods and expand on existing techniques of visualizing images and motion. The *Spaxels*[21] project, which utilizes a large number of networked drones equipped with LEDs, is one example of a hybrid approach that greatly extends the potential representation space. Animation software is also being used to control drones and robots, just as the animated frames of 3D characters are being printed as individual sculptures and then captured with stop-motion techniques to create an animation. Animation loops are integrated into physical sculptures and mutate into a moving sculpture using a zoetrope-based device, and three-dimensional animated holograms are generated using laser technologies. The fifth edition of the Expanded Animation Symposium examined and discussed such trends and current developments with a panel of international experts.

After jury member Sabine Hirtes kicked off the Prix Forum, Golden Nica winner David OReilly and Award of Distinction winners Emblematic Group (a next-generation media company) and Kimchi and Chips (an experimental art studio) presented their award-winning projects. All these pieces are prime examples of expanded animation: *Everything* is an experimental philosophical game that enables users to explore the

---

21 *Spaxels*, Ars Electronica Futurelab, https://www.spaxels.at/ (accessed December 18, 2018).

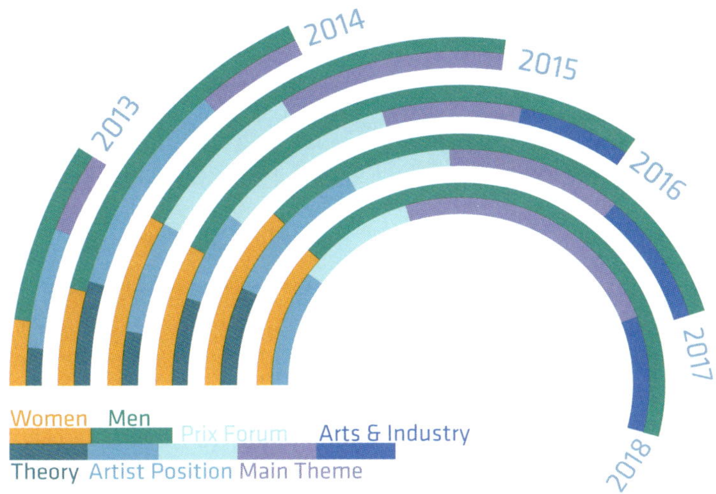

Figure 3: Expanded Animation from 2013 to 2018.

whole universe. *Out of Exile* is a VR experience based on a true story where VR users can take on the role of a young man who is confronted with his sexual orientation. Furthermore, *Light Barrier 3rd Edition* is an experimental light projection installation that creates volumetric drawings in the air using hundreds of calibrated video projections.

In the subsequent panel 3, artistic positions offered a prelude to the main topic "Amalgams of Technology and Aesthetics in Animation." Media artist Max Hattler discussed stereoscopic experiments and presented his approaches, including a screening at Ars Electronica's Deep Space 8K. Nikita Diakur talked about interactive animation and ugly aesthetic using his current animated short movie *Ugly* (Honorary Mention 2017). Job, Joris & Marieke, a Dutch studio for animation, illustrated character animation and music, gave insights into the production of their artistic work. The next two panels were specifically dedicated to the main topic, hybrid technologies in practice and theory. Media scholar Stephan Schwingeler addressed the topic of digital games as an artistic material and their hybrid forms. Lev Manovich, a pioneer in the application of data science for analysis of contemporary media culture, introduced his current research in the field of artificial intelligence and image culture and built a bridge to the festival theme: Artificial intelligence – The Other I. Artistic approaches regarding hybrids in

digital animation were provided by Hamill Industries and onformative in the next panel. Both studios are designing animations, installations and performances, using various technologies or custom-made animation tools. For instance, Hamill Industries developed an animation device to create animated light paintings; onformative designed a kinetic light sculpture called *true/false*, which is an animated sound frame composed of arrays of circular black metal segments, controlled by the computer. The final panel featured emerging Austrian artists struggling at the nexus of art and industry. Rafael Vangelis Mayrhofer gave an insight into the production of *Analog Loaders*, a hybrid stop-motion animation with 3D printed objects. Game designer Stefan Srb and motion designer Martina Stiftinger talked about the synergy of working on their own projects as well as a commissioned works. In addition to the talks, current works by many of the speakers were presented in the Animation Festival program and Deep Space 8K at Ars Electronica.

Speakers Expanded Animation 2017

Marieke Blaauw – Job, Joris & Marieke (NL) | Nikita Diakur (DE) | Hamill Industries – Pablo Barquín (ES), Anna Diaz (ES) | Max Hattler (DE/HK) | Sabine Hirtes (DE) – Juror 2017 | Onformative – Cedric Kiefer (DE) | David OReilly (IE) – Golden Nica 2017 | Lev Manovich (US) | Rafael Vangelis Mayrhofer (AT) | Stephan

Schwingeler (DE) | Stefan Srb (AT) | Martina Stiftinger (AT) | Eliot Woods (GB) – Award of Distinction 2017 | Jonathan Yomayuza (US) – Award of Distinction 2017

Expanded Animation 2018: Interfaces in Motion

How will future animated worlds be produced with and for new technologies like virtual and augmented reality? How will these interfaces change the way digital motion pictures are presented and received, and what role does the audience play in this? The 6th session of the Expanded Animation symposium was an inquiry into future interfaces in animation and presented approaches from the art world, the R&D field and the industrial sector, including artists, scientists, software developers and studios working in the fields of gaming, media design and animation.

The kick-off was the Prix Forum Computer Animation, where the Golden Nica winner Mathilde Lavenne, Boris Labbé (Award of Distinction), and Alex Verhaest (jury member) discussed currents positions. The forum was followed by 13 presentations. Vera-Maria Glahn talked about how generative design nourished their focus on "Visualizing the Invisible" illustrated by means of examples from the digital art studio FIELD. The Austrian artist duo DEPART presented their latest VR application *The Lacuna Shifts*, a surrealistic interactive journey inspired by Lewis Carroll's *Alice in Wonderland*. Hannes Rall elaborated on a current research project that illustrates how conventional animated productions can be expanded by VR technology. James Paterson presented *Norman*, an animation software that received a 2018 Honorary Mention for making it possible to bring the traces of movements left behind in a physical space to life in a VR environment. Volker Helzle offered insights into the latest research in virtual production, a complex field of postproduction in which the real and the virtual increasingly merge. Gerhard Funk's presentation highlighted interactive works subsumed under the title *Cooperative Aesthetics* that were developed for Deep Space 8K, and showed how their audience's collective movements can generate an animated world of imagery. Artistic experiments in the field of stereoscopic animation—from 3D noise to binocular rivalry—was the subject of Rainer Kohlberger's presentation. Chunning (Maggie) Guo talked about re-evolution as an interface in generative animation. Birgitta Hosea discussed works by artists in the expanded cinema movement and Sophie Mobbs reported on VR applications in medicine as well as artistic interventions in this field.

Rounding out the symposium was a making-of presentation about prizewinning and well-received works in the field of applied art. *Broken Rules*, an Austrian indie game studio, gave a speech about the emotional design of the computer game *Old Man's Journey*. Talks by Melt and FIELD, two design studios doing interdisciplinary work, and the ZEITGUISED / foam animation studio offered insights into the creative process—from VR experiences to large-format audiovisual projections. Plus, many of the presented works were shown in the Ars Electronica Animation Screening, in VRLab, and in Deep Space 8K at the Ars Electronica Center.

Speakers Expanded Animation 2018

Broken Rules – Felix Bohatsch (AT) | Depart – Leonhard Lass (AT) | FIELD – Vera-Maria Glahn (DE) | Gerhard Funk (AT) | Chunning (Maggie) Guo (CN) | Volker Helzle (DE) | Birgitta Hosea (GB) | Rainer Kohlberger (AT/DE) | Boris Labbé (FR) – Award of Distinction 2018 | Mathilde Lavenne (FR) – Golden Nica 2018 | MELT – Kuba Matyka (PL) | Sophie Mobbs (GB) | James Paterson (CA) | Hannes Rall (DE) | Alex Verhaest (BE) – Juror 2018 | ZEITGUISED / foam – Henrik Mauler (DE)

Retrospect and Perspective

The Expanded Animation symposium started in 2013 as a small event at Ars Electronica with a line-up of 10 speakers and 3 panels. The symposium was well received and expanded in the following years. Originally designed as a unique event, it has become an established part of the festival. Since 2014, it has been organized in cooperation with Ars Electronica and serves as an academic component of the Prix Ars Electronica and Ars Electronica Festival, featuring scientific, curatorial, and artistic perspectives. In the last six years, the symposium featured 74 experts from various fields, from animation, art, games, and science: media artists like John Gerrard or Alex Verhaest, scholars such as Lev Manovich or Susanne Buchan, curators like Ulrich Wegenast or Abigail Addison, animators like Mathilde Lavenne or Boris Labbé, experimental filmmakers (e.g., David OReilly and Max Hattler), game designers like Paolo Pedercini or Jonas Hansen, VR experts like Jonathan Yomayuza or Leonhard Lass, and media design- and animation studios such as ManvsMachine or Aixsponsa. As at the first conferences on computer animation at Ars Electronica in the 1980s, practice and theory are equally important. The symposium is open to experts in theory and practice including the Prix Forum, featuring the top prize winners in the category Computer Animation. Although the line between practice and theory is always fluid,

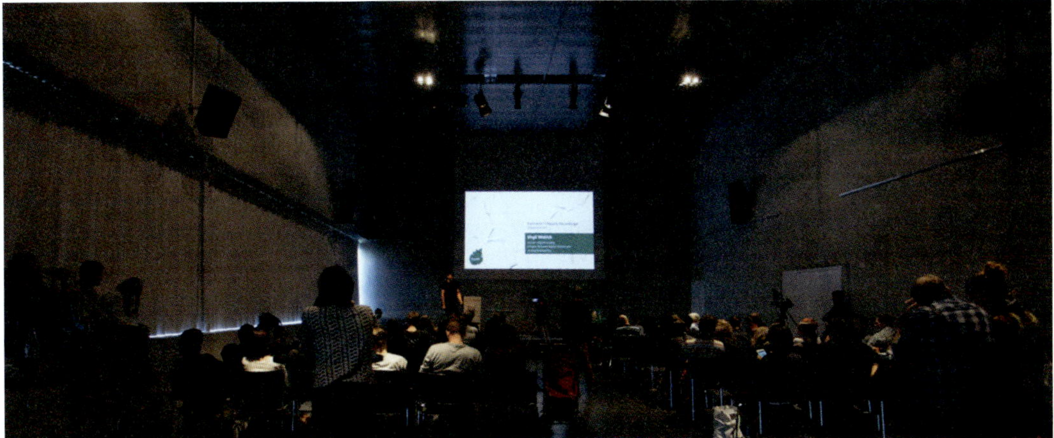

Figure 4: The very first Expanded Ainimation Symposium in 2013.

most of the speakers are active in both areas.

The Expanded Animation symposium picks up the idea of the initial conferences on computer animation at Ars Electronica in the 1980s, fosters the interplay between science and practice and seeks for artistic congruities. Expanded animation is not an academic conference, but more a hybrid between practice and theory that is open for a broad range of science, from humanities to applied and multi-disciplinary sciences, covering panels in media arts, animation, and film theory as well as computer science.

In general, in the past few years a trend has been observable towards a more intense interaction between established animation festivals and academic symposia.[22] Within the international animation festivals, Ars Electronica Animation festival represents an exceptional position, as its roots are in media arts and the focus is on computer animation. Between theory and art, the symposium additionally addresses the interaction between art and industry. Since 2016, the panel "Art & Industry" has featured artists and design studios like ZEITGUISED or Hamill Industries that are active in both areas. Therefore, the center of interest is the reciprocity between independent, artistic projects, and commissioned works.

However, what is striking is the fact that only about one quarter of the speakers at Expanded Animation are female. In the last sessions, a slight upward trend is recognizable. Furthermore, the ratio between male and female contributors at Ars Electronica and Prix Ars Electronica was not balanced at all. According to a data analysis of Prix Ars Electronica 1987–2016 about 33% are female (54% male, 13% group or organization, consisting of male and female contributors).[23] Altogether, the gender balance has improved significantly over the past few years. For example, in 2017 the ratio between female and male jury members at Prix Ars Electronica was equal for the first time and in 2018, the ratio between female and male award winners in the category Computer Animation was almost balanced, too. Regarding the gender balance in media arts, Ars Electronica started the initiative Women in Media Arts[24] in 2016 and established a symposium on the topic in 2017, also including a talk about women in animation.

However, it is remarkable that there is a slightly positive trend towards a better balance in the last years at the symposium. The initiative Women in Media Arts is also very gratifying and promising. The symposium in 2019 is already being planned, pursuing its original goals of providing an inspiring program about current trends in digital animation in an interdisciplinary context for students in the Digital Media department and for everybody who is interested in the expanded field at the interplay of art, technology, theory, and animation. As the history of Ars Electronica has shown, trends in media arts and technology come and go. Whereas computer animation was a main topic in

---

22 Juergen Hagler and Franziska Bruckner, "Reflecting Academic Symposia as a Trend at Animation Festivals, Media Art Festivals and Conferences on Computer Animation," in *Cartoon and Animation Studies*, Vol. 49, No. 4, 2017, pp. 611–632.
23 Christl Baur, Martin Hieslmair, Emiko Ogawa and Gerfried Stocker, Prix Ars Electronica Seeks Female Media Artists! https://www.aec.at/aeblog/en/2017/01/17/prix-ars-electronica-women/ (accessed December 18, 2018).
24 Women in Media Arts, Ars Electronica, https://archive.aec.at/womeninmediaarts/ (accessed December 18, 2018).

the 1980s and 1990s in the context of media art, it gradually slipped out of the focus for several years. In the last decade animation become pervasive and the boundaries between animation, game, film, media art, interactive art, architecture, sound art, et cetera are blurring more and more, and, at the same time, computer animation gained importance again. In fact, there has been a real boom in animation studies on expanded and experimental approaches in the last few years, and many conferences and symposia have emerged. The expanded animation symposium in conjunction with Ars Electronica features a unique focus on the intersection of animation and media art. In this regard, this vibrant multi-disciplinary interplay will probably spark many questions for further studies of the expanded field of animation. This book makes its contribution by summarizing these studies and examinations, although the selection presented here can only give limited, though essential, insights into the discussion. In addition to the book, the expanded animation archive provides a video documentation of all talks online at www.expandedanimation.com.

Bibliography

Bartlett, Mark. "Socialimagestics and the Visual Acupuncture of Stan Vanberbeek's Expanded Cinema." In *Expanded Cinema: Art, Performance, Film*, edited by A.L. Rees, Duncan White, Steven Ball, and David Curtis. London, 2011, pp. 50–61.

Buchan, Suzanne ed. *Pervasive Animation*. New York and London, 2013.

Cholodenko, Alan ed. *The Illusion of Life 2: More Essays on Animation*. Sydney, 2007.

Hagler, Juergen. "Animation, Kunst und Technologie. Evolution und Expansion am Beispiel Prix Ars Electronica." In *Im Wandel ... Metamorphosen der Animation*, edited by Julia Eckel, et al., Wiesbaden, 2017, pp. 171–185.

Hagler, Juergen and Franziska Bruckner. "Reflecting Academic Symposia as a Trend at Animation Festivals, Media Art Festivals and Conferences on Computer Animation." In *Cartoon and Animation Studies*, Vol. 49, No. 4, 2017, pp. 611–632.

Piene, Otto. "Sky Art Conference." In *ARS ELECTRONICA 82 im Rahmen des Internationalen Brucknerfestes Linz*, edited by LIVA, Linz, 1982.

Rean, Sheldon 1967. *An introduction to the American underground film*. London, 1967.

Russett, Robert, and Cecile Starr, eds. *Experimental and Expanded Animation: Origins of a New Art*. New York, 1976.

Russett, Robert. *Hyperanimation: Digital Images and Virtual Worlds*. United Kingdom, 2009.

Scheugl, Hans, and Ernst Schmidt. *Eine Subgeschichte des Films. Lexikon des Avantgarde-, Experimental- und Undergroundfilms*. Frankfurt a. M., 1974.

Smith, Vicky and Nicky Hamlyn, eds. *Experimental and Expanded Animation. New Perspectives and Practices*. Basingstoke, 2018.

Youngblood, Gene. *Expanded Cinema*. New York, 1970.

Zielinski, Siegfried. "Expanded Animation – A Short Genealogy in Words and Images." In *Pervasive Animation*. Edited by Suzanne Buchan, New York and London 2013.

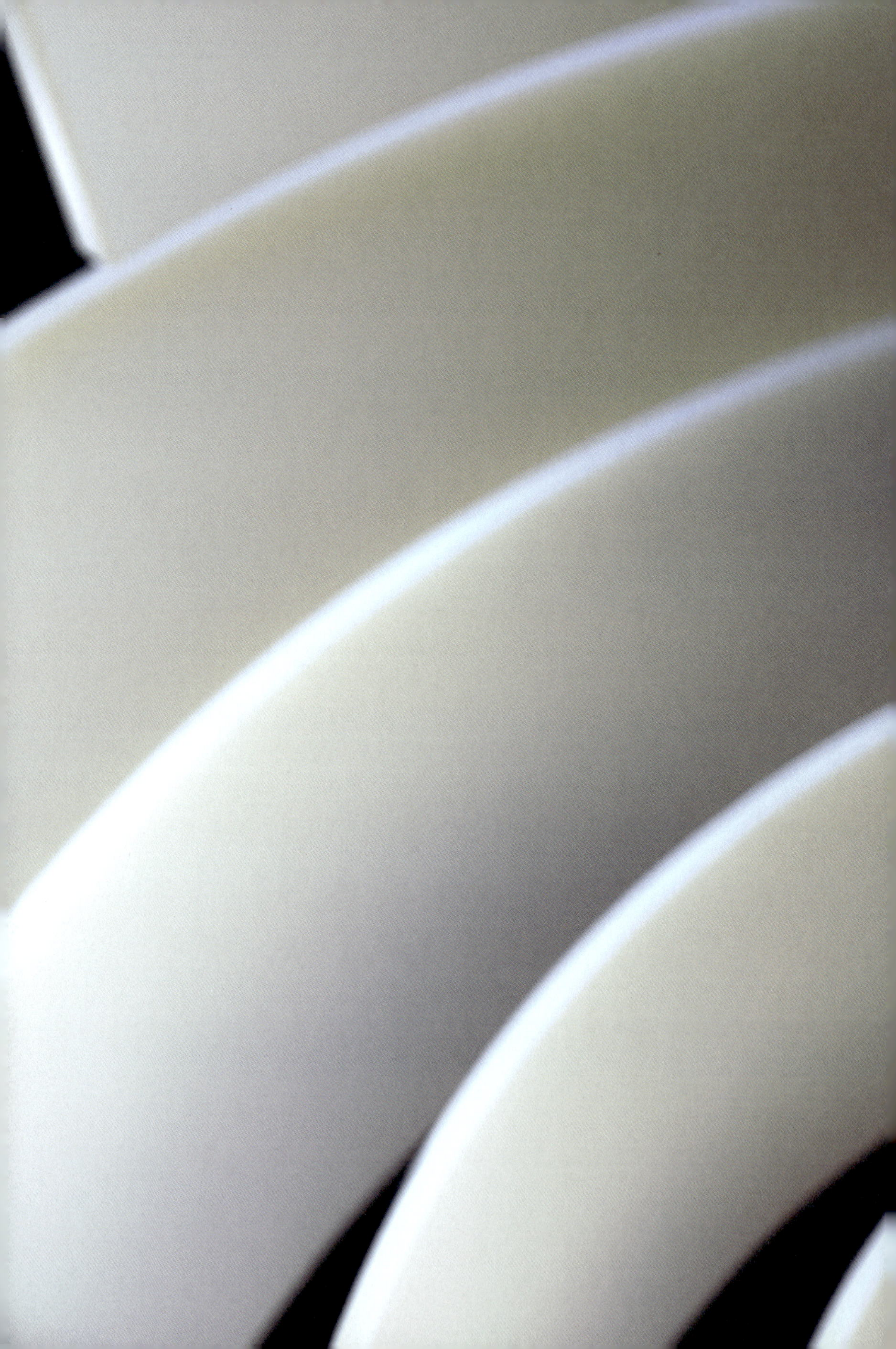

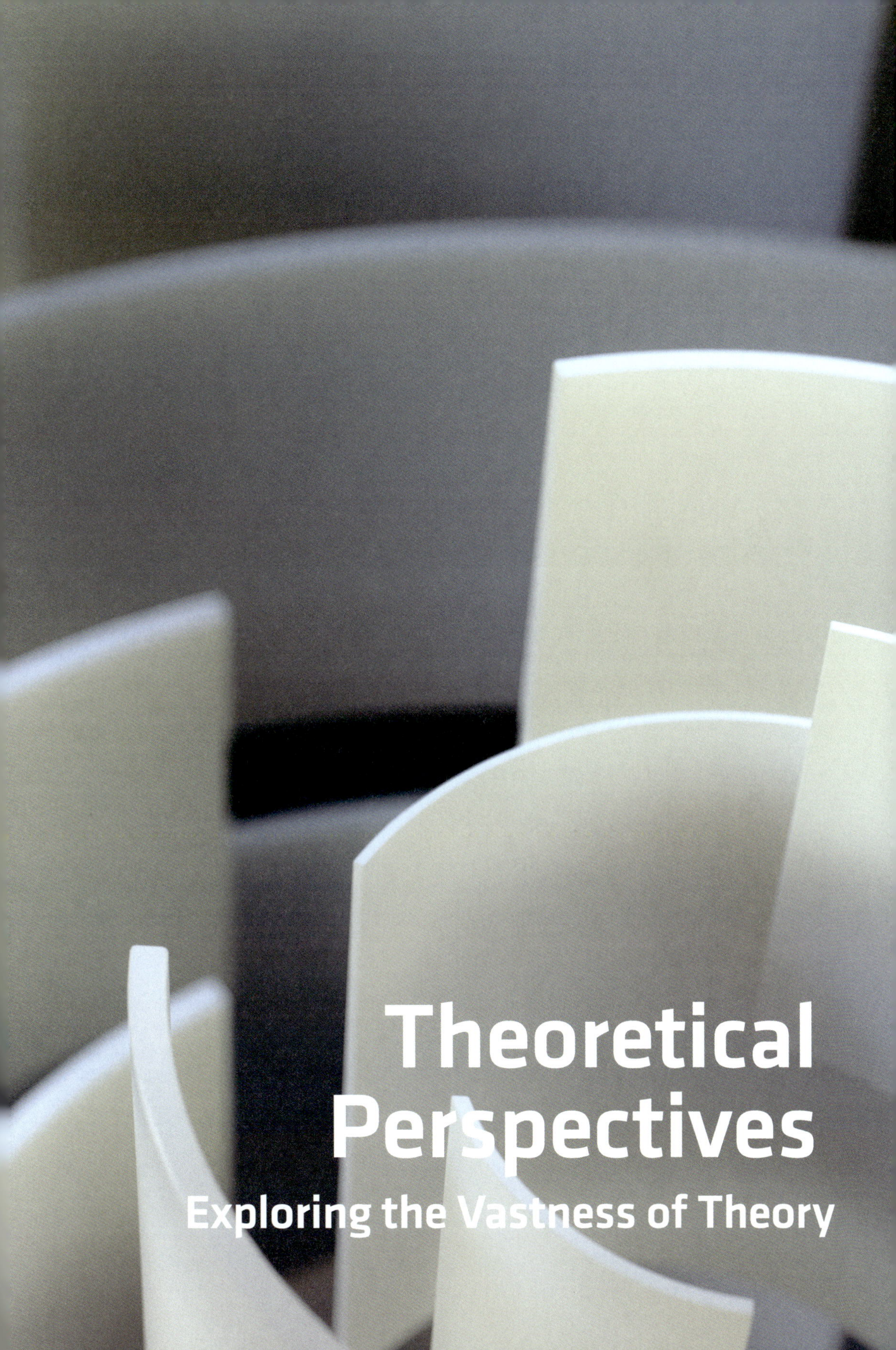

Theoretical
Perspectives
Exploring the Vastness of Theory

Ulrich Wegenast (DE)

Stan VanDerBeek: From Collage Film to Cybernetic Cinema

In the context of my research and teaching in Expanded Animation at Filmuniversität Babelsberg "Konrad Wolf," Stan VanDerBeek is an important reference point and artistic figure. His visions and concepts continue to resonate today in various film and media discourses, and his work has found a greater reception again in recent years. Despite his early death in the Orwellian year 1984, he developed a multitude of concepts ranging from subversive underground film to immersive dome cinemas and global networks to media performances and computer films. It is hardly possible within the constraints of this essay to provide even a rough introduction to the complex work of the American artist VanDerBeek, but his projects do contain a variety of approaches that are relevant to my work as a festival organizer, art scholar, and media manager.

Like other film, media, and animation artists of the sixties and seventies, Stan VanDerBeek (1927–1984) received hardly any attention from scholars of art despite his collaboration with artists such as Claes Oldenburg, Allan Kaprow or John Cage; for a long time after his death, he was almost completely forgotten.[1] Only during the Expanded Cinema Reception[2] of recent years has there been a renewed interest in VanDerBeek's multifaceted work.[3] The current film and animation theories of such artists as Chris Gehman, Steve Reinke[4] or Sean Cubitt,[5] as well as a general survey of today's film and cinema landscape, show that the post-cinematic approach taken by VanDerBeek in the sixties was a model that offered a glimpse into the future of cinema.

VanDerBeek studied architecture at the Cooper Union in New York, where he received his diploma in 1952. He also studied at Black Mountain College, where Oskar Fischinger was teaching, from 1949–51. He was already working in different media, such as drawing, from early on, and experimented with architectural forms inspired by Buckminster Fuller that looked like a cross between a spaceship and a cave structure.[6]

1 Bill Arning, "Stan VanDerBeek's Currency," in *Stan VanDerBeek. The Culture Intercom*, edited by Bill Arning, João Ribas, exh. cat. MIT List Visual Arts Center, Contemporary Arts Museum Houston (Cambridge MA, Houston, 2011), p. 64.

2 A. L. Rees, et al., eds. *Expanded Cinema: Art, Performance, Film* (London, 2011).

3 Maxa Zoller: Stan VanDerBeeks Movie Drome, in *Media-Space – Medien im Raum/Raum in Medien*, edited by Wand 5. Konferenzbroschüre. Stuttgart 2004. p. 9. A retrospective with the films of Stan VanDerBeek was presented during the media-space conference.

4 Chris Gehman and Steve Reinke, eds. *The Sharpest Point. Animation at the End of Cinema* (Toronto, 2005).

5 Sean Cubitt, *The Cinema Effect* (Cambridge, MA, London, 2004).

6 *Stan VanDerBeek, The Culture Intercom*, edited by B. Arning and J. Ribas. Exh. cat. MIT List Visual Arts Center, Contemporary Arts Museum Houston (Cambridge MA, Houston, 2011).

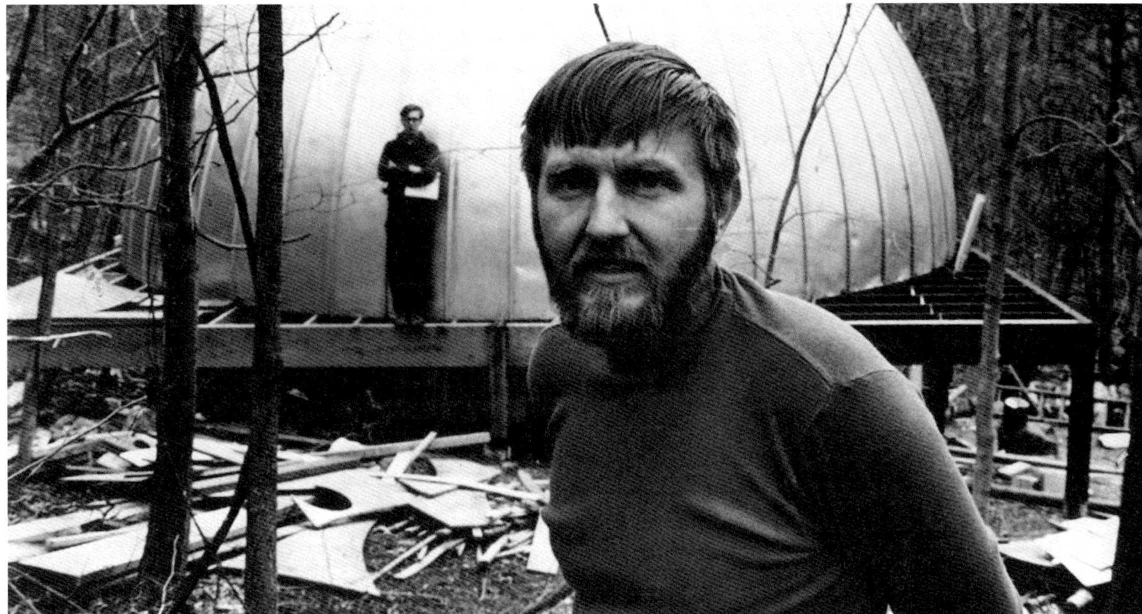

Figure 1: Stan VanDerBeek in front of his Movie Drome, 1963–65, an architectural prototype for mixed media events inspired by Buckminster Fuller.

During this time, he also adopted various film techniques and worked for television stations. In addition, he developed cinematic installations and—in cooperation with Robert Rauschenberg—experimental window displays for businesses such as Tiffany & Co. and Bonwit Teller. VanDerBeek took a greater interest than other animation filmmakers in the development and use of new technologies and developed immersive-cinema formats. However, his first films, such as *Science Friction*,[7] were mostly cut-out animations, which Hans Scheugl and Ernst Schmidt Jr. dismissed in their *Subgeschichte des Films* as "clumsily amusing collage films."[8] It was his stop-motion films, which were often relegated to underground status, that gained him a certain level of fame.

In their attitude to the mass media and their portrayal of the American Way of Life, these films do show strong parallels to Pop Art, e.g. to collage pictures such as *Just What Is It That Makes Today's Home So Different, So Appealing?* (1956) by British artist Richard Hamilton.

The principle of the collage and its appropriation can be seen in many of VanDerBeek's early films, such as *What Who How*[9] from 1957 and *A La Mode*[10] from 1958. The complex of science, the military, and the entertainment industry is featured in VanDerBeek's animated films in a similar way to the found-footage films of Bruce Conner or the collages of British pop artist Eduardo Paolozzi. The anarchic, socially critical humor in VanDerBeek's films was one of the inspirations for the Monty Python productions.[11] Terry Gilliam, Monty Python's long-time animator, explained in an interview:

I'd seen in New York—somewhere in the '60s—something by underground filmmaker Stan van der Beek, and he had done a pretty funny cartoon using cut-outs. The image I remember was Nixon with a foot in his mouth, and it really stuck with me. That was the thing that got me thinking, 'I've got to do cut-outs.' So that's what I did.[12]

---

7 *Science Friction*. Directed by Stan VanDerBeek, 1959.

8 Hans Scheugl and Ernst Schmidt jr., : *Eine Subgeschichte des Films. Lexikon des Avantgarde-, Experimental- und Undergroundfilms.* Vol. 2 (Frankfurt a. M. 1974), p. 1051.

9 *What Who How*. Directed by Stan VanDerBeek, 1957.

10 *A La Mode*. Directed by Stan VanDerBeek, 1958.

11 Ulrich Wegenast, "Die Aufhebung der Schwerkraft. Terry Gilliams Animationen bei Monty Python," *Schnitt. Das Filmmagazin.* Nr. 47 (March 2007), pp. 22–25.

12 Terry Gilliam, Interview by Kenneth Plume, https://movies.ign.com/articles/035/035923p1.html (accessed October 12, 2018).

A look at films such as *Science Friction* by VanDerBeek shows that there are in fact numerous elements that reappear in Gilliam's short animation clips. For one thing, there is a similar critique of science and society— *Science Friction* deals with the Space Race between the USA and the USSR—and VanDerBeek and Gilliam both often worked in collage style with found pictures from mass media. Gilliam was especially impressed by VanDerBeek's short film *Breathdeath*[13] made in 1964. Here VanDerBeek's penchant for slapstick and vaudeville, which he shared with Gilliam, comes to the fore. *Breathdeath* is a spectacular mix of partially distorted found footage, humorous performances VanDerBeek filmed himself, collage-style stop motion with photos from newspapers, and drawings that he found or made.

Many of VanDerBeek's parodies and satires are critiques of the affirmative techno-euphoria of the fifties and sixties as well as the competition between political systems during the Cold War. In the late fifties and early sixties, he produced a multitude of drawings and collages about the cult of celebrity, consumer fetishism, and the entertainment industry, continuing the approach of Joseph Cornell (while avoiding his enigmatic qualities).

Over the course of the 1960s, VanDerBeek increasingly turned his attention to Expanded Cinema projects with a utopian element while maintaining his critical awareness. According to Bill Arning, in addition to the many roles VanDerBeek took on, he was also a "lone wolf who sees the dark cloud behind techno-utopian thinking."[14] In the 1965 pamphlet "'Culture Intercom' and 'Expanded Cinema'. A Proposal and Manifesto," he emphasizes his approach, which was already established by then and represented an attempt to reflect on technological development in a critical, artistic way. As he wrote in his manifesto:

> The "technique power" and "culture-over-reach" that is just beginning to explode in many parts of the earth, is happening so quickly that it has put the logical fulcrum of man's intelligence so far outside himself that he cannot judge or estimate the results of his acts before he commits them.[15]

Based on this position and influenced by his architectural studies at the Cooper Union in New York, VanDerBeek developed a domed cinema with multiple projections, which he called a "Movie Drome," on a property in Stony Point near New York. On the grounds where the "Movie Drome" was located, also known as Gate Hill Cooperative Community, lived some alumni of Black Mountain College, including David Tudor, John Cage, and Merce Cunningham. The "Movie Drome" was to be the experimental prototype of a non-verbal international picture-language that would then develop into a world language. By eliminating words and dialog in his Expanded Cinema projects, VanDerBeek's cultural-technical approach comes very close to the understanding of animation as a form of visual communication and artistic expression and puts him in the company of film artists such as Oskar Fischinger, Harry Smith, and Norman McLaren, but also architects such as Charles and Ray Eames with their cinematic interior designs at the World's Fairs of the fifties and sixties.[16] Like Charles and Ray Eames, VanDerBeek sought to explore new intuitive forms of communication and reception in an international context with his simultaneous spatial films.

In VanDerBeek's "Movie Drome," audiences lay down to watch a conglomerate of many different films and slides that were intended to represent a kind of global language. The film material consisted partly of found footage. However, he also used reproductions of book illustrations and found photographs to create a collage projected into the dome of the 180-degree space. The images included Martin Luther King, Renaissance sculptures, archaic figures, masks, war photography, abstract shapes, and even isolated hand gestures. VanDerBeek's goal was to develop a network of various "Movie Dromes" that would later be provided with audiovisual information by satellite and deployed worldwide. VanDerBeek wished to "find the best combination of such machines for non-verbal inter-change."[17]

He described the prototype shows as "Movie Murals," "Ethos Cinema," "Newsreel of Dreams," "Feedback," and "Image Libraries,"[18] which demonstrates that his

---

13 *Breathdeath*. Directed by Stan VanDerBeek, 1964.
14 Bill Arning, "Stan VanDerBeek's Currency," in *Stan VanDerBeek. The Culture Intercom*, edited by Bill Arning, João Ribas, exh. cat. MIT List Visual Arts Center, Contemporary Arts Museum Houston (Cambridge MA and Houston, 2011), p. 65.
15 Stan VanDerBeek, "Culture Intercom, A Proposal and Manifesto" *Film Culture* 40, (Spring 1966).
16 Sandra Schramke, *Kybernetische Szenographie. Charles und Ray Eames – Ausstellungsarchitektur. 1959–1965* (Bielefeld, 2010).
17 Stan VanDerBeek, "Culture Intercom, A Proposal and Manifesto," *Film Culture* 40, (Spring 1966).
18 Ibid.

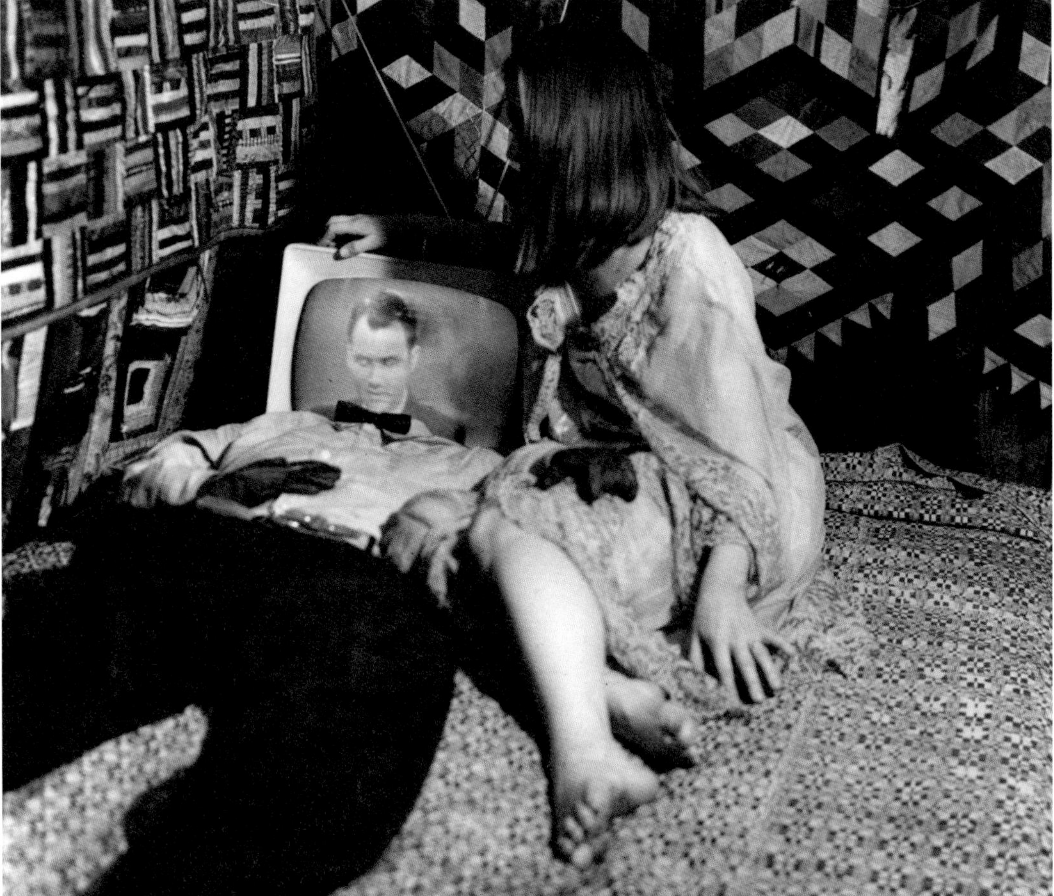

Figure 2: *Breath Death*, Stan VanDerBeek, USA, 1964, 10 minutes, B&W, sound, 16mm, surrealist experimental collage animation based on 15th century woodcuts.

concern was not to transmit factual information, but rather to create a poetic means of human communication and break down conventional categories in order to realize his concept of a worldwide "Culture Intercom." In the stream of images, each individual viewer was supposed to seek out the information and visual offerings that were relevant to him. This meant the "Movie Drome" project was paradoxically an immersive image space that completely surrounded the viewer in order to make available to him a selection of (film) images that was as associative and free as possible. In light of this, it is no surprise that VanDerBeek used the term "Newsreel of Dreams," drawing parallels to dreams and therefore also to the subconscious. In terms of content, VanDerBeek—in a way that was reminiscent of Canadian media theorist Marshall McLuhan's approach—tried to condense a kind of cul-

tural history of human civilization into a one-hour Movie Drome presentation beginning with the Egyptians, where "details are not important, it is the total scale of life that is ...".[19] All human endeavors from the natural sciences to geography to the arts were to be included. The image machine that VanDerBeek had in mind in the sixties was an aggregator intended to bring together all available visual information in an unmediated way, rather like what Google Images does today, in order to make the essence of civilization visible in a panorama.

It never went beyond a prototype. However, it was from this approach that he developed his theory of the "Culture Intercom." Echoing Marshall McLuhan, in 1965 he wrote in his aforementioned manifesto "'Culture Intercom' and 'Expanded Cinema,'" which was printed in the journal *Film Culture* No. 40 in 1966:

---

19 Ibid.

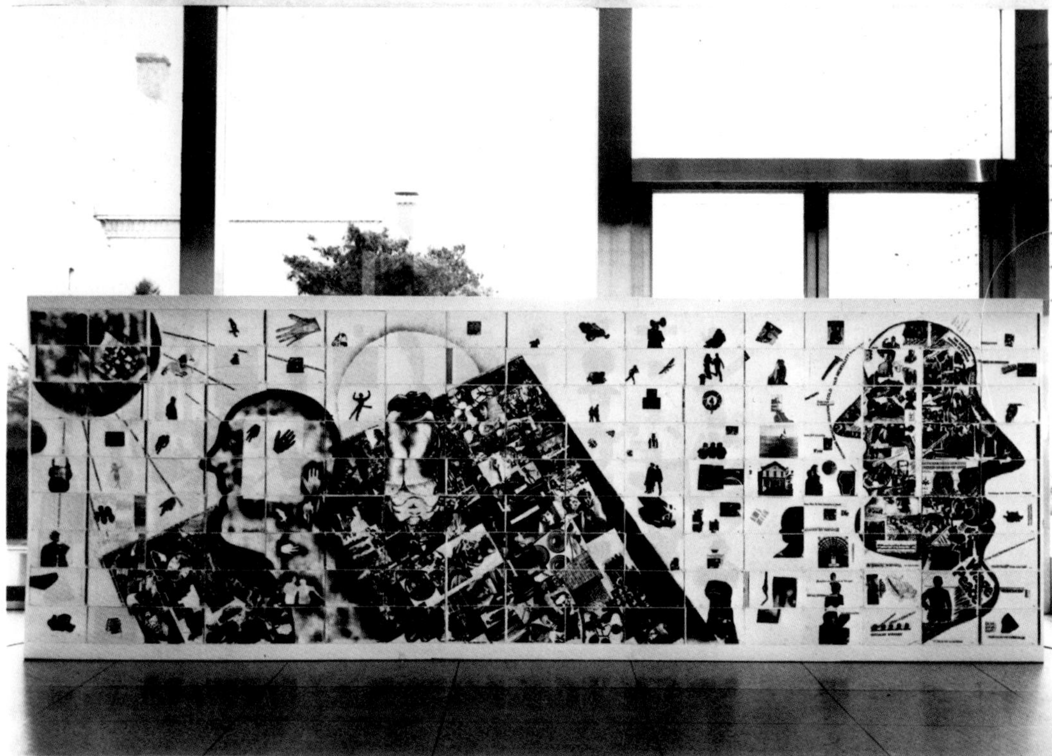

Figure 3: *Telephone Mural* by Stan VanDerBeek, produced in the context of the project "Panels for the Walls of the World" (1970). The images have been transmitted by fax machines to different museums where they have been put together as a mural collage.

It is imperative that we quickly find some way for the entire level of world human understanding to rise to a new human scale. This scale is the world ...[20]

With his technical know-how, experimental attitude, and utopian and communicative approach, VanDerBeek is more of a precursor to the media artist than a traditional animation filmmaker. His increasing engagement with computer-generated films was consistent with this. Between 1964 and 1970 he completed nine computer films with the specialist computer language and hardware BELFLIX, developed by Bell Laboratories. Ken Knowlton invented the BELFLIX System, which could display computer generated images through a Stromberg-Carlson 4020 microfilm recorder using an IBM 7094 Transistor computer and a special cutting method. This made it probably the first device to enable the transfer of images created on a computer directly to celluloid or microfilm. Many of the computer-generated films that VanDerBeek produced in this context are reminiscent of early computer games from the eighties. The experiment with computer films gave rise to printed graphics like the series "Mandell/as," which he published in short runs.

VanDerBeek also documented the performances and happenings of Claes Oldenburg, Allan Kaprow, and Robert Morris in the late fifties and sixties, becoming one of the chroniclers of actionist art. With the composer John Cage, he developed an interactive multimedia dance performance in collaboration with the Merce Cunningham Dance Company in 1965. The sound was controlled through ten photo cells developed by the pianist David Tudor and the engineer Billy Klüver. The dancers used their movements to manipulate the photocells, which controlled the tape recorders and shortwave radios. For this media performance, entitled *Variations V,*[21] VanDerBeek produced several films

---

20 Ibid.
21 *Variations V.* Media performance, Music by John Cage, Visuals by Nam June Paik and Stan VanDerBeek, 1965.

36

that were projected onto different screens distributed around the room. As in the "Movie Drome" project, VanDerBeek used archival material and pictures from the news. The multimedia performance, in which the synthesizer pioneer Robert Moog was also involved, took place on July 23, 1965, in the Philharmonic Hall at Lincoln Center in New York. In 1966, Norddeutsche Rundfunk produced an expanded fifty-minute version which integrated Nam June Paik's famous television manipulations into the background.

VanDerBeek's intention was to use the latest technology in a critical and subversive way and to connect the media to live performances. Because of that, his presentations tended to eschew cinemas and galleries in favor of colleges, planetariums, concert halls, or public television stations. Even NASA was among his partners. He used all the technologies available to him, such as the advanced BELFLIX system, telecopiers—the precursors to fax machines—and TV technology, appropriating them as if they were parts of a collage and combining them with other media such as drawing or photography. VanDerBeek completed the project *Panels for the Walls of the World (Phase I and II)* (1970) while working at MIT (the legendary Massachusetts Institute of Technology) in Cambridge. The work VanDerBeek named *Telephone Mural*[22] consisted of 153 individual pages, which were sent to the Walker Art Center in Minneapolis, the Smithsonian Institution in Washington, DC, and the Children's Museum by telecopier and assembled there into a large-format mural. The transfer of each individual picture took about ten minutes and the whole project lasted about four weeks. In his *Telephone Mural* project, VanDerBeek made new use of the concept of ubiquity and omnipresence from his "Movie Drome" idea, but also linked the work *Panels for the Walls of the World* with the longstanding tradition of state-commissioned murals in the United States and the socialist-inspired mural art of Mexican artists such as Diego Rivera and José Clemente Orozco. This form of public art had its heyday in the US during the New Deal period under Franklin Delano Roosevelt in the thirties, but also flowed into VanDerBeek's utopian ideas, which were intended to bring about a universal, international and omnipresent picture-language.

Unlike many experimental filmmakers of his time, such as Stan Brakhage or Ken Jacobs, he did not limit himself to the material aesthetic of celluloid, which sometimes led to pitched battles between filmmakers and video artists. His sociopolitical intentions made him open to developments in media technology that extended beyond the dispositive of cinematography, and even contributed to their advancement. VanDerBeek developed his film practice in tune with Dominique Willoughby's concept of a "cinéma graphiques" of the "mouvements image par image" and the "reproductions ciné-photographiques des mouvements réels" towards a "film synthetique."[23] His earlier films, such as *A La Mode* (1958) or *Science Friction* (1959), still represented the "frame by frame" concept and the reproducibility of real-world movements, while his later works were more concerned with aspects of real time and computer-aided image production and represent a decisive break with the black box of cinema. His own writings also emphasize this post-cinematic working assumption: in 1970 he wrote in the article "New Talent—The Computer" in *Art in America* magazine:

> Movie-making was for long the most revolutionary art form of our time. Now television touches the nerve ends of all the world; the visual revolution sits in just about every living room across America. The image revolution that movies represented has now been overhauled by the television evolution, and is approaching the next visual stage—to computer graphics to computer controls of the environment to a new cybernetic "movie art."[24]

Acting on this assertion in that same year, he produced *Violence Sonata*, an interactive television show broadcast on several TV channels.

These examples of Stan VanDerBeek's activities clearly show that his artistic practice extended far beyond animated film, encompassing spatial and performative practices that were intended to produce new forms of reception and distribution. Like Terry Gilliam of Monty Python, he can be termed an anti-animation filmmaker who used animation in a way that was

---

22 *Telephone Mural*. Directed by Stan VanDerBeek, 1970.

23 Dominique Willoughby, *Le cinéma graphique: Une histoire des dessins animés: des jouets d'optique au cinéma numérique* (Paris, 2009), p. 29.

24 Stan VanDerBeek, "New Talent—The Computer," *Art in America, No. 58*, (January–June 1970), quoted in Bartlett, Mark "The Culture: Intercom," in: *Stan VanDerBeek. The Culture Intercom* (Cambridge MA and Houston, 2011), p. 73.

as effective and anarchical as possible and avoided making technical virtuosity an end in itself. Like many experimental animation filmmakers up to the present day—for example, Oscar-winner Chris Landreth—VanDerBeek had a distinct visionary consciousness in addition to his technical experimentality. This can be seen in the fact that even in the mid-sixties he not only predicted the Internet and global digital social networks as well as real-time technologies,[25] but also the present age of server-based digital cinema:

> When I talk of the movie-dromes as image libraries, it is understood that such "life theatres" would use some of the coming techniques (video tape and computer inter-play) and thus be real communication and storage centers, that is, by satellite, each dome could receive its images from a worldwide library source, store them and program a feedback presentation to the local community that lived near the center, this newsreel feedback, could authentically review the total world image "reality" in an hour long show that gave each member of the audience a sense of the entire world picture ... "Intra-communitronics," or dialogues with other centers would be likely, and instant reference material via transmission television and telephone could be called for and received at 186,000 m.p.s. ... from anywhere in the world.[26]

In conclusion, this quote makes it clear that VanDerBeek was far more than an animator and media artist; he was a complex artistic figure who linked social and political discourse with technological innovation, cinematic experiments, humor, and subversion and understood himself as an author despite his numerous collaborations and participatory projects. Or as Bill Arning put it: "Throughout the 1960s, '70s and early '80s, VanDerBeek was an inspiring one-man research-and-development department for using untried forms and forcing them to reveal their interior poetics."[27]

---

25 Bill Arning, "San VanDerBeek's Currency," in *Stan VanDerBeek. The Culture Intercom*, edited by Bill Arning, João Ribas, exh. cat. MIT List Visual Arts Center, Contemporary Arts Museum Houston (Cambridge MA and Houston, 2011), p. 64.
26 Stan VanDerBeek, "Culture Intercom, A Proposal and Manifesto", *Film Culture* 40, (Spring 1966).
27 Bill Arning, "San VanDerBeek's Currency," in *Stan VanDerBeek. The Culture Intercom*, edited by Bill Arning, João Ribas, exh. cat. MIT List Visual Arts Center, Contemporary Arts Museum Houston (Cambridge MA and Houston, 2011), p. 68.

Bibliography

Arning, Bill. "Stan VanDerBeek's Currency," In *Stan VanDerBeek. The Culture Intercom*, edited by Bill Arning, João Ribas, exh. cat. MIT List Visual Arts Center, Contemporary Arts Museum Houston. Cambridge MA and Houston, 2011.

Cubitt, Sean. *The Cinema Effect.* Cambridge, MA, London, 2004.

Gehman, Chris, and Steve Reinke, eds. *The Sharpest Point. Animation at the End of Cinema.* Toronto, 2005.

Rees, A. L., Duncan White, Steven Ball, and David Curtis, eds. *Expanded Cinema: Art, Performance, Film.* London, 2011.

Scheugl, Hans, and Schmidt jr., Ernst: *Eine Subgeschichte des Films. Lexikon des Avantgarde-, Experimental- und Undergroundfilms.* 2. Bd. Frankfurt a. M. 1974.

Schramke, Sandra. *Kybernetische Szenographie. Charles und Ray Eames – Ausstellungsarchitektur. 1959–1965.* Bielefeld, 2010.

Sutton, Gloria: *The Experience Machine. Stan VanDerBeek's Movie-Drome and Expanded Cinema.* Cambridge MA and London, 2015.

VanDerBeek, Stan. "'Culture Intercom' und 'Expanded Cinema'. Ein Entwurf und ein Manifest (1965)," In *Avant-gardistischer Film 1951–1971: Theorie*, edited by Gottfried Schlemmer. München, 1973, p. 57–62.

Wegenast, Ulrich. "Die Aufhebung der Schwerkraft. Terry Gilliams Animationen bei Monty Python." Schnitt. *Das Filmmagazin*. Nr. 47, (March 2007), pp. 22–25.

Willoughby, Dominique. *Le cinéma graphique: Une histoire des dessins animés: des jouets d'optique au cinéma numérique.* Paris, 2009.

Birgitta Hosea (GB)

Paracinema and the Dematerialization of Animation

Introduction

Taking as a starting point the 2018 Expanded Animation symposium's theme of interface, this chapter
explores the sense of interface as a point of contact
between two different systems. The two systems
under consideration are, on the one hand, the live
experience—a unique, embodied event that takes place
in three-dimensions, and on the other hand, the cinema[1]—the recorded version of events that is encoded
as a stream of images and then reproduced as moving
image on a screen. To do this I will look at historical
and contemporary examples of avant-garde artists and
filmmakers who have engaged with questioning the
pre-recorded nature of film and how it might leave the
confines of the rectangular screen through expanded
cinema. I will be pointing out two different ways of
understanding the moving image: as an institution
bound to a set of tools, techniques, technologies and
material processes; as an idea conjured up in the mind
of the audience.

I will start by talking generally about expanded cinema and then refer more specifically to paracinema
with examples of work from historic and contemporary
artists.

Expanded Cinema

The term "expanded cinema" was coined by experimental filmmaker and pioneer of computer animation,
Stan VanDerBeek, in 1965[2] and popularized by Gene
Youngblood's seminal book *Expanded Cinema*, first
published in the USA in 1970. In this book, Youngblood
proposes a move away from the effect of brainwash-
ing and escapism that he considers to be produced
by viewing mainstream, story-led cinema. Instead,
he argues for a new synesthetic cinema that would
liberate the viewer's mind from the dulling effects
of mainstream realistic narratives that restrict the
imagination and offer a closed view on the world: "a
relatively closed structure in which free association
and conscious participation are restricted."[3] Instead
of the passive experience of popular entertainment,
expanded cinema would utilize multiple sensory stimuli to leave space for the individual's own free associations and thus expand their consciousness.[4] His book
gives examples of experimental films and live projection events by VanDerBeek and Carolee Schneeman,
amongst many others.

In Europe, expanded cinema took a slightly different
trajectory from that of America, argues A.L. Rees.[5]

---

1 I use the term cinema, rather than film or moving image, in order to reference the experience of a viewing event rather than getting
tied down to issues of materiality or medium.

2 Mark Bartlett, "Socialimagestics and the Visual Acupuncture of Stan Vanberbeek's Expanded Cinema," in *Expanded Cinema: Art,
Performance, Film*, edited by A.L. Rees, at al. (London, 2011), p. 50.

3 Gene Youngblood, *Expanded Cinema* (London, 1970), p. 64.

4 Gene Youngblood, *Expanded Cinema* (London, 1970), pp. 41–42.

5 A.L. Rees "Expanded Cinema and Narrative: A Troubled History," in *Expanded Cinema: Art, Performance, Film*, edited by A.L. Rees, at
al. (London, 2011), p. 14.

Rather than aiming to create an immersive, meditative and psychedelic experience, in general, the interpretation of "expanded cinema" in Europe tended towards a political attempt to deconstruct the illusionism and worldview of the mainstream cinematic experience. For example, this quote from Philip Drummond from a catalogue for the *Film as Form: Formal Experiment in Film 1910–1975* exhibition, held at the Hayward Gallery in 1979:

> As industrial products, mainstream films then have direct relationships to capital and class, through the restrictive patterns of ownership coupled with their 'mass' marketing and exploitation; by and large these films are 'dominant' precisely in the reproduction of dominant ideologies within this set of interests.[6]

The argument was that, as it was made by the ruling classes who hold the power in society, cinema presents their world view as "normal." Alternative viewpoints are not expressed or distributed. Within the pleasurable form of realist narrative, complex reality is reduced into simplified ways of understanding the world according to the ideas of the ruling class and the viewer is seduced into believing these representations to be truthful: "mainstream cinema 'dominates' not through coercion, but through seduction."[7] The viewer is brainwashed into escapism rather than action.

Consequently, the aim of avant-garde film was to oppose this system, to challenge the unreality of realism, to make the artifice of how the cinematic experience is constructed apparent, and to question narrative as a form and its stupefying effect on the viewer. The intention was to encourage a more politically aware and critical attitude towards the world and all its complexities. Structuralist-materialist filmmakers, such as Peter Gidal, created new, experimental work that questioned all aspects of illusionistic filmmaking. In addition to experimenting with the process, material and form of filmmaking, in the 1960s and 1970s, a number of live, expanded cinema events were held at which the cinematic event itself was investigated as an experience and deconstructed. Among the artist filmmakers involved were those associated with the

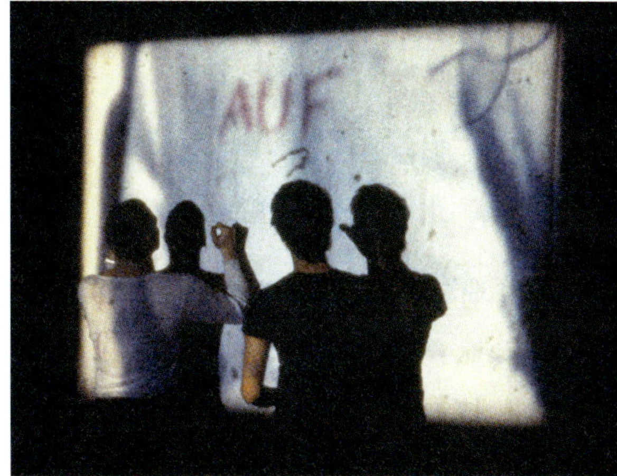

Figure 1: VALIE EXPORT, *Auuf+Ab+An+Zu*, 1968.

London Filmmakers Coop including Annabel Nicholson, Malcom Le Grice, William Raban, Anthony McCall, and Guy Sherwin; in Austria—Peter Weibel[8] and VALIE EXPORT; in Germany—Birgit Hein and Werner Nekes, in the USA—Paul Sharits and in Japan—Takahito Iimura. In their work, these artists sought to interrogate the components and experience of a cinematic screening event—the site of projection itself. Cutting, piercing, painting or scratching directly onto the surface of a film while the film was being projected onto different surfaces, in these live performances moving images were created in the present moment: the audience does not watch something being projected that was made in the past, but is witness to a process of becoming, images being created before their very eyes.

Paracinema

In a small number of expanded cinema projects, the subject of investigation was the cinematic experience, but the material of film was dispensed with altogether and other methods were used to create the basic essence or idea of cinema. Film theorist Jonathan Walley has adopted a term from filmmaker Ken Jacobs to refer to this kind of work as *paracinema*. The prefix "para" is used to denote something that is beside, adjacent to or beyond the root noun. Although the term paracinema is sometimes used in Film Studies to refer to cult cinema, Walley uses it to

---

6 Phillip Drummond, "Notions of Avant-Garde Cinema," in *Film as Form: Formal Experiment in Film 1910–1975*, edited by Hayward Gallery (London, 1979), p. 9.

7 Ibid., p. 9.

8 Peter Weibel presented his multimedia opera *The Synthetic Will* at Ars Electronica in 1984. He stayed on as head of the artistic committee for 10 years and was a core part of the festival's early artistic direction. Cf. Christine Schöpf, "The Making Of …," in *1974–2004 Ars Electronica The Network for Art, Technology and Society: The First 25 Years*, edited by Hannes Leopoldseder et al., (Ostfildern-Ruit, 2004), p. 21.

refer to something that goes beyond, but is connected to, conventional cinema. He argues that cinema is not defined by the medium of film alone:

> Paracinema identifies an array of phenomena that are considered "cinematic" but that are not embodied in the materials of film as traditionally defined. That is, the film works I am addressing recognize cinematic properties outside the standard film apparatus, and therefore reject the medium-specific premise or most essentialist theory and practice that the art form of cinema is defined by the specific medium of film. Instead, paracinema ... locates cinema's essence elsewhere.[9]

A.L. Rees explains the concept of paracinema more succinctly as a form in which: "the notion of the film medium is itself questioned, and the cinematic is sought outside or beyond the film machine. Here, expanded cinema is a form of live art, linked to theatre and performance rather than to recorded media as such."[10] For Jonathan Walley, paracinema is related to conceptual art practices in which the art object itself becomes much less important than the ideas behind it. The development and context to this kind of artwork is covered by Lucy Lippard's book *Six Years: The dematerialization of the art object from 1966 to 1972*. Walley uses the term paracinema in this context: in the sense of the dematerialization of film into idea, where cinema becomes a live event that questions the institution of cinema itself. It is a practice at the interface of live performance / happening and cinema.
 To summarize and clarify the definition of these key terms as used in this chapter: if *cinema* is thought of, in its classical sense, as being an institution where pre-recorded images are displayed on a screen in front of an audience; then *expanded cinema* is when artists seek to question this, to try to experiment with how the film is projected and what could happen during the act of projection; and finally, *paracinema* is when the material of film is dispensed with altogether and the moving image is dematerialized, in other words, it no longer takes a physical form but becomes a concept. These ideas will now be further elaborated with a series of examples.

Antony McCall

British artist Antony McCall had a multi-media background. While a student at Ravensbourne College of Art in the 1960s, he was part of a mixed-media performance group who used film and slide projections, live music and dance within an open structure.[11] After college, he collaborated on a number of different types of projects such as an interactive game, a 360° slide presentation and making films for dance performance. Through his relationship with American artist Carolee Schneeman, he came into contact with avant-garde performance practice such as Happenings, Fluxus, the Judson Dance Theater, and the work of John Cage. He became involved with the London Filmmakers Coop and the politics of film. He describes the ideas behind the films produced there:

> The work itself, sharing a methodology with the other visual arts, of reduction of means and attention to process, developed films that were continuous with the political critique implicit in the co-op structure. What was at issue was the politics of films, rather than film for politics.[12]

This context led him to question the experience of spectatorship, specifically the relationship of an audience to a film, whether sitting and looking at a conventional narrative film from a static position was a passive or an active experience and what the nature of projection was. In particular, he relates, "The specific idea that I was working on was that the projector's light beam was not only visible, but physical and space-occupying, and it could be shaped, both in space and in time, using film as the medium."[13]

This process of investigation lead to *Line Describing a Cone* (1973)[14] originally shown at the London Film-

---

9 Jonathan Walley, "The Material of Film and the Idea of Cinema: Contrasting Practices in Sixties and Seventies Avant-Garde Film," *October* 103 (October 2003), p. 18.
10 A.L. Rees "Expanded Cinema and Narrative: A Troubled History," in *Expanded Cinema: Art, Performance, Film*, edited by A.L. Rees, at al. (London, 2011), p. 12.
11 Scott MacDonald, "Anthony McCall," in *A Critical Cinema 2: Interviews with Independent Filmmakers*, edited by Scott MacDonald (Berkeley, 1992), p. 159.
12 Anthony McCall, "Film from the Other End," unpublished manuscript. New York. Archive of Malcolm Le Grice, Artists Film and Video Collection (Central Saint Martins, 1976), p. 1.
13 Scott MacDonald, "Anthony McCall," in *A Critical Cinema 2: Interviews with Independent Filmmakers*, edited by Scott MacDonald (Berkeley, 1992), pp. 160–161.
14 *Line Describing a Cone*. Directed by Anthony McCall, 1973.

maker's Co-op. In this film, a white line moves slowly across black exposed film to form a circular shape. This animation is projected onto smoke or dust particles, creating three-dimensional cones of light that fill the room as far as the reach of the projection. The audience does not look at the projected image on a screen, but at the beam of light emitted by the projector which slowly transforms from a line to a cone over thirty minutes. Thus, in this work, the animated line is no longer restricted to the screen but is extended into three dimensions. It is made manifest. It can be physically experienced.[15] McCall calls it a "solid light film."[16] Thus, the main focus of this work is about the act of projection in that particular time and space, about being able to walk through the projected cones of light, rather than on the content of what is shown on a screen.

Although he has been used by Noel Carroll as an example of a filmmaker who is preoccupied with the medium of film and its essential characteristics,[17] McCall's own writings demonstrate his intention to go beyond a narrow focus on film form and its material qualities. Moving to New York in 1973, McCall became disillusioned with what he saw as a stagnation in avant-garde, political filmmaking that was compromising any of its original political intentions through courting the international art establishment:

> Its very success has led ironically, to a stasis. Having decisively backed itself away from the values of the consumer film industry, it has slipped sideways into a network every bit as limiting, every bit as ideologically bound to a status quo as the movie business itself. The Museums of Modern Art have been our Odeon Leicester Square. Increasingly, the work is identified and practiced more as a visual style, than as a continuing exploration of the problematic of doing film, doing art, in this culture. Whatever political significance this work was beginning to acquire is now being negated by widespread promotion within the official system of art validation—one that occurs as

a pervasive abstract imprint on an international scale, without authentic connection to the special social geography of each city, region or country.[18]

With his own work, McCall wanted to reject the "'film-as-object' fixity"[19] and counteract audience passivity. In 1976, he wrote

> Film discourse—that of most film, is still locked into a blind obsession with what occurs within the frame, within the duration of the work, and a disregard of the circumstances surrounding the making and showing of these works... But suppose we see all audienceship as a special kind of passivity? 'Look there' is a call to your consciousness to perceive my problems, not yours, my relations to the world. In granting me an audience, the spectators surrender their personal cognizance of their own world, and in granting the audience over and over again, under all sorts of circumstances inside and outside art, in schools, work, civic and political life, they become captives to the habit of listening only to others. In art, where the form is made exemplary, the servitude of always being in a passive relation to action, is publicly reinforced.[20]

An outcome of this investigation can be seen in his *Long Film for Ambient Light* (1975),[21] an installation in which a specially prepared room had the windows on one side covered with translucent paper and in the center of the room a light bulb emits constant light. A "time-schema" depicting how the light sources would change over a period of fifty days ran along the wall. Most importantly, on the wall was a two-page statement entitled *Notes in Duration* that outlined the ideas behind the work. This text names the work in the room as a film.

With this work, McCall questions the nature of spectatorship: perhaps the notion of a film does not reside in the material of film, in a projector or a screen, but in

---

15 Birgitta Hosea, *Substitutive Bodies and Constructed Actors: A Practice-Based Investigation of Animation as Performance*, PhD Thesis (London: Central Saint Martins, University of the Arts London, 2012), pp. 100–101.

16 Scott MacDonald, "Anthony McCall," in *A Critical Cinema 2: Interviews with Independent Filmmakers*, edited by Scott MacDonald (Berkeley, 1992), pp. 160–161.

17 Noël Carroll, *Theorizing the Moving Image* (Cambridge., 1996), pp. 4–5.

18 Anthony McCall, "Film from the Other End," Unpublished manuscript. New York. Archive of Malcolm Le Grice, Artists Film and Video Collection (Central Saint Martins, 1976), p. 6.

19 Ibid., p. 7.

20 Ibid., p. 6.

21 *Long Film for Ambient Light*. Directed by Anthony McCall, 1975.

the eye of the beholder. Cinema is reduced to its bare essentials—light changing, time and an audience. Walley comments that what had begun in *Line Describing a Cone* as a process of minimalism had "reached a new level" and that "The film employed no camera, film strip, projector, or screen, taking instead space, light and duration as its parameters."[22] In other words, this work is about a live event in which light is witnessed changing in a room. It is an experience, created in the present moment in a specific time and place. The cinematic apparatus has been removed, but the work becomes a film because Anthony McCall has called it a film and, therefore, we perceive it as a film.

VALIE EXPORT

Another artist from the expanded cinema movement who has taken the concept of cinema and extended it beyond the material of film in a manner that can be described as paracinema is VALIE EXPORT. Based in Austria, VALIE EXPORT re-named herself in order to take ownership of her own representation and become a brand that she had designed herself.[23] For EXPORT, as with other post-war European artists, it was particularly important to mark a break with the past and to reconnect with the radical avant-garde movements of the 1920s, which had been exiled during the Second World War.[24] Having a background in painting, her work was created in an environment of happenings, student uprisings of May 1968, Fluxus, Dada, Situationism, structural film and Viennese Actionism.[25] EXPORT has described the influence on her work from the Cubism, Constructivism and Futurism paintings that she was exposed to in her formative years as a student thus: a "living, expanded" lineage of ways of seeing the image "with the form and extension of artistic expression in(to) space, and the related element, time; the interconnection between light and movement."[26]

EXPORT began experimenting with the idea of film together with Peter Weibel in 1967. Her *Tapp und Tastkino (Touch Cinema)*[27] (1968) is well known as an iconic

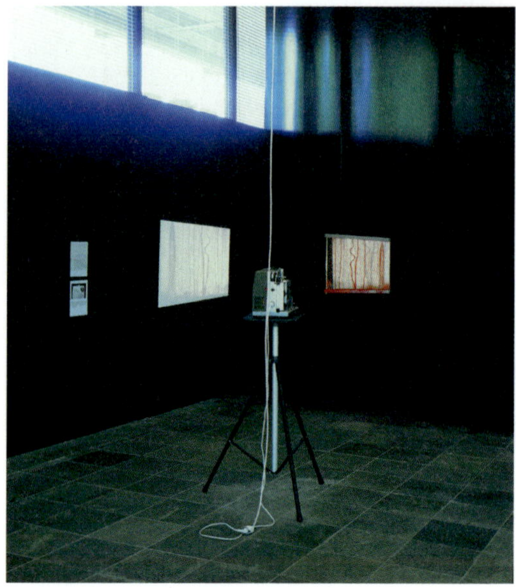

Figure 2: VALIE EXPORT, *Abstract Film n°1*, 1967/8.

feminist work in which the film industry's obsession with breasts is satirized. Her upper body encased by a mobile theater with two holes in it, photographs of this performance document her in the street with crowds of passers-by as she invites people to feel her breasts. This provocative work draws attention to the construction of woman as sex object and invites many responses—ranging from titillation by some to fears for her personal safety by others. Due to its sexual nature, it gets a lot of attention, but she also created a number of other important works around the same time that investigate the experience of cinema.

In *Abstract Film n°1* (1967/68),[28] a projector light shines on a mirror over which liquids are poured. The light bounces from the mirror onto a screen and abstract moving patterns are created.[29] As with McCall's work discussed earlier in the chapter, EXPORT has designated this a film and so it is experienced as a film, although this film is reduced to the most basic elements—a screen, a moving image and light travelling

<hr>

22 Jonathan Walley, "The Material of Film and the Idea of Cinema: Contrasting Practices in Sixties and Seventies Avant-Garde Film," October 103 (October 2003), p. 20.

23 VALIE EXPORT, *VALIE EXPORT: Works from 1968–1975. A Comprehension Catalogue* (Paris, 1975).

24 VALIE EXPORT, "Expanded Cinema: Expanded Reality," in *Expanded Cinema: Art, Performance, Film*, edited by A.L. Rees, at al. (London, 2011), p. 289.

25 Rosewitha Mueller, *VALIE EXPORT: Fragments of the Imagination* (Bloomington and Indianapolis, 1994).

26 VALIE EXPORT, "Expanded Cinema: Expanded Reality," in *Expanded Cinema: Art, Performance, Film*, edited by A.L. Rees, at al. (London, 2011), p. 288.

27 *Tapp und Tastkino (Touch Cinema)*, Performance by VALIE EXPORT, 1968.

28 *Abstract Film n°1*. Directed by VALIE EXPORT, 1967/68.

29 VALIE EXPORT, "Expanded Cinema: Expanded Reality," in *Expanded Cinema: Art, Performance, Film*, edited by A.L. Rees, at al. (London, 2011), p. 295.

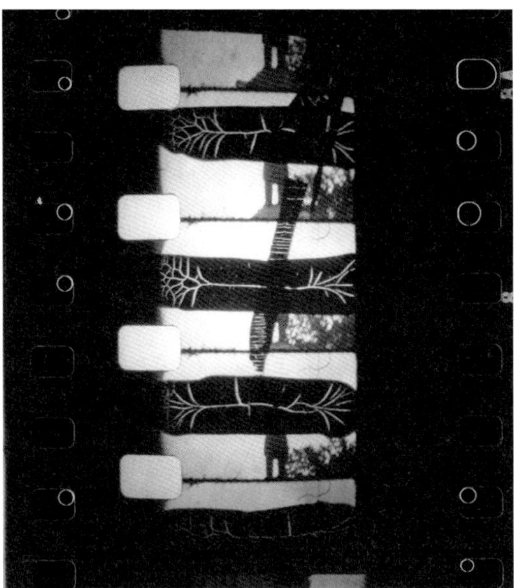

Figure 3: VALIE EXPORT, *Auuf+Ab+An+Zu*, 1968.

from a projector.

During *Auf+Ab+An+Zu (Up + Down + On + Off)* (1968),[30] a looped three-minute film shows a 360° camera view circling a monument. Some of the film footage is obscured by black geometric shapes. The film is pro-jected onto a paper screen and the audience is invited to draw upon this paper screen and, thus, complete the image in partnership with the artist. As the film loops, at intervals the drawings that are made on the screen momentarily fill the missing space. This description of the work from a 1975 catalogue shows the influence of Cubism:

> This film is an exercise in painting, an echo of the painting's cubistic desertion. Space as moment of time. From moving the camera in circles around the object to map, and by fixing all sides of a body on one and only one place, namely the screen, results a superimposition of static pictures. A performer who has to participate in the projection of the film in order that the film may be realized at all, completes with the crayon what is covered up with paint (painted over) on the celluloid. At

the end, there remain lines and signs in the white projection space.[31]

This expanded cinema performance questions the viewer as passive consumer. In reference to Bertolt Brecht's idea of a *Lehrstück* (a learning or instruc-tional play that aims to activate its audience out of passivity) EXPORT considers this a *Lehrfilm* (learning film), which eliminates the distance between creator and viewer in an effort to do away with the traditional hierarchal distinction between active, creative artists and passively receptive audiences.[32] Made by audi-ence members, EXPORT called these drawings that attempted to fill a series of absences—the real film.[33] Reflecting on her work and this process of questioning and breaking down the components that go into the experience of cinema EXPORT has said:

> ... in expanded cinema, the film phenomenon is initially split up into its formal components, and then put back together again in a new way. The operations of the collective union which is film— such as the screen, the cinema theatre, the pro-jector, light and celluloid—are partially replaced by reality in order to install new signs of the real. ... The filmic artwork was no longer understood only in its symbolic expression, but replaced by signs of the real.[34]

This demonstrates a search for a deeper truth beyond the illusionism and voyeurism of mainstream cin-ema. Like McCall she has always made the political intention behind her work clear, saying that her works "are always intended to be seen within the context of a social struggle, as an attack on state reality so as to destroy the limits of state reality and the tradi-tional concept of art, for expanded cinema also means expanded reality."[35]

Antony McCall and VALIE EXPORT are two artists involved with expanded cinema who have created

works that could be thought of as paracinema. Their practice goes beyond the confines of technology and the material of the film strip to deconstruct and ques-

30 *Auf+Ab+An+Zu (Up + Down + On + Off)*. Directed by VALIE EXPORT, 1968.
31 VALIE EXPORT, *VALIE EXPORT: Works from 1968–1975. A Comprehension Catalogue* (Paris, 1975).
32 Rosewitha Mueller, *VALIE EXPORT: Fragments of the Imagination. (Bloomington and Indianapolis, 1994)*, p. 11.
33 Dunja Schneider and Nina Kirsch. *VALIE EXPORT: Time and Countertime. Information Sheet*. Linz., 2011. https://www.lentos.at/images/Media/PK_VALIE_EXPORT_Presseunterlage_engl.pdf, p. 19. (accessed January 17, 2019).
34 VALIE EXPORT, "Expanded Cinema: Expanded Reality," in *Expanded Cinema: Art, Performance, Film*, edited by A.L. Rees, at al. (London, 2011), p. 290.
35 Ibid., p. 293.

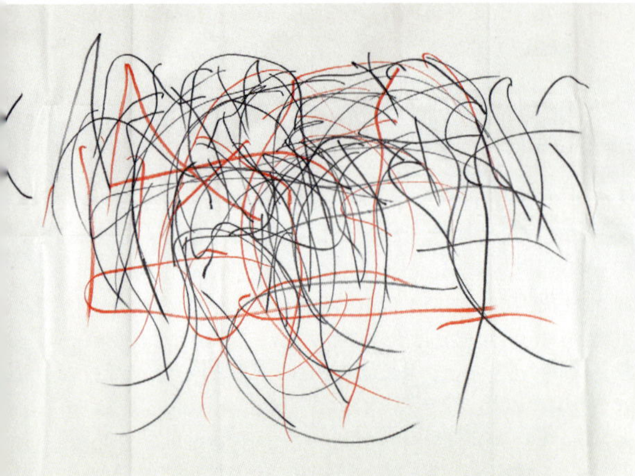

Figure 4: VALIE EXPORT, *Auuf+Ab+An+Zu*, 1968.

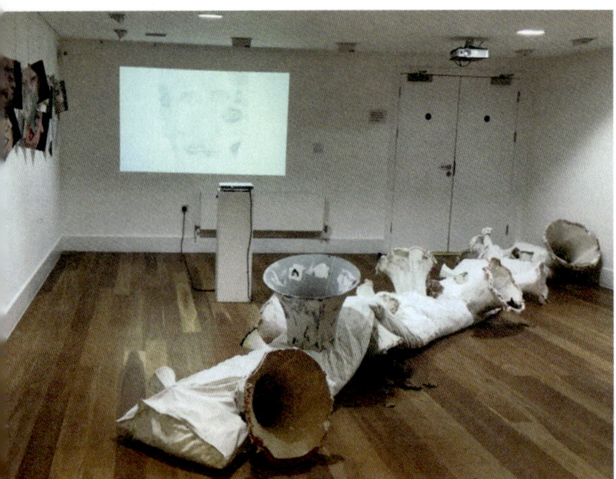

Figure 5: Tingting Lu, *Lisa*, solo exhibition, installation: 3-screen image, 8-meter device , 1-meter device, 32 x A3 composite photos; BUMF gallery, University of the Arts Bournemouth, UK,12/2016

tion the mainstream institution of cinema.

Animation as Concept: Expanded Animation / Post Animation

Inspired by the legacy of artists experimenting with expanded cinema, for a while I conceptualized my own practice in this way, as expanded animation—animation that expands out of the screen and into live events—and I have been keeping a blog with this name since 2011.[36] However, I began to move on from this position and to consider my work as a form of post-medium practice. Rather than expanding on the

conventional concept of animation, I wanted to go beyond it and to be free of disciplinary boundaries. However, I remain deeply influenced by the history and practices of animation, so I started to call my work post animation and, inspired by the work of Alan Cholodenko, to name it as a conceptual practice that seeks to interrogate and de-territorialize animation. In opposition to definitions of animation as something that is made by particular techniques and processes or as a kind of a film, animation theorist Alan Cholodenko argues that what animation is goes beyond this. He makes a case for a broader theorization of animation that goes beyond being defined by how it is made or the form it takes and is, instead, seen as an "idea, concept or process" that is:

> ... not delimited to and by the animation film (and conventional ideas of it) but as a notion whose purchase would be transdisciplinary, transinstitutional, implicating the most profound, complex and challenging questions of our culture, questions in the area of being and becoming, time, space, motion, change—indeed, life itself.[37]

Cholodenko contends that what is fundamental to animation is that it is a process by which something that is still and dead is brought into movement and apparent life. Animation is not just a technique, but a concept which raises fundamental issues about what is real and what it means to be alive: "... the basis of animation is that it is a process in which the inanimate is transformed into the animate through 'endowing with movement' or even 'endowing with life".[38]

Bringing together Cholodenko's notion of animation as a concept and Walley's notion of paracinema, I now propose not only expanded animation and post animation, but also para-animation. I will now give some examples.

Post Animation / Anti Animation: Tingting Lu

I first met Tingting Lu at the *Beyond Noumenon* exhibition and forum at Sichuan Fine Arts Institute, Chongqing, China, in 2016, for which she was Director and Head Curator and discovered that she is also working with this notion of post animation. *Beyond Noumenon*[39] aimed to question the ontology of animation with a series of speakers and artists show-

---

36 Now at expandedanimation.net (accessed January 17, 2019).

37 Alan Cholodenko, *The Illusion of Life: Essays on Animation* (Sydney, 1993) p. 15.

38 Ibid., pp. 15–16.

39 *Beyond Noumenon*. Directed by Tingting Lu, 2016.

ing work that troubled the edges of animation as a practice and as an idea; exploring the possibility of a new language beyond the single screen; exploring how animation might be experienced by an audience. In her closing speech, Lu concluded that we need to go beyond technique and shallow aesthetics. She argued for anti-animation that rejects commercial values; for dissolving the boundaries between disciplines; for post animation, a post medium practice where animation is used as an adjective or adverb instead of a verb or a noun. Tingting Lu was originally trained in animation at Sichuan Fine Arts Institute, but she now works in a post medium context embracing a number of different art forms. The form that her work takes cannot be contained by a single screen and explores different ways in which an audience can encounter animation. At the core of each piece is a conceptual investigation of movement through space and time, but this is expressed through a number of media such as painting, sculpture and installation as well as animation. Her installation *Lisa*[40] can be considered as a work of expanded animation, since the animated imagery was not originally designed as a standalone piece, rather as simply one of the components within a monstrous installation. It was first shown as a part of a solo exhibition at the BUMF gallery, University of the Arts, Bournemouth. For this installation, Lu contacted a number of women called Lisa, searched for women called Lisa online and drew an animated composite portrait of all of them. What had been a number of real women became a monster. The room is filled with a twisted sculpture made of fabric and old lampshades that resembles a decaying lifeform encrusted in barnacles. The animation is shown projected on a wall alongside a number of composite portraits drawn on paper. The sculptural objects and drawings in the room extend the world of the animation out of the screen and into the room. Lu has subsequently developed this work into a multi-screen installation.

Rather than expanded animation, *The Person in the Gap*,[41] her piece for the *Beyond Noumenon* exhibition, can be seen as a work of para-animation as it dispenses altogether with the playback of moving images and features a series of monitors located on the ceiling that each display a different still from her animation. In doing this, she wants to express the idea that people are in the gaps of time, that it is people who make time

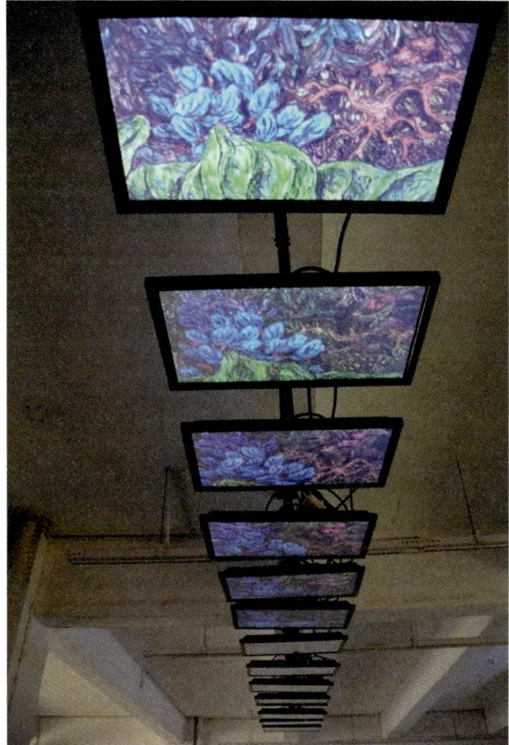

Figure 6: Tingting Lu, *The Person in the Gap*, installation: digital screens, animation sequence of frames from *The Person in the Gap; Beyond Numenon* exhibition, Sichuan Institute of Fine Arts, Chongqing,China, 10/2016

happen. This calls to mind Norman McLaren's famous definition of animation:

> Animation is not the art of drawings that move, but rather the art of movements that are drawn. What happens between each frame is more important than what happens on each frame. Animation is therefore the art of manipulating the invisible interstices that lie between the frames.[42]

In other words, animation is foregrounded as a cognitive process that is completed in the mind. It is our mind that connects a series of still images and experiences an illusion of movement. Through walking underneath the images to experience them all, the viewer is made to do the work of animating the sequence of stills through their physical act of walking and this brings into question traditional ways of experiencing animation. As we gaze upwards with an

---

40 *Lisa*. Installation by Tingting Lu, 2016.
41 *The Person in the Gap*. Installation by Tingting Lu, 2016.
42 Georges Sifianos, "The Definition of Animation: A Letter from Norman McLaren," *Animation Journal 3 (2)*, 1995, p. 62.

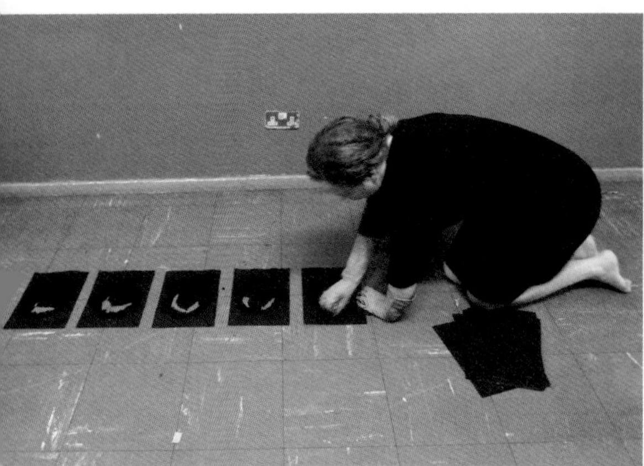

Figure 7: Birgitta Hosea, *Rosary Drawing XII*, live performance: water, scouring pads, black paper, rosary beads; *51% Remember Her* exhibition, Tower Gallery, London, 2017.

almost religious awe, dwarfed by the images above, this action also references the God-like power of the animator to create their very own time and spaces that transgress the rules of nature. The content of the film also explores gender—the idea of being in between male and female realities.

Expanded Animation / Para-animation: Birgitta Hosea

In *Erasure*,[43] my 2018 solo exhibition at the Hanmi Gallery, Seoul, South Korea,[44] the different artworks all explore ideas about the visualization of manual labor, an activity which forms the world around us and yet remains invisible. The show is named after my short film, *Erasure*, which was originally commissioned for EMPIRE II, an exhibition of artists' films at the Venice Biennale in 2017 that formed part of the UK's Collateral art events. The multiple meanings of the word "erasure" inspired the works, as it could refer to removing part of a drawing, cleaning away dirt, censorship or obliteration. The following three works *Scrubbed Clean*[45] (2018), *Warping the Weft*[46] (2017) and *Rosary Drawing XII*[47] (2015) are all part of this exhibition.

Scrubbed Clean is an installation of animation projected over 112 panels made from scrubbing through layered sheets of paper with a scrubbing brush using bleach, bicarbonate of soda, plain flour and abrasive cleaning products. An animation, made from charcoal drawings (in negative) of my hand scrubbing with the same brush that was used to make the panels, is projected over the paper panels. The disembodied hand scrubs away at the wall endlessly, repeating the gestures that I used to make the panels. It roams across the wall unconstrained by a frame. It never stops.

Warping the Weft was commissioned by the curator Zhang Xiaotao for an exhibition of contemporary artists' responses to traditional weaving at the Chengdu Museum of Contemporary Art in 2017. Combining a string picture nailed to the wall with projection mapped animation that plays over it, the installation forms a moving drawing. My response to the brief was originally inspired by Freud's observation that women had never invented any technology of their own, apart perhaps from weaving, but that this was only an unconscious and compulsive process based on recreating pubic hair to cover their shameful deficiency at not having a penis.[48] The title of the work refers to the process of weaving in which the *"Weft"* is the name given to the thread going across the cloth and the *"Warp"* is the thread that runs vertically. The word *"warped'* in English also has the sense of something that is twisted or bent from its usual shape or even something that is abnormal or strange. The string in the picture is distorted into a pubic triangle from the conventional rectangular shape that woven cloth takes. The projection of animated drop shadows onto it creates the optical illusion that the string itself is moving and breathing: as if it has a life of its own. Thus, the work explores distortion and the difficulty in telling the difference between reality and illusion. *Scrubbed Clean* and *Warping the Weft* experiment with projection, but they involve pre-recorded animated movies as one component within a field of linked items created with different media[49] and, so, I would call them expanded animation. The following two works I would call para-animation.

Conceived of whilst on a residency in a former convent in Italy, *Rosary Drawing XII* is a performance that takes place in an art gallery. After removing all make-up and jewelry, I scrub away a hole from a series of sheets of black paper on my hands and knees while counting down the beads of my deceased Grandmother's bro-

43 *Erasure*. Exhibition by Birgitta Hosea, 2018.

44 https://www.hanmigallery.co.uk/exhibitions/current/birgitta-hosea-erasure/

45 *Scrubbed Clean*. Installation by Birgitta Hosea, 2018.

46 *Warping the Weft*. Installation by Birgitta Hosea, 2017

47 *Rosary Drawing XII*. Performance by Birgitta Hosea, 2015.

48 Sigmund Freud cited in Sadie Plant. *Zeros + Ones: Digital Women + The New Technoculture* (London, 1998), p. 23–24.

49 I am grateful to Tianran Duan for this insight about the use of animation as one component amongst others in installation art.

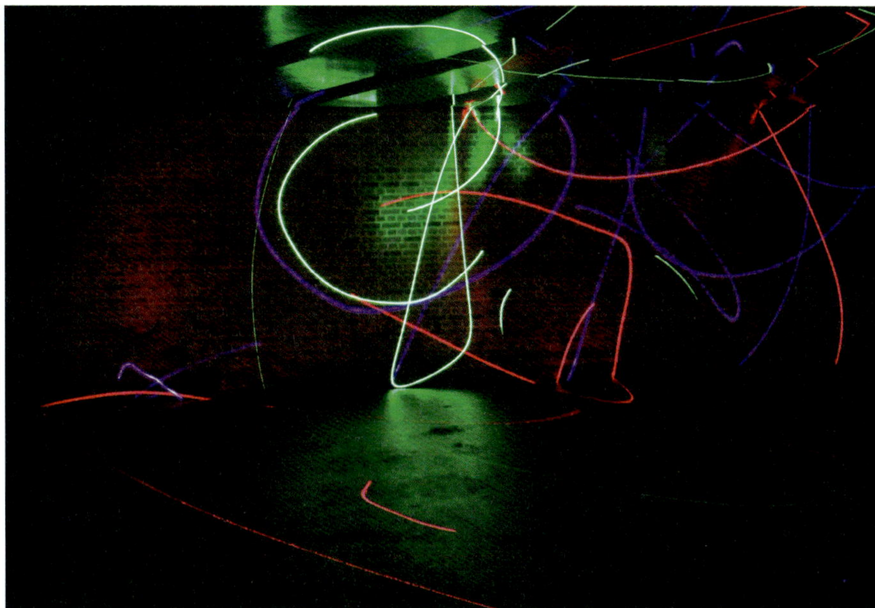

Figure 8: Birgitta Hosea, *dotdot dash*, participatory performance: red, green, purple laser pointers, live vocals; Inspiral-London event for London as Park City Festival in Regents Canal Tunnels, Kings Cross, London, 2018.

ken rosary. One act of scrubbing on one sheet for each bead. Going from one side of the gallery to the other, I leave behind a trail of paper resembling a filmstrip on which my actions have been recorded frame-by-frame. The scoured marks resemble the highlights shining on the black beads of the rosary. An "artist" is not supposed to get down on their hands and knees and scrub in a gallery. It is a homage to all women who clean endlessly and are forgotten. Another recent work of para-animation is *dotdot dash*[50] (2018), which was commissioned for the Night Walking North Kent festival by InspiralLondon, a collaborative artists' project led by Charlie Fox of Counterproductions. The project is based on a 300-mile walking trail around London in the shape of a spiral created by Charlie Fox and divided into 36 different walks. Determining a route by chance through this drawing of a line means that each walk cuts through unpredictable parts of London. *dotdot dash* was created to be experienced by walkers as part of a series of site-specific artworks at the end of the trail in Gravesend. My intention was to create a work of animation that could be made collectively by the participants on the walk; that was mobile and would not involve carrying any heavy equipment and that would reclaim the night through light and noise for people who may not normally feel safe to walk at night.

The route of the walk involved going through light industrial areas that are desolate and deserted at night, walking through a caged walkway over a sheer drop to a chalk pit, through bushes and undergrowth, past burnt out motor bikes, across another caged walkway over a railway line and then to a tunnel through a disused chalk pit near Ebbsfleet International station. Everyone on the walk was given two laser pens and together we created a live performance of animation. To orchestrate the composition, I gave instructions from a chance-based score I had made as to what colors and types of marks they should make and encouraged the participants to sing along in a choral manner. Although many other artists have done light painting before, such as Pika Pika and even Picasso, this was something very different. It was not a set up for a photograph, but a performed, live animation of lights that was created communally and looked like a scratched-on film, abstract animation. The work was repeated in a tunnel on the Regents Canal at Kings Cross, London for another InspiralLondon night walk for the *London as Park City Festival*, Friday, July 20, 2018. A different group of walkers participated in the work. The addition of the water going through the tunnel added an extra element of bounced light and reflection to the mark making possibilities.

---

50 *dotdot dash*. Participatory performance directed by Birgitta Hosea, 2018

Conclusion

To conclude, the roots of expanded animation lie in the avant-garde experimental work of expanded cinema. The aim behind this was not for escapist and immersive entertainment, but to be critical of mainstream forms of cinema and the political ideas and values embedded within them. This often is forgotten or overlooked in the rush of enthusiasm to learn new techniques and adopt new technologies. New immersive technologies such as VR and AR offer an opportunity to build on these ideas, to go beyond simply recycling the same type of mainstream content from one technology into another, and, instead, imagine new ways in which animation might expand from out of the screen and into three-dimensional space and what the politics of this might be like. In the words of VALIE EXPORT "transformed media produce a transformed world, and a world pressing towards transformation presses toward transformed media."[51]

---

51 VALIE EXPORT, "Expanded Cinema: Expanded Reality," in *Expanded Cinema: Art, Performance, Film*, edited by A.L. Rees, et al. (London, 2011), p. 293.

Bibliography

Bartlett, Mark. "Socialimagestics and the Visual Acupuncture of Stan Vanberbeek's Expanded Cinema." In *Expanded Cinema: Art, Performance, Film*, edited by A.L. Rees, Duncan White, Steven Ball, and David Curtis. London, 2011, pp. 50–61.

Carroll, Noël. *Theorizing the Moving Image*. Cambridge at al., 1996.

Cholodenko, Alan. *The Illusion of Life: Essays on Animation*. Sydney, 1991.

Drummond, Phillip. "Notions of Avant-Garde Cinema." In *Film as Form: Formal Experiment in Film* 1910–1975, edited by Hayward Gallery. London, 1979.

EXPORT, VALIE. *VALIE EXPORT: Works from 1968–1975. A Comprehension Catalogue*. Paris, 1975.

EXPORT, VALIE. "Expanded Cinema: Expanded Reality." In *Expanded Cinema: Art, Performance, Film*, edited by A.L. Rees, Duncan White, Steven Ball, and David Curtis. London, 2011.

Hosea, Birgitta. *Substitutive Bodies and Constructed Actors: A Practice-Based Investigation of Animation as Performance*. PhD Thesis, London: Central Saint Martins, University of the Arts London. 2012.

Lippard, Lucy. *Six Years: The Dematerialization of the Art Object from 1966 to 1972*. Berkeley et al., 1997.

MacDonald, Scott. "Anthony McCall." In *A Critical Cinema 2: Interviews with Independent Filmmakers*, edited by Scott MacDonald, Berkeley, 1992.

McCall, Anthony. "Film from the Other End." Unpublished manuscript. New York. Archive of Malcolm Le Grice, Artists Film and Video Collection, Central Saint Martins, 1976.

Mueller, Rosewitha. *VALIE EXPORT: Fragments of the Imagination*. Bloomington and Indianapolis, 1994.

Plant, Sadie. *Zeros + Ones: Digital Women + The New Technoculture*. London, 1998.

Rees, A.L. "Expanded Cinema and Narrative: A Troubled History." In *Expanded Cinema: Art, Performance, Film*, edited by A.L. Rees, Duncan White, Steven Ball, and David Curtis. London, 2011.

Schneider, Dunja, and Nina Kirsch. VALIE EXPORT: Time and Countertime. Information Sheet. Linz: LENTOS Kunstmuseum, 2011. https://www.lentos.at/images/Media/PK_VALIE_EXPORT_Presseunterlage_engl.pdf.

Schöpf, Christine. "The Making Of …" In *1974–2004 Ars Electronica The Network for Art, Technology and Society: The First 25 Years*, edited by Hannes Leopoldseder et al., Ostfildern-Ruit, 2004.

Sifianos, Georges. "The Definition of Animation: A Letter from Norman McLaren." Animation Journal 3 (2), 1995, pp. 62–66.

Walley, Jonathan. "The Material of Film and the Idea of Cinema: Contrasting Practices in Sixties and Seventies Avant-Garde Film." October 103 (October 2003): pp. 15–30.

Youngblood, Gene. *Expanded Cinema*. London, 1970.

Juergen Hagler (AT)

Anomalies at the Intersection of Animation, Media Art and Technology

Introduction

The interplay of art and technology is a fundamental theme of media art. Accordingly, one of its central questions is: how can technology and therefore science influence artistic processes, and how can artistic research and experimentation advance technological and scientific developments? Ars Electronica has been concerned with that question since its beginning—a current selection of artworks dedicated to that topic can be found in the book *The Practice of Art and Science*.[1] On the one hand, technology is developed specifically for certain applications and these are used accordingly. On the other hand, technological innovations of any kind are the impetus for experimental paths, are modified and used in a new form or are incorrectly employed or deviate from their actual purpose.

These interactions are also evident in the field of expanded cinema,[2] experimental animation[3] and "hyperanimation,"[4] a term introduced by Robert Russett for expanded forms that use advanced digital technologies. A current comprehensive collection is provided by the book *Experimental and Expanded Animation*,[5] edited by Vicky Smith and Nicky Hamlyn. Any form of animation is primarily linked to one or more techniques and, in an expanded sense, to technology. The history of animation is characterized by the invention of numerous techniques, from early devices for creating and displaying moving images like the praxinoscope to the movie camera, from various stop-motion techniques to the latest animation software tools. New technologies such as sound film, color film, television or the advent of computer animation and interactive art have expanded the forms of animation. A look back at the history of computer animation shows two tendencies: technologies and techniques that were developed for animation or technological innovations of any kind have been the trigger

---

1   Cf. Gerfried Stocker et al., eds., *The Practice of Art and Science* (Ostfildern-Ruit, 2017).

2   Cf. Gene Youngblood, *Expanded Cinema* (New York 1970).

3   Cf. Robert Russett and Cecile Starr, *Experimental Animation: Origins of a New Art* (New York, 1976). Hans Scheugl and Ernst Schmidt, *Eine Subgeschichte des Films. Lexikon des Avantgarde-, Experimental- und Undergroundfilms* (Frankfurt a. M., 1974).

4   Robert Russett, *Hyperanimation: Digital Images and Virtual Worlds* (United Kingdom, 2009).

5   Vicky Smith and Nicky Hamlyn, eds., *Experimental and Expanded Animation. New Perspectives and Practices.* (Basingstoke, 2018).

for experimental pathways within animation. In the context of art, various subversive strategies for using technology in the service of animation can be seen, which can be described as a kind of anomaly. Based on recent examples from the Prix Ars Electronica category Computer Animation, different forms of anomalies at the intersection of animation and technologies are analyzed here.

Anomalous Links between Animation and Technology One of the first computer generated films—a simulation of a satellite orbiting a planet—came out of a research project produced by Edward E. Zajac in 1963 at Bell Labs.[6] This was followed by a number of other milestones that strived to further develop computer animation. At the same time, while working at Bell Labs Ken Knowlton developed a software language for computer production of still and moving pictures called Beflix that was used for numerous artistic animated short films by Knowlton, Stan VanDerBeek and Lilian Schwartz.[7] The first artistic use of computer animation involved the repurposing of military equipment and can thus be considered an anomaly of an established technology. John Whitney, Sr. and his brother James modified analog computing devices that served as anti-aircraft gun directors and combined these with cameras to produce their first computer animations,[8] for instance, *Catalog*,[9] in 1961. War machines became an artist's animation toolset.

These ways of using technology have been a prevalent theme in computer animation ever since, relying on deviations and a deliberate exploitation of flaws and errors.

Anomalies: Art & Technology

The etymological root of the word anomaly, from Latin *anomalia*, means in general a "[d]eviation from the common rule; an irregularity; anything anomalous"[10] and is synonymous with abnormality, deviation, exception, inconsistency, irregularity, or error. The term is used in various areas like computer science, astronomy, medical and natural science, or physics with different meanings. For instance, an anomaly can

---

6   Herbert W. Franke, *Computergraphik Computerkunst* (Munich, 1971), p. 94.
7   Robert Russett and Cecile Starr, *Experimental Animation: Origins of a New Art* (New York, 1976), p. 193.
8   Ibid., p. 184.
9   *Catalog*. Directed by John Whitney, Sr., 1961.
10   "Anomaly," https://www.websters1913.com/words/Anomaly (accessed December 18, 2018).

be a deviation in a quantity from its expected value, a genetic disorder, a rift in the space-time continuum, or an error in a computer program.[11] Deviations of technologies—in terms of using technology in other forms—are usually referred to by the term "spin-off." For example, NASA spin-off technologies are "commercial products and services which have been developed with the help of the NASA."[12]

The phenomenon of anomalies requires a concept of normality. In the context of human beings, the concept of normality was established in the early 19th century, after the foundation of European nation-states. Since then, standard values are constantly being determined and serve as the basis for varied and controversial definitions of abnormalities in manifold forms, for instance physiognomy, intelligence or disability.[13] In the world of art there is a different approach to imperfect humans, or rather to abnormal bodies, ranging between the poles of spectacle and entertainment, and critical deconstruction.[14]

In the field of art, the term "anomaly" does not have a particular meaning. However, the concept of deviation is basic pillar in many artistic examinations, for instance in the context of found footage, appropriation art or remix culture. Experimental exploration of errors in visual art, predominantly for aesthetic purposes, are termed as glitch art. These engagements range from experimental film to video or game art and can become a critical or rather political intervention beyond aesthetic effects.[15]

Deviations in the field of art, technology and science can be seen throughout the entire history of media art and were tackled for instance at the Ars Electronica festival in 2005, entitled *Hybrid—Living in Paradox*.[16] According to Roger Clark's thoughts on a taxonomy of hybridization, ranging from mimicry to mutation, dysfunctionality is one of the characteristics of hybrid forms.[17] In 2018, failures and deviations became the main festival theme: *Error – The Art of Imperfection*.[18]

The goal of the 2018 edition was to examine possibilities, risks and dangers of artificial intelligence (AI), machine learning, data mining, and deep learning as well as future technologies. Gerfried Stocker, artistic director of Ars Electronica, emphasizes the possibilities of errors and deviations from the norm: "... what is the norm and who establishes it? An error doesn't have to be a mistake; it can be an opportunity!"[19]

The proposed concept of anomalies at the intersection of animation, media art and technologies constitutes an alternative to common approaches in computer animation and spinoff-technologies. Artistic anomalies are experimental, self-reflective, and artistic interventions, beyond the aesthetics of errors like glitch art and datamoshing.

The focus is on the subversive examination of the technology that is used in an unintended way, in most cases a way diametrically opposed to its own purpose. In doing so, the subversive strategy addresses a critical reflection on technology and in most cases these interventions take on a political dimension. The anomalies are located in the technology itself and show hidden or rather suppressed or totally new qualities that become visible through the artistic intervention: an unexplored dimension emerges.

Misuse of Army Property

As history has shown, the development of new technologies is mostly connected with the development of army technology. Media theorist Friedrich Kittler determines three phases in the development of the media system, in particular AM radio, film and computer.

Phase I, beginning with the American Civil War, developed storage technologies for acoustics, optics, and script: film, gramophone, and the man-machine system, typewriter. Phase 2, beginning with the First World War, developed for each storage content appropriate electric transmission

11   "Anomaly," Wikipedia, last modified September 19, 2018, https://en.wikipedia.org/wiki/Anomaly (accessed December 18, 2018).

12   Nasa, "Nasa Spinoff," https://spinoff.nasa.gov/ (accessed December 18, 2018).

13   Petra Lutz, et al., "Einleitung," in *Der (im-)perfekte Mensch. Methamorphosen von Normalität und Abweichung*, edited by Petra Lutz, et al. (Cologne, 2003), pp. 10–11.

14   Ibid., pp. 14–15.

15   Cf. Michael Betancourt, "Glitch Art in Theory and Practice. Critical Failures and Post-Digital Aesthetics," (New York and London, 2016), pp. 102–122.

16   Ars Electronic festival 2005, https://90.146.8.18/de/archives/festival_archive/festival_overview.asp?iPresentationYearFrom=2005 (accessed December 18, 2018). In 2005 an ongoing discussion about hybridity within art and science started, supplemented by the Prix Ars Electronica category Hybrid Art (2007–2018).

17   Roger Clarke, "Hybridity—Elements of a Theory," in *Ars Electronica 2015. Hybrid – Living in Paradox* (Ostfildern-Ruit, 2005) p. 32.

18   Ars Electronic festival 2018, https://ars.electronica.art/error/en/ (accessed December 18, 2018).

19   Gerfried Stocker, "ERROR – The Art of Imperfection," in *ERROR – The Art of Imperfection* (Ostfildern-Ruit, 2005) p. 19.

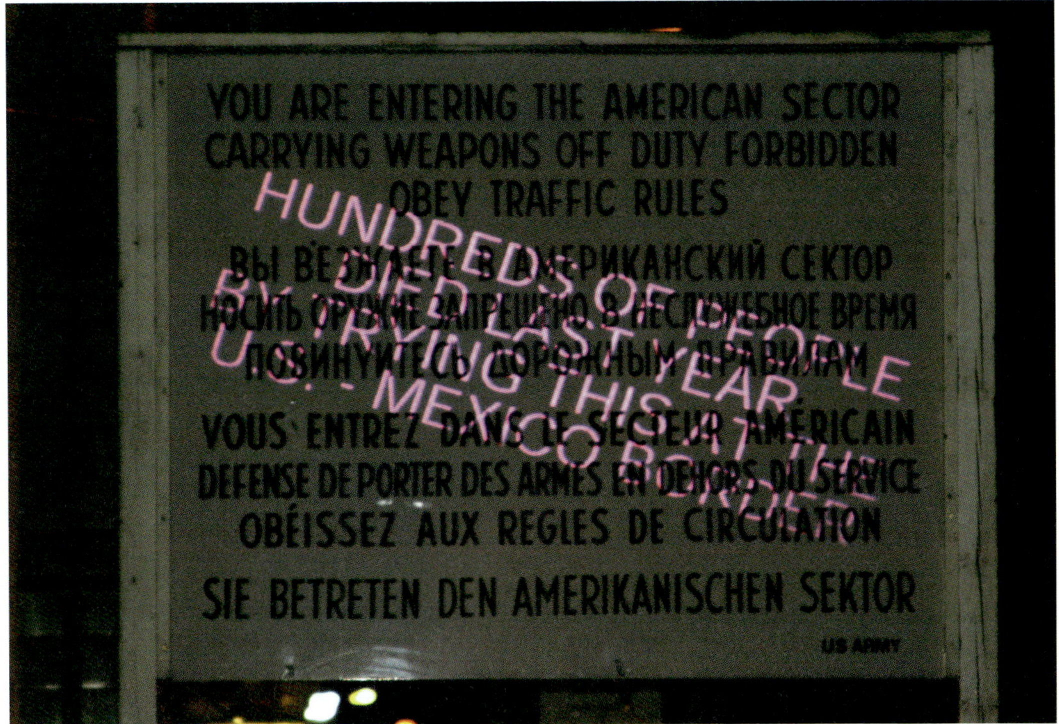

Figure 1: *Image Fulgurator*, projection onto the Replica of the sign at the former East–West Berlin border, 2007.

technologies: radio, television, and their more secret counterparts. Phase 3, since the Second World War, has transferred the schematicof a typewriter to a technology of predictability per se; Turing's mathematical definition of computability in 1936 gave future computers their name.[20]

Kittler adds that unlike film and radio, the computer would not even have been invented without World War II. He identifies a strong link between wars and the development of technologies for the media system and the entertainment industry. He provides two examples: radio, or rather rock music, and film. Through these case studies, Kittler illustrates that war can trigger a push for the innovation of new media and, subsequently, for the entertainment industry. He calls that phenomenon "misuse of army property."[21] Just like radio, which first operated through illicit use of "military radios," rock music is also a consequence of a subversive use of military equipment in violation of the norm:

A nice symmetry holds: just as the misuse of military equipment that had been constructed for the positional warfare of 1917 led to medium-wave monophony, the misuse of military equipment that had been devised for tank divisions, bomber squadrons, and packs of U-boats led to rock music.[22]

Through the example of film, Kittler identifies an ambivalent relationship between the medium and army property. Looking at the history of the film camera, he points out its diametrically opposed function, as seen at the beginning of the moving images. Etienne-Jules Marey's chronophotographic gun (1883) is not a weapon, it is a movie camera with a riflescope to capture serial images, for example of a flying bird. Instead of killing the bird, the bird will be alive in the image sequence forever. The purpose of the technology is reversed. As has been shown, there has always been a lively interaction between military technology and computer animation. Whether analog computing

---

20   Friedrich A. Kittler, *Grammophon, Film, Typewriter* (Stanford, California, 1999), p. 243.

21   Ibid., 218.

22   Friedrich A. Kittler, "Rock Music: A Misuse of Military Equipment," in *The Truth of the Technological World: Essays on the Genealogy of Presence* (Stanford, California, 2013), p. 160.

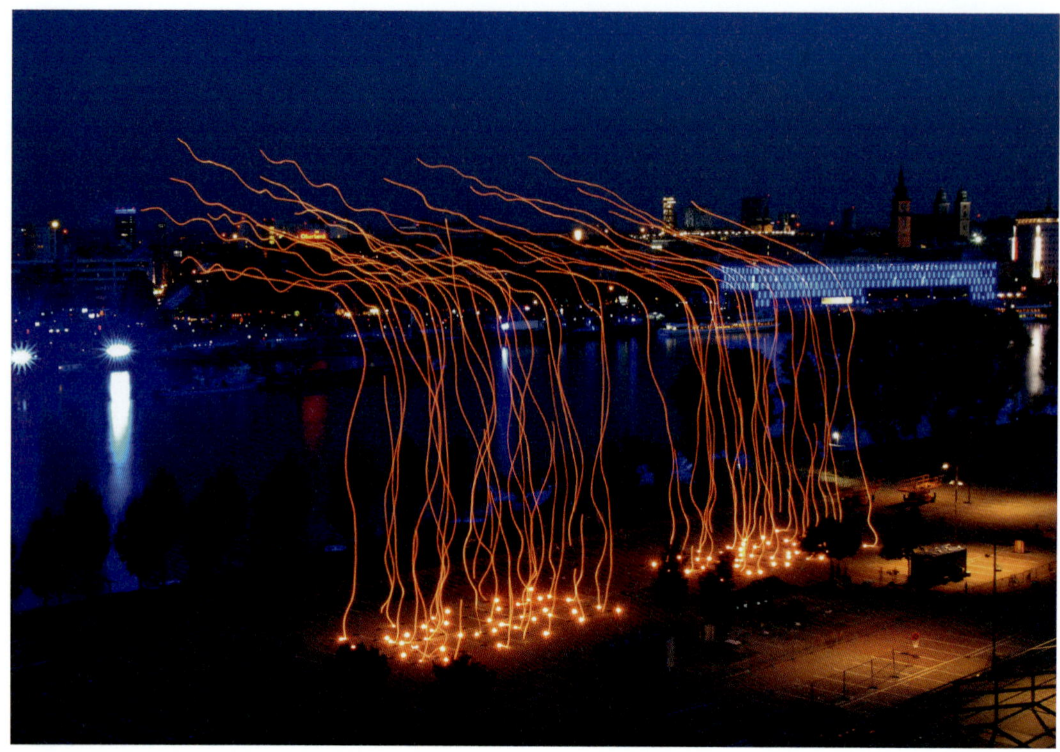

Figure 2. *Drone 100 – Spaxels over Linz*, Ars Electronica Futurelab, 2016 (Photo credit: Ars Electronica / Martin Hieslmair).

devices for anti-aircraft gun directors, flight simulators, or computers developed for the army, all these technologies provide the basis for digital filmmaking.

Fulguration: Subversive Reversal of Technology

Subversive forms of using technology reveal a great potential for reflecting on the technology itself. Through a subversive interplay of its components, new qualities of the technology can emerge and critical reflection can take place, as seen in many examples at Prix Ars Electronica. A vivid example from outside the field of computer animation, but closely linked to Kittler's reflections, is *Image Fulgurator*,[23] a device for physically manipulating photographs, developed by artist Julius von Bismarck in 2007. It was a top-prize Winner in the category Interactive Art.

In principle, the Fulgurator can be used anywhere where there is another camera nearby that is being used with a flash. It operates via a kind of reactive flash projection that enables an image to be projected onto an object exactly at the moment when someone else is photographing it. .... Every photo another photographer takes of an object at which the Fulgurator is also aimed, is affected by the manipulation. Hence, visual information can be smuggled unnoticed into the images of others.[24]

By means of this subversive installation, Julius von Bismarck addresses the issue that people do not question the reality of photographic reproductions. "The Image Fulgurator represents a manipulation of visual reality and so targets the very fabric of media memory," according to the artist. Bismarck performed various interventions, for instance if a tourist takes a photo of the replica of the sign at Checkpoint Charlie at Berlin, the Fulgurator will project the text "HUNDREDS OF PEOPLE DIED LAST YEAR BY TRYING THIS AT THE U.S. – MEXICO BORDER" (see fig. 1). The *Image Fulgurator* reverses the function of the photo camera, resulting in a new characteristic of the medium. The term "ful-

---

23 *Image Fulgurator*. Developed by Julius von Bismarck, 2007.

24 "Image Fulgurator," Ars Electronica Archive (website) https://archive.aec.at/prix/showmode/12122/ (accessed December 18, 2018).

guration," from Latin "fulguratio," meaning "flash," refers to the new purpose and the reverse function of the camera.

Misuse of Army Property: from Anomaly and Spin-off

A current example of an artistic anomaly and misuse of army property in the field of expanded animation are the so called Spaxels, first introduced by Ars Electronica Futurelab in 2012.[25] Spaxels, a conjunction of space and pixel, are "a novel display paradigm … based on the control of a swarm of unmanned aerial vehicles equipped with RGB lighting and a positioning system that can be coordinated in three dimensions to create a morphing floating display."[26] In short, a controlled swarm of quadrocopters with LEDs. In 2015, Ars Electronica Futurelab and Intel Corporation presented *Drone 100*, a drone show with 100 quadrocopters. Since then both companies have developed light shows with drone technologies all around the world.

If we look at the evolution of drones, or rather unmanned aerial vehicles, from balloons equipped with bombs—an Austrian invention from 1846—to flying objects that currently make it to Mars, one thing will become obvious: the initial intention of the drones—to attack or observe enemies—has changed. Instead of bombs or cameras, the spaxels are equipped with LEDs. The unmanned aerial vehicles transform into a controllable luminous pixel in physical space. The spaxels were first presented at Ars Electronica during the "Linzer Klangwolke" under the motto *The Cloud in the Web* in 2012. This big open-air show told the story of our increasingly networked world from the first telephone to current social media. By using the drones in a subversive form, this show provides the impetus for inspiration and reflection on the initial purpose of the unmanned aerial vehicles. The further development and commercialization of the spaxel shows—for instance, in 2018 Intel broke a world record by creating the biggest-ever choreographed drone light show with 2,018 drones[27]—reveals another characteristic, possibly the initial purpose: as animated rocket flares, the spaxels replace fireworks arts, a technology that has its roots in army property as well. Quadrocopers and

LEDs replace gunpowder and pyrotechnical propellant. This use for the spaxels was already apparent at the Klangwolke 2012, as fireworks have been part of the show since the beginning. The artistic anomaly turns into a spin-off and becomes a prime example of the interplay between art, science, and industry.

Types of Animation Anomalies at Prix Ars Electronica

The forms of play and experimentation with anomalies at the intersection of animation and technology are quite diverse. On the basis of the remarks and suggestions made on this subject, some types of artistic anomalies based on examples from Prix Ars Electronica's category Computer Animation since 1987 will be introduced. These approaches to artistic anomalies are discussed below.

Deconstruction – Substance and Materiality

Animation can be self-reflective, specifically addressing its own substance and materiality as a theme. The deconstruction of animation in any form is a basic topic, a generic specificity[28] since the beginning of moving images. It was first discussed in a detailed and comprehensive manner in the anthology *Experimental Animation*[29] by Robert Russett and Cecile Starr. Pioneers in experimental computer animation like John and James Whitney, Ken Knowlton, Stan VanDerBeek, Peter Foldes, or Lillian Schwartz[30] developed and explored ways and means for making digital animation, not just to simulate traditional animation technique. They primarily investigated the language of computer animation and digital filmmaking. This was one of the main topics in the early days of Ars Electronica and was discussed at the very first editions of the festival in the early 1980s in the context of media art. Artists and scholars like Otto Piene, Stan VanDerBeek, Gene Youngblood or Peter Weibel as well as computer scientists like Alvy Ray Smith and David Di Francesco were invited to address current positions in art and science. In 1987 the international competition for media art Prix Ars Electronica was established and since then the competition has called for entries in the category Computer Animation.

---

25   Horst Hörtner et al., "Spaxels, Pixels in Space – A Novel Mode of Spatial Display," SIGMAP 2012, pp. 19–24.

26   Ibid. p. 19.

27   "Celebrating 50 Years of Innovation," Intel (website) https://www.intel.com/content/www/us/en/technology-innovation/aerial-technology-light-show.html (accessed December 18, 2018).

28   Cf. Paul Wells, *Animation. Genre and Authorship*, (London and New York, 2002), pp. 67–71.

29   Robert Russett and Cecile Starr, *Experimental Animation: Origins of a New Art* (New York, 1976).

30   Ibid., p. 178–208.

One of the first examples in the archive of Prix Ars Electronica that foregrounds the substance of digital production is *Calculated Movements*[31] by Larry Cuba, honored with a mention in 1987. Cuba developed his own animation software and before he produced his own artworks, he supported John Whitney producing digital animation.[32] In *Calculated Movements* ribbon-like figures are animated and connected to electronic music to explore the basic ideas behind the software for animation and sound. By bringing the nature of the artificial production and the procedures behind the software to the surface, the authorship of the animator is questioned. *Time as Code: Chronokratie*[33] by Peter Weibel, an Austrian Media Artist and well-known representative of expanded cinema, implies the same question and reveals anomalies caused by the system. In his work Weibel animates multiple layers of grid of horizontal lines to create artefacts like moiré, rings, et cetera. In that sense, this work shows "automatic, self-executing pattern making processes … as well as auto-colouring based upon the principles of colour addition and colour subtraction" and reveals the "Consciousness of the Machines," according to Weibel.[34] Current artists working in the field of self-reflective procedural animation are Casey Reas, Memo Akten or Quayola. Reas creates procedural and minimal artworks with the Processing programming language, which he developed together with Ben Fry.[35] Media artist Quayola investigates new modes of visual synthesis between art, nature and technology in a series of works entitled Nature-Process-Synthesis including installations like *Jardins d'Été*[36] and *Pleasant Places*.[37] Inspired by the work of Vincent van Gogh and Claude Monet, Quayola recorded several movies of landscapes in the area where both painters lived and worked, like trees and flowers moving slightly in the wind. By means of image processing software, the images are transformed into a van Gogh- or Monet-like painting solely and exclusively by the captured movement. The result is an artificial animation based on the natural motion of trees and flowers. Memo Akten goes a step further: he uses state-of-the-art Machine Learning algorithms to create artworks like *Deep Meditations*,[38] which will be discussed later.

Flaws and Artifacts

Apart from deconstruction, flaws or artefacts created by established technologies are not simply covered up but subtly become a conceptual part of the work. In this context, several strategies can be pursued. A first distinction can be made when flaws and artefacts are used for storytelling based on aesthetic reasons. A prime example is David OReilly, who intentionally explores artefacts and characteristics of 3D animation. In his essay *Basic Animation Aesthetics*[39] he introduced the idea of coherence of all aspects of filmmaking and defines basic aesthetic rules through the short movie *Please Say Something*.[40] The key question here is: how can the substance and materiality of computer animation serve the narrative? Many of those nodes comprise aesthetic decisions that could be understood as mistakes in general. However, in OReilly's oeuvre, these supposed errors are made intentionally, for instance, when 3D objects intersect or renderings are not anti-aliased. In most cases common techniques and procedures are deconstructed and conceptually used for storytelling. With his works, OReilly outlines a concept as an alternative to the "rapidly expanding aesthetic library."[41] As already explained, making artefacts visible by deconstructing the medium can lead to critical reflection on the medium, as seen in the works of Peter Weibel, Quayola or Case Reas.

The installation *The Augmented Hand Series*[42] by Golan Levin and his team also addresses flaws and

---

31   *Calculated Movements*. Produced by Larry Cuba, 6. Minutes, 1985. Prix Ars Electronica Honorary Mention 1987.

32   Neesa Sweet, "Animating the Death Star Trench," *The Very Best of Fantastic Films: The Magazine of Imaginative Media* (February 1981), p. 27.

33   *Time as Code: Chronokratie*. Directed by Peter Weibel, 1988.

34   "Time as Code: Chronokratie," Ars Electronica Archive (website) https://archive.aec.at/prix/showmode/21075/ (accessed December 22, 2018).

35   https://reas.com/ (accessed December 22, 2018).

36   Jardins d'Été, produced by Quayola, Series of 4k videos, 2016, https://www.quayola.com/jardins/ (accessed December 22, 2018).

37   *Pleasant Places*, https://www.quayola.com/pleasant-places/ (accessed December 22, 2018).

38   *Deep Meditations*. Developed by Memo Akten, 2018, https://www.memo.tv/portfolio/deep-meditations/ (accessed December 22, 2018).

39   David OReilly, *Basic Animation Aesthetics* https://www.davidoreilly.com/downloads/ (accessed December 18, 2018).

40   *Please Say Something*. Directed by David OReilly, 2008–2009, Honorary Mention 2008.

41   David OReilly, *Basic Animation Aesthetics* https://www.davidoreilly.com/downloads/ (accessed December 18, 2018).

42   *The Augmented Hand Series*. Developed by Golan Levin, Chris Sugrue, and Kyle McDonald, 2014, Honorary Mention 2015. For more details see p. 184.

artefacts, but not by deconstructing or reflecting on the medium. This interactive software system transforms the hand of the visitors in real time. The user can explore about twenty different malformations of their own hands, altered by various dynamic and structural digital mutations, such the hand receives an additional finger, or the fingers get twisted or turn into rubber fingers. This playful installation is appealing but at the same time provokes thoughts about the human body. The artist duo Joe Gerhardt and Ruth Jarman, aka Semiconductor, encourages us to think about anomalies at the intersection of art and science, when working with raw scientific data. For instance, in *Black Rain*[43] Semiconductor worked in collaboration with space scientists and used data from two Heliospheric Imagers. This pair of cameras is designed to image the solar wind between the sun and the earth. *Black Rain* shows the original collected data transferred into a single channel installation.

> As in Semiconductor's previous work 'Brilliant Noise', which looked into the sun, they work with raw scientific satellite data, which has not yet been cleaned and processed for public consumption. By embracing the artefact's calibration and phenomena of the capturing process, we are reminded of the presence of the human observer, who endeavours to extend our perceptions and knowledge through technological innovation.[44]

The scientists involved routinely cleaned the data because they thought that the noise was not relevant for science and for the general public. Semiconductor's artistic intervention resulted in a reciprocal effect: through this collaboration the scientists started to rethink the cleaning process of scientific data.[45]

Abnormal Spin-off Technology

As described using the examples of Whitney's first computer animation and Ars Electronica Futurelab's project *Drone 100*, army property or new technologies in general can become a spin-off technology for animation. Technologies like robotic or 3D printing, new devices such as virtual (VR) and augmented reality (AR), or interactive tools can extend the world of animation and become the topic of an artistic examination at the same time. To give another example for drones: the music video *Nosaj Thing / Cold Stares ft. Chance The Rapper + The O'My's*,[46] produced by Rhizomatiks Research, uses drones to visualize the message in the lyrics of the song—the blurring of boundaries between reality and illusion. A dance performance was captured with six cameras mounted on drones to enable fluid transitions between the performance by the dancers and the computer-generated delusional world.

Apart from unmanned aerial vehicles, VR and AR are being increasingly utilized in animation, a technology that also has its roots in army property. Current VR-installations like *Out of Exile*[47] or *489 Years*[48] are pioneering works in the field of immersive storytelling. Both works use VR to address sensitive and political issues: in *Out of Exile* the user is involved in a dispute about a young man coming out as gay based on a real story. In *489 Years* the user explores a personal journey of a former soldier walking through the Demilitarized Zone between North and South Korea. Moreover, VR and AR technology can be utilized to animate virtual worlds in physical space. For instance, James Patterson developed the animation VR software *Norman*,[49] which enables artists to animate hand-drawn virtual sculptures frame by frame, using VR devices in physical space. This new approach to digital animation expands the possibility of VR devices.

Another spin-off technology can be found in the field of robotics. Animating physical objects in the real world is not a new idea when we think of early animatronics or robots. However, the boundaries between real and virtual animation are blurring, as seen in the research project *BOX*[50] by Bot&Doly, a unique combination of computer animation software, projection mappings and two robots. A similar blending between real and digital objects can be observed with 3D printing. Meanwhile 3D printed replacements are common within stop motion productions.

43   *Black Rain*, Semiconductor, Joe Gerhardt and Ruth Jarman, 2009, Honorary Mention 2011. For more details see p. 162.

44   Semiconductors, "Black Rain," https://semiconductorfilms.com/art/black-rain/ (accessed December 22, 2018).

45   Semiconductors "A-Z of Noise," Expanded Animation (website), https://vimeo.com/107897788 (accessed December 22, 2018).

46   "Nosaj Thing / Cold Stares ft. Chance The Rapper + The O'My's," Ars Electronica Archive (website) https://archive.aec.at/prix/showmode/52881/ (accessed December 22, 2018). For more details see p. 200

47   *Out of Exile*. Directed by Nonny de la Peña, produced by Emblematic Group, 2017, Award of Distinction 2017.

48   *489 Years*. Directed by Hayoun Kwon, 2015, Award of Distinction 2018. For more details see p. 200.

49   *Norman*. Developed by James Paterson, 2017–2018, Honorary Mention 2018. For more details see p. 234.

50   *Box*. Developed by Bot & Dolly, 2013, Award of Distinction 2013.

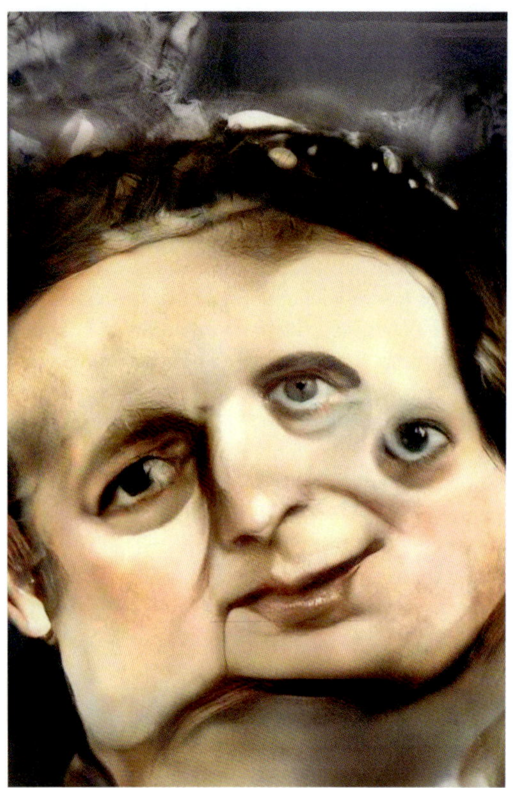

Figure 3. *79530 Self Portraits*. Mario Klingemann, 2018.

A completely different approach is taken by Akinori Goto in a series of animation sculptures called *toki-*.[51] Goto uses 3D printing to capture motion in one sculpture for a 3D zoetrop. A ray of light directed onto the twisted sculpture makes the animation or rather the captured traces visible. A much more critical examination of the technology can be seen in the experimental stereoscopic artwork *Shadowland*[52] by Japanese filmmaker Kazuhiro Goshima. He transferred recordings from moving shadows created by the lights of driving cars into three-dimensional stereoscopic image. This was achieved by combining two single frames with a temporal offset of 1 to 5 frames to a stereo image. In this respect, stereoscopy serves a different purpose: the parallax is created by a temporal shift of the recorded images. Instead of reproducing images with a spatial sense of depth, new 3D images emerge that do not exist in the real world. Stereoscopy is deconstructed and expanded at the same time. Further anomalies within stereoscopy are experiments with binocal rivalry, a phenomenon where different images for the left and the right eye are provided. Current artists who are investigating that phenomenon in the field of animation are Max Hattler, Sebastian Buerkner and Memo Akten.[53] In Akten's installation *Fight*,[54] the user can explore interactive binocal rivalry in a painful virtual tour that reveals the limits of human perception. Experiments with binocal rivalry as well as Goshima's shadow experiments are, therefore, literally deconstruction and explorations of the imperfection. The core topics are manipulation of space and time, reversal of function, and subversion of stereoscopic perception.

All these examples have one thing in common: experimental, self-reflective approaches to animation derived from technologies in different areas, like drones, robotic, 3D printing, stereoscopy or VR, while reflecting the medium itself.

Subversive Animation Software

Software that is not common in the field of animation can be adapted or modified. A vivid example can be seen in the late 1990s when artists started to hack game engines and explore new methods of digital filmmaking: a subversive initiative called Machinima. Nowadays it seems that the phenomenon has become obsolete, since game engines, real-time rendering and animation tools are merging. A current example is *Adam*,[55] a film that was produced entirely in the game engine Unity. Apart from that, however, artists like David OReilly, Friedrich Kirschner or Nikita Diakur still explore experimental approaches and use game technology in a slightly different way. The origin of the source is not hidden, but shown on a display. Friedrich Kirschner was quite active as a machinima artist and is now a researcher in the field of digital puppetry and interactive game performances. OReilly's artwork ranges from games to interactive animations to animated films. Diakur uses game soft- and hardware, for instance game controllers and ragdolls for character animation, as well as game aesthetics and real-time

---

51 *toki-*. Installation by Akinori Goto, 2017. *toki-* serves the basis for *Rediscovery of Anima*, Honorary Mention 2018. For more details see p. 236.

52 *Shadowland*. Directed by Kazuhiro Goshima. 2013. Award of Distinction 2014. For more details see p. 174.

53 Cf. Max Hattler, "Rupturing Visions: Towards an Expanded Stereoscopy," pp. 73.

54 *Fight*. Directed by Memo Akten, VR installation, 2017, https://www.memo.tv/portfolio/fight/ .

55 *Adam*. Directed by Veselin Efremov, 2016.

rendering. His animated short film *Ugly*[56] addresses the possibilities between staying in control and leaving room for coincidences by the computer, exploring the unpredictability of artefacts and errors.

Animation software can also become the object of experimental investigations, such as when motion capture data is not used for characters, but instead is applied to abstract forms, as seen in the project *Forms*[57] by Memo Akten and Quayola. The artists used motion analysis software and applied the human locomotion captured from video sequences from former Olympic games onto abstract forms. Whereas most of the artists use current tools, Swiss artist Yves Netzhammer creates animations with an early version of a 3D visualization software from the 1990s, for instance *Die Gegenwart sucht ihren Mund in der Spiegelung der Suppe*.[58] Instead of recreating the rough aesthetics of early computer graphics with current software, he prefers an authentic way and struggles with limited features.

A special kind of subversive form can be seen when the artist uses malware, and virus-like programs. A current example is *Descent*[59] by Peter Burr, Mark Fingerhut, and Forma, which is an animated film, presented as software, a downloadable exe. The virus takes control of the computer and manipulates the desktop, showing the picture *The Triumph of Death* by Flemish artist Pieter Bruegel the Elder.

An interesting aspect is the fact that the artwork is done by the computer and the artist relinquishes a large degree of control. Building on the knowledge of artificial life, artists and scientists started to investigate procedural models and evolutionary techniques for computer graphics and animation in the late 1980s. For instance, Karl Sims developed software based on artificial evolution[60] and produced short films like *Evolved Virtual Creatures*[61] to demonstrate new approaches in animation, so called "simulated Darwinian evolutions of virtual block creatures."[62] Those early experiments were of poor quality and subsequently were abandoned in the field of animation. Since AI has reached a higher level in general in the last few years, software of this kind has gained importance for artists. One of the first examples in the archive of Ars Electronica is *Blade Runner—Autoencoded*[63] by Terence Broad, a film based on a research project on autoencoding video frames.[64] In this film a type of artificial neural network called autoencoder recreates frames from the film *Blade Runner*.[65] After the computer was trained to see the film, the software reconstructs the film from its memories. "The resulting sequence is very dreamlike, drifting in and out of recognition between static scenes that the model remembers well, to fleeting sequences—usually with a lot of movement—that the model barely comprehends."[66]

A similar approach can be seen in recent artworks by Mario Klingemann and Memo Akten. In *79530 Self Portraits*,[67] by Klingemann, the computer was trained on thousands of painted "old masters" portraits captured from various European collections by means of loops of generative adversarial neural networks (GANs). In *Deep Meditations* by Akten, the computer analyzes a series of images found on photo sharing website Flickr under the term "everything." Both projects explore how the computer generates new meaning by learning and analyzing a series of images. For the human eye the result is an unexpected aesthetic anomaly, an accumulation of errors and flaws. Both projects raise the questions of who the author of the artwork is, and at the same time, if computers can be creative and animate at all. Weibel's investigation of the consciousness of the computer is more relevant than ever.

These questions will be heatedly discussed in the next few years at Ars Electronica. The festival started the

---

56   *Ugly*. Directed by Nikita Diakur, Honorary Mention 2017. For more details see p. 216.

57   *Forms*. Developed by Memo Akten & Quayola, 2012, Golden Nika 2013. For more details see p. 166.

58   *Die Gegenwart sucht ihren Mund in der Spiegelung der Suppe*. Directed by Yves Netzhammer. 2014, Honorary Mention 2016. For more details see p. 194.

59   *Descent*. Directed by Peter Burr and Mark Fingerhut, sound design by Forma, 2017. For more details see p. 228

60   Karl Sims, "Artificial Evolution for Computer Graphics," ACM SIGGRAPH '91 Conference Proceedings, Las Vegas, Nevada, *Computer Graphics*, 25(4), July 1991, pp. 319–328. https://www.karlsims.com/papers/siggraph91.html (accessed December 22, 2018).

61   *Evolved Virtual Creatures*, Karl Sims, 1994, https://www.karlsims.com/evolved-virtual-creatures.html (accessed December 22, 2018).

62   Ibid.

63   *Blade Runner—Autoencoded*. Developed by Terence Broad, 2016, Honorary Mention 2017. For more details see p. 202.

64   *Autoencoding Video Frames*, Dissertation, Goldsmiths, University of London, 2016.

65   *Blade Runner*. Directed by Ridley Scott, 1982.

66   "Blade Runner—Autoencoded," Ars Electronica Archive (website) https://archive.aec.at/prix/showmode/55653/ (accessed December 22, 2018).

67   *79530 Self Portraits*. Directed by Mario Klingemann, 2018.

examination with *AI – The Other I*[68] in 2017 and continued a year later with *Error – The Art of Imperfection*,[69] featuring various artists and researchers, exploring the effects and errors caused by such software. A new Prix category Artificial Intelligence & Life Art, introduced in 2019, underlines the importance of the topic.

Conclusion

The subversive usage of technology in animation offers not only a great potential for experimenting with forms and aesthetics, but also for reflecting on the medium itself. In particular, the reversal of the technology's function, as seen in many examples—from James Whitney to recent artists—serves as a good starting point for that. These artistic interventions are examinations of anomalies of soft- and hardware that cause new qualities to emerge. In this regard, the critical engagement can take on a political dimension to question established norms and structures.

The types of animation anomalies presented here are a first attempt to illustrate a variety, ranging from deconstruction, self-critical reflection, flaws and artefacts as a concept as well as subversive examinations of technology, from animation software to stereoscopy, VR or AI. Furthermore, these anomalies at the interface of animation, media art and technology can provide new qualities which can drive further developments in science, art and the economy.

68   Ars Electronica festival 2017, https://ars.electronica.art/ai/en/ (accessed December 22, 2018).
69   Ars Electronica festival 2018, https://ars.electronica.art/error/en/ (accessed December 22, 2018).

Bibliography

Betancourt, Michael. *Glitch Art in Theory and Practice. Critical Failures and Post-Digital Aesthetics.* New York and London, 2016.

Clarke, Roger "Hybridity—Elements of a Theory." In *Ars Electronica 2015. Hybrid – Living in Paradox,* edited by Gerfried Stocker and Christine Schöpf, Ostfildern-Ruit, 2005, pp. 30–44.

Franke, Herbert W. *Computergraphik Computerkunst.* Munich, 1971.

Hörtner, Horst et al. "Spaxels, Pixels in Space – A Novel Mode of Spatial Display." *SIGMAP 2012,* pp. 19–24.

Kittler, Friedrich A. *Grammophon, Film, Typewriter.* Stanford, California, 1999.

Kittler, Friedrich A. *The Truth of the Technological World: Essays on the Genealogy of Presence.* Stanford, California, 2013.

Lutz, Petra, et al., eds. *Der [im-]perfekte Mensch. Methamorphosen von Normalität und Abweichung.* Cologne, 2003.

Russett, Robert, and Cecile Starr. *Experimental Animation: Origins of a New Art.* New York, 1976.

Russett, Robert. *Hyperanimation: Digital Images and Virtual Worlds.* United Kingdom, 2009.

Scheugl, Hans, and Ernst Schmidt. *Eine Subgeschichte des Films. Lexikon des Avantgarde-, Experimental- und Undergroundfilms.* Frankfurt a. M., 1974.

Smith, Vicky and Nicky Hamlyn, eds. *Experimental and Expanded Animation. New Perspectives and Practices.* Cham, 2018.

Smith, Vicky and Nicky Hamlyn. "Introduction." In *Experimental and Expanded Animation. New Perspectives and Practices.* Edited by Vicky Smith and Nicky Hamlyn. Basingstoke, 2018.

Stocker, Gerfried et al., eds. *The Practice of Art and Science.* Ostfildern-Ruit, 2017.

Stocker, Gerfried. "ERROR – The Art of Imperfection." In *ERROR – The Art of Imperfection.* edited by Gerfried Stocker et al., Ostfildern-Ruit, 2018, pp. 19–21.

Wells, Paul. *Animation. Genre and Authorship.* London and New York, 2002.

Youngblood, Gene. *Expanded Cinema.* New York, 1970.

Franziska Bruckner (AT)

Virtual Hybrid Image, Virtual Hybrid Montage: Notes on the Hybridization of Live Action and Animation within Virtual Reality Environments

Introduction

Animation is a very broad and heterogeneous media form. Often associated with cinema and television, animated images have entered many areas of life, taking on operative, communicative, epistemic, and didactic tasks, among other things. In this context, Suzanne Buchan[1] speaks of pervasive animation, a media world in which animated images are omnipresent. Paul Wells[2] also promotes a broader notion of animation. His *Animation Spectrum* includes moving images like films and TV series, animation as applied tools such as motion capture and motion graphics, as well as animation in expanded formats particular to games, installations, data visualization and real-time interaction. Also, in the newest and most innovative field of motion picture production, augmented (AR), and virtual reality (VR), animation is an integral part of artistic, scientific and economic applications. As in conventional filmic formats, the animation parts may

range from purely animated forms to hybrid mixtures with live-recorded footage. The goal of this paper is to identify some of the possibilities and challenges of animated content in virtual reality environments. In order to do so, a film-analytical method designed for animation-film studies will be expanded to VR content. The analytical starting point is a typology called *Hybrid Image, Hybrid Montage*[3] that illuminates the formal characteristics of live action/animation hybrid films. By reference to six categories, the combination of animation and live action is explored on the level of the cinematic time and space. Originally, the adaptable set of parameters should be applicable to films as well as different sequences within cinematic moving images. By applying it to two VR projects—*Out of Exile*[4] and *Zero Days VR*[5]—that received awards at the Ars Electronica Festival in 2017, the paper will map animation and hybrid forms within VR, and expand the knowledge of media scholars in this research field.

---

1 Suzanne Buchan, "Introduction," in *Pervasive Animation* (New York, 2013), pp. 1–21.

2 Paul Wells, "Animation in the Gallery and the Gestalt. György Kovàsnai and William Kentridge," in *Global Animation Theory. International Perspectives at Animafest Zagreb* (New York, 2018), p. 15.

3 Franziska Bruckner, "Hybrid Image, Hybrid Montage: Film Analytical Parameters for Live Action/Animation Hybrids," *animation: an interdisciplinary journal* 10 (March 2015), pp. 22–41.

4 *Out of Exile*. Developed by Emblematic Group, 2017, https://emblematicgroup.com/experiences/out-of-exile/ (accessed October 20, 2018), Software. For more details see p. 212.

5 *Zero Days VR*. Developed by Yasmin Elayat, James George, Alexander Porter, Scatter, Mei-Ling Wong, Elie Zananiri, 2017, https://www.zerodaysvr.com/ (accessed October 20, 2018), Software. For more details see p. 220.

A short history of AR/VR at Ars Electronica

The combination of VR and art is older than the medium itself. Media theorist Oliver Grau[6] traces a historical genealogy of the immersive "image spaces of illusion," ranging from ancient examples of fresco painting and 19th century panoramic devices to expanded cinema and VR applications. The technological development of VR can be traced back to the 1960s. As part of his work on immersive technologies, Ivan Sutherland describes his invention of the head-mounted display (HMD) as early as 1965. In the 1980s, Jaron Lanier and his colleague Thomas Zimmermann with their company VPL developed both a "DataGlove" and a data helmet called "EyePhone." Lanier also used the term "virtual reality" for the first time in 1987. According to his definition, a VR system requires the technical components of a computer, a head-mounted display, headphones and motion sensors.[7] On a visual level, most of the VR applications consist of computer generated and therefore computer animated content.

The Ars Electronica Festival, which started in 1979 as a small conference on media art and soon expanded rapidly, took an early interest in the subject of virtual reality. In 1990, the theme of Ars Electronica was "Digital Dreams – Virtual Worlds" resulting in a highly anticipated symposium on VR including contributions by the aforementioned VR pioneers Ivan Sutherland and Jaron Lanier, as well as talks by e.g. Brenda Laurel, Timothy Leary, Warren Robinett or Bruce Sterling.[8] While Sterling emphasized the "power of the computer … that allows it to melt and mix other machines and other media, creating strange hybrids,"[9] Robinett's presentation was technologically groundbreaking. His "See-through HMD" for a medical XR-Application[10] is one of the earliest concepts for AR.[11] In addition to HMD devices, projection based representations in the field of VR were also developed in the early 1990s. The system CAVE (CAVE Automatic Virtual Environment), which was purchased by the Ars Electronica Center as early as 1996, consisted of four screens and allowed one spectator the correct perspective perception within a room.[12] In recent years, the technological progress has significantly advanced the possibilities of VR applications and Ars Electronica has also established new virtual systems: in 2009, the Ars Electronica Center installed "Deep Space," an interactive 16-by-9-meter wall and floor projection, for VR environments as well as 2D and 3D cinematic experiences.[13] Originally equipped with a resolution of 4K, it was upgraded to 8K in 2015.

Advances in smartphone and mobile computing technology have spurred a development of HDM devices, too.[14] One of the new media formats now supported by all major platforms are 360° videos, which are sometimes referred to as VR. But while in interactive VR and AR the users are able to move freely and change the environment, in cinematic 360° videos, whether they are animated or recorded with live action, the opportunities for interaction are limited.[15] The Ars Electronica Center also reacted to this trend by opening a VRLab in 2017 stating: "The enthusiasm that accompanied the dawn of this new high-tech age in the 1980s and 90s is back, with the technology deployed in today's data glasses … finally seeming to be able to live up to the visions that preceded it."[16]

6 Oliver Grau, *Virtual Art. From Illusion to Immersion* (Cambridge, London, 2003).

7 Ralph Dörner et al., "Einleitung," in *Virtual und Augmented Reality (VR/AR). Grundlagen und Methoden der Virtuellen und Augmentierten Realität* (Berlin, Heidelberg 2013), p. 20.

8 Gottfried Hattinger et al. ed., *BAND II VIRTUELLE WELTEN*, exh. cat. Ars Electronica (Linz 1990).

9 Ars Electronica 1990, VR-Symposium with Jaron Lanier, Warren Robinett, Brenda Laurel, Marvin Minsky, Timothy Leary, Vimeo video, 18:16 min., uploaded by "ars history," Sept 11, 2010, https://vimeo.com/14888138 (accessed October 20, 2018).

10 Warren Robinett, "Head Mounted Display Project," in *BAND II VIRTUELLE WELTEN*, exh. cat. Ars Electronica (Linz 1990), pp. 119–122.

11 In general, augmented reality (AR) is understood as a "combination (superimposition) of reality and virtuality that is interactive, in which the representation takes place in real time and in which 3D objects are (geometrically) registered." Wolfgang Broll, "Augmentierte Realität," in *Virtual und Augmented Reality (VR/AR). Grundlagen und Methoden der Virtuellen und Augmentierten Realität*, (Berlin and Heidelberg 2013), p. 245.

12 Ralph Dörner et al., "Einleitung," in *Virtual und Augmented Reality (VR/AR). Grundlagen und Methoden der Virtuellen und Augmentierten Realität*, (Berlin and Heidelberg 2013), p. 20.

13 Daniela Kuka et al., "Deep Space: High Resolution VR Platform for Multi-user Interactive Narratives," in *Interactive Storytelling. Second Joint international Conference on Interactive Digital Storytelling*. ICDS, (Guimarães 2009), p. 186.

14 A variety of different cost-effective AR/VR HMD systems are on the market: For VR, among others, Oculus Rift2, HTC Vive or Sony PlayStation VR, for AR Magic Leap One, Microsoft HoloLens and Google Glass.

15 Nevertheless, most of AR/VR and 360 contents are consumable e.g. on online platforms or apps, directly on the computer via the smartphone screen and can be transformed—in conjunction with the Samsung Gear VR or Google Cardboard—to a large-scale virtual experience.

16 Ars Electronica VRLab, https://ars.electronica.art/ai/en/vrlab/ (accessed October 20, 2018).

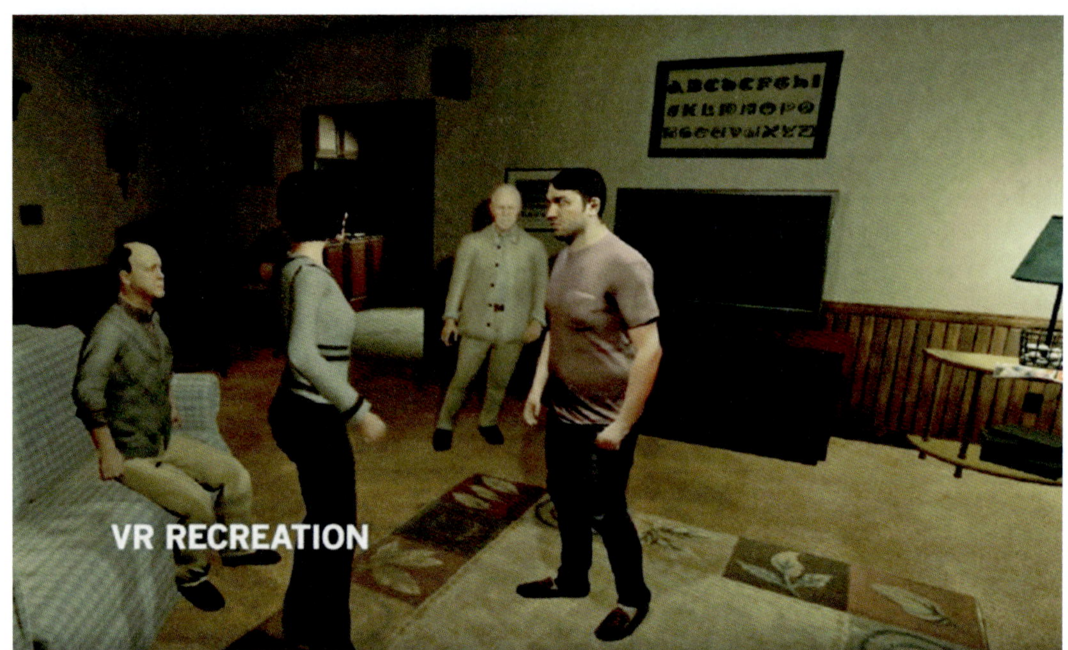

Figure 1: VR Recreation of *Out of Exile* , Nonny de la Peña, Emblematic Group.

Hybrid Image, Hybrid Montage goes VR

The analytical starting point of this paper is a set of parameters called *Hybrid Image, Hybrid Montage* that was developed elsewhere. It illuminates various characteristics of hybrid forms of animation and live action within films, without necessarily referring back to technical details. The original categories include the following questions: A) Animation techniques – Which and how many animation techniques are used? B) Hybrid Images: Image plane – On which layers are animation and live action elements located within a single image? C) Hybrid images: Disparities/transitions within images – To what degree is hybridity visible within single frames? D) Hybrid montage: Combination of image types – In which ways are animated, live action or hybrid images combined in montage? E) Hybrid montage: Duration and frequency – With which frequency do live action, animated or hybrid images/elements alternate? F) Hybrid transitions – Which kinds of transition between the different image types are chosen in editing?[17] In order to summarize those findings for this paper, the original categories B and C are condensed to one section called Virtual Hybrid Image, also, E and D are summarized to one chapter

about Virtual Hybrid Montage. Although the focus of the original typology on visual markers of animation and live action is transferable to augmented and virtual reality content, the focus here will be on cinematic and interactive VR experiences.

The case studies are two VR projects called *Out of Exile* and *Zero Days VR* which were both exhibited at the Ars Electronica Festival in 2017. In the thirteen-minute interactive VR room-scale experience *Out of Exile*, by Nonny de la Peña and Emblematic Group, a virtual re-enactment is addressing the confrontation of Daniel Ashely Pierce about his sexual orientation, staged by his family. The first part is based on the real audio footage of this aggressive intervention, and the VR environment enables the viewer not only to witness the events, but to walk freely in the room endowed with its own holographic body (see fig. 1). In the second part, Daniel and other members of the LGBTQ community are recorded via volumetric videos and give direct insights into their thoughts and lives. *Zero Days VR* by Yasmin Elayat, James George, Alexander Porter, Scatter, Mei-Ling Wong, and Elie Zananiri is a twenty-two-minute VR documentary based on the feature length participative media documentary *Zero Days*,[18] directed by Alex Gibney. In five chapters the user fol-

---

17 Franziska Bruckner, "Hybrid Image, Hybrid Montage: Film Analytical Parameters for Live Action/Animation Hybrids," *animation: an interdisciplinary journal 10* (March 2015), pp. 24–32.

18 *Zero Days*. Directed by Alex Gibney, 2016, Film.

lows a self-replicating computer virus named "Stuxnet" that travels through different virtual spaces. The cinematic VR environments range from graphics of the virus' processes, to news-breaking reveals from an NSA informant, to the visualization of public news archives (see fig. 2).In order to analyze the VR environments, both case studies were first watched with VR HMD devices combined with descriptive audio-recording,[19] but for practical reasons both were transferred to screengrabs for the close readings, later on.

Animation Techniques: A) Which and How Many Animation Techniques Are Used?

The first step towards a set of parameters is to define the animation technique, as certain visual markers are inherent in different kinds of animation. In hybrid films, analogue animation techniques such as cell animation, direct film, various stop-motion techniques such as object and puppet animation, pixilation cutout or modified base animation are frequently used as computer animation.[20] Some VR projects like Uri and Michelle Kranot's *Nothing Happens*,[21] also incorporate digitalized drawn animations that share a similar aesthetic to their analogue counterparts. However, most VR contents are designed with three dimensional, computer generated images (CGI) and are often realized through a combination of keyframe animation, performance capture or live action recordings.

Both *Zero Days VR* and *Out of Exile* incorporate CGI, but in *Out of Exile* the movements of the protagonists are created by performance capture and videogrammetry.[22] *Zero Days VR* uses a "hybrid approach,"[23] too: it incorporates live action footage and photos in animated VR environments, as well as volumetric live action point cloud videos of actors. At the end of the experience a camera is broadcasting the user's own image into his/her own virtual experience—although this feature is not included in all versions of the application.[24]

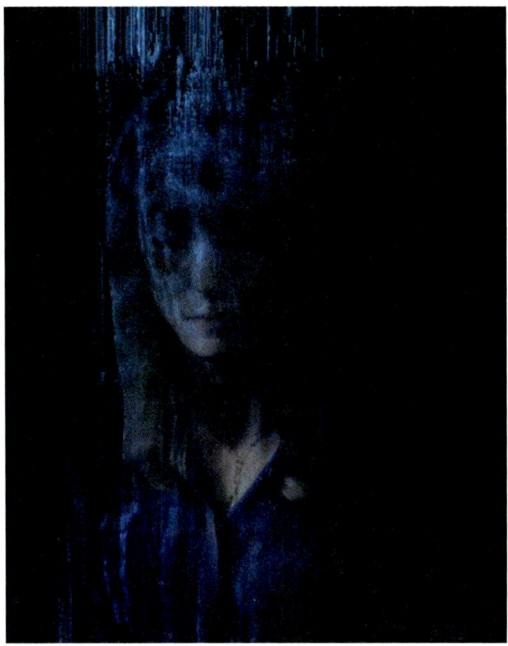

Figure 2: *Zero Days VR* image of the NSA Informant, one of the two key characters in the documentary.

Virtual Hybrid Image B) On Which Image Planes Are Animation and Live Action Elements Located Within the Virtual Space? C) To What Degree Are Disparities/ Transitions of Animation and Live Action Visible?

Considering the relation between animation and live action within the cinematic space, a significant aspect of hybrid images deals with the question of on which image layer different techniques are located: animated parts can be placed in the foreground in front of a live action background, or live action elements are in front of animated backgrounds; in other films, either the animated and live action elements are located on the same image layer, separated, for instance, by split or multi-screen, or the hybridization occurs simultaneously on all image layers. Equally important is the visibility of the disparity between animation and live action in filmic as well as virtual content. While for

19 *Out of Exile* was watched with Oculus Rift and Zero Days VR with Oculus Go.

20 Franziska Bruckner, "Hybrid Image, Hybrid Montage: Film Analytical Parameters for Live Action/Animation Hybrids," *animation: an interdisciplinary journal 10* (March 2015), pp. 24–26.

21 *Nothing Happens*. Developed by Michelle and Uri Kranot 2017, Software.

22 *Out of Exile: Daniel's Story*, YouTube video, 02:19 min., uploaded by "Emblematic Group," March 23, 2017, https://www.youtube.com/watch?time_continue=22&v=TiSKz2Wa9w8 (accessed October 20, 2018).

23 *Blackout by Scatter and DepthKit* | Expanding Storytelling in VR on Intel® Core™ i7 | Intel Software, YouTube video, 01:01 min., uploaded by "Intel Software," May 1, 2017, https://www.youtube.com/watch?time_continue=12&v=jwx5JvExDNY (accessed October 20, 2018).

24 This feature is not included in the version for the Oculus Go available to us and will therefore not be considered in this analysis. Beckett Mufson, "How to See Stuxnet? 'Zero Days' Filmmakers Find an Unlikely Answer in VR" https://creators.vice.com/en_us, January 26, 2017, https://creators.vice.com/en_us/article/pgq7v8/zero-days-vr-sundance-debut (accessed October 21, 2018).

some filmic examples the applied animation technique already predetermines its in/visibility, other techniques, like stop-motion or CGI, require additional parameters in order to determine how seamless the transition between different elements actually is.[25]

By transferring these film-analytical standards to VR, some interesting changes occur. First, in contrast to a cinematic space, the fore-, middle and background of a virtual space has to be defined as concentric circles or spheres. Second, a virtual space with fixed fore-, middle and background only exists within cinematic VR experiences, or 360° videos, that offer no interactive mobility. Although *Zero Days VR* is described as "hybrid format" that "allows for interactivity while staying true to the project's purpose as a documentary conveying true events"[26] it is actually a cinematic VR experience, where the action almost exclusively takes place at an angle of 180 degrees. The viewer cannot change position, but is led through the environment via pan and zooms. However, three types of live action sources can be traced. First, 2D images of found-footage news, showing, for example, a speech by president Barack Obama or George W. Bush, which are clearly discernible and placed on 2D screens in the fore-, middle, and sometimes in the background, but always embedded into an animated virtual space. They also could be classified as a virtual form of split- or multiscreen. Most of the images are distorted on the edges and seem to expire into infinity. Second, the volumetric recording of a female informant that is first placed behind a desk in the middle ground, but later appears in the foreground in front of a black backdrop. Her image is distorted via the already mentioned cloud-point optic, but is still detectable as live action recording. Third, a city being destroyed by the impacts of the Stuxnet virus, which is spread from the fore- to the background of the virtual space. It could be entirely generated, but could also incorporate the structure and footage of one or more real cities.

As soon as an interactive VR room-scale mode is activated, and the user has the flexibility to move freely in their environment, the fore- and background depend on the behavior and location of each user. The first part of *Out of Exile* appears, like many interactive VR experiences, to be entirely animated, while a hybridization of live action and animation is incorporated by motion capture. While the user can freely change position, at the very beginning he/she is placed in the middle of a living room surrounded by Daniel and his family. Therefore, the "live action" component is still happening in the foreground, unless the spectator decides to walk away to the edge of the room and watches the scene from a distance. However, in the second part, the recordings can be classified as volumetric live action recording in front of a black background, and animation is not an integral part of this section.

Virtual Hybrid Montage: D) How Are Animated, Live Action or Virtual Hybrid Images Combined in the Virtual Montage? E) In Which Frequency Do Live Action, Animated or Virtual Hybrid Images/Elements Alternate?

The parameters for filmic hybrid montage question if hybrid images, detected in the cinematic space, are edited with entirely live action or animated sequences, or if only animated and live action images are being combined in the montage. At times, it was observed that one hybrid image type dominates a film entirely. However, several different hybrid image types can also interact, varying either their A) animation technique B) their distribution within the cinematic space or C) their visibility. The next step is to determine the length of the single segments as well as the frequency with which they alternate. It can be long, entirely detached and stylistically separated sequences. Changes also occur within a sequence or scene, with hybrid images, animation and live action alternating on almost every shot. Images types are also able to vary several times within one single take, often without visible cuts. At times, the shift between image types happens repeatedly within a few frames, which results in the highest possible alteration frequency.[27] If used within a split- or multi-screen or as translucent hybrid image, the editing frequency of the animated part can be faster or slower than the one within the live action part of the image.

In order to fit a virtual analysis, the analytical instruments need some adjustments, too. While in interactive VR the change of shot-types within one sequence is no longer necessary because the user can decide on

---

25 Franziska Bruckner, "Hybrid Image, Hybrid Montage: Film Analytical Parameters for Live Action/Animation Hybrids," animation: an interdisciplinary journal 10 (March 2015), pp. 26–28.

26 "Ars Electronica Archive – Zero Days VR" https://archive.aec.at/prix, https://archive.aec.at/prix/showmode/55657/ (accessed October 21, 2018).

27 Franziska Bruckner, "Hybrid Image, Hybrid Montage: Film Analytical Parameters for Live Action/Animation Hybrids," animation: an interdisciplinary journal 10 (March 2015), pp. 28–31.

which part he/she wants to focus, changes of perspective that could be associated with a kind of montage, appear useful to transfer users from one place to the other. This occurs either by teleporting within a room or even to a new location.[28] As the first part of *Out of Exile* is set in one particular room-scale environment, and does not work with a teleporting option, the virtual hybrid image type classified before, stays more or less the same during the whole experience and the user can simply choose the "camera-angle." Also, the second part is taking place in one environment: while the user stays in the same black room, different LGTBQ witnesses appear one after another to talk directly to the user.

Although *Zero Days VR* is a cinematic VR experience, the distribution of the hybrid images is more diverse, not only because the story is structured in five chapters with different visual styles, but also because not all of them incorporate hybrid content. The live action recorded NSA informant is set in the first two minutes of chapter three, "The Whistleblower." A blonde woman appears in the middle ground behind a table, simulating a conversational situation. While she is talking to us, official government buildings are placed in the foreground, followed by miniature versions of tubes from an Iranian nuclear facility, and a flat white map of the world that is "occupied" by the orange virus. The agent reappears at the end of chapter five, "The Fourth Dimension of War," this time more distorted, but in the foreground before a black background. In the same sequence, but before the whistle blower, the nocturnal city builds up: it looks like the urban center of a typical American city, including generated traffic. In the background, the city as well as a power plant on the left side begin to burn, some houses in the center turn red, before the city dissolves again.

The virtual hybrid 2D images are spread through three sections: in the first minute of the experience the found footage is discernible. News reports appear, left, right and in the center, moving either to the background, or appearing in the background, as the spectator moves closer, it shifts to a bar above us. At the end of chapter two "Inside Stuxnet," a video shot of President Obama is visible and at the end of Chapter Three "The Whistleblower" pictures of further politicians are appearing in the background, coming closer, until they dissolve again. Interestingly, in almost all

described hybrid sequences of *Zero Days VR*, different editing frequencies for various parts of the virtual images seem to be the norm rather than the exception. Fades-to-black are only used occasionally, between the sequences.

Virtual Hybrid Transitions: F) Which Kinds of Transition Between Different Virtual Image Types Are Chosen?

The final step of the original typology analyses transitions between the individual image types within filmic content. In film editing the most frequent form of transition is the straight cut, followed by simple fade ins, fade outs and dissolves. For a hybrid perspective, the latter are especially interesting because, for the duration of a dissolve—for instance from a fully animated to a live action image—hybrid images emerge that are constantly changing. Particular attention should also be drawn to animated dissolves and morphs.[29]

In *Out of Exile* cuts and dissolves still appear useful within the title sequence and in the second part of the experiences, especially when Daniel and the other interview partners are slowly fading out after each of their testimonies; however, as no teleporting option was applied during the first part of *Out of Exile*, no cuts or dissolves appear at all.

In terms of dissolves, in *Zero Days VR's* city sequence only two parts are interesting to mention: at the beginning, the city is slowly building up from the bottom to the top in front of the black background, while at the end the city is dissolving very quickly, from top to bottom.

The whistleblower is fading in very slowly at the beginning of the first sequence, and dissolving from the fringes of the figure to the center, while the rest of the picture is fading out later. In the second sequence, the NSA informant appears in a straight cut and is dissolving in blue lines at the end of the film. But in terms of hybrid transitions, interesting to mention are the glitches within her speech, distorting her for seconds at a time. They appear when the whistleblower is changing the subject. They are used instead of regular jump-cuts. The most diverse aesthetics are noticeable in terms of virtual 2D images, aka the found footage news. They either appear with a dissolve in the virtual space, or sometimes different news reports alternate with each other by straight cuts. The disappearance

---

28 In some applications the VR experience alternates with short 360 videos, often representing a meta-level like memories or dreams.
29 Franziska Bruckner, "Hybrid Image, Hybrid Montage: Film Analytical Parameters for Live Action/Animation Hybrids," animation: an interdisciplinary journal 10 (March 2015), pp. 31–33.

is also solved via straight cuts, regular dissolves or dissolves into the color bars mentioned above. In all cases, the animated environment stays more or less the same. In some cases, even the 2D live action sequences stay, but as the viewer is led through the environment via a steady pan, the live action footages just disappear out of the focus, but could be traced again, if the user decided to take look back.

Conclusion

The fundamental goal of this paper was to expand a film analytical typology about the hybridization of animation and live action film to virtual environments. The already established categories served as guidelines, but were modified and adapted in order to work for cinematic and interactive VR applications.

Furthermore, the focus of the original typology on visual markers of animation and live action was transferred to virtual reality content. One of most obvious changes from the filmic anthology was the definition of virtual spaces as concentric circles or spheres, in opposition to the fixed cinematic space. In interactive VR room-scale applications, where the user has the flexibility to move freely in the environment, the fore- and background also depend on the behavior and location of each user. Furthermore, cuts and dissolves only still appear if users are teleporting from one place to the other—which was not applicable within our case studies. In cinematic VR applications, the filmic montage analysis is more useful. Various editing frequencies for different parts of the virtual hybrid images, seem to be the norm rather than the exception.

By applying a film analytical hybrid grid to the two VR projects *Zero Days VR* and *Out of Exile*, first notes for and expanded notions of a Virtual Hybrid Image and Virtual Hybrid Montage were established. But in order to verify those media analytical instruments, more applications, not only including VR but also AR and 360° videos, have to be considered. Furthermore, it should be noted that an analytical method for the media analysis of VR experiences is not established yet, and a standardized practical workflow for that should be developed in the future.

Bibliography

Broll, Wolfgang. "Augmentierte Realität." In *Virtual und Augmented Reality (VR/AR). Grundlagen und Methoden der Virtuellen und Augmentierten Realität,* edited by Dörner Ralph et al., Berlin and Heidelberg, 2013, pp. 241–295.

Bruckner, Franziska. "Hybrid Image, Hybrid Montage: Film Analytical Parameters for Live Action/Animation Hybrids." *animation: an interdisciplinary journal* (March 2015), pp. 22–41.

Buchan, Suzanne. "Introduction." In *Pervasive Animation* edited by Buchan Suzanne, New York, 2013, pp. 1–21.

Dörner, Ralph et al. "Einleitung." In *Virtual und Augmented Reality (VR/AR). Grundlagen und Methoden der Virtuellen und Augmentierten Realität,* edited by Ralph Dörner et al., Berlin and Heidelberg, 2013, pp. 1–33.

Grau, Oliver. *Virtual Art. From Illusion to Immersion.* Cambridge MA, London, 2003.

Hattinger, Gottfried et al. eds., *BAND II VIRTUELLE WELTEN,* exh. cat. Ars Electronica 1990, Linz, 1990.

Kuka, Daniela et al. "Deep Space: High Resolution VR Platform for Multi-user Interactive Narratives." In *Interactive Storytelling. Second Joint international Conference on Interactive Digital Storytelling. ICDS,* edited by Ido Iurgel et al., Berlin, Heidelberg, 2009), pp. 186–196.

Robinett, Warren. "Head Mounted Display Project." In *BAND II VIRTUELLE WELTEN,* exh. cat. Ars Electronica, edited by G. Hattinger et al., Linz, 1990, pp. 119–122.

Wells, Paul. "Animation in the Gallery and the Gestalt. György Kovàsnai and William Kentridge." In *Global Animation Theory. International Perspectives at Animafest Zagreb,* edited by Franziska Bruckner et al., New York, 2018, pp. 11–27.

Max Hattler (DE/HK)

Rupturing Visions: Towards an Expanded Stereoscopy

This article develops from and expands upon talks I presented at Ars Electronica Festival's Expanded Animation Symposium[1] and Bucheon International Animation Festival's Asia Animation Forum.[2] It investigates the potential of stereoscopic imagery to create engagements and experiences for the audience that go beyond the mere re-creation of three-dimensional space, creating visual ruptures as well as confusion in spatial perception. Through the lens of today's artistic practices, particularly new media arts including digital animation and virtual reality (VR), these broken visions or expanded abstractions are envisaged on one hand as an expression of a new realm of technologically induced sublime, while on the other hand pointing towards the lived abstraction of a future saturated by alienating mass media technologies. The aim of the essay is to explore, through a number of works by selected artists, the artistic potentials and poetic possibilities of *expanded stereoscopy*. It will also bring to light the partial lack of historical contextualization of, and trust in, moving image work by contemporary artists, whose experimental investment in "stereoscopies" provokes the homogeneous moving image space afforded by electronic media technologies, together with accompanying institutional regimes and discourses. Working at the periphery of vision, these artists incite the hegemonic media ecology of "visualities" that dominate our moving image consciousness since at least the mid-nineteenth century. Based on these premises, the hypothesis is that new modes of binocular vision, conditioned by seeking alternative uses of stereoscopy, enable and further expedite ways of seeing which are impossible in the real world. Hence, they truly expand the senses, firstly by re-asserting the subjective, personal viewer and their particular positioning in relation to the screen, and secondly by opening up our thinking about what constitutes the very "real" as in "real world."[3]

Breaking the Hegemony of Stereoscopic Realism

Since the commercial success of James Cameron's stereoscopic film *Avatar*,[4] much film and animation created for cinematic release has embraced stereoscopic vision and the three-dimensional depth it creates for the viewer. The maturation of consumer-level VR technology since 2014 has simultaneously spurred a wave

---

1 Max Hattler, "Broken Visions in Stereo." Expanded Animation Symposium, Ars Electronica Festival, Linz, Austria, September 8, 2017. Websites: https://ars.electronica.art/aeblog/en/2017/08/04/animation-festival-2017/, https://www.expandedanimation.com (accessed November 20, 2018).

2 Max Hattler, "From Broken Visions to Expanded Abstractions," Asia Animation Forum, Bucheon International Animation Festival, Bucheon, South Korea, October 22, 2017. Website: https://www.biaf.or.kr:47436/2017/en/index_forum_new.php (accessed November 20, 2018).

Max Hattler, "From Broken Visions to Expanded Abstractions," in *Cartoon and Animation Studies,* vol. 49 (2017), pp. 697–712.

3 On systems of reality and alternative reality systems, see Federico Campagna, *Technic and Magic: The Reconstruction of Reality* (London and New York, 2018).

4 *Avatar.* Directed by James Cameron, 2009.

of media productions set within three-dimensional space, ranging from computer games to Google Cardboard-enabled pornographic VR videos, and short film productions such as the first Academy Award-nominated animated VR project, the short film *Pearl*[5] by Patrick Osborne. Despite their different political, economic and cultural conditions, all of these works rely technically and aesthetically on stereoscopic fusion through stereopsis, that is, the perception of depth produced by the brain from left and right images with the amount of binocular parallax that corresponds to our eyes. They aim to emulate, as closely and comfortably as possible, three-dimensional human vision.[6] However, within more experimental moving image practices, and specifically abstract film and experimental animation, a fully rendered three-dimensional space might not always be desirable. The negotiation with, and abundance of, such "total space" links to the attack on the "figurative" and representational more widely, which has been and continues to be exploited to varying degrees in art, film and media histories—among the most prominent being Modernist artists and designers who added their significant contribution

to the field. Those visionaries of the visual culture of the twentieth century undermined mimetic or perspectival notions of vision and representation at large. And the emerging imaginary realm aimed at nothing less than the reduction of perceptual depth toward flatness and abstraction; where those new two-dimensional environs on screen resonated with the shifts in social power, together with their institutions and discourses, already at play since the nineteenth century.[7] Within that culture, the legacy of early avant-garde abstract film and animation is arguably engrained in our animation consciousness. We know of artists including Len Lye, Hans Richter, Marcel Duchamp, and Germaine Dulac, for example, whose concerns with visual rhythms or film poetry—"to create a *film poetry* with all the means provided by the transposition of objective reality by the camera"[8]—provided grounds for a growing artistic vocabulary around a dynamic filmic image surface, or painting in time, abstract universal signs in motion, and movement material; which was partly conditioned by investing "the dual nature of the camera as both a tool to record and a medium of expression through which to transform. .... What was

---

5 *Pearl*. Directed by Patrick Osborne, VR animated film, 5:38 min., USA, 2016.

6 Groundwork in this field has been undertaken firstly by the German physician and physicist Hermann von Helmholtz (1821–1894), who initiated his research on binocular vision when he invented the telestereoscope in 1857. However, major experiments with binocular eye movements, including the horopter, and stereoscopic vision happened in the early 1860s. The challenge of perceiving space was interestingly addressed by Wilhelm Wundt, Helmholtz's assistant between 1858 and 1862. See Guest Editorial, Perception (1994), and also Hermann von Helmholtz, *Treatise on physiological optics*, vol. 3: The perceptions of vision (New York, 1825).

7 Jonathan Crary, *Techniques of the Observer: On Vision and Modernity in the Nineteenth Century* (Cambridge, 1990). In this book Crary emphasizes the significance of optical apparatuses, including the stereoscope and precinematic devices, in how they exemplified the production of new physiological knowledge.

8 Hans Richter, *The Struggle for the Film, Towards a Socially Responsible Cinema* (Hampshire, 1986), p. 59.

at stake in avant-garde projects was testing the camera for its possibilities and limits, experiments which sometimes led to the complete separation of the two forms of film-making, like [Richter's] abstract *Rhythm* films and films where the camera records objective reality."[9]

Although these works resonate with me, I also depart from them in my own moving image practice, where I tend to favor two-dimensional flatness and the relative obfuscation of spatial relations it affords. Whether the moving image space is constructed from the "cameraless" digital non-objectivism of computer-generated vector shapes, as in my works *Collision*,[10] *Sync*[11] or *Divisional Articulations*,[12] or is derived from an abstraction of photographed realism, such as in stop-motion films *AANAATT*[13] or *Shift*;[14] in both cases a denial of 3D depth perception usually helps to underline the pursued visual abstraction. The aim of this abstraction is generally a distancing from the everyday, a reduction or removal towards an "abstracted heterotopia":[15] a thinking space from which to reflect upon and critically comment back on reality. To this end, many of my works utilize optical tricks of shifting scales and folding perspectives, spatial conflations and confusions, which would be void or weakened if presented stereoscopically. The work, then, is bolstered by two-dimensionality's inherent denial to immediately visually comprehend what one sees on the screen, what is spatially in front and what is behind.

In late 2015, new media artist and researcher Jeffrey Shaw invited me to create a stereoscopic work for Animamix Biennale 2015–16, an exhibition he co-curated in Hong Kong.[16] I took the Biennale's theme "Directed Towards Knowledge" as a call for challenging and expanding my own knowledge and visual vocabulary of the in/animate, by exploring the artistic potential of stereoscopic imaging: the incentive prompted me to question how stereoscopy, rather than hyper-defining space within three dimensions, might itself be used to achieve a confusion of spatial perception.[17] It appeared pertinent at this stage, to put forward the possibility of a heterotopic, stereoscopic situation; that is, speculatively positing stereoscopy as a heterotopia itself, and as one that is in search of yet unexplored pathways to new knowledge. Or to put it differently, asking in what ways an expanded stereoscopy can be taken as a model for the creation of new knowledge. In addition, my desire was to find resistances to and ruptures in the current, hegemonic media ecology, read as an ever-increasing, all-encompassing, uncanny space of reality, as it were. As such, it seemed urgent to enquire the ways abstract and experimental moving image practices might benefit from stereoscopy both conceptually and aesthetically for opening up "new opportunities for radical abstractions, poetics, disruptions"[18] if used in ways that break with, or go beyond, stereoscopic fusion. If there is something like an alternative stereoscopics that may exceed mass media and the falsely supreme, commercially driven moving image environment, then what must this doubling vision look like? What would it encompass, what affects would become powerful, and what kind of viewer–and subjectivities–would it stage or imply? And I was contemplating that this other stereoscopy, which hovers in the shadows of the dominant regime, must perform the task of a kind of prophet. Of something or someone forecasting in imaginative, revealing, very real yet magic modes.

Given this apparent promise that an expanded stereoscopy holds for the present observer, one can perhaps hypothesize that truly new "visionary" experiences (a reference to Crary) are on the way that dislocate the domineering visual-sensorial-experiential regime. To underline what is at stake here, a few noteworthy works which exemplify a range of non-traditional, expanded artistic approaches to binocular vision will

9 Verina Gfader, *Adventure-Landing* (Berlin, 2012), pp. 60–61.

10 *Collision*. Directed by Max Hattler, Animation, UK / Germany, 2005.

11 *Sync*. Directed by Max Hattler, Animation, Denmark / Holland / UK / Germany, 2010.

12 *Divisional Articulations*. Directed by Max Hattler, Animation, Hong Kong / UK / Germany, 2017.

13 *AANAATT*. Directed by Max Hattler, Animation, UK / Japan / Germany, 2008.

14 *Shift*. Directed by Max Hattler, Animation, UK / Germany, 2012.

15 Based on Michel Foucault's concept of 'heterotopia.' Cf. Michel Foucault, "Des Espaces Autres (Of Other Spaces)," *Architecture, Mouvement, Continuité*, no. 5, 1984, pp. 46–49; translated by Jay Miskowiec in Diacritics 16, no. 1. 1986, pp. 22–27.

16 *POST PiXEL. Animamix Biennale 2015-16*, Run Run Shaw Creative Media Centre, Hong Kong, March 22–April 17, 2016 (Curated by Jeffrey Shaw and Ivy Lin, presented by the Leisure and Cultural Services Department, co-organised by City University of Hong Kong and Hong Kong Visual Arts Centre. Website: https://www.acim.cityu.edu.hk/archive/post-pixel/ (accessed November 20, 2018).

17 Max Hattler, "III=III," in *POST PiXEL, Animamix Biennale 2015-16*, exh. cat. Leisure and Cultural Services Department (Hong Kong, 2016), p. 34.

18 Blake Williams, "3D in the 21st Century. Becoming 3D." Mubi.com, 2015, https://mubi.com/notebook/posts/3d-in-the-21st-century-becoming-3d (accessed October 10, 2018).

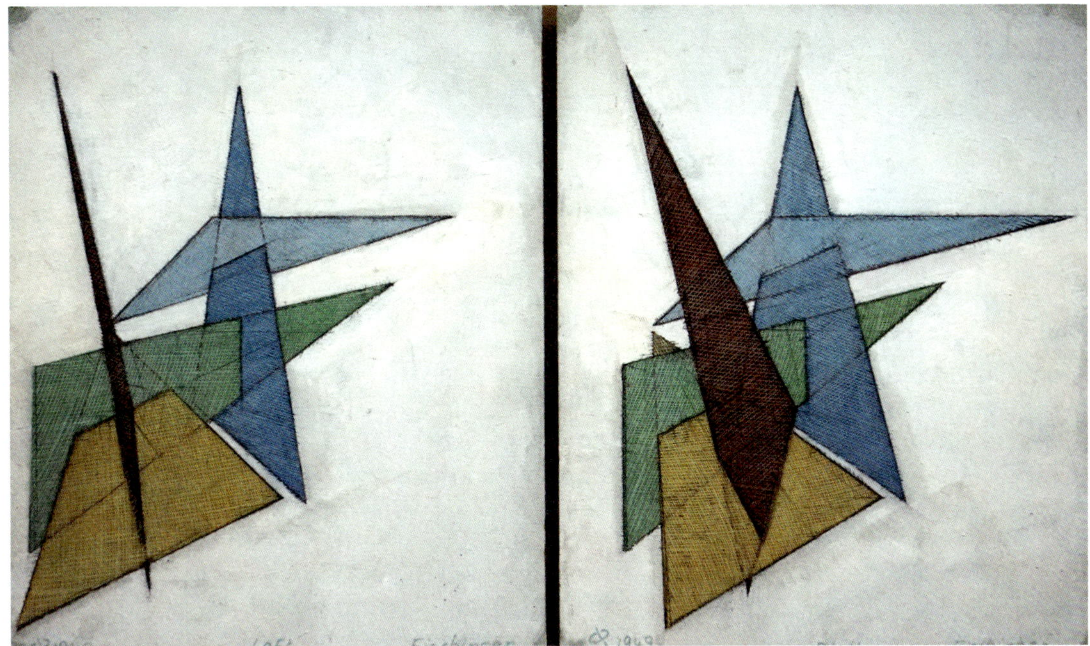

Figure 1: Oskar Fischinger, *Stereo No. 49*, 1949.

be discussed below, followed by a brief introduction of my own moving image work in this area, which started with the creation of stereoscopic animation loop *III=III*[19] for the Animamix Biennale 2015–16. The techniques employed in these works might serve as a toolkit for artists interested in exploring a more experimental, expanded engagement with stereoscopy. And by way of a toolkit for the critic, for a critical reviewer they may open up unknown elements from within the discourses linked to their own investigations in the field.

Tracing the history of avant-garde film and animation, there are few documented examples of experimental stereoscopy. Among the most interesting voices on the topic, William Moritz[20] importantly points to Harry Smith, Hy Hirsh, Norman McLaren, Dwinell Grant and Oskar Fischinger. These artists all delved into the realm of three-dimensional phenomena on screen in the late 1940s and early 1950s, around the time of the first theatrical 3D craze, using various devices and technologies such as coded prisms, oscilloscopic patterns, or visual disparities coming together stereoscopically in unusual ways. What was at stake in these early experiments was always the complex perceptual and cognitive relationship between two separate images or screens as they were experienced simultaneously as a stereoscopic image: right–left at once, but forever split. And within that, we see a first application of the experimental artistic impulse to the domain of stereoscopy, that is, an impulse to transcend established norms, and provoke or stipulate new experiences. While Grant creates three-dimensionally believable interactions between his shifting abstracted forms of stop-motion animation in *Composition 4*[21] *(Stereoscopic Study No. 1)*, Hirsh explores in *Come Closer*[22] what Moritz calls "'realistically' impossible relationships,"[23] as his oscilloscope-drawn objects pass through each other in unpredictable, poetic, rhythmic ways–like an ensemble of dots, lines, and shapes rehearsing and dancing to the music.

19 *III=III*. Directed by Max Hattler, Stereoscopic animation loop, 2:12 min., Hong Kong / Germany, 2016.

20 William Moritz, "Stereoscopic Abstract Film William Moritz's notes for 1999 lecture," https://www.centerforvisualmusic.org/WMlecstereo.pdf (accessed October 12, 2018).

21 *Composition 4*. Directed by Dwinell Grant, 1944–45.

22 *Come Closer*. Directed by Hy Hirsh, 1953.

23 William Moritz, "Stereoscopic Abstract Film William Moritz's notes for 1999 lecture," https://www.centerforvisualmusic.org/WMlecstereo.pdf (accessed October 12, 2018).

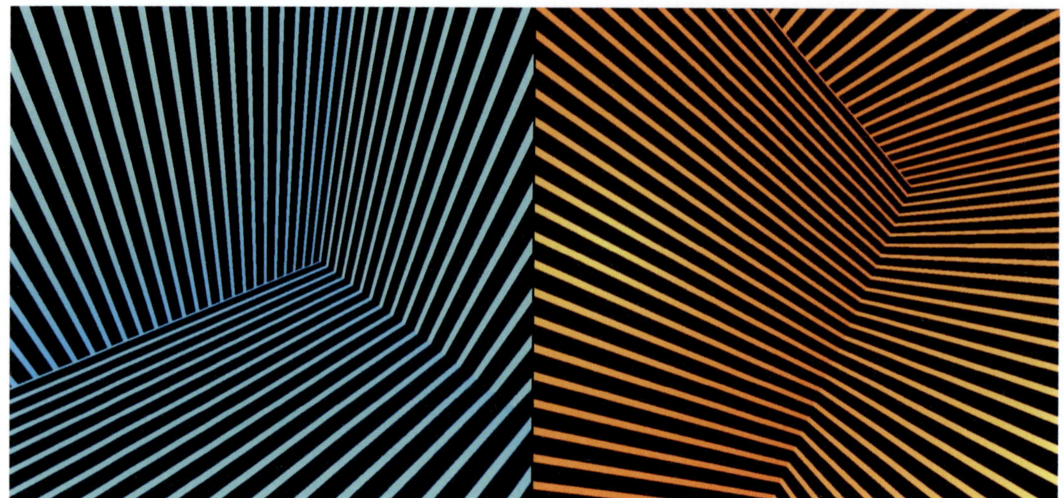

Figure 2: Memo Akten, *Fight*, 2017.

Binocular Rivalry

Fischinger's abstract stereoscopic paintings similarly present the viewer with spatial relations that go beyond the realistic recreation of three-dimensional space. In the late 1940s, straight after completing his film *Motion Painting No. 1*,[24] he spent four years creating a series of side-by-side pairs of paintings designed for 3D free-viewing–without the help of a stereoscope. One such "space painting"[25] is *Stereo No. 49*.[26] Using cross-eye viewing, a well-defined 3D image emerges. Other paintings of the series however seem to present the viewer with differently spaced parallax information within one image pair that goes beyond the "norm" of acceptable parallax difference. In *Circles in Circle*,[27] for example, some objects in left and right images are closer together and easily fusible into a coherent stereoscopic space, while others are so far apart or differently spaced, that they require an active re-adjustment effort on the part of the observer. As such, the presented "illusive painting in the middle,"[28] synthesized by the viewer from left and right images, does not hold together as one stereoscopic construct.

Instead, it presents competing yet co-existing versions of spatial depth within itself. As a result, the three-dimensional space shifts and re-aligns as the viewer actively negotiates the "space painting." Such unorthodox use of stereoscopy can lead to surprising artistic outcomes, viewer engagements, and the creation of improbable, paradoxical stereoscopic spaces.

However, when the difference between the images presented to left and right eye is so large that they cannot be fused into a singular image, the viewer experiences an unstable, volatile composite image. This phenomenon of visual perception, where perception alternates between different images presented to each eye, is called binocular rivalry.[29] Gregory Garvey's *Homage to the Square: Stereoscopic Suprematist Composition II*[30] investigates the effects of binocular rivalry. Following a long tradition of "the square" in the arts, from Kazimir Malevich to Joseph Albers, to the later minimalism of Ellsworth Kelly, Garvey's investment in the square picks up this reductionist impulse and celebration of the square as the most elementary formal element of an art striving towards the "supremacy of pure sensa-

24 *Motion Painting No. 1*. Directed by Oskar Fischinger, 1947.

25 Oskar Fischinger, "A Statement About Painting," 1951, https://www.oskarfischinger.org/Fisch1951Painting.htm (accessed October 10, 2018).

26 Oskar Fischinger, *Stereo No. 49*, Oil on cardboard stereo painting, each painting 32.4 x 23.4 cm, 1949, courtesy of The Elfriede Fischinger Trust, Long Beach, CA (Inv. No. 433a and 433b).

27 Oskar Fischinger, *Circles in Circle*, Oil on masonite stereo painting, each panel 30.48 x 30.48 cm, 1949.

28 Oskar Fischinger, "A Statement About Painting," 1951, https://www.oskarfischinger.org/Fisch1951Painting.htm (accessed October 10, 2018).

29 Randolph Blake and Nikos K. Logothetis, "Visual competition." Nature Reviews Neuroscience. 3 (1): 13–21 (2002), https://www.nature.com/articles/nrn701 (accessed October 14, 2018).

30 Gregory Garvey, *Homage to the Square: Stereoscopic Suprematist Composition II*, Inkjet print, Stereoscope, 2005.

tion."[31] But Garvey revisits the square through the lens, quite literally, of cognitive and perceptual psychology. *Homage to the Square* is a print work containing differently sized grey squares positioned side by side, which, when viewed with a stereoscope, are fused into a single image of nested squares. Due to the degree of binocular rivalry however, the resulting image is not three-dimensional. Instead, "(t)he squares appear to slowly slide over or behind the other as the brain's visual apparatus strives to maintain a single coherent view that exists 'only in the mind's eye.'"[32] Through the use of binocular rivalry, the modernist flattening is not reversed into a three-dimensional geometric space, but instead, Garvey pushes the perceptual boundaries of the square's sensations by adding this "internal," unstable, semi-spatial dimension that is only experienced within the viewer: "It is not a stereoscopic 3D illusion. Instead, a kind of 2.5D space is perceived."[33] Forwards in time, and developed from within today's cultural-technological conditions, in Memo Akten's virtual reality artwork *Fight*[34] the use of a VR headset underlines the effect of binocular rivalry, as each eye is completely forced into its respective view. Akten's meditative, introspective exercise in visual perception probes the limits of binocular rivalry, taking the viewer through different chapters which start out in a stereoscopically fused, three-dimensional space. Partly through the viewer's own head movements, the space then folds into two increasingly opposed directions. As stereopsis is denied, a forever-shifting image presents itself, making those who encounter the work acutely aware of their own image processing mechanism and the "fight" between left and right eyes.

> Presented with rival signals, the conscious mind "sees" an unstable, irregular, animated patchwork of the two images; with swipes and transitions. The nature of these irregularities and instabilities depend on the viewer's physiology.[35]

The mostly abstract content of *Fight* underlines this collapsing of a total image/space as the two parts of a once stereoscopically fused image drift apart. This experience of extreme binocular rivalry can be dislocating and highly uncomfortable, as the viewer loses all reference points to a sense-making pictorial space, however abstract. Deliberately closing one eye gives temporary respite by reverting back to the un-broken space of monocular two-dimensionality.

However, when used with geometry that is displayed with the right amount of parallax to allow for stereoscopic fusion, binocular rivalry can be leveraged to generate particular visual effects unique to stereoscopic vision, such as the display of luster, which results from color disparities between the images presented to left and right eyes. One of the less extreme chapters in Akten's *Fight* is composed of three-dimensionally fused diamond-like particles which are "drawn" on the image space through the viewer's head movements. The colors of these diamond shapes are different for left and right eyes (their red and blue colors can be understood as a nod to the anaglyph process, which will be discussed further below). This color difference gives the objects a luminous sheen in the viewer's perception, which is distinctly different from any other color perception possible with 2D or non-expanded stereoscopic means.

In the 1970s, the Spanish artist Salvador Dalí had already created a series of stereo pairs of paintings which explore similar effects. Working from within the Surrealist movement with its focus on how the unconscious mind reveals and releases the power of imagination, it is no surprise that Dalí probed the binocular rivalry potential of stereoscopy to tease out perceptual possibilities that go beyond our everyday cognition, to create new and expanded optical illusions and experiences. By using different colors for certain elements in the left and right paintings of an otherwise stereoscopically fusible image pair, the corresponding parts appear to glow with a velvety luster, when the pair of paintings is observed through a stereoscope. This luster can be observed in a number of works including *Dali's Hand Drawing Back the Golden Fleece in the Form of a Cloud to Show Gala the Dawn, Completely Nude, Very, Very Far Away Behind the Sun*[36] or *Dali*

31 Gregory Garvey, "Gregory Garvey," In ACM SIGGRAPH 2005 Electronic Art and Animation Catalog (SIGGRAPH '05). New York, NY, USA: ACM, 2005, pp. 66–67, https://dl.acm.org/citation.cfm?doid=1086057.1086089 (accessed October 15, 2018).
32 Ibid.
33 Ibid.
34 *Fight*. Directed by Memo Akten, VR artwork, 2017.
35 Memo Akten, "FIGHT (2017)," Memo Akten Official Website, 2017, https://www.memo.tv/portfolio/fight/ (accessed October 15, 2018).
36 Salvador Dalí, *Dali's Hand Drawing Back the Golden Fleece in the Form of a Cloud to Show Gala the Dawn, Completely Nude, Very, Very Far Away Behind the Sun* (two stereoscopic panels, oil on canvas, 60 x 60 cm), 1977.

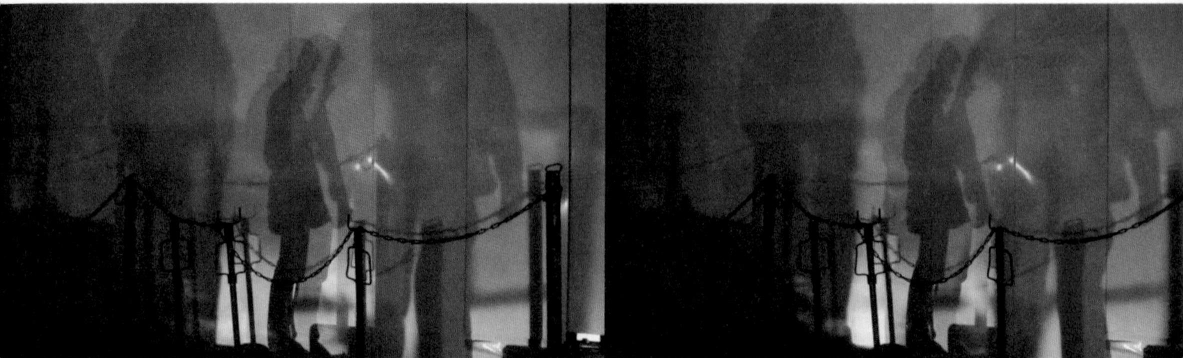

from the Back Painting Gala from the Back Eternalized by Six Virtual Corneas Provisionally Reflected in Six Real Mirrors.[37] Other paintings from Dalí's series such as *Athens Is Burning! The School of Athens and the Fire in the Borgo*[38] display both stereoscopic fusion and extreme binocular rivalry. In *Athens*, large parts of the left and right paintings (which are comparatively intimate, at about thirty by forty centimeters each) are completely different, making it impossible to see a coherent image, while some sections display elements of stereoscopic fusion, which partially anchor the viewer back into the image space.

Camera-Based Binocular Poetics

Further to binocular rivalry we discover the Pulfrich effect, named after the German physicist and instrument inventor Carl Pulfrich.[39] As a researcher at the Carl Zeiss company in Jena around 1880, Pulfrich achieved major advances in the improvement of optics and in developing stereoscopic techniques. In 1922, Pulfrich was the first to describe the phenomenon that came to bear his name. The Pulfrich effect is a psychophysical percept wherein three-dimensional depth is perceived in two-dimensional lateral motion, if the vision of one eye of the viewer is slowed down through a dark filter such as one-eyed sunglasses. This creates a relative difference in signal timings between the two eyes,

leading to the perception of three-dimensional depth. Following this direction, the Japanese experimental filmmaker Kazuhiro Goshima created an intriguing series of stereoscopic works which play with the time difference between left and right eye in imaginative ways to create three-dimensional space from two-dimensional source material. Goshima's short film *Shadowland*[40] is shot with a fixed 2D camera and depicts a two-dimensional city at night, in which only the shadows, created from the time-difference parallax of moving car headlights, take on a three-dimensional form. Goshima (2014) emphasizes that,

> The essential factor of 3D vision is binocular parallax. I derive parallax from the slight time lag between the movies projected onto the right and left eyes. There are no digital special effects. I show the same movies to each eye but there is slight time lag (one–five frames).[41]

The outcome of this rather simple transformation is highly effective and surprising, as the ephemeral by-products of urban traffic—the wandering reflections and fleeting shadows—are poetically reimagined as sculptural characters three-dimensionally emerging from the cinema screen. *Shadowland* really comes into its own when viewed on a large-scale stereoscopic

---

37 Salvador Dalí, *Dali from the Back Painting Gala from the Back Eternalized by Six Virtual Corneas Provisionally Reflected in Six Real Mirrors* (stereoscopic paintings, left and right, unfinished), 1972-73.

38 Salvador Dalí, *Athens Is Burning! The School of Athens and the Fire in the Borgo* (stereoscopic paintings, left and right), 1979-80.

39 Carl Pulfrich, "Die Stereoskopie im Dienste der isochromen und heterochromen Photometrie," *Die Naturwissenschaften*, 10, 1922, pp. 553–564.

40 *Shadowland*. Directed by Kazuhiro Goshima, Stereoscopic film, 14:32 min., Japan, 2013. see also p. 174.

41 Kazuhiro Goshima, "Shadowland," in *CyberArts 2014: International Compendium Prix Ars Electronica*. Edited by Leopoldseder, Hannes, et al., (Berlin, 2014), p. 27.

Guest Editorial. Perception, 1994, vol. 23, pp. 981–89. https://journals.sagepub.com/doi/pdf/10.1068/p230981 (accessed October 18, 2018).

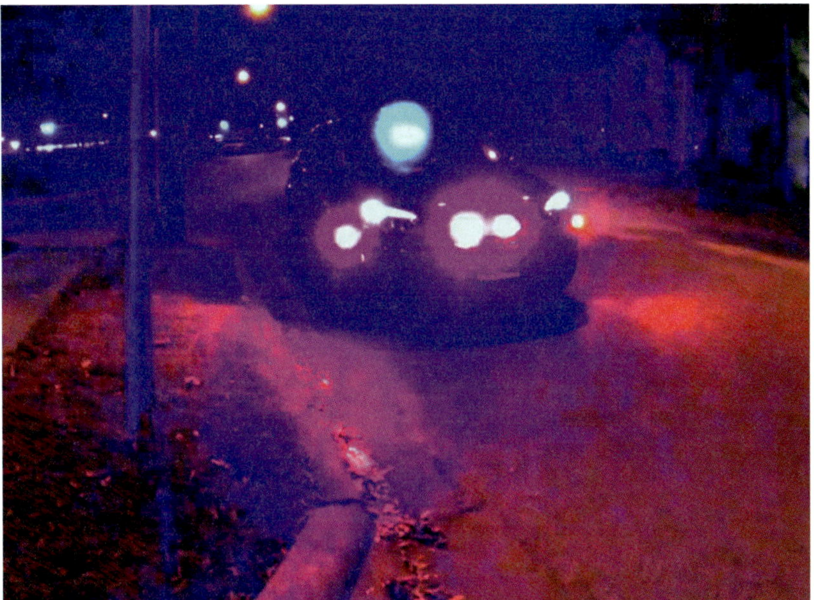

Figure 4: Blake Williams, *Red Capriccio*, 2014.

screen such as Ars Electronica Center's Deep Space 8K floor-to-ceiling projection environment. Then the shadows truly rise up from the screen and enter the room, which is all the more impressive since the city from which they emerge remains at a safe, two-dimensional distance from the audience. As the film unfolds and envelops us, we witness the beauty of time passing by, and we forget that it is time itself, through the different signal timings, which create the film's magic. *Shadowland* feels like a meditation on life and fleeting, in-between moments, on what is hardly noticed and mundane. Rather than a shadow play or shadow theater the work evokes the urban as a shadowy organic body in becoming, and as a site for hidden treasures, a poetry of light rhythms, impermanent, cursory figures appearing and disappearing like dancers against the city's concrete surfaces.

Vancouver-based artist Blake Williams also takes advantage of left-right time difference to create three-dimensional parallax in sections of his film *Red Capriccio*.[42] The film's main focus, however, lies elsewhere. Made entirely from found two-dimensional video footage, and created specifically for anaglyphic 3D glasses, the film plays with, and intensifies, the color-specific binocular rivalry built into the anaglyphic

process. Through color correction and solarization of the separated red and cyan stereo channels, *Red Capriccio* creates intense eye-asynchronous flicker effects and duotone luster.

> The image, distilled through the Anaglyph filters—one bloodshot and the other frigid—grants each eye its moment; one fills in the blanks for the other, the two share together but then finally fight for exclusivity, blinding the other before being blinded right back.[43]

Again, here is the image of the fight, which Akten addressed in his film. Williams takes this fight for dominance between left and right, and playfully develops multiple open-ended strands of meaning from it, constructing *Red Capriccio* around polar opposites of machines and landscape, motion and stasis, crescendos and glissandos, and of course the multiple blinding reds and blues. Set in a desolate urban environment, the three movements of the film depict nighttime scenes of a parked Chevrolet Caprice Police Pursuit Vehicle, the Turcot three-level stack freeway interchange in Montréal, and an empty room illuminated only by moving disco lights. Through these juxtaposi-

---

42 *Red Capriccio*. Directed by Blake Williams, Anaglyph stereoscopic video, HDV, 6 min. HD, USA / Canada, 2014. Featured on Blake Williams's Website, https://blakewilliams.net/red-capriccio-2014/ (accessed October 15, 2018).
43 Blake Williams, "3D in the 21st Century. Becoming 3D." Mubi.com, 2015, https://mubi.com/notebook/posts/3d-in-the-21st-century-becoming-3d (accessed October 10, 2018).

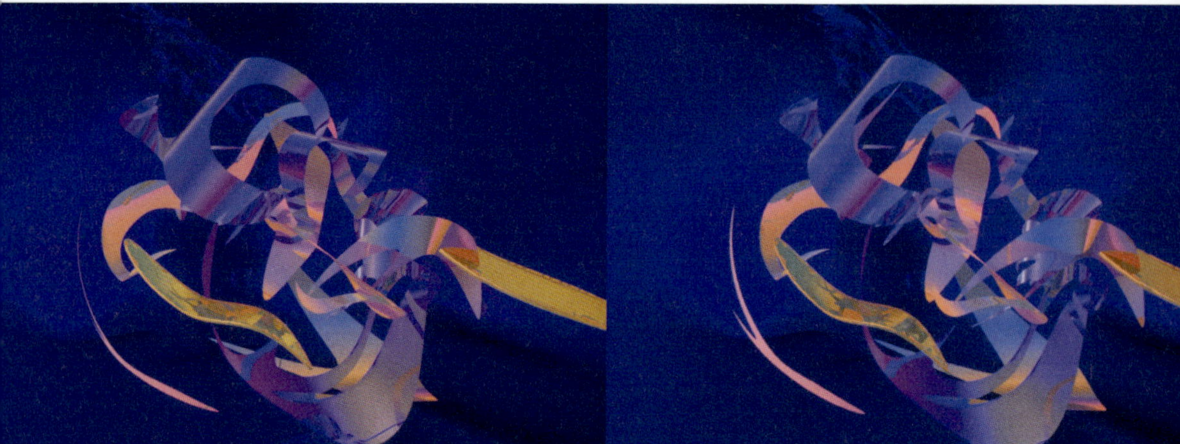

Figure 5: Vibeke Sorensen, *Maya*, 1993.

tions of the emptiness of his subject matter and the visual intensity of anaglyph flicker and luster, Williams manages to present a strangely manifold visual-narrative space. This red-blue color sphere is more like an afterimage or image behind the closed eye: an image of trauma or intoxication, a dreamlike remembrance of an event that might have never happened. Pulsating thoughts. Nightmarish, but so very real.

Williams's expanded exploration of anaglyph imagery also loosely relates back to Smith's *Film No. 6*[44] *[Untitled 3-D Abstraction]* from 1951, which creatively works with the red and green anaglyph process it relies on for stereoscopy. *Film No. 6* presents a recording of a live performance in which paper cut-outs are suspended in space and lit by red and green lights to create anaglyphic shadow images on the screen. These are combined further with red-green depth displaced projections of pre-recorded images to create multi-layered abstractions. "Smith's interest in Alchemy led him to design "magical" configurations that do not necessarily correspond to ordinary experiences,"[45] notes Moritz.

Paradoxical Digital Spaces

An early example of digital moving image work which features expanded approaches to stereoscopy is Vibeke Sorensen's computer-generated short film *Maya*.[46] This atmospheric abstract animation of organic shapes was produced at the San Diego Supercomputer Cen-

ter's Advanced Scientific Visualization Laboratory and exploits mirroring and reflection within the three-dimensional image space to create spatial ambiguities and confusions. The film's title *Maya*, of course, refers to the Sanskrit word meaning "illusion" or "magic," or more precisely the conflict between illusion and reality. In Hinduism, the whole world is Maya: a veil that covers divine reality behind the materialist entrapment, which constitutes the illusion we perceive to be real. According to Sorensen,[47] the film is a reflection on representation and illusion, partly provoked by the quest for increased realism in computer graphics. Sorensen saw this emergent computer graphics realism as a surface illusion, that should not be confused with reality. Instead, computer graphics should be understood on its own terms, with its own specificities, which offer the potential for new experiences. In *Maya*, some of this new potential is explored through stereoscopic visual abstraction. Here, photorealism and "objective correlative" are removed, to focus the viewer's attention purely on the perception of space and how it unfolds over time within the three-dimensional computer environment. Some of this spatial exploration is done in novel, medium-specific ways, leading to contradictory, paradoxical spaces: for example, Sorensen maps 3D images inside of other 3D images, which leads to fractal-like spatial recursions, where objects become windows into other spaces.

---

44 *Film No. 6 [Untitled 3-D Abstraction]*. Directed by Harry Smith, 1951.

45 William Moritz, "Stereoscopic Abstract Film William Moritz's notes for 1999 lecture,"https://www.centerforvisualmusic.org/WMlecstereo.pdf (accessed October 12, 2018).

46 *Maya*. Directed by Vibeke Sorensen, Stereoscopic animation film, 7:15 min., USA, 1993.

47 Sorensen, Vibeke, "Art-Science / Art-Engineering Interactions: Four Decades of Experimentation," (Masterclass), Punto y Raya Festival 2018, CeTA Centrum Technologii Audiowizualnych, Wrocław, Poland, October 26, 2018

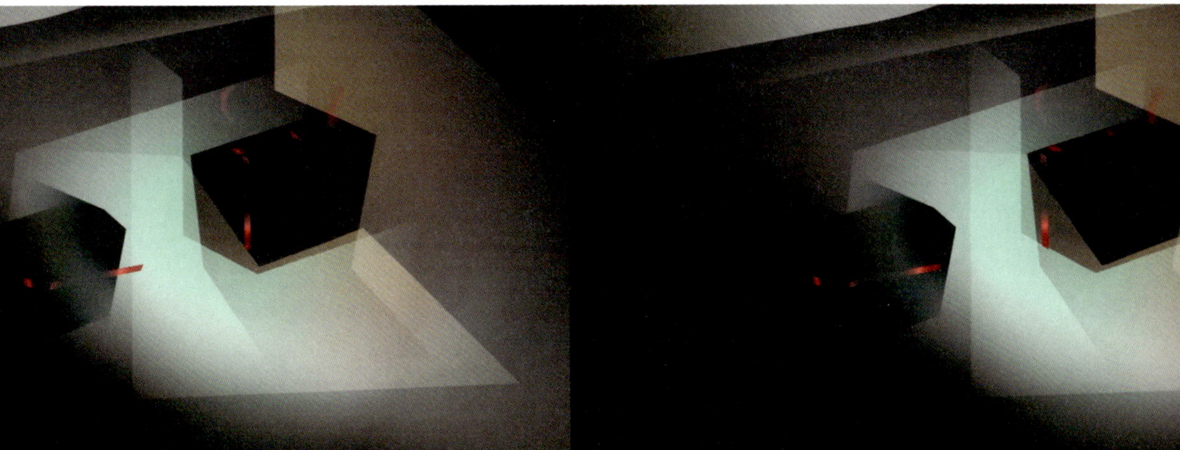

Figure 6: Sebastian Buerkner, *The Chimera of M.*, 2013.

In one scene stereoscopic images are projected onto flat discs making up a small sculpture. Each disc is a circular window to another 3-D space. The result is a perceptual paradox: you see the edges of the disks in a sculpture made up of flat surfaces. But when you look at each separate, "flat" disc, you see windows to spaces that extend far beyond the space of the sculpture. The two spaces contradict each other, but the mind holds them together.[48]

The artist also made use of the computer's ability to adjust the interaxial separation between left and right eyes: "By using interaxial separation to scale up or down objects and scenes, I was able to better understand the structure and continuity of space and to have very fine control over the abstract visual elements that I used to compose *Maya*."[49] This was, for example, employed in a "3D cross-dissolve," where there are two sets of 3D cameras, and Sorensen controls the moving apart (increasing depth) and moving together (decreasing depth, flattening, and appearing farther away) to modulate spatial perceptions. As a result of this "3D cross-dissolve," the 3D scene on screen flattens and becomes the surface of an object of the next scene. This play with surface and depth, where three-dimensional spaces become surfaces of objects, and objects become windows into other dimensions, breaks and probes our preconceptions of space, and indeed, by extension, reality itself.

A more recent computer-generated work which re-configures and questions our perceptions of space is Sebastian Buerkner's 25-minute long stereoscopic digital animation film *The Chimera of M.*[50] Here, three-dimensional space appears malleable and disjointed, otherworldly yet strangely familiar. Ephemeral elements such as shadows, floating specks of light, and reflections are spatially foregrounded. Through the orchestration of multitudes of overlapping 2D-animated layers within three dimensions, Buerkner creates an unstable post-Cubist visual universe, which celebrates an abstracted, multi-perspectival version of space. This highly expressive use of stereoscopy, while pushing and distorting, or making malleable, the conception of reality, reinforces the spatial and visual ambiguity of the film's narrative.

In *The Chimera of M.*, the viewer is put in the position of an elusive protagonist who moves through obscure spaces as he reengages with his past relationships. If there are faces in this loose abstracted narrative, they have the quality of an animated, unstable Francis Bacon portrait, where details are brushed over, giving the impression that there may have never been a face in the first place. There is a lack of clear identification of a person or character, with Buerkner's use of stereoscopy supporting this dissolution of a stable visual coherence, of a reliable figure–of any reliable figuration. In this work this is beautifully posed in an atmospheric, soft, sometimes almost cartoonish and humorous manner, with the viewer being allowed to

48 Vibeke Sorensen, "Maya," Vibeke Sorensen Official Website, 1993, https://vibeke.info/maya/ (accessed October 15, 2018).

49 Vibeke Sorensen and Robert Russett, "Computer Stereographics: The Coalescence of Virtual Space and Artistic Expression," *Leonardo*, 32(1), 1999, p. 45.

50 *The Chimera of M.* Directed by Sebastian Buerkner, Stereoscopic animation film, 25:12 min., color, UK, 2013.

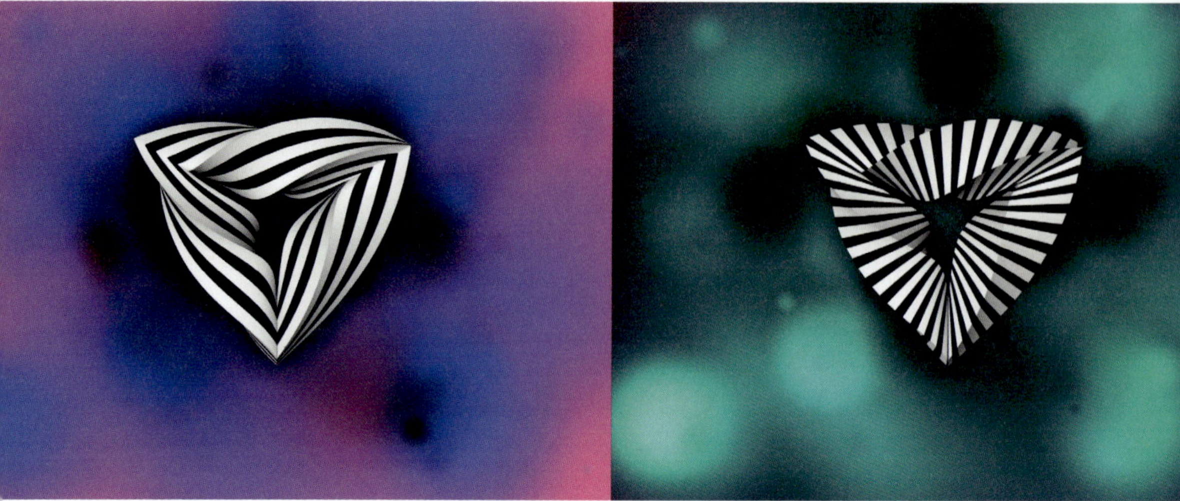

Figure 7: Max Hattler, *III=III*, 2016.

retreat into the unseen protagonist. There is also a sensation of, or hinting at, the sphere of a painterly scene we might find in Luc Tuyman's oeuvre. Such scene is in fact never a scene in the sense of being staged or deliberately constructed, but is a noticing of moments and givens in one's surroundings. And this is then reduced by the artist to showing us only bare visual clues.

Space in *The Chimera of M.* is reminiscent of Cubism, but equally connects to surreal futuristic film worlds. We want to be *in* the work precisely *because of* its deluding environment. And there is both a sculpturing dynamic as well as a flattening or schematizing motive in the way the film draws the viewer in. It wants you to be there, but at the same time occludes access. In that sense, the stereoscopic prospect is enticing as it underlines this process: dreamland in reality, imaginative, blending abstraction and the figurative in combinations virtually never seen before. This is a deliberately false construct, wherein the viewer's contorted relationship both with the uncertain spaces in the film, and the multi-dimensional film space itself, as well as with the protagonist's point of view, adds to the effect of absorption and disorientation. The sound supports the confused narrative. There are voices, splinters of conversations, motors, muffled techno beats and thunder, the door creaking as someone enters.

With *The Chimera of M.*, then, stereoscopy must be considered as expanded, as it becomes a means to underline viewer affect and narrative expressiveness in a contemporary spatiotemporal visual poetics. Visual abstraction and expression come together, as they merge in the exposition of the film's unfulfilled, inconclusive narrative. The spatial and visual ambiguity of the film's narration is reinforced by a vehement stereoscopic reconfiguration of space and spatial compounds as it were: and there is a sensation of a kind of mind game, or image of the deepening plasticity of the brain.

Lastly, random-dot stereograms should be mentioned here briefly, as a further approach towards paradoxical digital stereoscopic spaces. Invented by Christopher Tyler[51] and popularized by the *Magic Eye* book series,[52] random-dot autostereograms constitute single images of random dots which are computer-encoded with a depth map. When seen with the correct binocular convergence, the two-dimensional noise patterns open up into a fully three-dimensional scene hidden within. The revealed 3D space itself is not "expanded" as such; it relies on parallax and stereoscopic fusion to appear. However, the effect of something tangibly spatial appearing out of two-dimensional noise is so surprising and unique, that it warrants being included in this section, as it may open up avenues for further artistic experimentation. It was, in fact, one of the techniques I took up in my own artistic stereoscopic explorations.

---

51 Christopher Tyler and Clarke Maureen, "The Autostereogram," Stereoscopic Displays and Applications Conference, Proc. SPIE Vol. 1258, 1990, pp. 182–196.
52 N. E. Thing Enterprises, *Magic Eye: A New Way of Looking at the World* (Kansas City, 1993).

III=III and beyond

My animation piece *III=III* was developed for Animamix Biennale 2015–16 as an experiment, as a first approach towards expanded stereoscopic spaces.[53] The work was projected on a four-by-three-meter silver screen in the gallery space. It presented the viewer with a series of ten-second vignettes appearing in a looped sequence, which explore different stereoscopic effects ranging from subtle to extreme. The aim was to incorporate binocular rivalry while maintaining enough parallax-based geometry to ensure stereopsis. Several scenes explore different colors in left and right eye images to create luster. This effect is at times almost unnoticeable, as it does not draw too much attention to itself. A stronger binocular rivalry percept is achieved when a 3D object remains stereoscopically fused, while its textures are considerably different in the left and the right image. The viewer can process the image as three-dimensional, while simultaneously being confronted with the destabilizing sensation of binocular rivalry. Only in one scene, used for "shock value," the rivalry is so extreme that the image becomes completely unfusible, creating a conflicted visual space that is hard to watch and difficult to endure. Here, wireframe tubes, one per eye, rotate in *opposite* directions. At this point viewers in the Animamix exhibition often took their 3D glasses off to escape the jarring sensation. In other scenes, 3D depth maps are employed to create deformations and invisible, inverted spaces: in one scene, clusters of cubes move towards the viewer. When seen in motion and through 3D glasses, an opposite movement of invisible counter-cubes reveals itself. In two scenes, I adapted the random-dot stereogram *Magic Eye* technique with animated stereo pairs of random dot images. Here, the viewer only sees random noise on the screen, as they approach the work in the gallery space. Yet a fully three-dimensional, animated space "magically" appears when 3D glasses are donned. These sections were the most commented on by the Animamix audience, as they elicit the greatest amount of surprise, derived from the extreme difference between watching the screen with 3D glasses and without. Since the creation of *III=III*, I have continued to explore expanded stereoscopy in and through my moving image work. In 2018, some of the *III=III* scenes were adapted to a Unity-based VR environment. While the use of a VR headset made the binocular experience stronger, it simultaneously weakened some of the compositional aspects I am used to working with, through the open-endedness inherent in the VR space. My current moving image work picks up and continues some of these issues by further experimenting and exploring, with both camera-based and computer-originated stereoscopic approaches. At the same time, experimental stereoscopy has found its way into my audiovisual performance practice, in the form of another iteration of the Hattlerizer setup, namely *Hattlerizer 4.D.*[54]

Conclusion

Stereoscopy holds the potential for expanded uses that go beyond the emulation of human vision and the faithful recreation of perspectival space. This can take the form of spaces where depth relations are disjointed and appear to be paradoxical. Or spatial manifestations where new dimensionality and visual intensity is excavated, carved out from flat source material. This is a sculptural process with implications: what is considered flat–and is also often seen as secondary and minor to perspectival space–hosts space or cosmos. In that sense the "flat" holds the potential of re-ordering hierarchies and power relations in new and unpredictable ways. Beyond this speculative note around an animation of the yet-to-come, the use of binocular rivalry stipulates and bears unique perceptions ranging from the subtle observation of luster to the uncomfortable, destabilizing experience of a complete breakdown of stereopsis. The promise an expanded stereoscopy holds, especially when it develops from artistic practitioners or film makers, comes as a promise of the imaginative, as it channels our desires for unexplored and unthinkable realms against or beyond "realism." There is a drive towards rupturing familiar narratives that the expanded stereoscopic is drawn to. This is fascinating, especially when it maintains its power of being something marginal and liminal, actual and virtual at once; escaping precise categorizations and forensic readings. Having been reluctant about stereoscopy and its relevance to my work in the past,

---

53 To be precise, there is one earlier stereoscopic experiment, an animated loop for Pulfrich effect 3D glasses entitled *Forms II (Karate)* (directed by Max Hattler, 2011). Here, motion capture data is abstracted inside a polyhedron mirror, creating complex spatial confusions. It was produced at CalArts with a group of Experimental Animation students and guided by technical and inspirational advice from Michael Scroggins.

54 *Hattlerizer*. Audio-visual performance by Max Hattler, length variable, 2010–. See also "Live and Direct," Max Hattler (website), https://www.maxhattler.com/live/ (accessed October 15, 2018).

this research has opened up many new lines of inquiry beyond my comfort zone, as it were. And I am excited by the still relatively untapped potential for artistic expression. In conclusion, alternate uses of stereoscopy constitute modes of an expanded cinema which allow for novel ways of seeing that are at once deeply personal and subjective–individual to each viewer–and unique to technologically aided binocular vision. These approaches, with flatness and new depth, spatio-visual abstractions and confusions, and a re-empowered viewer in essence, compel ways of seeing which are exceptionally *impossible* in the real world. As such, they can be seen as a true, "magical" as well as real, expansion of the senses. How this expanded cinema registers the technological and the ways we narrate the human and in/animate as it evolves further remains to be seen. One strategy might be to continue to try and rupture things, and carefully observe if and how the broken remnants are exploded into space to create new spatial configurations.

Acknowledgements

This research was supported by grants from City University of Hong Kong (Projects No. 7005173 and 7200562) and the Centre for Applied Computing and Interactive Media (ACIM) of the School of Creative Media, City University of Hong Kong.

Bibliography

Campagna, Federico. *Technic and Magic: The Reconstruction of Reality.* London and New York, 2018.

Crary, Jonathan. *Techniques of the Observer: On Vision and Modernity in the Nineteenth Century.* Cambridge, MA, 1990.

Foucault, Michel. "Des Espaces Autres (Of Other Spaces)." *Architecture, Mouvement, Continuité*, no. 5, 1984, pp. 46–49; translated by Jay Miskowiec in *Diacritics* 16, no. 1. 1986, pp. 22–27.

Gfader, Verina, *Adventure-Landing*. Berlin, 2012, pp. 60–61.

Goshima, Kazuhiro. "Shadowland." In *CyberArts 2014: International Compendium Prix Ars Electronica*. Edited by Leopoldseder, Hannes, et al., Berlin, 2014, pp. 26–27.

Hattler, Max. "III=III." In *POST PiXEL, Animamix Biennale 2015–16*, exh. cat. Leisure and Cultural Services Department, Hong Kong, 2016, pp. 32–34.

Hattler, Max. "From Broken Visions to Expanded Abstractions." Asia Animation Forum, Bucheon International Animation Festival, Bucheon, South Korea, October 22, 2017. Website: https://www.biaf.or.kr:47436/2017/en/index_forum_new.php

Hattler, Max. "From Broken Visions to Expanded Abstractions." In *Cartoon and Animation Studies*, vol. 49. Seoul: Korean Society of Cartoon and Animation Studies, 2017, pp. 697–712.

Helmholtz, Hermann von. *Treatise on physiological optics*, vol. 3: The perceptions of vision. New York, 1825. Available from Echo, Cultural Heritage Online, https://echo.mpiwg-berlin.mpg.de/ECHOdocuView?url=/permanent/library/HS7FH69N/pageimg&viewMode=index&pn=9&mode=imagepath (accessed October 12, 2018).

N. E. Thing Enterprises, *Magic Eye: A New Way of Looking at the World*. Kansas City, 1993.

Pulfrich, Carl. "Die Stereoskopie im Dienste der isochromen und heterochromen Photometrie". *Die Naturwissenschaften*, 10, 1922, pp. 553–564.

Richter, Hans, *The Struggle for the Film, Towards a Socially Responsible Cinema*. Romhild, Jürgen, ed. Hampshire, 1986.

Sorensen, Vibeke, and Robert Russett. "Computer Stereographics: The Coalescence of Virtual Space and Artistic Expression." *Leonardo*, 32(1), 1999, pp. 41–48, https://www.mitpressjournals.org/doi/10.1162/002409499552984 (accessed October 15, 2018).

Tyler, Christopher, and Maureen Clarke. "The Autostereogram". Stereoscopic Displays and Applications, Proc. SPIE vol. 1258, 1990, pp. 182–196.

Stephan Schwingeler (DE)

Radical Action and Pure Joy: David OReilly's Video Game *Everything* in the Context of Game Art, Art History, and a new Gamic Avant-garde

In the beginning I was an elephant. My first play-through of David OReilly's videogame *Everything*[1] started in the pachyderm's thick skin. Shortly after that I entered a beetle's body, transformed into pollen, and back into a beetle. I controlled tufts of grass and turned into a palm tree. At one point I became a rubber duck, a snooker table, a set of conga drums, an electric guitar. I transformed into an island, a sun, a galaxy, becoming everything at once, incorporating everything that is included in it at the same time.

On the one hand, David OReilly's *Everything* plays with this permanent change of perspective, enabling the player to experience the game's world as another entity. On the other hand, the game utilizes change of scale resulting in the fact that the object incarnated before becomes the measure of the following object. The outcome is a journey from a small into a large universe, from micro- to macrocosmos, and back again, comparable to Ray and Charles Eames's famous experimental film *Powers of 10* from 1977.

A main difference, of course, is that *Everything* is not a film—it is a game, an interactive piece, in which no individual traverse, playthrough, or free navigation is comparable to another player's experience. *Everything's* reception is a personal, individual journey depending on the path through the game's cosmos chosen by the player. This path is not laid out linearly leading from A to B, but is rather comparable to a web, a network, a rhizome. The player moves through this very system of objects and rules and thus navigates the system itself, wielding influence over it. In the following remarks I will discuss OReilly's *Everything* from different perspectives and situate it in art history. First the piece will be situated in the broader context of game art. After that I will lay out some basic remarks about the video game as a new material in art history: the video game's entry into the art world as a new material and genre is outlined in a short overview using examples from the nineteen-eighties and nineties such as Toshio Iwai's *Otocky* (1987)[2] and the video game modification *Arsdoom* (Orhan Kipcak, Reinhard Urban, 1995)[3]. In the course of describing early video game pieces various artistic strategies are indentified that are used by artists mainly in the nineteen-nineties to appropriate

---

1 *Everything*. Directed by David OReilly, Produced by Double Fine Productions. 2017. see also p. 206

2 *Otocky*. Developed by Scitron & Art SEDIC. Published by ASCII Corporation. 1987.

3 Orphan Kipcak, "ARSDOOM – art adventure," in *Mythos Information: Welcome to the Wired World*, edited by Karl Gerbel, Peter Weibel, and Ars Electronica, exh. cat. Brucknerhaus Linz. Vienna, New York, 1995, pp. 262–264.

video games in the context of art. As a consequence, the opportunity arises to step further into art history by highlighting various strategies of appropriation that are relevant to artists beginning to use video games as their material. It becomes clear that the first artists using video games mainly in the nineteen-nineties cultivated a rather aggressive approach towards the material tending to analyze it by disruption, interference, and eventually destruction. These tendencies are addressed by the concept of countergaming. The term coined by media scholar Alexander Galloway[4] can be used to frame the strategies and tendencies to rebel against established forms of convential game design resulting in a new form of gameplay eventually leading to a new gamic avant-garde: radical action. *Everything* can serve as an example for this new form of radical gameplay being one of the first games to truly embrace the potentialities of videogames as artistic, hybrid material and one fine example of a new gamic avant-garde.

Video Games and Art

In the art context, *Everything* can be seen as belonging to a larger field that curators call game art[5]. In the following remarks I will critically discuss the term game art, integrating David OReilly's work into a larger context of art practice including video games as material. While the label game art makes sense from a curatorial perspective, it is problematic from a scholarly one. One definition of game art was proposed by Matteo Bittanti.[6] Bittanti understands game art as *every kind* of artistic expression in which digital games play a significant role:

Game art is any art in which digital games played a significant role in the creation, production, and/ or display of the artwork. The resulting artwork can exist as a game, painting, photograph, sound, animation, video, performance, or gallery installation.

---

4 Alexander R. Galloway, *Gaming. Essays on Algorithmic Culture* (Minneapolis, 2006).
5 According to current scholarship, the concept game art was first used as a curatorial label in 2002. Curator Rebecca Cannon used it for her exhibition *Trigger: Game Art from 14–25* May 2002 in Melbourne, Australia. *Game Art* functioned as the title of and as a sort of label in an exhibition at Völklinger Hütte in Völklingen near Saarbrücken in 2003 (cf. Meinrad M. Grewenig et al., eds., GameArt, exh. cat. Völklinger Hütte (Ostfildern, 2003)). The concept game art refers in the context of game design to the implementation of graphics from the first sketch to the final product. Game art thereby encompasses the classical techniques of fine art as well as computational visualistics.
6 Matteo Bittanti, *Per una cultura dei videogames. Teorie e prassi del videogiocare* (Milan, 2002).

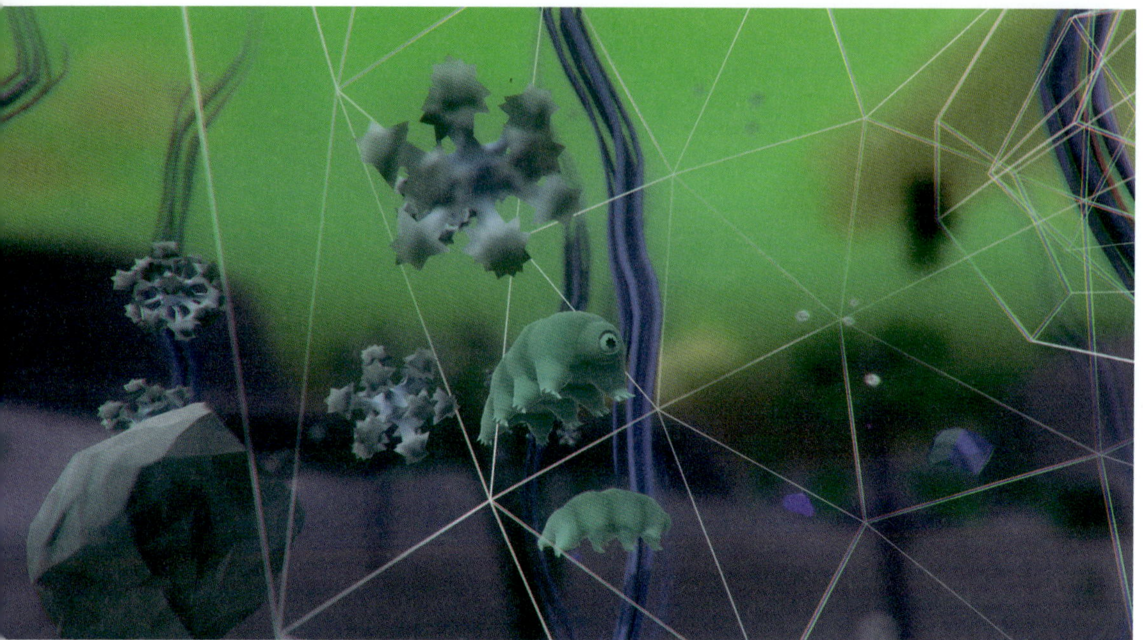

Figure 1: OReilly, David: *Everything* (2017), screenshot. Here the player's avatar is depicted as a tardigrade. https://www.everything-game.com/presskit/ (accessed on July 27, 2018).

He then adds a further attempt at a definition ex negativo:

> It is true that game art often defines itself against commercial games. Its ambivalent nature lies in the fact that it both celebrates and condemns its source material.[7]

According to Bittanti,[8] then, artists can help themselves to the whole field of fine art and all its wealth of resources in producing game art. Bittanti's game art is independent of genre, materials, media, and technology. The only restriction in terms of content involves the observation that such works of art are often directed *against*, or are critical of, commercial games and the computer game industry.[9]
A further attempt to define game art was made by Corrado Morgana,[10] who opens the genre up even further to include (analogue) *games* as such:

> Game art does exactly what it says on the tin: it is art that uses, abuses and misuses the material and language of games, whether real world, electronic/digital or both. The imagery, the aesthetics, the systems, the software and the engines of games can be appropriated or the language of games approximated for creative commentary.[11]

Such a broad conceptualization of the area of inquiry and the generalization it entails lead to significant methodological problems. Game art thus becomes a heterogeneous field of artifacts of wide-ranging artistic strategies and techniques, means, media, and materials. The field can be divided into three groups: to the first group belong adaptations and appropriations of the audiovisual surface of games that implement a "computer-game aesthetic" (which is not further defined) in painting, graphic design, sculpture, photography, film, video, performance, et cetera. What we have here is a *reception* of computer game images and their use in other media and genres of fine art. Computer games as *sujet*.

7 Matteo Bittanti, "Game Art – (This is not) A Manifesto, (this is) A Disclaimer," in *Gamescenes. Art in the Age of Videogames*, edited by M. Bittanti and D. Quaranta (Milan, 2006), p. 9.
8 Ibid., pp. 7–15.
9 Ibid., p. 11.
10 Corrado Morgana, "Introduction," in *Artists Re:Thinking Games*, edited by Ruth Catlow, Marc Garrett, and Corrado Morgana (Liverpool, 2010), pp. 7–14.
11 Ibid., p. 12.

The second group consists of forms of expression that originate directly in the field of computer games without being computer games themselves, like machinima[12] or demos,[13] for example. In the case of machinima, the computer game becomes more of a *tool* for the production of an artifact.

The third group includes all modifications (or mods) and independent productions of computer games (sometimes called art games) explicitly under the sign of art. When it comes to modifications of already existing games, one could speak of "art with computer games." In this case the computer game itself constitutes the artistic genre. The strategy of modification was the "first attempt to approach the phenomenon of the computer game within its own medium."[14] OReilly's *Everything* is an artistic computer game produced from scratch and thus falls into the category of production. To be sure, a substantial scholarly work could be written just on the artistic production of computer games—art games—which have become increasingly prevalent in recent years. It could be theorized that in the field of artistic computer game production, in contrast to modification, a second generation is developing that works less (with a partially aggressive impetus) *against* the medium of the computer game and instead adopts a more conciliatory attitude towards the specific features of the genre, exploiting them much more intensively as means of artistic expression instead of slaving away at them. Art games cultivate less incoherencies, dysfunctionalities, and counter-strategies than artistic game modifications from the nineteen-nineties and around the year 2000. Examples of outstanding protagonists in the field of art games include the artist couple Tale of Tales (Auriea Harvey, * 1971; Michaël Samyn, * 1968), Jason Rohrer (* 1977) and Bill Viola (* 1951), whose project *The Night Journey*[15] takes up the genre of the computer game. Begun in 1998, the first concrete concepts came about in 2005.[16] Most recently in this category, David OReilly earned acclaim and delivered new impulses with his games *Mountain*[17] (2014) and *Everything* (2017). As a pinnacle *Everything* was awarded the Golden Nica at Ars Electronica. From autumn 2018, a new version of the game will be shown in a 540-degree full dome as part of the *New Infinity* program of the Berliner Festspiele and depart from there on a world tour through various international planetaria, partly based on the initiative of the author.

Video Games as a new Material in the Art World

After these more programmatic and basic remarks I would like to outline the video game's entry into the realms of the art world in a cursory historical summary. *Otocky* from 1987 is one of the first video games designed by a media artist, namely Toshio Iwai. The Japanese video game for the rather obscure platform Famicom Disk System called *Otocky* is clearly situated in the context of the entertainment industry and outside the art world. It is still a great example for pushing boundaries and blurring lines considering the connection between video games and art. The game is a side-scrolling shooter and contains generative music, meaning the soundtrack is being generated by playing the game in the first place. The music and sound effects are dependent on the player's actions and the way she is interacting with the rule set of the game and the algorithms of the computer program. In this regard *Otocky* very clearly is a predecessor of and source of inspiration for the famous musical shooter

---

12 Machinima are animated films created in real time by computer game technology. Friedrich Kirschner defines the technique as "shooting film … in a realtime … 3d virtual environment." He adds: "Cameras record the action going on. … [T]he time needed for the computer to transform the abstract data into a 3-dimensional visible representation is so little that you do not notice it. The whole calculation takes less than 1/10th of a second. Thus the term 'realtime'. … [T]he actors aren't human, but virtual Avatars or Objects, controlled by user input or scripting and act in a virtual world that is simulated using a computer game." Cf. Friedrich Kirschner's personal website at: https://www.zeitbrand.de/machiniBlog/WhatIsMachinima.html (accessed July 26, 2018). Machinima can be played either in real time within a game environment or as videos. They thus result in audiovisual, linear, non-interactive artifacts that follow the logic of films or music videos with a linear, usually narrative structure. Machinima originated in computer games and are thus rooted in their technology and aesthetics. If a machinima is played live in real time for an audience, it approaches the vicinity of the performing arts—theater, puppetry. Cf. Henry Lowood and Michael Nitsche, eds., *The Machinima Reader* (Cambridge, Mass. et al., 2011).

13 Demos look and often sound like music videos, despite being something different. They are computer programmes which, when run, appear as audiovisual, non-interactive, linear artefacts, that are are computed in real time. Demos are executable files. Cf. on the so-called Demoszene, Daniel Botz, *Kunst, Code und Maschine: die Ästhetik der Computer-Demoszene* (Bielefeld, 2011).

14 Gerrit Gohlke, "Genre i. Gr. Computerspielkunst als Gegenentwurf zu einer technikentfremdeten Kunst," in *Games: Computerspiele von KünstlerInnen*, edited by Tilman Baumgärtel (Frankfurt am Main, 2003), pp. 21 and 23.

15 *The Night Journey*. Directed by Bill Viola, 2007–2018.

16 Cf. Tracy Fullerton, "Reflections on The Night Journey: an Experimental Video Game," in *The Ludic Society. Kritische Berichte 2/2009*, edited by Ulrike Gehring and Stephan Schwingeler (Marburg, 2009) pp. 72–83.

17 *Mountain*. Directed by David OReilly. Published by Double Fine Productions. 2014.

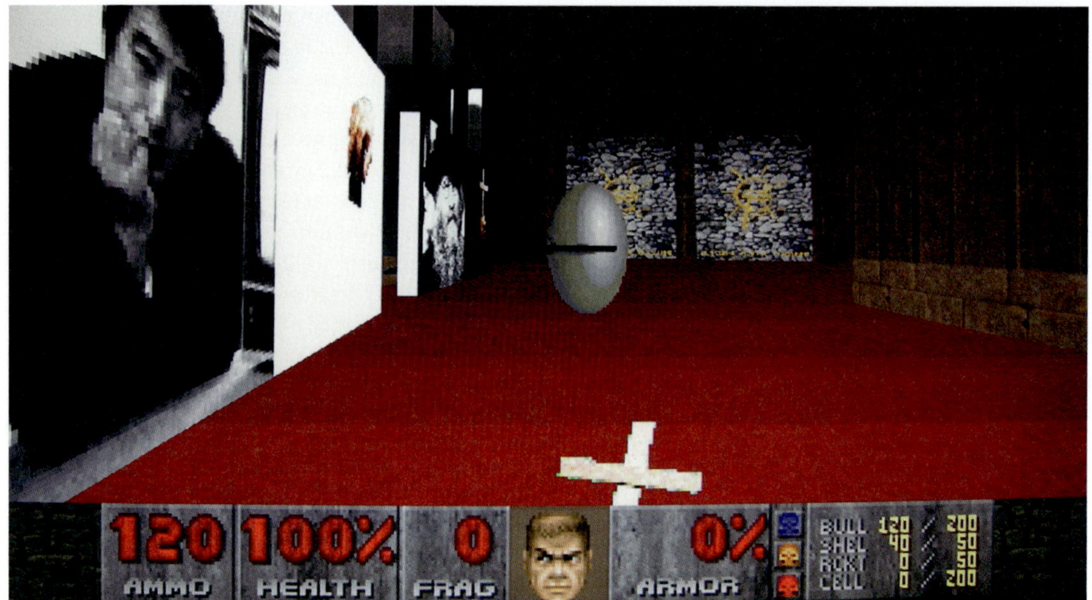

Figure 3: Kipcak, Orhan and Urban, Reinhard: *Arsdoom* (1995), Screenshot. Nam June Paik's portrait is visible in the foregreound. The player is equipped with the weapon associated with Joseph Beuys in the game: his shooting cross. https://www.gamescenes.org/2009/11/interview-orphan-kipcak-arsdoom-ars-doom-ii-1995.html (accessed on July 27, 2018).

REZ[18] (2001) by Tetsuya Mizuguchi. The topic of generative music and sound is the main theme in Toshio Iwai's body of work. He varied the theme in almost all of his pieces. Iwai did variations on the theme in his large scale interactive installations that anticipate his endeavor in the context of commercial video game design. *Piano – As Image Media* (1995) for example is targeted on synaesthesial effects, mainly the interplay of visual and auditive sensations. These proven concepts from the realm of media art are included in commercial yet experimental video games by Toshio Iwai, for example *SimTunes* from 1996 and *Elektroplankton* from 2005. Iwai's oeuvre emphasizes that interactive media art and video games are extremely closely related but are happening in different contexts: the art world and the entertainment industry. A further example for a video game in art history is the artistic video game modification *Arsdoom*.[19] 1995 the Austrian architect Orhan Kipcak was commissioned by Peter Weibel, the artistic director of Ars Electronica at the time, to produce an interactive piece for the festival. The result was *Arsdoom*, a video game mod based on *Doom II* and its id Tech 1 engine that he designed with his colleague Reinhard "Reini" Urban.[20] [21]

Arsdoom is a digitally constructed model of the Brucknerhaus in Linz, the venue where Ars Electronica took place back in 1995. The replica was constructed with the help of the original blue prints of the Brucknerhaus. Players navigate the spatial structures of the game. There they encounter giant heads coming closer to the players. These monsters are the portraits of artists who were part of Ars Electronica. Peter Weibel can be seen and shot in the game, too.[22] The weapons in this first-person shooter refer to artists from recent art

---

18 *REZ*. Directed by Jun Kobayashi. Developed by United Game Artists. 2001.

19 Orhan Kipcak, "ARSDOOM – art adventure," in *Mythos Information: Welcome to the Wired World*, edited by Karl Gerbel, Peter Weibel and Ars Electronica, exh. cat. Brucknerhaus Linz (Vienna and New York, 1995), p. 263.

20 Ibid., pp. 262–264.

21 Orhan Kipcak remarks: "All the modules were then assembled technically by Reini Urban. Reini also programmed a little extension that bypassed the limitations of the Doom Level Editor: the original editor could only design squared rooms. But we needed a room with pointed angles in order to reproduce the complex geometry of the physical design of the Ars Electronica center, the Brucknerhaus." Jansson, Mathias: Interview: Orhan Kipcak (*ArsDoom, ArsDoom II*) (1995–2005), in: www.gamescenes.org, 2009, https://www.gamescenes.org/2009/11/interview-orphan-kipcak-arsdoom-arsdoom-ii-1995.html (accessed on January 6, 2011).

22 The following artists participated: "Seichi Furuya, Peter Kogler, Heimo Zobernig, Peter Weibel, Jörg Schlick, Stephen Pusey, Michael Smith, Sabine Bitter, Stefan Nessmann, Ecke Bonk, Manfred Wolff-Plottegg, Curd Duca, Orhan Kipcak + Special Guests. Ein Raum wird von Studenten der Meisterklasse Visuelle Medien gestaltet: Norbert Pfaffenbichler, Wolfgang Hilbert, Andrea Mayr, Katharina Copony, Rich.Art" Cf. Orhan Kipcak, "ARSDOOM – art adventure," in Mythos Information: Welcome to the Wired World , edited by Karl Gerbel, Peter

history. For example players can shoot with Nam June Paik's remote control or Joseph Beuys's cross, or they use Arnulf Rainer's thumb. The game is about entering and penetrating the structures of Ars Electronica as an institution of art standing for the art world's system. Players become iconoclasts and destroy artworks and artists alike in the iconography of a first-person shooter. Kipcak commented on the aggressive impetus of the piece: "I chose those artists because they were well known and their art had a brutal aspect to it. This is important for a first-person-shooter: with Arnulf Rainer you paint over artworks, with Nitsch you soak them in blood, with Baselitz you turn them upside-down."[23]

The game is an "inside joke, a tongue-in-cheek take on the art world."[24] The theme of entering and penetrating a system is multilayered in the piece: first of all the players invade the space of Ars Electonica. Secondly *Arsdoom*'s creators, Kipcak and Urban entered the very structures of the software *Doom II* in order to appropriate and alter them and thirdly: with *Arsdoom* a new material entered the system of art, namely the video game as a new artistic hybrid material.

There are two main reasons why video games managed to enter the art world around 1995. The first reason is rather obvious: in 1995 there were artists who knew video games from their childhood since the beginning of the video game industry was in 1972. This is the first generation of artists with explicit video game literacy.[25] They discovered the potentials of video games against the background of emerging media art and net art scenes and begin to reflect their characteristics. The second reason is that in the nineteen-nineties users gained access to the material of video games. Before 1995 tinkering with video games as computer programs required a large amount of specialized know-how and skill. In the nineteen-nineties the video game company id Software opened its software products for everybody to use freely. It published the source code of *Doom* in 1997. Before that users discovered that 1992 shooter *Wolfenstein 3D* was easily modifiable using simple tricks and primitive hacking routines. Thus modding as a cultural practice emerged out of the early gaming communities on the Internet leading to the fact that artists began using this new techniques, too. Thus modification of found games historically developed as a first approach for artists to gain access to the new material of the videogame.

Since the beginning of the nineteen-seventies the video game has been a product in the context of a commercialized and professionalized industry. In the course of its professionalization, access to the products' code was denied; the video game as a product was closed by the industry and literally put into cases, cabinets, consoles, cartridges, and boxes. The concept of proprietary software was developed. Blocking access means that the first historical approach to use video games as an artistic material lies in their almost parasitical appropriation—hence breaking open these boxes and gaining access again. In an interview Orhan Kipcak, the creator of *Arsdoom*, commented on these circumstances. He emphasizes the thesis that artists began using video games in the moment that they gained access to their code.

Kipcak remarks: "And then id Software opened up the *Doom* engine, allowing everybody to tinker with the level editor. It was such a powerful tool! It was an epiphany. … Last but not least: I chose a video game for technical and practical reasons. The *Doom* engine was an open-source solution, easy to handle and very popular at the time. It made our life so much easier!"[26] Kipcak answers the following question with only one word "Why did you choose *Doom* for your art project?": "Availability."[27] Media scholar Claus Pias[28] summarises these processes:

Die einst oppositionellen Computerspiele wurden also in den 1970ern selbst zu einer Institution, gegen die KünstlerInnen erst seit den späten 90er Jahren wiederum Verfahren der Appropriation und Umwidmung einzusetzen beginnen.[29]

Weibel and Ars Electronica, exh. cat. Brucknerhaus Linz (Vienna and New York, 1995), p. 264.

23 Mathias Jansson, Interview: Orhan Kipcak (*ArsDoom, ArsDoom II*) (1995–2005), in: www.gamescenes.org, 2009, https://www.games-cenes.org/2009/11/interview-orphan-kipcak-arsdoom-arsdoom-ii-1995.html (accessed on January 21, 2011).

24 Ibid.

25 Mark Tribe et al., eds., *New Media Art* (Cologne et al., 2006), p. 10.

26 Mathias Jansson, Interview: Orhan Kipcak (*Arsdoom, Arsdoom II*) (1995–2005). Gamescenes.org URL: https://www.gamescenes.org/2009/11/interview-orphan-kipcak-arsdoom-arsdoom-ii-1995.html (accessed on April 12, 2012).

27 Ibid.

28 Claus Pias, "Appropriation Art & Games: Spiele der Verschwendung und der Langeweile," in Games: *Computerspiele von KünstlerInnen*, edited by Tilman Baumgärtel, exh. cat., Hartware Medienkunstverein, Phoenix Halle Dortmund (Frankfurt am Main, 2003), pp. 26–32.

29 Ibid., pp. 26–32.

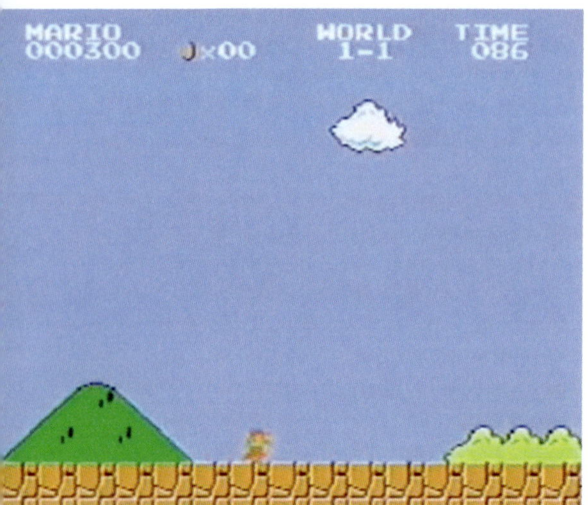

Figure 4: *mario battle no.1* (Myfanwy Ashmore, 2000), screenshot of the Vimeo video, https://vimeo.com/18502121 accessed on 05.05.2012 (accessed on January 05, 2012).

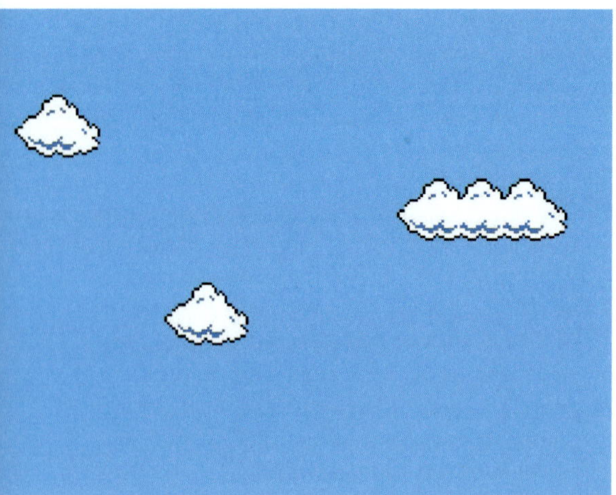

Figure 5: *Super Mario Clouds* (Cory Arcangel, 2002/2009), screenshot from a ROM-file.

[“The formerly opposititional videogames became an institution themselves in the nineteen-seventies. Only in the late nineties did artists begin applying methods of appropriation and reallocation against it.” Translated from the German by the author.]

Today—as OReilly's *Everything* shows as an example—we can as well identify the artistic practice of video game production on larger scale than in the nineteen-nineties and around 2000, implying that artists not only gained access to modifying found media as in the early days but also gained access to specific skills that are crucial for producing a video game. This development can be put in context of new possibilities of education (computer science, informatics, coding, and the emerging discipline of game design) and a general opening and accessibility of know-how and high capacity tools (hard- and software) leading to various emerging independent game scenes.

Artistic Strategies

While video games established themselves as an artistic material in the context of the art world, artists developed different artistic strategies dealing with the new material. In the following passage various artistic strategies are laid out and described:

A first strategy could be termed “re-decoration of the source material.” This strategy describes the modding of existent video games and their audio-visual interfaces, as is the case in the total conversion *Arsdoom* (1995), which was the first video game modification in the context of the art world.

Reduction and abstraction of the source material functions as a second strategy. Artists cultivate voids and imperfections as, for example, in Myfanwy Ashmore's *mario battle no.1*[30] (2000). In Ashmore's modification, all obstacles and opponents are deleted from *Super Mario Bros.*[31] (1985). In Cory Arcangel's *Super Mario Clouds*[32] (2002), what remains of the original game are the clouds passing by the viewer from right to left in front of the pale-blue background. The strategy of abstraction, on the one hand, aims at highlighting the games' interfaces and thus on a staging of the audio-visual, as in the *Quake III Arena*[33] (1999) mod *QQQ*[34] (2002) by British artist Tom Betts, which is consciously

---

30 *mario battle no.1.* Developed by Myfanwy Ashmore. 2000.
31 *Super Mario Bros.* Directed by Shigeru Miyamoto. Published by Nintendo. 1985.
32 *Super Mario Clouds.* Developed by Cory Arcangel. 2002.
33 *Quake III Arena.* Published by id Software. 1999.
34 *QQQ.* Developed by Tom Betts. 2002.

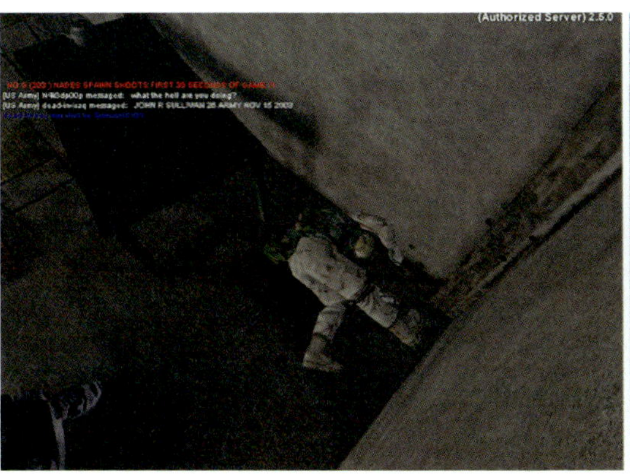
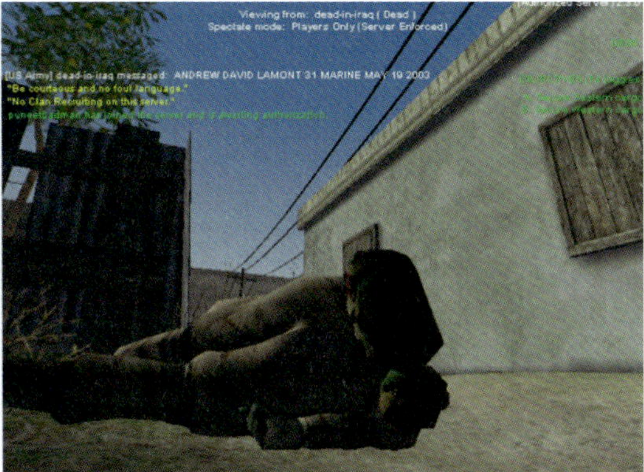

Figure 6: Screenshots from Jeoseph DeLappe's perfromance *dead-in-iraq* (2006–2009), https://www.delappe.net/project/dead-in-iraq/ (accessed on July 27, 2018).

saturated with graphics glitches. On the other hand, it aims at (and partly complements) the process of image and sound development and highlights the representation of the code and the computing process, as in Margarete Jahrmann and Max Moswitzer's *nybble-engine-toolZ*[35] (2002), an installation which "converts information (text, images, sound) on the hard disk into three-dimensional abstract movies and projects these onto a 180 degrees circular screen."[36]

Modifications of the rules of the game and game-discordant actions in the source material itself form a third strategy. For example, in *Velvet-Strike*[37] (Brody Condon, Anne-Marie Schleiner, and Joan Leandre, 2001), pacifist images are attached to the walls of *Counter-Strike*[38] (2000) maps, while in Joseph DeLappe's online gaming performance *dead-in-iraq*[39] (2006), the artist staged an online protest against the war in Iraq during a session of *America's Army*[40] (2002) by posting the names of soldiers killed in action in the Iraq War via the game's chat function.

The combination of these strategies may produce paradoxical artifacts: unplayable games. JODI's *Wolfenstein 3D*[41] mod *SOD*[42], the map *Arena* from the series

Untitled Game, and the game *Glitchhiker*[43] (2011) provide examples of this most extreme form of obstinacy. Unlike the other two examples, *Glitchhiker* is not a modification but an original game. As such, it is not based upon a commercial game and has appropriated it; instead, *Glitchhiker* is an independent computer game production that was developed during a game jam within a couple of days.All of these artistic strategies disrupt the operating principles of their source materials. These strategies aim at raising awareness of the video game's technical limits through formal-aesthetic experiments, the construction of dysfunctionalities, incoherence, and the limitation of interactivity.

Art-Historical Traditions of Interference and Disruption

Historically video game art appropriates its source material. To this end, artists working with video games employ modification practices such as parasitic repurposing and appropriation to highlight video games' specific media-immanent characteristics and structures.[44] Thus, errors and glitches are programmed into video games' codes, disrupting them and limiting

---

35 *nybble-engine-toolZ*. Developed by Margarete Jahrmann and Max Moswitzer. 2002.

36 "Nybble-Engine-Toolz," V2_, Lab for the Unstable Media, https://v2.nl/archive/works/nybble-engine-toolz/ (accessed on July 18, 2017).

37 *Velvet-Strike*. Developed by Brody Condon, Anne-Marie Schleiner, and Joan Leandre. 2001.

38 *Counter-Strike*. Published by Valve. 2002.

39 *dead-in-iraq*. Developed by Joseph DeLappe. 2006.

40 *America's Army*. Published by United States Army, Ubisoft. 2002.

41 *Wolfenstein 3D*. Developed by id Software. 1992.

42 *SOD*. Developed by Jodi. 1999.

43 *Glitchhiker*. Created by ceMelusine, Lucas J. W. Johnson, Andrew Grant Wilson, Claris Cyarron. 2011. https://glitchhikers.com/ (accessed on January 28, 2019).

44 Cf. Anne-Marie Schleiner, "Parasitic Interventions: Game Patches and Hacker Art," Opensorcery.net: Annie-Marie Schleiner (accessed July 18, 2012), https://opensorcery.net/patchnew.html; Claus Pias, "Appropriation Art & Games: Spiele der Verschwendung und der Langeweile," in *Games: Computerspiele von KünstlerInnen*, edited by Tilman Baumgärtel (Frankfurt am Main: Revolver, 2003), pp. 26–32; Axel Stockburger, "From Appropriation to Approximation," in *Videogames and Art*, edited by Andy Clarke and Grethe Mitchell (Bristol, 2007), pp. 25–38.

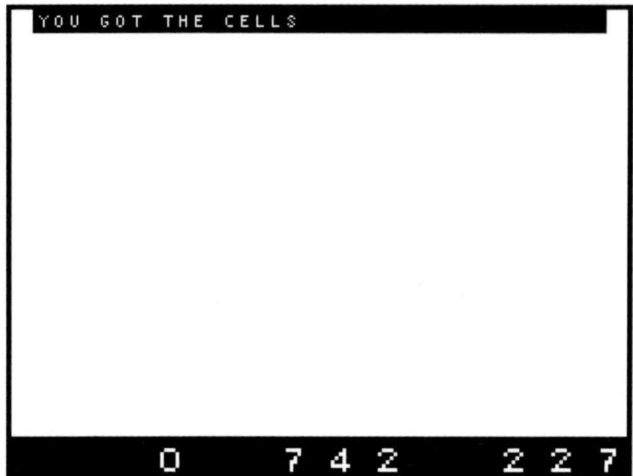

Figure 7: Negation of the image: *Arena* from the series *Unitled Game* (JODI, Joan Heemskerk und Dirk Paesmans, 1998–2001). The artists modified the game *QUAKE* in an iconoclastic manner resulting in a stripped, "opaque" game without any representation at all. The HUD and audio are still intact. Players can still navigate *QUAKE*'s game world but do not see anything. https://www.untitled-game.org/ug2.html (accessed on July 27, 2018).

their interactivity to the point of unplayability. In this way, artists act as spoilsports, as video games simply stop being games. Artists alienate players and viewers from the expected gaming situation and thus relocate video games into artistic contexts through the practice of *détournement*, the "overturning of the established order" accomplished through the "unforeseen activity within the institution, utilizing its tools and imagery."[45] This practice of appropriation is also key to hacker culture and ethics. After all, an essential element of hacking is making things work differently from the way they were meant to. Indeed, as Corrado Morgana explains:

> *Détournement* is … central to hacker culture; taking "stuff" and making that "stuff" do things it wasn't meant to do. By modding, hacking, exploiting and other strategies of intervention, artists, game designers and players have responded to preset game limits and other practical and creative boundaries. They have responded by producing artifacts and activity that re-appropriate

dominant culture, where normative tropes and memes are subverted and détourned to produce a counter to expected "normal.[46]

As a result, the testing, expansion, and crossing of boundaries as well as the breaking of rules ensures a particular hack value. Appropriation opens up links to other artistic traditions. The Situationist movement embraced an aggressive-destructive impetus which drove them to intervene with the structures of (mass) media and apparatuses. This is, for example, evident in Wolf Vostell's variations of *dé-coll/ages* of TV sets and Nam June Paik's TV modifications from the nineteen-sixties.

The modification of games (i.e., their rules, aims, et cetera.) up to unplayability has a distinct tradition in art history. Indeed, games and the playful became important ideas in the twentieth century, as surrealists, Dadaists, and Fluxus artists dealt with games and used them as material. Variations of the chess game illustrate this utilization of games as artistic resource. Man Ray and Marcel Duchamp, for example, produced

---

45 Corrado Morgana, "Introduction," in *Artists Re:Thinking Games*, edited by Ruth Catlow et al., (Liverpool, 2010), p. 9. For a discussion of détournement in connection to computer game art, see Anne-Marie Schleiner, "Dissolving the Magic Circle of Play: Lessons from Situationist Gaming," in *From Diversion to Subversion: Games, Play, and Twentieth-Century Art*, edited by David J. Getsy (Pennsylvania, 2011), pp. 149–58.

46 Corrado Morgana, "Introduction," in *Artists Re:Thinking Games*, edited by Ruth Catlow et al. (Liverpool, 2010), p. 10; Roberto Simanowski (2008) sees a similar connection between *détournement* and hacker culture: "The transformation of a commercial product of digital media into a critical-reflexive artwork is a popular form of *détournement* in the context of hacktivism ('hacking' and 'activism') and artivism ('art' and 'activism') inside and outside digital media" p. 87.

and interpreted chessboards and pieces.[47] Representatives of the Fluxus movement such as Takako Saito and Yoko Ono followed in their footsteps. Saito has produced modified chess sets since the nineteen-sixties, including chess sets that are played with spices or vials. On the other hand, Yoko Ono's all-white chess sets lead the game and its objective ad absurdum, while simultaneously acting as anti-war metaphor and political statement. Like *Velvet-Strike*, this modification accentuates metaphors of war and combat which are deeply entrenched in many analog and digital games. Video game art often employs a rhetoric of negation: as soon as the video game does not perform as expected anymore, its operating principles are acknowledged *ex negativo*. As ideas such as Bertold Brecht's "alienation effect" suggest, interferences render the immanent characteristics of a medium explicit. Artists thus develop alternative models to commercial video games and break their rules. In this way, their artworks reflect not only on the design of computer games as defined by what Gerrit Gohlke has called a "performance-oriented, hyperreal culture," [translated from the German: *hyperrealistische Leistungskultur*] but also on the general relation between man and machine in the circuit of cybernetics and in the magic circle of play.[48]

Countergaming

Media theorist Alexander R. Galloway calls the described tendencies to rebel against established forms of gaming countergaming.[49] Galloway borrows this term from film theory and the concept of *Nouvelle Vague's Countercinema*. The characteristics of countergaming aesthetics are the following:

1. *Transparency versus foregrounding*. (Removing the apparatus from the image versus pure interplay of graphics apparatus or code displayed without representational imagery.)
2. *Gameplay versus aestheticism*. (Narrative gameplay based on a coherent rule set versus modernist formal experiments.)
3. *Representational modeling versus visual artifacts*. (Mimetic modeling of objects versus glitches and other unexpected products of the graphics engine.)
4. *Natural physics versus invented physics*. (Newtonian

laws of motion, ray tracing, collisions, etc., versus incoherent physical laws and relationships.)
5. *Interactivity versus noncorrespondence*. (Instant, predictable linkage between controller input and gameplay versus barriers between controller input and gameplay.)
6. *Gamic action versus radical action*. (Conventional gamic poetics versus alternative modes of gameplay.)[50]

In many early artistic video game modifications we see pure interplay of graphics without any representational imagery. This is how the apparatus and ultimately the code become visible.

Secondly narrative gameplay based on a coherent rule set is radically neglected. Further by neglecting the dogma of photographic hyperrealism and the illusionary and immersive aspects of playing a video game is broken. The graphical glitch can become the image's only content thus resulting in concrete video games.

Often the programmed physics are neglected as well. Newtonian laws become absurd.

These modifications generate absurd outcomes: input does not generate the expected output. Control gets debarred and undermined.

This results in a new kind of gameplay. The game is not played in the intended way. It is playing with a generative, algorithmic engine that randomly produces abstract (or more precise: concrete) imagery.

Countergaming is centred around breaking the established and accepted forms of coherence, illusion, interactivity, and immersion and focusing on the material itself and its concretion. It is about revealing the media-immanent characteristics of video games—it is about showing the constructedness of virtual environments. In the sense of Bertold Brecht users should reflect about the fact that they are playing a video game—being immersed in a cybernetic circle. Here: it is all about breaking the rules.

When Galloway identified these characteristics more than ten years ago in 2006, he pointed out that the last point—radical action—in the sense of a true gaming avant-garde has not there arrived yet. He criticized that most of artistic video game pieces focused on destruction of gameplay and the audiovisual surface rather than embracing the very potentials of the medium

---

47 Cf. Francis M. Naumann et al., *Marcel Duchamp: The Art of Chess* (New York, 2009).

48 Gerrit Gohlke, "Genre i. Gr. Computerspielkunst als Gegenentwurf zu einer technikentfremdeten Kunst," in *Games: Computerspiele von KünstlerInnen*, edited by Tilman Baumgärtel (Frankfurt am Main, 2003), p. 19.

49 Cf. Alexander R. Galloway, *Essays on Algorithmic Culture* (Minneapolis, 2006), pp. 107–127.

50 Ibid., pp.124–125.

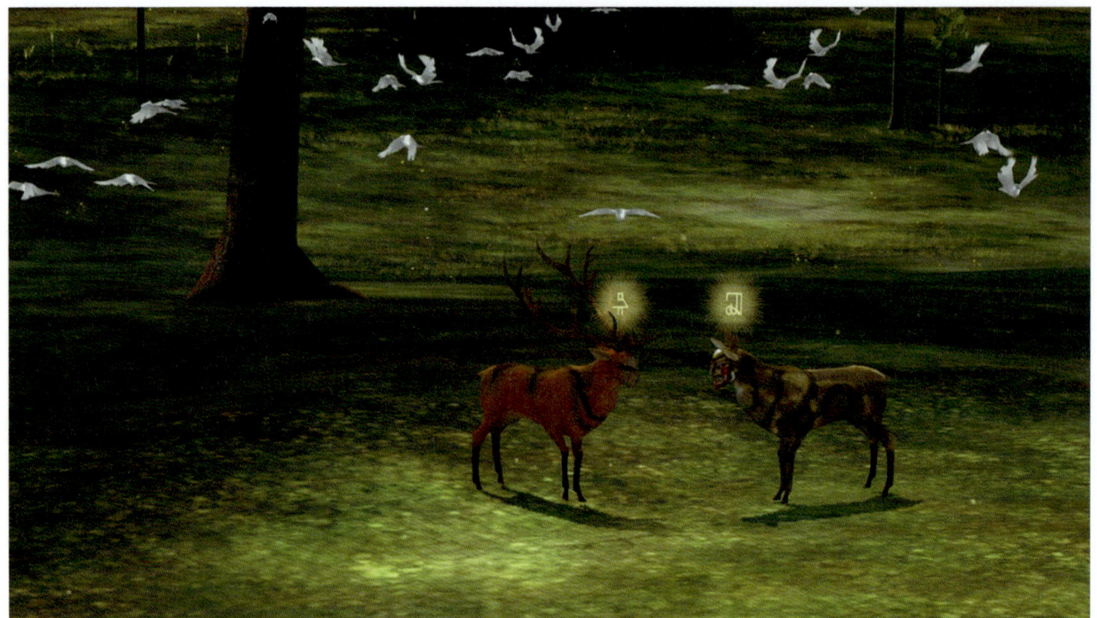

Figure 8: Tale of Tales, Auriea Harvey and Michaël Samyn: *The Endless Forest* (2005), screenshot, https://tale-of-tales.com/TheEndlessForest/ (accessed on July 27, 2018).

by the means of radical action in a positive, constructive way: in other words, countergaming is essentially progressive in visual form but reactionary in actional form. It serves to hinder gameplay not advance it. It eclipses the game as a game and rewrites it as a sort of primitive animation lacking any of the virtues of game design.

> … We need an avant-garde of video gaming not just in visual form but also in actional form. We need radical gameplay, not just radical graphics. … By radical action, I mean a critique of gameplay itself. … Artists should create new grammars of action, not simply new grammars of visuality. … So countergaming is an unrealized project. An independent gaming movement has yet to flourish … This will be a realization of countergaming as gaming …. The countergaming movement should aspire to a similar goal [as countercinema], redefining play itself and thereby realizing ist true potential as a political and cultural avant-garde.[51]

At the moment we are witnessing a shift. The first approach of using video games as an hybrid, artistic material was to appropriate, remix, reprogram, and even destroy found commercialy available mainstream video games with a rather destructive attitude. This is most clearly visible in the strategies of JODI and Cory Arcangel, for example. In the last few years there has been another develpment in another context, or other gaming scenes.

Standing outside the context of media art, we have witnessed an emerging independent video game scene in the last fifteen years. Parts of the emerging independent video game scene have experimented a lot with exactly the concept of radical action in mind. While the first generation of artists working with video games tended to break found games, the second generation tends to build meaningful games of their own. *Everything* is a fine example for these tendencies and developments.

Radical Action: Pure Joy

As a path to true radical action of a gamic avant-garde Galloway programmatically identifies the creation of pure joy during gameplay. By focussing on joy rather than destruction of found structures new forms of gameplay can be established that fall into Galloway's category of radical action. As an example he uses Tale of Tales' (Auriea Harvey, * 1971; Michaël Samyn, * 1968) game *The Endless Forest*[52] (2005):

---

51 Ibid., pp.125–126.
52 *The Endless Forest*. Designed and directed by Auriea Harvey and Michaël Samyn. 2005. https://tale-of-tales.com/TheEndlessForest/

It is pure joy: *The Endless Forest.* ... It is a dream of the Garden of Eden before the fall, a vision of art as communion. The game is life and beauty, a fantasy exchange in a forest beyond, connected in a living environment of many souls distributed across as many worlds.[53]

Related to this manifestation of radical action in *The Endless Forest* David OReilly creates his game world. He does not turn against the medium of the video game in an aggressive manner but rather embraces the possibilities of the material. Rather than deconstructing a found game's audiovisual surface and destroying its interactive structure OReilly builds something up. Rather than aggressively deconstructing the apparatus- and code-based nature of mainstream video games, OReilly is actively building his own alternative setup. Rather than destroying the graphics and simulated physics of a found videogame and scratching the surface he is building a simulation—a world—of its own. A side note: for the new 540-degree installation version of *Everything* that was commissioned by Berliner Festspiele's *New Infinity* program[54] OReilly focussed on the game mechanics and dynamics of dancing, a joyful, playful, free act that undermines video game conventions such as violent behavior, competion, and challenge. OReilly is part of a second generation of artists using and misusing the material of the video game. While the first generation had a destructive approach OReilly understands video games as a medium with its own potentialities embracing their qualities in a positive manner. Therefore it might be one of the first games truly embracing Galloway's concept of radical action in countergaming. Interestingly *Everything* is a game that does not need a player to funtion properly.

The game has a mode in which it begins to play itself after no player input is detected after a while. *Everything* develops almost a life of its own as an algorithmic, simulated ecosystem. Here the player becomes a spectator comparable to the reception of living pieces of art by Pierre Huyghe.

In media theory the process occurring in this case can be specified as a so-called ambience act. This term describes the diegetic existence of a game world without interaction and influce by the player. In many games the change of the time of day, change of weather, and behavior of NPCs is programmed and determined in the game's structure.[55] Ambience acts keep the diegesis alive, they sustain the fictional universe and thus the diegetic machine acts without an active, acting player/operator. Metaphorically speaking the player is in pause mode while the video game's apparatus keeps on acting in a computing state of limbo.[56]

Surely there is a difference between games and play that needs to be addressed here. Games follow certain rules while *play* can be described as a free activity.[57] This ludic range can be described as *ludus* and *paidia*, following Roger Caillois.[58] While a game forms the structure for play, "play is free movement within a more rigid structure."[59]

Within the boundaries of *Everything*'s game rules the players navigate freely, respectively the game flows freely without player input. In the center of *Everything*'s structure stands the free change of scale and perspective between the representation of objects, meandering between micro- and macrocosmos, strolling from avatar to avatar. In the 540-degree version the main game mechanic is dancing: dancing is *paidia* par excellence.

Games are rule-based systems. Regarding video games these systems are coded as software. *Everything* is not only a rule-based system on a ludic and

---

(accessed on January 28, 2019).

53 Alexander R. Galloway, "Unfun," in *Homo ludens ludens: Third Part of the Gaming Trilogy*, edited by Erich Berger, and Industrial, LABoral Centro de Arte y Creación, exh. cat. (Gijón, 2008), p. 495.

54 Cf. https://www.berlinerfestspiele.de/en/aktuell/festivals/immersion/programm_immersion/immersion18_the_new_infinity/immersion18_the_new_infinity_detail.php (accessed on July 27, 2018).

55 Alexander Galloway describes the Ambience Act referencing the game *Shenmue* (Sega, 1999): "One plays *Shenmue* by participating in its process. Remove everything and there is still action, a gently stirring rhythm of life. ... When games like *Shenmue* are left alone, they often settle into a moment of equilibrium. Not a tape loop, or a skipped groove, but a state of rest. The game is slowly walking in place, shifting from side to side and back again to the center. It is running, playing itself, perhaps. The game is in an ambient state, an ambience act." Alexander R. Galloway, *Essays on Algorithmic Culture* (Minneapolis, 2006), p. 8.

56 "The machine is still on in an ambience act, but the operator is away. ... The ambience act is the machine's act. The user is on hold, but the machine keeps on working. ..., it is the operator who is paused in an ambience act, leaving the machine hover in a state of pure process." Alexander R. Galloway, *Essays on Algorithmic Culture* (Minneapolis, 2006), p. 10.

57 Cf. Roger Caillois, *Die Spiele und die Menschen: Maske und Rausch* (Frankfurt am Main et al., 1982), p. 20.

58 Ibid., p. 20.

59 Katie Salen and Eric Zimmerman, *Rules of Play: Game Design Fundamentals* (Cambridge, MA et al., 2004), p. 304.

algorithmic level, but it also depicts a system: it is the representation of a fantastic, fictional eco-system, developing a life of its own, in which in Alan Watts's sense everything is incorporated in everything and everything influences everything. The small scale correspondends with the large scale, whereas the other is not conceivable without the other and cannot exist in the first place. Thus, *Everything* finds its perfect medium in the form of the digital game.[60]

---

60 For an in-depth analysis of practices and strategies in the context of art with videogames and videogames as artistic material cf. Stephan Schwingeler, *Kunstwerk Computerspiel* (Bielefeld 2014), pp. 39–53.

Bibliography

Bittanti, Matteo. *Per una cultura dei videogames. Teorie e prassi del videogiocare.* Milan, 2002.

Bittanti, Matteo. "Game Art – (This is not) A Manifesto, (this is) A Disclaimer." In *Gamescenes. Art in the age of videogames*, edited by Matteo Bittanti and Domenico Quaranta. Milan, 2006, pp. 7–15.

Botz, Daniel. *Kunst, Code und Maschine: die Ästhetik der Computer-Demoszene.* Bielefeld, 2011.

Caillois, Roger. *Die Spiele und die Menschen: Maske und Rausch.* Frankfurt am Main et al., 1982.

Fullerton, Tracy. "Reflections on The Night Journey: an Experimental Video Game." In *The Ludic Society. Kritische Berichte 2/2009*, edited by Ulrike Gehring, and Stephan Schwingeler, Marburg, 2009, pp. 72–83.

Galloway, Alexander R. *Gaming. Essays on Algorithmic Culture.* Minneapolis, 2006.

Galloway, Alexander R. "Unfun." In *Homo ludens ludens: Third Part of the Gaming Trilogy*, edited by Erich Berger and Industrial, LABoral Centro de Arte y Creación, exh. cat. Gijón, 2008, pp. 494–495.

Gohlke, Gerrit. "Genre i. Gr. Computerspielkunst als Gegenentwurf zu einer technikentfremdeten Kunst." In *Games: Computerspiele von KünstlerInnen*, edited by Tilman Baumgärtel, Frankfurt am Main, 2003, pp. 18–26.

Grewenig, Meinrad M. et al. *GameArt*, Exh. Cat. Völklinger Hütte. Ostfildern, 2003.

Kipcak, Orhan. "ARSDOOM – art adventure." In *Mythos Information: Welcome to the Wired World*, edited by Karl Gerbel, Peter Weibel, and Ars Electronica, exh. cat. Brucknerhaus Linz. Vienna, New York, 1995, pp. 262–264,

Lowood, Henry, and Michael Nitsche, eds.*The Machinima Reader*. Cambridge, Mass. et al., 2011.

Morgana, Corrado. "Introduction." In *Artists Re:Thinking Games*, edited by Ruth Catlow et al., Liverpool, 2010, pp. 7–14.

Naumann, Francis M. et al., eds. *Marcel Duchamp: The Art of Chess*, New York, 2009.

Pias, Claus. "Appropriation Art & Games: Spiele der Verschwendung und der Langeweile." In *Games: Computerspiele von KünstlerInnen*, edited by Tilman Baumgärtel, exh. cat., Hartware Medienkunstverein, Phoenix Halle Dortmund, Frankfurt am Main, 2003, pp. 26–32.

Pias, Claus. "Children of the Revolution. Video-Spiel-Computer als Kreuzungen der Informationsgesellschaft." In *Zukünfte des Computers*, edited by Claus Pias, Zürich and Berlin, 2005, pp. 217–241.

Salen, Katie, and Eric Zimmerman. *Rules of play: game design fundamentals.* Cambridge, MA et al., 2004.

Schleiner, Anne-Marie. "Dissolving the Magic Circle of Play: Lessons from Situationist Gaming." In *From Diversion to Subversion: Games, Play, and Twentieth-Century Art*, edited by David J. Getsy, Pennsylvania, 2011, pp. 149–58.

Schwingeler, Stephan. *Kunstwerk Computerspiel – Digitale Spiele als künstlerisches Material: eine bildwissenschaftliche und medientheoretische Analyse.* Bielefeld, 2014.

Simanowski, Roberto. *Digitale Medien in der Erlebnisgesellschaft: Kultur–Kunst–Utopien.* Reinbek bei Hamburg, 2008.

Stockburger, Axel. "From Appropriation to Approximation." In *Videogames and Art*, edited by Andy Clarke and Grethe Mitchell, Bristol, 2007, pp. 25–38.

Tribe, Mark et al., eds. *New media art.* Cologne et al., 2006.

Diana Arellano (DE/ES)

The Other Face of Animation

Animating believable 3D faces that fulfill the expectations of an audience is a hard problem that has taken many researchers an enormous amount of time and effort to solve. Early attempts from companies like the no longer extant *LifeFX* proved that facial animation could be feasible,[1] as was the case with the short film *The Jester*,[2] selected for the SIGGRAPH Electronic Theatre in 1999. This was considered by the graphics community to be a milestone in computer generated humans.[3] More recently the quality of character facial animation has increased to a level that spectators cannot tell the difference between a real actor and a computer generated one. Some examples are the live-action movies *Rogue One*[4] or *Blade Runner 2049*,[5] where iconic actors were brought to life as their younger selves thanks to CG facial replacement. However, it is not only in entertainment where we can find good examples of character facial animation. More scientific fields such as autism research[6] or computational creativity have benefited from the use of real-time facial animation.

In this essay, we will present the work we have made in facial character animation at Animationsinstitut, Filmakademie Baden-Württemberg, in Germany; from the tools developed to animate the faces of virtual characters, to the projects and applications of these animations.

Facial Animation Toolset

We cannot talk about facial animation without explaining the technology behind facial rigging. In its simplest form, 3D rigging is the process of creating a skeleton for a 3D model so it can be moved, or animated. To this end, we developed our own *Facial Animation Toolset*

---

1 Sami Lais, "Is It Real, or Is It LifeFX?" https://www.computerworld.com/article/2590570/app-development/is-it-real--or-is-it-lifefx-.html (accessed February 2019).
2 *The Jester*. Directed by Paul Charette and Mark Sagar, 1999.
3 Mike Seymour, "fxpodcast: Dr. Mark Sagar," https://www.fxguide.com/fxpodcasts/fxpodcast-dr-mark-sagar (accessed July 2018).
4 Jordan Zakarin, "'Rogue One' VFX Head Promises CGI Won't Drive Actors Extinct," https://www.inverse.com/article/26295-rogue-ones-tarkin-vfx-won-t-replace-actors-ilm-promises (accessed July 2018).
5 Richard Clegg, Interview by Vincent Frei, "BLADE RUNNER 2049: Richard Clegg – VFX Supervisor – MPC," https://www.artofvfx.com/, October 20, 2017, https://www.artofvfx.com/blade-runner-2049-richard-clegg-vfx-supervisor-mpc/ (accessed June 15, 2018).
6 Cf. Suzan Anwar and Mariofanna Milanova, "Real time face expression recognition of children with autism," Proceedings Int. Acad. Eng. Med. Res. 1 (1) (2016), pp. 1–7.
Jeff Cockburn et al., "SmileMaze: A Tutoring System in Real-Time Facial Expression Perception and Production in Children with Autism Spectrum Disorder," Proceedings International Conference on Automatic Face and Gesture Recognition, Workshop on Facial and Bodily expressions for Control and Adaptation of Games (2008).
Iris Gordon et al., "Training Facial Expression Production in Children on the Autism Spectrum," Journal of Autism and Developmental Disorders, 44 (2014), pp. 2486-2498.

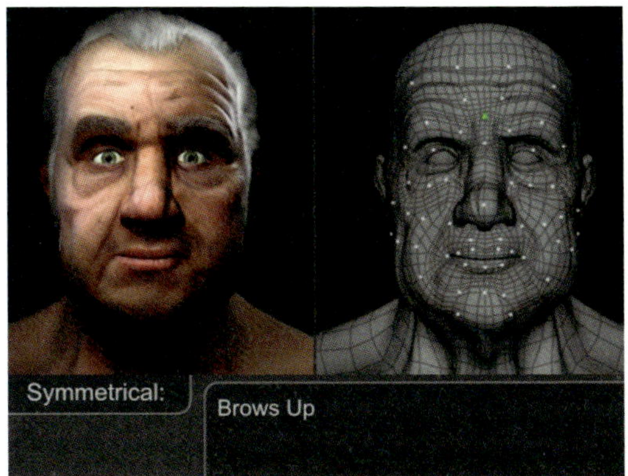

Figure 1: Character performing the *FACS* Action Unit "Brows Up".

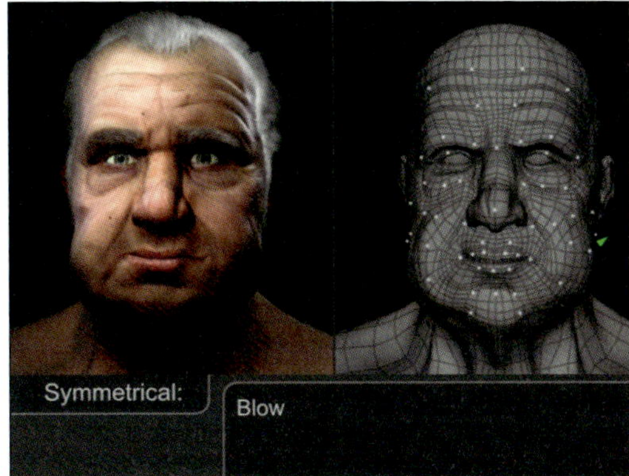

Figure 2: Character performing the *FACS* Action Unit "Blow".

(FAT), a set of plugins for the Digital Content Creation tool *Maya®*, capable of reducing the amount of work associated with the creation of high-quality, ready-to animate facial rigs.[7] This not only provides a comprehensive foundation for the fast and efficient creation of facial animation rigs, but also offers increased performance and stability that demonstrates the rigging and animation capabilities of the tools.

The rigs for our characters' faces were created using the *Facial Action Coding System* (FACS),[8] resulting in a parameterizable rig that was easy to transfer to any other character with a similar FACS-based rig.

The Facial Animation Toolset comprises five modules, each with a unique function:

- *Adaptable Facial Setup* (AFS),[9] which allows the automation of the most time-consuming aspects of the facial setup process, while offering comprehensive control over all facial regions. The foundation of the technique is a complete motion-capture-based library of facial deformations that is able to deform any humanoid geometry.
- *Geometry Matcher* is a Maya plugin that clones weights from the skin of one geometry to another (can be topologically different), avoiding tedious weight modification (*weight painting*).
- *Corrective Blendshape Manager* allows the creation of corrective blendshape targets by interactively moving vertex positions of a rigged, skinned mesh, and having these corrective blendshapes triggered (driven) by a specific joint (driver).
- *Conditional Blend Weighted* allows for more complex blending of animation parameters.
- *Performance Solver* is a plugin that dissolves facial motion-captured data into a structured set of face clusters. The Performance Solver was added to exploit the real-time capabilities of our in-house development framework Frapper (Filmakademie Application Framework).[10]

Figures 1 and 2 show some of the facial deformations achieved in one of our animated characters using FAT.

Animation 2.0

Animation 2.0 is the working title that bring together all those applications that use character animation for purposes other than entertainment, for instance: computational creativity or autism research.

To this end this we used the Agent Framework,[11] a subset of functionalities within Frapper, which allowed real-time interaction with the animated characters. The Agent Framework was designed for the rapid prototyping of agent-centric applications. While it offers the user an intuitive and easy-to-use interface based on nodes, it gives the developers a powerful platform where they can add new functions and integrate new libraries or devices according to the needs

7 Filmakademie Baden-Württemberg, "Facial Animation Toolset," https://animationsinstitut.de/de/forschung-rd/tools/facial-animation-toolset/info/ (accessed July 3, 2018).

8 Cf. Paul Ekman Group, "Facial Action Coding System," https://www.paulekman.com/product-category/facs/ (accessed February 2019), Paul Ekman and Wallace V. Friesen, "Facial Action Coding System: A Technique for the Measurement of Facial Movement." (Palo Alto, 1978).

9 Volker Helzle et al., "Adaptable Setup for Performance Driven Facial Animation," Proceeding SIGGRAPH '04 ACM SIGGRAPH 2004 Sketches (August 2004).

10 Filmakademie Baden-Württemberg, "Frapper, the Filmakademie Application Framework," https://animationsinstitut.de/de/forschung-rd/tools/frapper/info/ (accessed July 3, 2018).

11 Diana Arellano et al.. "Animated Faces, Abstractions and Autism," Proceedings of Intelligent Virtual Agents (September 2004).

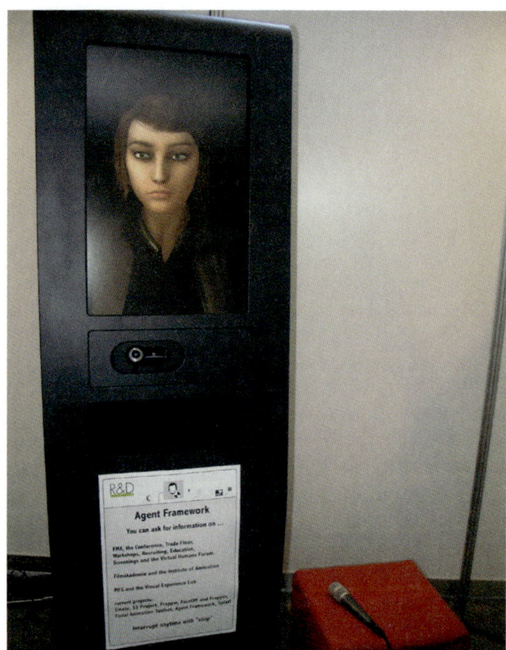

Figure 3. Agent Terminal – Interactive Conference Presenter: the visitors interacted with the virtual character using voice recognition and asked questions about the topic of the FMX conference, main tracks or weather in the host city (Stuttgart, Germany).

of their deployments. The following applications were created using the Agent Framework within the scope of Animation 2.0.

Early Proof of Concept: *Conference Guide* and *Emote*

One of the first use cases of the Agent Framework was the creation of a "terminal agent conference guide" named *Nikita*, who answered questions of the attendees in reference to the conference they were visiting (FMX) and the city where it was held. The questions and answers were scripted in an XML file, so the user was limited in the number of questions and how they could ask them. The system used voice recognition and voice generation, setting the basis for real-time interactive characters. Figure 3 illustrates the conference agent.

Another application was *Emote*, a web-based messaging service, which instead of delivering plain text

messages, synthesizes the information using the text-to-speech technology. In this way, it helps to overcome the exclusion of emotion in modern electronic messaging applications.[12]

To use *Emote*, the user has to access a webpage (on the computer or mobile device) that represents the front-end and interface for the user to create the message by typing text and emoticons into a text box. The system generates synthetic speech from the text. The emoticons are divided into basic emotions (happiness, sadness, angry, and surprise) and additional animations (e.g. wink, big smile, wave). The basic emotions define the emotional state throughout the message, while the additional animation options consist of prepared clips, such as winks or smiles, which are blended into the animation. Figure 4 shows the interface and animations generated by *Emote*.

The Muses of Poetry

The Muses of Poetry was an interactive installation that combined dynamically generated character animation, semantic analysis, natural voice interaction and emotions in poetry. This project served to explore how interactive animated characters can effectively transmit to an audience the intrinsic emotions conveyed in poems, broadening in this way the act of reciting poetry. The installation was also intended to be a step forward in the direction of computational creativity, by bringing into existence a "virtual poetry interpreter."[13]

Some previous works in this area combined poetry and artificial intelligence in order to "generate written poetry," instead of "automatically read poetry." Examples of these are Colton et al.,[14] who came up with a corpus-based poetry generation system that constructs poems according to a given rhyme, sentiment, word frequency and similarity; David Cope, who created the program *Alena* (Artificial Life Evolving Natural Affinities) to automatically write haiku, which were subsequently published in the ebook *Comes the Fiery Night*;[15] Pablo Gervás, who created WASP, a reasoning rule-based system that takes as input a set of words in Spanish and verse patterns and returns a set of vers-

---

12 Filmakademie Baden-Württemberg, "Emote," https://animationsinstitut.de/index.php?id=529 (accessed July 3, 2018).

13 Diana Arellano et al., "The Muses of Poetry – In search of the poetic experience," Symposium: Artificial intelligence and Poetry – AISB2013 (April 2014).

14 Simon Colton "Full face poetry generation," Proceedings of the Third International Conference on Computational Creativity (2012).

15 David Cope, *Comes the Fiery Night* (New York, 2011).

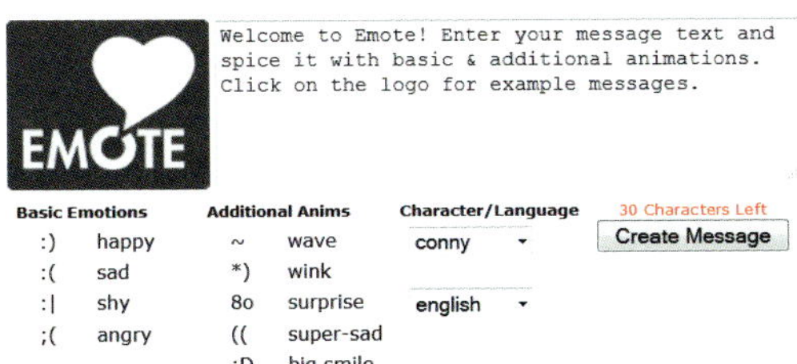

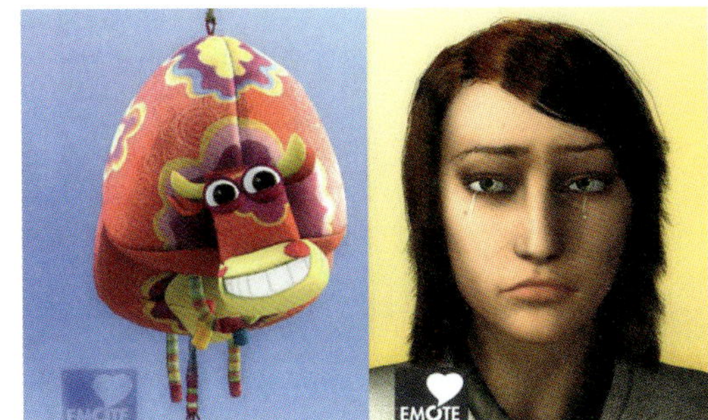

Figure 4. *Emote* web interface (top) and characters generated according to the emoticons in the message (middle).

es;[16] or Toivanen et al.,[17] who made used of text mining methods, morphological analysis, and morphological synthesis to generate poetry in Finnish. Figure 5 shows the modules that constitute the system architecture of our installation. The interaction with *The Muses* was conceived as a conversation between the user and the character. It was initiated with the user greeting the installation: "Hello Muses." To this, the character replied: "Hello, I am one of the muses of poetry. Select two words and I will recite a poem for you." This natural voice interaction was implemented in the *Voice Recognition* module. To avoid the use of a hand microphone, we hid a clip microphone in one of the physical installation slides above the head of the participant, so they could talk freely without noticing the device. The "two words" mentioned by the animate characters were selected from a pool of words shown on the display. It was configured by the *Word Cloud Display* module in a "word cloud" arrangement, generated dynamically in every interaction with the most repeated words in all the poems in the *Poems Repository*. After a word was selected, the *Poems Selector* reduced the number of candidate poems to those containing only that first word. Once the two words were recognized, the character recited the poem containing those two words.

The *Poem Affect Analysis* module was the one that carried on the semantic analysis of each of the poems available in the installation, in order to automatically extract their emotional content. A detailed insight of how this module was implemented is given in the work of Arellano et al.[18]

The extracted emotions were used as expression tags, which were then interpreted by the real-time *Dynamic Facial Animation* module, triggering the corresponding facial movements. The considered states were: pleasant, nice, fun, unpleasant, nasty and sad. For changes in the speech, tags with prosody elements like "pitch" and "speech" were added before the words with the line's prevailing emotional state: unpleasant, happy, or sad. These tags were processed by the text-to-speech tool, which was part of the *Affective Speech Synthesis* module, modulating the generated voice and enhancing the emotionality in the poem.[19]

The installation contained six animated characters that covered the wide spectrum of animated characters: a realistic human-like female who expressed emotions through facial expressions; an abstract character made of moving disc particles, the velocity of which depended on the emotions from the poem; a 2D cartoon character, who was a round shape with two points for eyes and a line for a mouth, named Myself; a 2D full body cartoonish monster named Krel; a character made of clay who looked like a sailor; and a character that had its face made with branches and stones, named Woody.

The clay character and Woody were actually physical characters that had to be photographed performing the different visemes (shape of the mouth when pronouncing different phonemes), in a Stop-Motion style. Woody and Krel expressed emotions by changing their color. Myself had small emotional animations (e.g. he would turn into a line if confused, or would explode if

---

16 Pablo Gervás, "Wasp: Evaluation of different strategies for the automatic generation of Spanish verse," Symposium on Creative & Cultural Aspects and Applications of AI & Cognitive Science (2000).

17 Jukka M. Toivanen et al., "Corpus-based generation of content and form in poetry," Proceedings of the Third International Conference on Computational Creativity (2012).

18 Diana Arellano and Volker Helzle, "The muses of poetry," Proceedings of CHI'14 Extended Abstracts on Human Factors in Computing Systems (April 2014).

19 Diana Arellano et al, "Automatic Speech for Poetry – The Voice behind the Experience," Proc. Workshop "Emotion and Computing" in KI 2013 (2013).

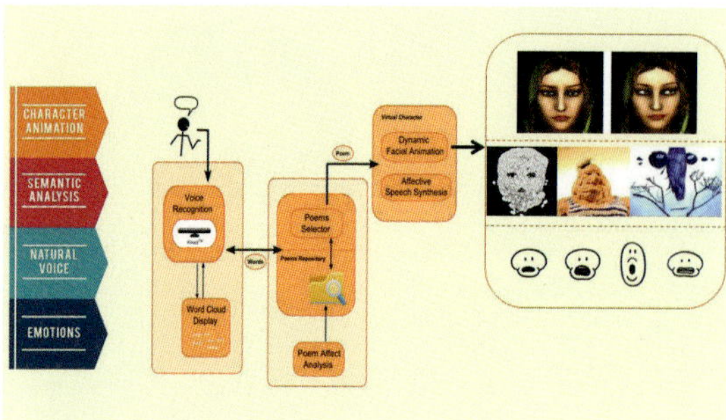

Figure 5. System architecture of *The Muses of Poetry*.

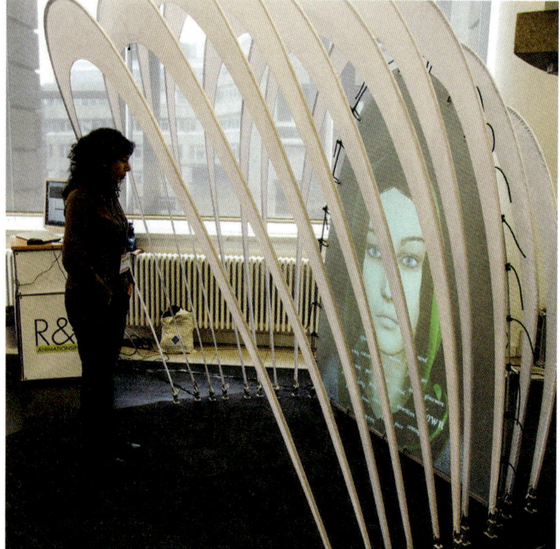

Figure 6. Interaction with the *Muses of Poetry*.

poems and the characters. Figure 6 shows the physical installation and the interaction with the characters.

SARA – Stylized Animations for Research on Autism

The ability to perceive emotions and other affective traits from human faces is considered the result of a "social training" that occurs from early childhood and develops during the adolescence and adulthood. However, individuals with Autism Spectrum Disorders (ASD) present difficulties not only when judging someone's emotions from their facial expressions,[20] but also when it comes to processing faces in general.[21] There are different theories that attempt to explain the causes of these impairments, but so far there is little consensus in this regard.[22]

Motivated by the divergence in these findings and the increasing number of individuals diagnosed with ASD,[23] we proposed *SARA* (Stylized Animations for Research in Autism), a project that investigated the causes behind communication and emotion perception deficits in children and adolescents with high-functioning ASD. To achieve this, SARA combined the expertise from three different German institutions: clinical psychology, from the University Medical Center Freiburg; real-time non-photorealistic rendering (NPR), from the University of Konstanz; and 3D facial animation and eye tracking technology, provided by the Filmakademie Baden-Württemberg.

On the one hand, the goal was to assess how abstracted faces with different levels of detail were categorized by children and adolescents with ASD, in comparison to the so-called neurotypically developed (NTD) participants (i.e. people without ASD). On the other hand, we wanted to determine how eye gaze behavior is related to ASD and those deficits in emotion perception.

The reasoning behind the use of NPR was that it allows a variation in the level of abstraction and visual information, adapting images to "focus the viewer's attention".[24] Thus, the information load in the characters' facial expressions can be reduced, conveying the emotional information more efficiently.[25][26] To

vangry) triggered when a strong emotion in the poem was elicited. Each character can be seen in Figure 5.

After presenting this installation in different venues and conferences, we concluded that the perception of the audience is very tied to their level of expertise. For instance, people working in computer graphics, animation or VFX focused mainly on the visual features of the character, while the audience coming from human-computer interaction focused mostly on the interaction, as well as on the feelings elicited by the

20 D.P. Kennedy and R. Adolphs. "Perception of emotions from facial expressions in high-functioning adults with autism," Neuropsychologia (2012).

21 Madeline B. Harms et al., "Facial Emotion Recognition in Autism Spectrum Disorders: A Review of Behavioral and Neuroimaging Studies," Neuropsychology Review (September 2010).

22 Marc Spicker et al., "Emotion recognition in autism spectrum disorder: does stylization help?", Proceedings of the ACM Symposium on Applied Perception (SAP '16), (July 2016).

23 Center for Disease Control and Prevention. "Facts About ASD (2014)," https://www.cdc.gov/ncbddd/autism/facts.html (accessed April 6, 2015).

24 Bruce Gooch, Amy Gooch, *Non-Photorealistic Rendering* (Natick, 2001).

25 Doug DeCarlo and Anthony Santella, "Stylization and abstraction of photographs," ACM Trans. Graph. 21, 3 (July 2002).

26 Bruce Gooch et al., "Human facial illustrations: Creation and psychophysical evaluation," ACM Trans. Graph. 23, 1 (January 2004).

this end, a set of virtual characters were used in an interactive computer based psychological test, named DECT (Dynamic Emotional Categorization Test)[27] where each character displayed emotional facial animations generated in real-time. The test was a computer-based test consisting of a number of trials, each consisting of the following parts:

(1) Fixation cross (0.5 seconds).
(2) Stylized character animation.
(3) Response screen with 6 possible emotions.
(4) Screen for cognition loading (white noise).

Figure 7 shows the different screens presented during a trial of DECT. The way the test was realized was by the participant sitting in front of the computer and being assisted by the researcher to select the emotion that would correspond to the animation previously seen. Figure 8 shows a DECT session.

The characters' faces were rigged using the Facial Animation Toolset and animated to portray emotions corresponding to the six universal emotions: happiness, sadness, anger, fear, disgust and surprise with different intensity levels.[28] Figure 6 shows two animated characters used in the DECT test: an elderly man (Hank), and a younger woman (Nikita).

The core test of the project was the NPR-DECT, where we used non-photorealistic rendering (NPR) algorithms to abstract and manipulate visual information in the faces of our virtual characters. It not only constituted a way to reduce information load in the characters' facial expressions, but also a way to include more artistic approaches to investigate how these abstractions affected the recognition of the facial expressions of emotions, in comparison to their more realistic representations. In total, four different styles (watercolors, pencil drawing, image abstraction, and sketching) plus the original (non-abstracted), in 2 different levels of abstraction (medium and high abstraction) were evaluated. Figure 7 shows different facial abstractions in the character Nikita.

In the final test, i-DECT, we provoked a visual interaction between the participant and the virtual character. The aim of this test was to clarify even further the differences in eye contact and mutual gaze between neu-

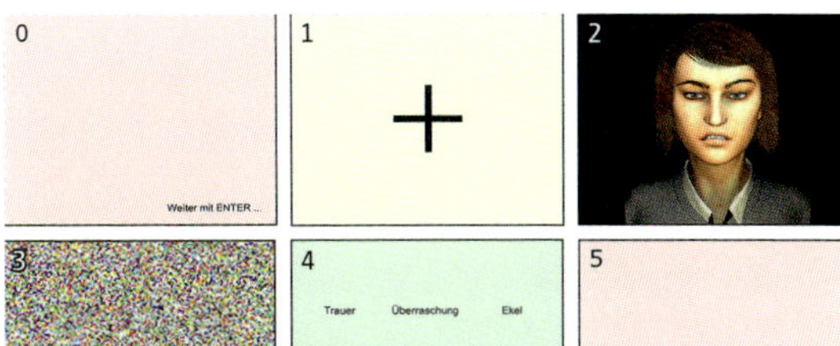

Figure 7: Screens presented in a DECT trial: (0) Initial screen, (1) fixation cross, (2) real-time animated character, (3) white noise for cognition loading, (4) emotional options, (5) Initial screen for following trial.

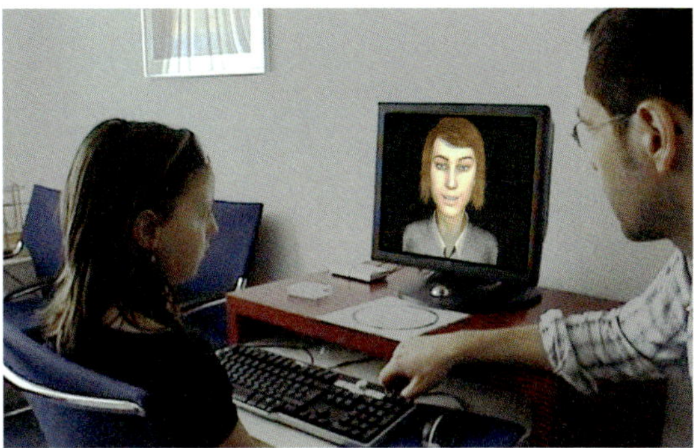

Figure 8: DECT session.

rotypical subjects and subjects with ASD. In the "passive" modality of the test, the character appeared with the head facing the user, but the gaze was diverted and the character never looked in the eyes of the participant. During the "interactive" mode the character appeared with both gaze and head averted (to the left or right); after approximately 2 seconds the character rotates their head and gaze, looking in the eyes of the participant. At the same time, the head movements of the virtual characters can be steered using the coordinates of the participant's pupils, which are obtained through an eye tracker. For instance, if the participant looked to the upper-left corner, then the head of the character moved towards the upper-left. The gaze of the character remained fixed on the participant.

It is worth mentioning that this level of interactivity was achieved thanks to the real-time characteristic of our Frapper framework. It provided the flexibility and opportunity for more elaborate interactive experiments.[29]

---

27 Reinhold Rauh and Ulrich M. Schaller, "Categorical perception of emotional facial expressions in video clips with natural and artificial actors: A pilot study," Tech. rep., University of Freiburg (2009).

28 Diana Arellano et al, "Generation and visualization of emotional states in virtual characters," Computer Animation and Virtual Worlds 19 (September 2008).

29 Diana Arellano et al., "Interactive testbed for research in autism – The SARA project," Universal Access in the Information Society (March 2018).

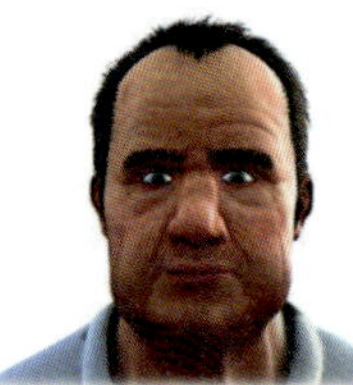 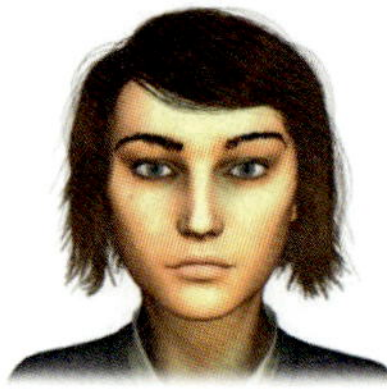

Figure 9: Hank (left) and Nikita (right). Characters created, rigged and animated at the Filmakademie Baden-Württemberg.

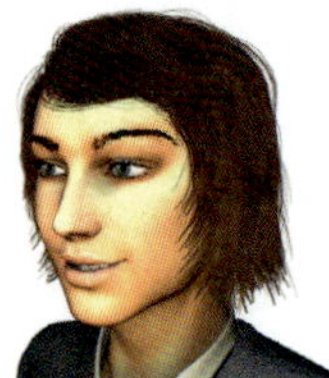 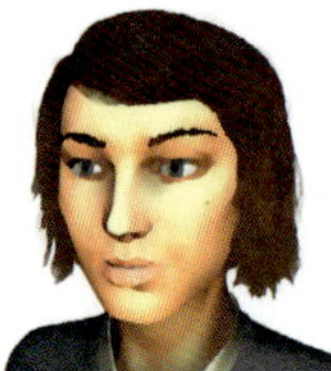 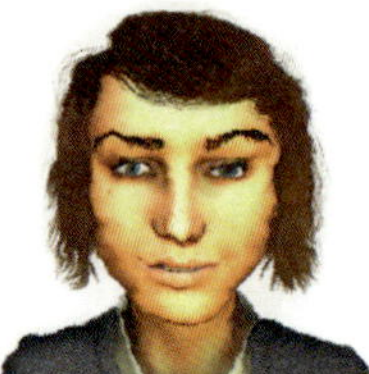 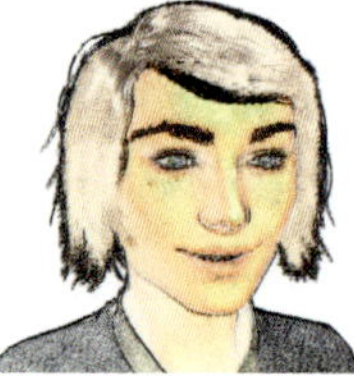 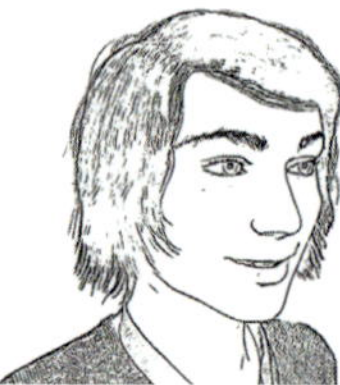

Figure 10. From left to right: original, image abstraction, watercolors, sketching, pencil drawing.

Regarding evaluation, in this compilation we report the results of the NPR-DECT, because it was the test that constituted the core of our research. We evaluated 62 participants with ages between 13 and 18, and an IQ > 85. The primary participants were individuals with ASD (16 subjects), and two control groups: ADHD (Attention Deficit Hyperactivity Disorder, 24 subjects) and NTD (22 subjects). The reason why we included subjects with ADHD in the trial groups is because ADHD shares some traits with ASD, such as difficulty categorizing emotions in faces. Additionally, we carried out a questionnaire to assess the recognizability and likeability of the characters in their original style and in abstracted styles.

In the end the results showed that there was indeed a significant difference in the categorization of emotions between the NTD and ASD groups, with the latter group showing impairments in facial emotion categorization.

However, it was not possible to say which emotion(s) contributed to this general difference. As for the NPR styles, no decisive conclusions were achieved regarding which abstraction method leads to better emotional categorization. Nevertheless, all versions of the DECT tests are distributed as open source.[30] This opens the door for other researchers or artists who want to create new interactive applications or tests considering HCI elements that contain NPR elements and artistic abstraction techniques.

Final words

Facial character animation has come a long way, but by no means it has reached its destination. Our research at the Animationsinstitut, Filmakademie Baden-Württemberg demonstrates that even with a limited budget it is possible to create technology that can serve to advance fields that are not necessarily linked with films or entertainment. In the case of autism research, it was important to try understanding the process behind the categorization of emotions and eye gaze behavior in individuals with high-functioning ASD. Therefore, it would be possible to design and implement methodologies and interventions that can aid people with ASD to improve their social skills. Additionally, the use of a real-time interactive environment, like the one we provided, broadens the possibilities for experimentation and research that otherwise would not be possible (e.g., with pre-rendered animations).

---

30 Filmakademie Baden-Württemberg. "SARA Stylized Animations for Reserach on Autism," https://animationsinstitut.de/de/forschung-rd/projects/animation-20/sara/info/ (accessed July 7, 2018).

Bibliography

Arellano, Diana et al. "Animated Faces, Abstractions and Autism." *Proceedings of Intelligent Virtual Agents (IVA)* (September 2004).

Arellano, Diana et al. "Generation and visualization of emotional states in virtual characters." *Computer Animation and Virtual Worlds* 19 (September 2008).

Arellano, Diana et al. "Automatic Speech for Poetry - The Voice behind the Experience." *Proc. Workshop "Emotion and Computing" in KI 2013* (2013).

Arellano, Diana et al. "The Muses of Poetry - In search of the poetic experience." *Symposium: Artificial intelligence and Poetry - AISB2013* (April 2014).

Arellano, Diana, and Volker Helzle. "The muses of poetry." *Proceedings of CHI'14 Extended Abstracts on Human Factors in Computing Systems* (April 2014).

Arellano, Diana et al. "Interactive testbed for research in autism - The SARA project." *Universal Access in the Information Society* (March 2018).

Colton, Simon et al. "Full face poetry generation." *Proceedings of the Third International Conference on Computational Creativity* (2012).

Cope, David. *Comes the Fiery Night*. New York, 2011.

DeCarlo, Doug, and Anthony Santella. "Stylization and abstraction of photographs." *ACM Trans. Graph.* 21, 3 (July 2002).

Ekman, Paul, and Wallace V. Friesen. "Facial Action Coding System: A Technique for the Measurement of Facial Movement." Palo Alto, 1978.

Gervás, Pablo. "Wasp: Evaluation of different strategies for the automatic generation of Spanish verse." *Symposium on Creative & Cultural Aspects and Applications of AI & Cognitive Science* (2000).

Gooch, Bruce, and Amy Gooch. *Non-Photorealistic Rendering*. Natick, Massachusetts, 2001.

Gooch, Bruce, et al. "Human facial illustrations: Creation and psychophysical evaluation." *ACM Trans. Graph.* 23, 1 (January 2004).

Harms, Madeline B. et al. "Facial Emotion Recognition in Autism Spectrum Disorders: A Review of Behavioral and Neuroimaging Studies." *Neuropsychology Review* (September 2010).

Helzle, Volker et al. "Adaptable Setup for Performance Driven Facial Animation." *Proceeding SIGGRAPH '04 ACM SIGGRAPH 2004 Sketches* (August 2004).

Kennedy, D.P. and R. Adolphs. "Perception of emotions from facial expressions in high-functioning adults with autism." *Neuropsychologia* (2012).

Rauh, Reinhold, and Ulrich M. Schaller. "Categorical perception of emotional facial expressions in video clips with natural and artificial actors: A pilot study." Tech. rep., University of Freiburg (2009).

Spicker, Marc et al. "Emotion recognition in autism spectrum disorder: does stylization help?" *Proceedings of the ACM Symposium on Applied Perception* (SAP '16), (July 2016).

Toivanen, Jukka M. et al. "Corpus-based generation of content and form in poetry." *Proceedings of the Third International Conference on Computational Creativity* (2012).

Artistic Perspectives

Traversing the Borders of Art, Science & Play

Markos Kay (GB)

Simulation Scientific Observation

As a visual artist exploring the intersection of art and science, my aim is to create public engagement with scientific theory by communicating it in a visually intuitive way. With a background in fine arts and communication design, I am drawn to the artistic implications of the natural sciences and to finding ways to communicate the complexities of scientific observation and theory.

I am particularly interested in the shift in perspective that happens through scientific methods when studying those parts of reality that lie beyond "direct" observation. Specifically, I have focused on methods of observation used in cellular biology and particle physics, such as scientific instruments, simulations, and visualizations. The underlying theme of my work is the idea that physical information is transformed into increasing orders of complexity and levels of abstraction when observed, a theme which can been seen throughout the scientific narrative. My work takes the form of virtual experiments using generative and procedural methods such as 3D physics engines and particle simulations. In using computational visualization methods as an artistic medium, I am referring to the contemporary paradigm in physics that posits that our reality can be described in terms of information, with the implication that it is potentially computable. This investigation starts with the act of observation, which can be defined as the abstraction of information from a source. Observation is considered a physical process that involves amplification of information, a thermodynamically irreversible process that causes an increase in entropy. In visual perception, light information is transformed, amplified, processed and reinterpreted through various structures of the brain to create a representation of phenomena. This process is not just a translation of data, it also involves the abstraction of this information that is dependent on our internal model of the world. The original light information that the eyes receive is actually very low in quality and the processing it undergoes until it becomes conscious experience leads to a huge increase in complexity. Essentially new information is created in every step of this process in order for the original information to be perceived. There is a paradox at play here because while "information is the reduction in uncertainty regarding the state of a variable ... conversely (it) is what increases in specifying a variable with a growing number of possible states."[1]

Our brain takes raw sense data and manipulates them to create a rich, detailed representation or simulation, the phenomenological world.

When it comes to scientific observation, our instruments intervene to translate information from aspects of reality that cannot be directly observed into per-

---

1 Giulio Tononi, "An information integration theory of consciousness," *BMC Neurosci.* 5 (November 2004) p. 42.

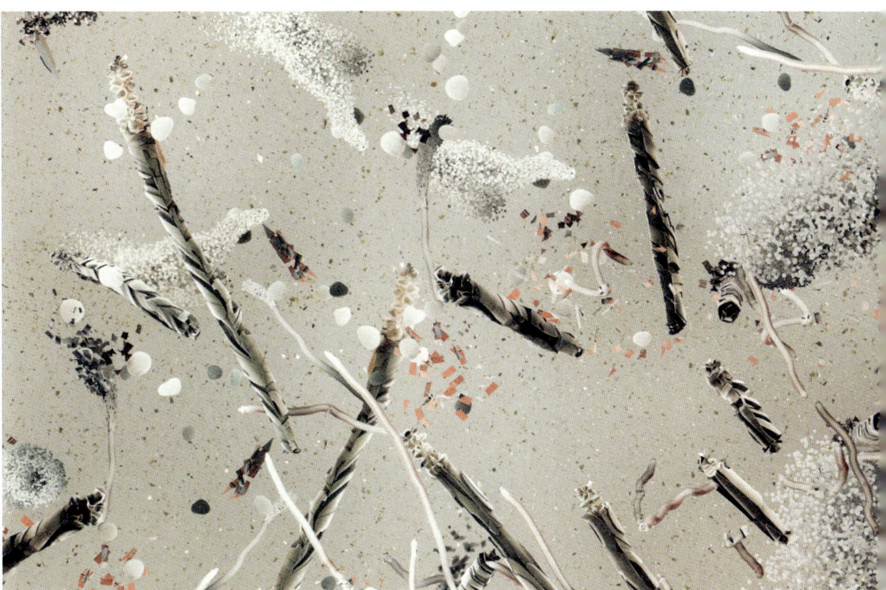

Figure 1: *Cytoplasmic Playgrounds* (2013) – Conceptual visualization and simulation of macromolecular crowding in the cytoplasm of a cell.

ceptible forms, going beyond the capabilities of our senses. Instruments such as microscopes, telescopes, and particle accelerators transform and process information into intelligible forms just like our brain does. The tools used for scientific observation mediate information, transforming it into emergent orders of complexity which is organized into the systematic body of knowledge we call science. This knowledge continuously changes as new discoveries take place and theories are proven or disproven. The scientific method itself is a continuous process of purposeful revision of knowledge, as new information is recovered or reinterpreted. This transitory quality echoes Mackenzie's etymology of information as *in formation,*[2] a process in a continuous state of becoming.

A further level of abstraction is added when this knowledge is communicated in visual form. Scientific visualization has its own language and iconography as expressed in illustrative, diagrammatic and imaging methods. These visualizations communicate scientific observations, guiding and forming the way this knowledge is perceived and understood. There is another critical shift in perspective and increase in complexity that occurs in the process of verifying theory through tools of observation such as sensors and simulations when that information is communicated through visualization. Just as our brain reinterprets sense data into perceptions, so do our visualizations interpret scientific data into forms we can perceive and engage with intuitively.

In the study of cells there are instruments of observation which result in such visualizations, such as imaging, computer modelling and simulations. One example is acoustic microscopy which uses ultrasounds that are processed by a computer to create a visual representation that is richer in detail than a traditional light microscope, revealing new information about the cells studied. In electron cryotomography, cells are frozen and scanned using an electron microscope; the computer processes the reflected electrons to render 3D visualizations of the cell that enable us to study its intricate structure.

Lattice Light Sheet Microscopy,[3] pioneered by Nobel prize-winning Eric Betzig, takes this even further by using sheets of light that scan cells that are processed to reveal a detailed view of cellular processes in motion. These are then translated into animated 3D computer models which allow scientists to study

---

2 Howard Hughes Medical Institute, "New Microscope Captures Detailed 3-D Movies of Cells Deep Within Living Systems," *www.hhmi. org*, April 19, 2018, https://www.hhmi.org/news/new-microscope-captures-detailed-3-d-movies-cells-deep-within-living-systems (Last accessed October 15, 2018).
3 Tadashi Ando and Jeffrey Skolnick, "Crowding and hydrodynamic interactions likely dominate in vivo macromolecular motion," *PNAS* 107 (October 26, 2010), https://www.pnas.org/content/107/43/18457 (Last accessed October 15, 2018).

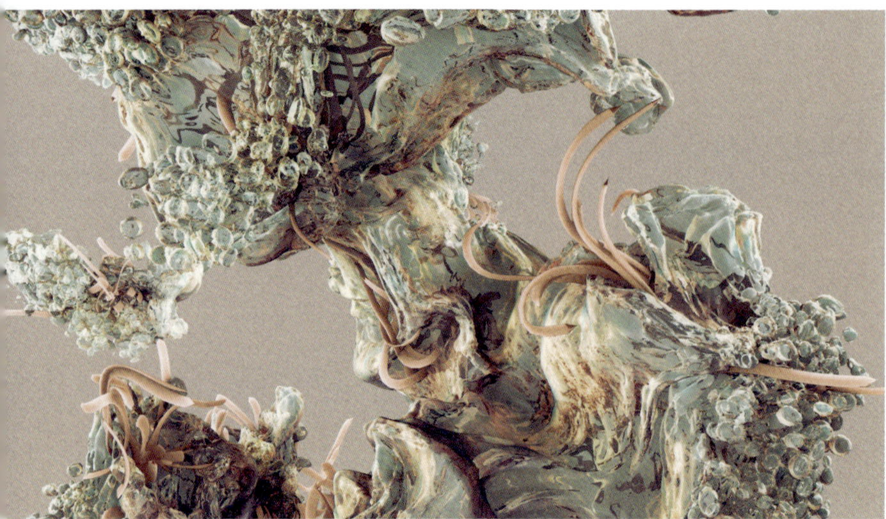

Figure 2: *Microscopic Leaps* (2015) – Conceptual visualization and simulation of microtubule dynamics in multinucleate D. discoideum cells.

the structure and movement of cells from a new perspective. We see here a complex transformation of information, going from light data to computer image processing to 3D models which are virtual representations of the original cells. In other words, scientists are using computer generated simulations as a method of observation. In fact, the dynamic molecular systems present in cells that are revealed through Lattice Light Sheet Microscopy are studied through the use of computer simulations, such as the work done at the Center for the Study of Systems Biology at Georgia Tech as part of the growing field of Computational Biology.[4] Simulations today play an important role in modern science and are often studied like laboratory phenomena, aiding and guiding observation and theory.

In *Microscopic Leaps* (2015)[5] I was commissioned by the Howard Hughes Medical Institute to create conceptual visualizations based on the recordings of cells using Lattice Light Sheet Microscopy. The recordings of biological processes using this technique were artistically reinterpreted and recreated as computer simulations which were then used to extract images for print. In my work these simulations are used as the brush and paint to create abstract representations of scientific narratives. The Betzig Lab provided their 3D computer models of cells which I incorporated into conceptual simulations of their recordings with feedback from the scientists. This was a seamless transition which goes to show how similar these scientific processes are to the design process. Creating visual simulations based on Betzig Lab's recordings was also quite straightforward, as our computational models are designed to mimic these dynamic systems we see in nature. The short film *Microscopic Leaps* was created out of these simulation experiments. Using simulations as an artistic tool requires a lot of trial and error. It involves setting initial conditions such as the physical forces, properties and entities of a virtual environment, running the simulation to see how it evolves, then going back and adjusting the parameters to create different iterations. This leads to unexpected and often beautiful results that look like they have a life of their own. There is a selection process involved here, where a particular iteration is selected among many for rendering. I like to see it as similar to a nature documentary, where events are recorded with no intervention, and the best shots are chosen. Similarly, with simulations there is no control over the way the virtual events unfold although there is control over their initial parameters. I first explored this technique in my short film *aDiatomea* (2008),[6] where virtual organisms were set loose in a simulated environment and their movement was recorded using randomly placed cameras that were also subject to the forces of the simulation.

---

4 Adrian McKenzie, *Transductions: Bodies and Machines at Speed* (London, 2002).
5 *Microscopic Leaps. Directed by Markos Kay, 2015.*
6 *aDiatomea*. Directed by Markos Kay, 2008.

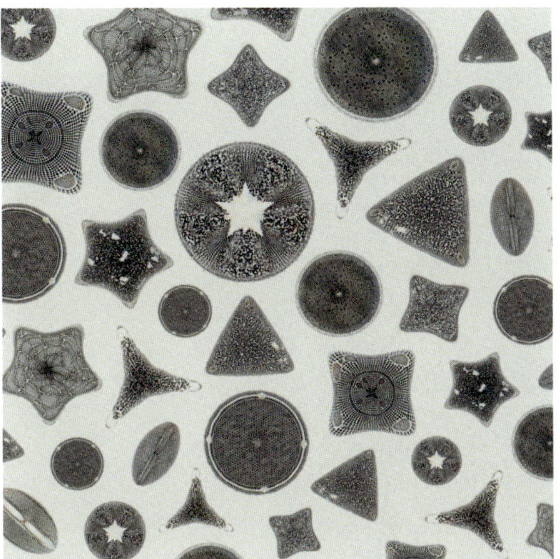

Figure 3: *aDiatomea* (2008) – Procedurally generated virtual organisms based on the form of diatoms.

The idea of transformation of information can also been seen in the bigger picture of the scientific narrative. In the Big Bang story we see the transformation of fundamental forces into particles, nucleons, atoms, stars and so on. If we look at ourselves we see a similar story, we are made of quarks that make up atoms that construct molecules and cells, the story of supervenience and emergence. Looking at the greater picture we can see information increasing in complexity as it transforms from one level to the next, each with its own emergent properties. If we look at the smallest picture we can see the same thing, fields that interact with each other through the exchange of information in the form of particles. In other words, *"information is any type of pattern that influences the formation or transformation of other patterns."*[7] The idea of supervenience is best exemplified visually in the seminal art & science short film *The Powers of Ten* (1977)[8] by Ray and Charles Eames, which has been a great influence on my work. I had the opportunity to be a part of an international collaboration funded by the Gates Foundation to reimagine this film for its thirty-fifth anniversary.

In the short film *The Flow* (2011)[9] I set out to visualize the theory behind these transforming layers of matter. I looked at scientific iconography such as textbook illustrations and how these differ from our observations and theories. For example, the traditional icon for an atom shows electrons orbiting around the nucleus, whereas the theory talks of electrons existing in probability clouds around the nucleus as described by the hydrogen wave function, observed through quantum microscopy and visualized as 3D atomic orbitals. Similarly, the classic textbook illustration for a proton shows three quarks bound together by spirals that represent the strong force. However, the theory tells us that in fact within the proton there is an infinite number of virtual quarks and gluons in flux or again, *in formation.*[10]

In the film I tried to create visualizations that better matched the theory, engaging the viewer with the intricacies of the scientific theory in a more intuitive way. The moving image and the procedural methods lend themselves to the complexity of the subject matter, which is very hard to describe in a diagram. Visually, I was inspired by scientific imaging of biological processes, using biomorphism to inject life into these visuals and to refer back to the visual language of science. The medium of moving image helps to illustrate the idea that the flow of information from one integral level to the next is a continuous process. Through the use of computational simulations I wanted to show

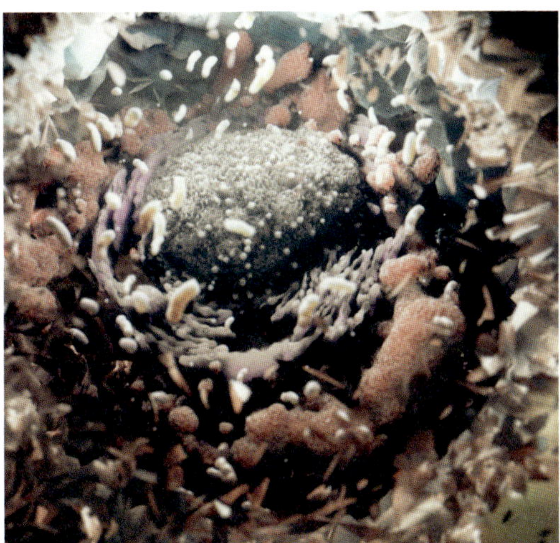

Figure 4: *The Powers of Ten: Lymphocyte* (2012) – Conceptual visualization and simulation of a Lymphocyte for the reimagining of the Eames classic *The Powers of Ten* (1977).

---

7 Claude E. Shannon, The Mathematical Theory of Communication (Cambridge, 1949).

8 *Powers of Ten*. Directed by Charles Eames and Ray Eames, 1977.

9 *The Flow*. Directed by Markos Kay, 2011.

10 Howard Hughes Medical Institute, "New Microscope Captures Detailed 3-D Movies of Cells Deep Within Living Systems," www.hhmi.org, April 19, 2018, https://www.hhmi.org/news/new-microscope-captures-detailed-3-d-movies-cells-deep-within-living-systems (Last accessed October 15, 2018).

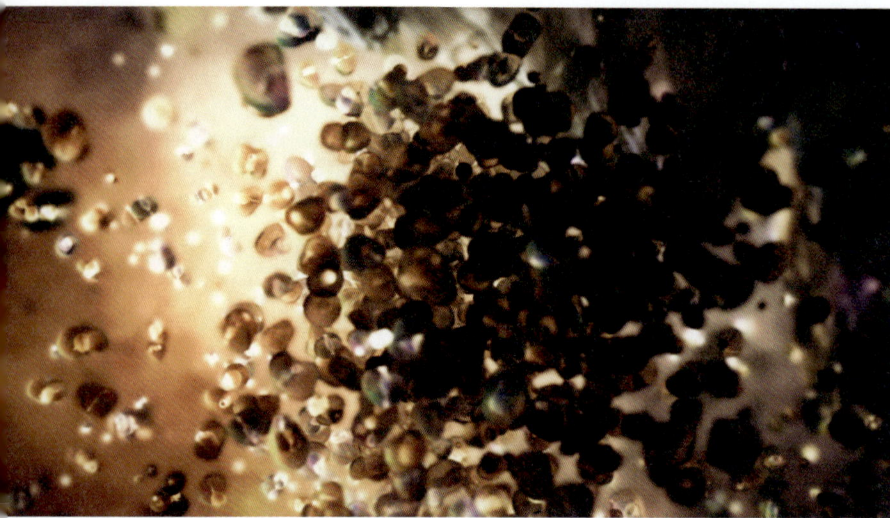

Figure 5: *The Flow* (2011) – Conceptual visualization and simulation of virtual gluons and quarks fluctuating around a valence quark.

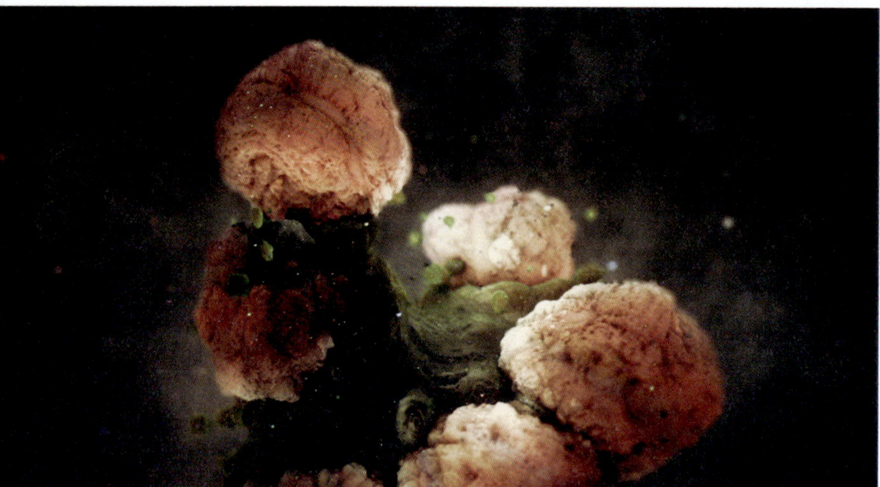

Figure 6: *The Flow* (2011) – Conceptual visualization and simulation of hadrons held by the residual strong force in the atomic nucleus via the exchange of pairs of quarks.

how information is embedded or implicated within this process. David Bohm, one the most significant physicists of the twentieth century whose concepts of *Wholeness and the Implicate order* are increasingly becoming relevant in modern physics, echoes this Heraklitian sentiment: "Not only is everything changing, but all is flux. That is to say, what *is* is the process of becoming itself, while all objects, events, entities, conditions, structures, etc., are forms that can be abstracted from this process."[11]

The informational paradigm is put into practice in particle accelerators where supercomputer simulations are used to verify observations of particle interactions, something I explore in *Quantum Fluctuations* (2016).[12] The quantum world is impossible to observe directly and to even visualize; in fact Heisenberg adamantly renounced the case of visualization in his Nobel Lecture in 1933.[13] The presence and properties of elementary particles are ascertained by measuring the minute changes they make on instruments such as the

---

11 David Bohm, Wholeness and the Implicate Order (London, 1980).

12 *Quantum Fluctuations*. Directed by Markos Kay, 2016.

13 Nobel Lectures, Physics 1922-1941, Elsevier Publishing Company, Amsterdam, 1965

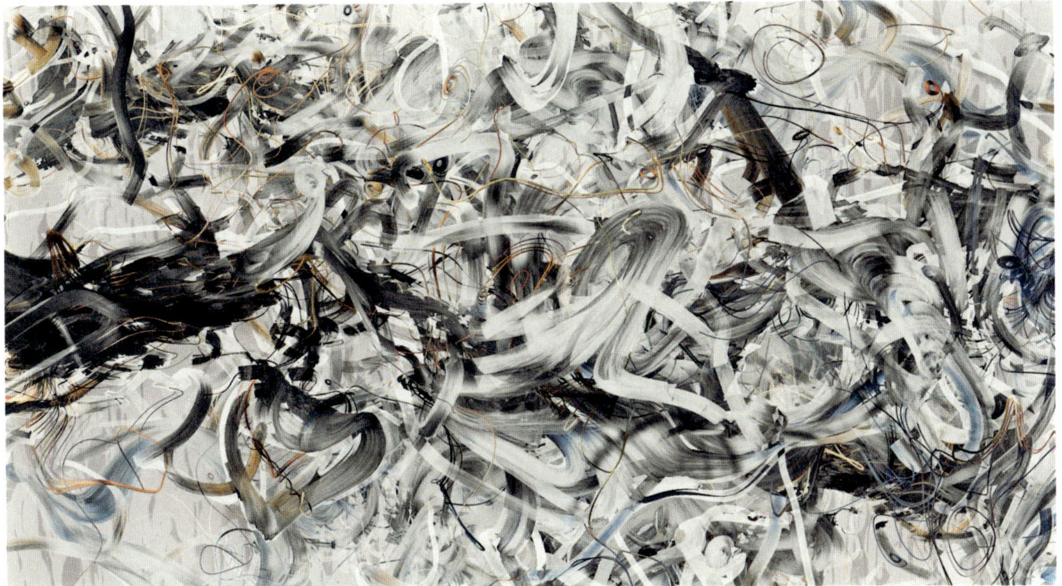

Figure 7: *Quantum Fluctuations* (2016) – Conceptual visualization and simulation of the Underlying Event, the background of particle interactions in the Large Hadron Collider.

Large Hadron Collider (LHC) which are then compared to data collected from supercomputer simulations. Essentially "simulations ... stage interactions between virtual entities from which properties, tendencies, and capacities actually emerge ... (playing) the role of laboratory experiments."[14] This is perhaps the most indirect method of observation imaginable, a non-representational form of observation mediated by supercomputer simulations.

The theory tells a story of particles rapidly moving, interacting and transforming into different states which I imagined as repeating structures that form patterns. I looked at abstract expressionist paintings and other gestural abstraction art, because I wanted the artwork to have this element of spontaneous action. The film in fact opens with rapidly moving brush strokes that represent the random wave fluctuations that underlie all of reality. I also drew influence from classic scientific iconography such Feynman diagrams and other diagrams that show quantum particle interactions and movement, images of wave interference patterns and electric discharge patterns (Lichtenberg figures), particle dynamics simulations and microscopy images of chemicals and crystal growths.

Moving on to the computer I recreated these patterns using 3D particle simulations that work on the same underlying principle as the simulations at the CERN.

This 3D simulation software generates streams of particles in random configurations. These particles have properties such as spin and velocity, they can scatter off each other, attract or repulse, split into more particles and form groups. Adjustment of all these parameters results in intricate structures and patterns made out of systems of millions of particles pushing computational power to its limits. These conceptual simulations work on the same principle as the Monte Carlo simulations that run at the LHC which are computational algorithms that rely on repeated random samplings to obtain numerical results. As visualized virtual experiments, they illustrate the computational paradigm behind the observational methods at the LHC.

These simulations were used to create abstract moving paintings which visualize the distinct microevents that occur in the LHC during a proton collision. The events described by the theory involve multiple particle interactions in the background of a collision called the *Underlying Event*: the *Proton Beams* that are accelerated to speeds near the speed of light, the *Hard Subprocess* which is the main collision, *Parton Showers* which is radiation in the form of virtual quarks and gluons caused by the energy of the collision, *Hadronization* where these particles become composite hadrons and finally *Hadron Decay* where unstable composites

14 Manuel De Landa, Philosophy and Simulation: The Emergence of Synthetic Reason (London, 2011).

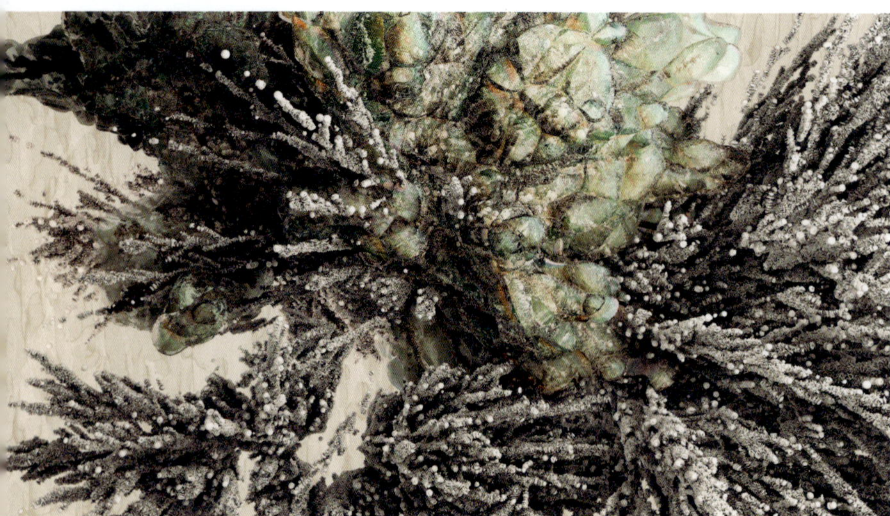

Figure 8: *Quantum Fluctuations* (2016) – Conceptual visualization and simulation of the Hard Subprocess—the main collision event during a high energy particle collision.

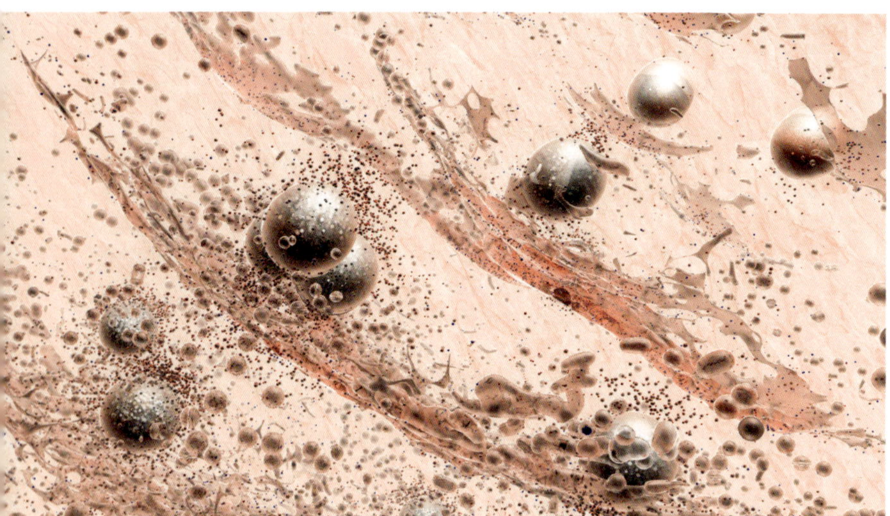

Figure 9: *Quantum Fluctuations* (2016) – Conceptual visualization and simulation of Parton Showers, the outward radiation of particles after a collision.

break apart and light is emitted. There is a narrative at play here, the story of these elementary particles, carriers of information that continuously transform from one state to the next. And then there we are, tampering with this ephemeral world that lies on the edge of reality and understanding, creating simulations in order to understand it. In a way, "simulations present themselves not only as mechanisms of control, or spectacles, but … in the form of visualized knowledge."[15]

Due to the complexity of the subject matter I needed to make sure that it made sense to scientists and that it had merit as a public engagement piece for their work. While the work was in progress, I sent my concept and visuals to scientists at the CERN who were involved in the art & science documentary *Sense of Beauty* (2018),[16] which featured parts of my work. They were kind enough to go over my work in progress and gave their approval for my efforts to evoke viewer imagination on the happenings of particle collisions.

---

15 Yuk Hui, The Plane of Obscurity – Simulation and Philosophy (London, 2011).
16 *Sense of Beauty*. Directed by Valerio Jalongo, 2018.

What is so fascinating about the quantum world is that this most fundamental aspect of reality exists in a constant state of flux that is so rapidly changing that it can only be understood in probabilistic and statistical terms like those expressed in the Monte Carlo simulations. What follows are interpretations of quantum mechanics that have epistemological and ontological implications for how we understand nature. It becomes a deeply philosophical endeavor, and in many ways an existential one, dealing with fundamental questions that have a direct impact on how we understand ourselves.

I consider my art-science experiments as ways of looking at the bigger picture. What interests me is to find the underlying patterns that repeat in all aspects of reality from the microcosm to the macrocosm. There is an emerging academic discipline called Big History[17] that brings together different disciplines, from particle physics to astrophysics to geology to biology to humanities and everything in between. The aim is the same, to find those patterns that emerge from observations of the universe in all scales. An interdisciplinary approach between the arts and science could help lead to important paradigm shifts by helping scientists and laypeople to engage with scientific theory from a different perspective.

Science is able to profoundly change the way we understand the universe but also our societies and our minds. From an artistic perspective science is an extremely powerful metanarrative and is therefore a subject that needs to be deconstructed through art. The scientific method itself can be seen as an artistic process—it aims to answer questions about how the world works but, more importantly, it creates more questions about reality. It deconstructs and reconstructs knowledge and it uncovers beauty, complexity, and simplicity, just as art does. The desire of artists to find ways to understand, represent and reinterpret the world they live in gives rise to an investigation of nature, perception and thought—which is exactly what a scientist does. With my work I aim to challenge ideas on how knowledge is formed and to highlight its constantly transforming nature. On an intuitive level I hope to engage viewers with the beauty of quantum mechanics and molecular biology and evoke their imagination about what happens behind the scenes of our reality.

---

17 David Christian, Maps of Time: An Introduction to Big History (London, 2004).

Bibliography

Bohm, David. *Wholeness and the Implicate Order.* London, 1980.

Tononi, Giulio, "An information integration theory of consciousness." *BMC Neurosci.* 5 (November 2004).

McKenzie, Adrian. *Transductions: Bodies and Machines at Speed.* London, 2002.

Shannon, Claude E. *The Mathematical Theory of Communication.* Cambridge, 1949.

De Landa, Manuel. *Philosophy and Simulation: The Emergence of Synthetic Reason.* London, 2011.

Hui, Yuk. *The Plane of Obscurity – Simulation and Philosophy.* London, 2011.

Christian, David. *Maps of Time: An Introduction to Big History.* London, 2004.

Abigail Addison (GB)

Silent Signal – Exploring Visionary Science through Experimental Animation

Silent Signal (2013–17)[1] was devised and produced by Animate Projects[2] with scientist Bentley Crudgington and was supported by a Wellcome Trust Large Arts Award[3] and the Garfield Weston Foundation.[4] It was a project that brought together six artists working with animation and six biomedical scientists who collaborated to produce six experimental animated artworks that explore new ways of thinking about the human body and the signals that enable our bodies to operate and to adapt to fight disease. Collectively the works explore the science of genetics, cell biology, immunology and epidemiology.

The project was intended to be accessed through exhibition in galleries, cinemas, public screens, and online at silentsignal.org[5] where the films, interviews and educational resources are still accessible. The project launched publicly in February 2016 with the opening of the *Silent Signal* exhibition at the QUAD arts center in Derby, UK. *Silent Signal* then toured for a year in the UK and internationally, as both a single screen program and a gallery installation. *Silent Signal* was designed to take the viewer on a journey: starting at the microcosm of the infection fighting internal landscapes of our cells, through the personal experiences and opinions of individuals and scientists, to the application of the research in the wider world of infectious disease modelling and genome code sequencing. The works were intended to raise questions about what our genetic code is, how our immune system functions, how disease is spread, and what the future applications and impact of the research into these areas might be for us all.

The works are artistic, aesthetic, abstracting—rather than visualizing, illustrating, or interpreting the science, as animation is often employed to do, they seek to bring a different perspective, allowing space for contemplation on the subject at hand. All of the works are made using digital technology, whether that be programming a game engine, manipulating Kinect[6] technology, or using animation software and a drawing tablet, though some have more of a hand-crafted or traditional animation feel than others. The project

1 Silent Signal, https://www.silentsignal.org (accessed June 20, 2018).

2 Animate Projects, https://www.animateprojects.org (accessed June 20, 2018).

3 Wellcome Trust, https://wellcome.ac.uk/home (accessed June 20, 2018).

4 Garfield Weston Foundation, https://garfieldweston.org/ (accessed June 20, 2018).

5 Animate Projects, https://animateprojects.org/portfolio/silent-signal/ (accessed June 20, 2018).

6 Microsoft, https://developer.microsoft.com/en-us/windows/kinect (accessed June 20, 2018).

first began with a thorough research and development phase supported by the Wellcome Trust, a large medical research charity in the UK which, as part of its remit, chooses to support artistic public engagement projects inspired by biomedical science. As part of the development process, scientist Bentley Crudgington was approached to partner with the team on developing the project, and to give crucial advice on the scientific research areas being explored. He continued to collaborate throughout the project and aided us with contextualizing the work, producing educational resources and activities that could be shared with schools and science communicators.

An open call for scientists was shared online, while simultaneously artists recommended by UK-wide curators and producers were approached. Both the artists and scientists were required to write short proposals outlining their interest in the project and their suitability. From the proposals a variety of potential collaborators were selected and brought together in a lab afternoon (which included some speed dating) to identify those who were suitable to work with and those who would work well together. From this process the six collaborative pairings were selected who then went on to spend two years in constant dialogue.

Each work is the result of a close collaboration, with the artist and scientist jointly developing ideas, and exploring the similarities and differences in the way they work and the imaging technologies they each use. There was also much discussion both within the collaborative pairings and in group roundtable sessions about how the artists were responding to the research and how the scientists were feeding into the creative process.

Each project will be discussed in terms of how it has evolved and been explored by each pairing, with a brief introduction to each animation technique and each research area. As this is being presented from a non-scientist perspective, if you wish to find out more about the research areas it is recommended to take a look at the video interviews[7] with the scientists, and the science guide[8] that Bentley Crudgington and educational consultant Gillian Pearson produced for the project. It is also worth noting that since completing the project in 2017, some of the scientists have

moved on to different positions and different organizations but are cited here in relation to the roles and the research in which they were involved at the time of making the animations.

Afterglow

Each project will be introduced individually, starting with the artwork *AfterGlow*,[9] made by artists boredomresearch (Vicky Isley and Paul Smith) in collaboration with Dr. Paddy Brock (Research Associate, Institute of Biodiversity, Animal Health and Comparative Medicine, University of Glasgow). The piece exists in two versions: a real-time animation that is ever evolving, and a single-screen animated short film.

Dr. Brock uses statistics and mathematical modeling to identify patterns in malaria transmission between animals and humans, so he can help determine where medical intervention needs to happen. *AfterGlow* essentially abstracts his data, and the beautiful spirals at the heart of the piece are generated by code written by boredomresearch based on the code used by Dr. Brock in modeling infectious disease transmission scenarios.

Each party brought to the project their own experience with coding, and discovered through conversation that they work with similar coding environments and algorithms. Having found a common language, they were able to make sense of each other's practice.

boredomresearch honed in on the unknown elements that Dr. Brock faces in modeling data. They were interested in how they as artists could give visual form to something unseen, to explore the unknown in a creative fashion. In addition, a mutual interest in landscape, and discussions around satellite imagery and the drones used in Dr. Brock's research, brought the artists to the idea of creating an ever-evolving malaria transmission scenario in which the viewer is led around by a virtual camera traversing an island landscape. Patterns emerge as the infection spreads across the terrain, with the trail of infection left by the mosquitos presented as glowing trails of light, as the artists make the invisible visible.

Dr. Brock was pleased that boredomresearch chose to imagine his data in 3D, as spatial variation is an area that has been discussed in epidemiology modeling, but

---

7 "Meet the Scientist interviews," Vimeo videos, uploaded by Animate Projects, https://vimeo.com/album/3701273 (accessed June 20, 2018).

8 Bentley Crudgington and Gillian Pearson, "Silent Signal Science Guide," Silent Signal website, https://www.silentsignal.org/science-guide (accessed June 20, 2018).

9 boredomresearch, https://boredomresearch.net/wp/portfolio/afterglow/ (accessed June 20, 2018).

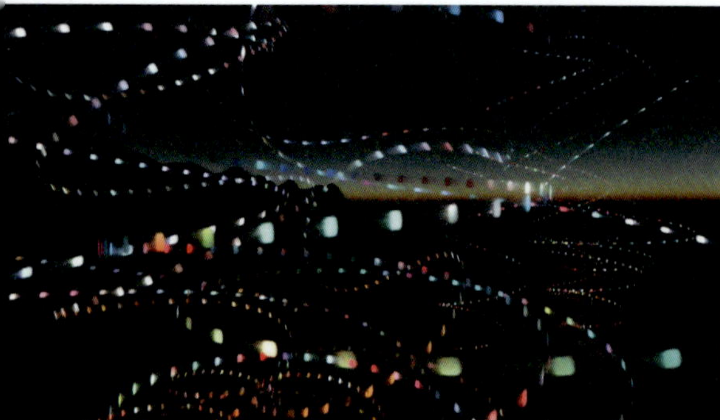

Figure 1: *Afterglow*, Credit: boredomresearch, courtesy of Animate Projects.

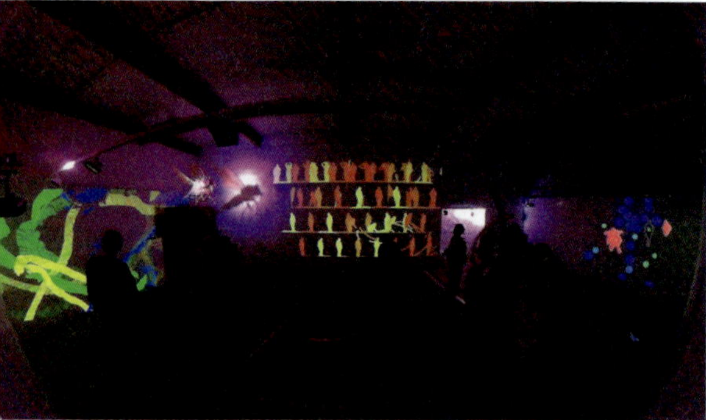

Figure 2: *Battle of Blister*, Credit: Genetic Moo, courtesy of Animate Projects.

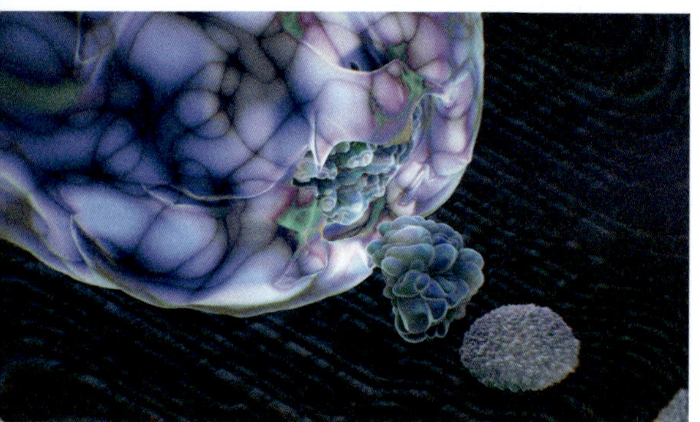

Figure 3: *Immunecraft*, Credit: Eric Schockmel, courtesy of Animate Projects.

at that time had not yet found its way into the models that Dr. Brock and his colleagues employ. He also appreciated that the piece did not attempt to visualize his modeling data, or provide results, but instead used an aesthetic approach to give visual expression to his complex research.

The island created by the artists is based on the Banggi Island in Malaysia where Dr. Brock was carrying out field research. Banggi is a very flat island, so boredomresearch brought a height map of the island into the game engine and then added their own mountains to the piece to create a more visually appealing environment. Dr. Brock was initially a bit shocked by this manipulation of the terrain, but upon reflection he saw its similarity to the way researchers scale variables so they are easier to understand.

In Dr. Brock's work he has to hypothesize how scenarios might play out, and he has to think creatively about how real scenarios could evolve. Before this project he had not considered how creative his work is; it was only through participating in this interdisciplinary project and having conversations with the artists that he perceived his way of working in a new light.[10]

Battle of Blister

In a similar vein to *AfterGlow* (and to *Immunecraft* which will be discussed later) is *Battle of Blister*,[11] where we also witness how infection spreads and how the resolution could either end in infection or recovery, success or defeat.

Battle of Blister by artistic duo Genetic Moo (Nicola Schauerman and Tim Pickup) is a film that explores innate immune response through the blister model that Dr. Neil Dufton uses in his research. Dr. Dufton, Research Associate, National Heart & Lung Institute, Imperial College London, looks at individual cells to learn how and why disease is spread, and how cells might be mobilized to fight disease. This research inspires the narrative and the structure of the film, which explores the complex processes that happen inside a blister caused by an insect bite. The artists and scientist worked together on how best to artistically represent the different stages of the immune response, often sharing drawings with one another that created the storyboard for the film.

10 Dr. Paddy Brock, "Understanding Monkey to Human Malaria Transmission," Cambridge Core Blog, March 9, 2016 https://blog.journals.cambridge.org/2016/03/09/understanding-monkey-to-human-malaria-transmission (accessed June 20, 2018).
11 *Battle of Blister*. Genetic Moo, 2016, Silent Signal website, https://www.silentsignal.org/Collaborations/battle-of-blister (accessed June 20, 2018).

The blister was chosen to be the focus of the film as it is a fundamental model in immunology research, and is also an injury that most people can relate to. However, Genetic Moo, who are known for their vibrant immersive installations, have taken this seemingly simple condition and created a "fantastic voyage" into the inflammation process.

Both the scientist and the artists use imaging technology, and while they are looking at the same process in this project, much in the same way that boredomresearch and Dr. Brock found a parity with the computer programs they employed, they are ultimately producing very different outputs.

The artists Genetic Moo work primarily in interactive art, where they engage people to experiment and play. They saw that the cascades of information being passed from cell to cell inside a blister had a similarity with the cascades they brought in their own work. They were keen to represent the drama going on inside our bodies physically, bringing real performance into the piece, with performers working together to represent how the different cells work together to battle disease. *Battle of Blister* is made up of several performances captured in the artists' interactive workshops, the "Blister Cinema." They are performed by acrobats, dancers, actors, scientists and children, who are all experimenting with movement and with props. The performers were given gentle direction as to the different stages of the inflammation process they should try to represent, but were able to bring their own interpretations to the work. Their performances were captured through a Kinect sensor into a program designed by the artists, and from there the animated avatars were selected to represent different stages, layered and edited together to make the final work.

Dr. Dufton was surprised by the parallel between the experimentation that is at the heart of Genetic Moo's art creations and the experimentation in his scientific research. He saw it as both model scenarios, setting parameters and seeing how variables affect the outcome, but where Dr. Dufton might be deleting a gene, Genetic Moo might be allowing performers to generate their own individual interpretations. Alongside each *Silent Signal* exhibition, Genetic Moo and Dr. Dufton have led interactive public workshops, allowing anyone to take part in the battle between bacteria and immune cells and learn a bit about their bodies at the same time.

Immunecraft

Another film that explores the immune response is *Immunecraft*,[12] where artist Eric Schockmel has created a trailer for a fictional, futuristic video game, where users are able to control real cell cultures. The work combines gameplay functionality with immunology, where the abilities and roles that the different cells in the immune system have are translated to the functions of a game: the player's base could be likened to the spleen or the lymph nodes that send out the "soldier cells" around the body to deal with invading pathogens, and the upgrades available in the game mimicking the immunological memory function where cells learn from their environment and become better at fighting pathogens. (Owing to budgetary constraints the work was realized as a single-screen piece rather than an interactive game.)

In order to make the research relatable to a non-scientific, young audience, the artist decided to speak in the language of gamers, sci-fi and popular culture. He references multiplayer games *World of Warcraft* and *Minecraft* in the choice of title, and chose to make the language and visuals playful, while at the same time creating interest in the underlying scientific research. At one of the *Silent Signal* events a young man in the audience raised his hand and commented on his experience of the film, saying that when he played video games from now on it would remind him about the combat going on in his immune system.

All of the gameplay functions presented in the film were developed through conversations between the artist and his scientist partner Dr. Megan MacLeod, Research Fellow, Institute of Infection, Immunity and Inflammation, University of Glasgow, while again trying to find a common language. Together they worked on uniting gaming terminology and immunology concepts in the language used in the film. Dr. MacLeod found it interesting to compare how they work with imaging technology: whereas the artist can generate and manipulate the imagery in the software, the cell imagery the software generates for her can only be employed for the analysis of data in order to inspire further questions.

The cells were designed so as to appear organic, but were not intended to be direct replicas of the cells that inspired them. Dr. MacLeod was particularly pleased that through Eric's design experiments, he produced

---

12 *Immunecraft*. Eric Schockmel, 2016, Silent Signal website, https://www.silentsignal.org/Collaborations/immunecraft (accessed June 20, 2018).

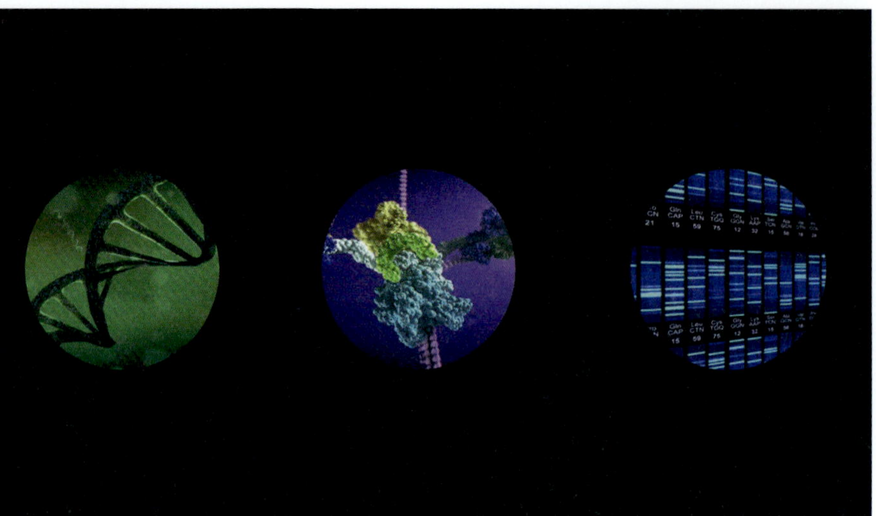

Figure 4: *The Signal and the Noise*, Credit: Charlie Tweed, courtesy of Animate Projects.

a texture and a movement that reminded her of the way the receptors, the proteins on the surface of a cell, behave, which was a visual representation that Dr. MacLeod had not experienced in scientific animations that she uses in her research.

Dr. MacLeod's research focuses on the auto-immune disease rheumatoid arthritis. In her research, Dr. MacLeod tries to understand why the T cells in our body can sometimes go awry, and instead of protecting us, they tell cells to attack healthy tissue. This idea is presented in the film through one of the key characters, the "zombie" cell that the gamer can deploy to make their opponent's cells go rogue and, like zombies, start attacking the cells in their own team/culture.

At the end of the film it is revealed that the cell cultures that the players are controlling are being kept alive in an artificial environment, similar to a server farm. This bigger picture reveal is included in order to prompt conversation about the future of how our biological information might be used, how our biology may be commodified, and the ethical considerations around this. There is much discussion going on in the scientific community on how cell lines and DNA can be decoded and shared digitally with scientists around the world,[13] and the use of artificial DNA to store data is already being trialed.[14]

The Signal and the Noise

This future facing ethical theme is also explored in *The Signal and the Noise*[15] by artist Charlie Tweed, which is inspired by research undertaken by Dr. Darren Logan, Group Leader at the Wellcome Sanger Institute. Dr. Logan looks to understand through his research which genes influence our behavior. He uses DNA sequencing to discover why some people have certain unusual characteristics, such as rare genetic disorders. The artist found through visiting the Institute, seeing the banks of DNA sequencing machines, and talking in depth to Dr. Logan about his research and the tools he uses, that their mutual interests in technology and the evolution of our machines was key to this project. The artist assembled stock footage of server farmers, computer code, 3D computer generated scientific visualizations, and Dr. Logan's research footage, to question the authenticity of what we are visually presented daily, and to question our relationship with our machines. He chose to mask some of the clips with constructed shapes, in order to create an interface into the "code space," and also to reference ways of looking in research such as microscopy. The voices in the film are of futuristic hybrids—part organic, part machine—a

13 Clive Cookson, "DNA decoding initiative to involve 500,000 middle-aged Britons," *Financial Times*, March 23, 2017. https://www.ft.com/content/9a5c8472-0efc-11e7-a88c-50ba212dce4d (accessed June 20, 2018).

14 Robert F. Service, "DNA could store all of the world's data in one room," *Science*, March 2, 2017. https://www.sciencemag.org/news/2017/03/dna-could-store-all-worlds-data-one-room (accessed 20 June, 2018).

15 Charlie Tweed, *The Signal and the Noise*, 2016, Silent Signal website, https://www.silentsignal.org/Collaborations/the-signal-and-the-noise (accessed June 20, 2018).

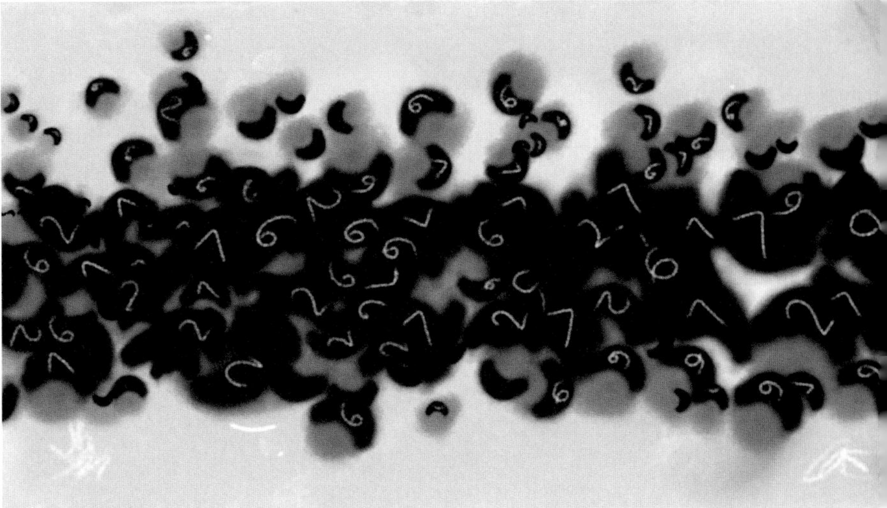

Figure 5: *Loop*, Credit: Samantha Moore, courtesy of Animate Projects.

suggestion of what an advanced, sentient descendent of the current sequencing machines might be. In the film, the narrator talks about its lineage via the discoveries of Turing (computational) and Crick (molecular), the evolution of computers and genetics happening simultaneously. The artist's research into the history of machines and our relationship to them, as well as his interest in the similarities between genetic and computer coding fed into the script, which was developed collaboratively between the artist and the scientist over several months.

The machinic narrator discusses ways to improve the imperfect human, and one it mentions is a gene editing tool called CRISPR Cas9.[16] Over the two years of making the film this tool went from a nascent idea to a tool now widely used by scientists. Something the artist originally chose to include as a futuristic sounding technology became something very real, very quickly. By looking at this "hybrid machine" future scenario, *The Signal and the Noise* shines a light on ethical concerns that are prescient today. Particularly around how our genetic code may be accessed and edited in the future, who should have control of this technology, and that the idea of hybrid computing[17] might also one day move from the realm of science fiction to reality, as science continues to advance at a rapid rate.

Loop

Humanizing scientists working on cutting-edge research is one of the aims of *Loop*,[18] by Samantha Moore, a maker of animated documentaries. The focus of the film shifted over time from the research to the perspectives of scientists working in the lab. Her partner on the project, Dr. Serge Mostowy, Research Fellow, MRC Centre of Molecular Bacteriology and Infection, Imperial College London, with his team, is looking at septin cage assembly, trying to discover new ways to control the bacterial infection process happening at a cellular level, using the zebrafish model to do so. The artist approached the lab team by first introducing her work through an animation workshop with the scientists in the lab, before she began interrogating the researchers about their work.

Faced with the complexity of the scientific field, the artist became interested in the way that each team member spoke about their research, and how it betrayed a subjectivity that is rarely presented when scientists are represented or quoted in the media. The imagery in the film is based on the drawings made by the scientists while they were explaining what septin cage assembly entails to the artist during lab visits. As a visual artist it made sense to ask each of the lab members to make explanatory drawings of their

---

16 What is CRISPR-Cas9?, *yourgenome*, https://www.yourgenome.org/facts/what-is-crispr-cas9 (accessed June 20, 2018).

17 Sharon Gaudin, "DARPA: We're on cusp of merging human and machine," *Computerworld*, February 13, 2017. https://www.computerworld.com/article/3168840/artificial-intelligence/darpa-we-re-on-cusp-of-merging-human-and-machine.html (accessed June 20, 2018).

18 Samantha Moore, *Loop*, 2016, Silent Signal website, https://www.silentsignal.org/Collaborations/loop (accessed June 20, 2018).

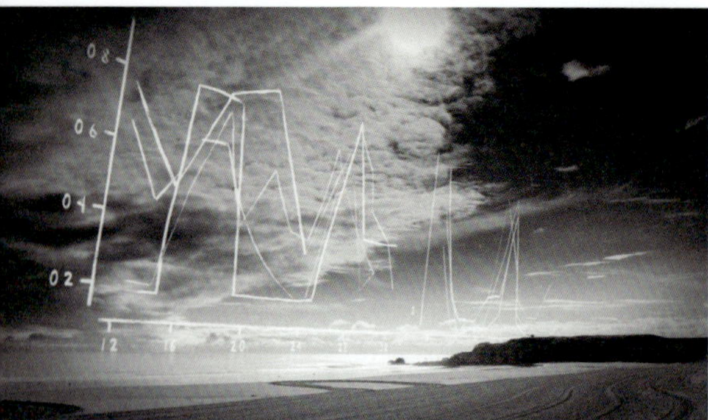

Figure 7: *Sleepless*, Credit: Ellie Land, courtesy of Animate Projects.

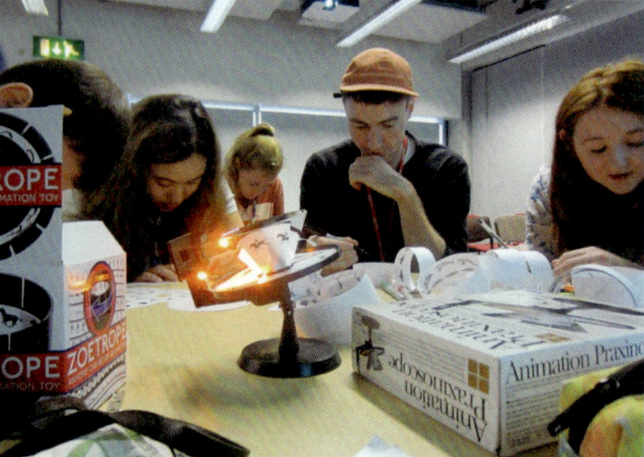

Figure 8: Zoetrope workshop with the Mostowy Lab team, Credit: Samantha Moore, courtesy Animate Projects.

complex scientific ideas. And through this process the artist was amazed at how varied each scientist's interpretation was of the research area. The sketches benefitted the scientists as much as the artist, as they were able to see for the first time how each person visualized and understood the process, and Dr. Mostowy was able to discover where some younger members of his team may need to review their understanding of the science. The artist used the scientists' drawings as the basis for the 2D animated sequences of the film, so that coupled with their voices, which make up the audio track of the film, the viewer is presented with a version of the science that is authentic to the individual speaking. With one researcher the artist chose to use stop motion to bring to life what felt like a very 3-dimensional view of the process that the researcher described, as she felt this was the best medium to present his interpretation of what happens when the septin proteins join together.

Loop also demonstrates how science is a constantly evolving process. In the film the artist captures the moment when a new scientific discovery occurs. The artist chose to keep this breakthrough moment in the film, showing a necessary revision to her animation, to highlight the point at which the scientists had to revise the way they viewed the assembly process and adapt their ideas to take the research forward.

Dr. Mostowy felt that his role on the film was to keep the science responsible, while at the same time putting his faith in the way the artist represented their research. Both he and the team found it inspiring to have the artist in the lab, enabling them to think about how to convey their work in new ways. And as with the other projects, integrating continuous feedback from the scientific contributors ensured that the scientists were happy with how their voice, their ideas, and their research were being portrayed.

The artist was once again interested in the opportunity to make visible the invisible, the unseen, the unknown. The jellybean image in the film references a well-known scientific illustration of the septin cage assembly process that scientists working in this field would recognize. But from talking to the researchers, and what is captured in the film, it is evident that there is another side to this jellybean—only no one yet knows what happens there, so it is left out of illustrations. And this was something that fascinated the artist and that she felt she had to acknowledge it in the film. However, who knows how long before this unknown will be identified and science will once more move on?

Sleepless

Another relatively new area of science explored in the *Silent Signal* project is sleep science. The film *Sleepless*,[19] by animated documentary maker Ellie Land, is based on the research being conducted by Professor Peter Oliver, Associate Professor of Neuroscience, Department of Physiology, Anatomy and Genetics, University of Oxford. Professor Oliver primarily studies the mechanisms in the brain that control sleep and the circadian rhythms that control our daily lives. According to Professor Oliver, sleep disturbance is a common feature of many neurological disorders, of degenerative diseases such as Alzheimer, autism, and psychiatric disease such as schizophrenia.

Throughout the film a wave travels across the screen signifying the circadian rhythms going on inside our bodies, based on the scientist's explanatory draw-

---

19 Ellie Land, *Sleepless*, 2016, *Silent Signal* website, https://www.silentsignal.org/Collaborations/sleepless (accessed June 20, 2018).

ings. In the film its rhythm becomes disrupted, as does the audio, as the participants speak about their problems sleeping and how it affects their lives. Professor Oliver's gene expression profiling graphs have been woven into the visuals. (These graphs present a global picture of cellular function by analyzing the patterns of thousands of genes.) In this way the viewer is conscious of the research that underpins the research without the complexities being directly explained by a scientist.

Light is a key element in the film, as it is in our circadian biology, where the suprachiasmatic nucleus in the brain that is our internal clock reacts to light and sends out signals for the rest of the body to react to. In reflecting this there are many references to light and dark, day and night throughout the film, including time lapse footage of the shadows cast by the sun's movement over the course of a day.

Through conversations between the artist, the scientist, and a group of mental health service users, the narrative for the film was created around accounts of good and bad sleep, with four of the contributors interviewed to provide the voiceovers in the film. For Professor Oliver, working with real subjects was a valuable experience, as his research takes place in the lab, and does not involve speaking with patients directly. For the artist to be able to collaborate with participants who gave feedback on their voiceover and the animation throughout the process was key to producing a truly collaborative piece.

The first person you hear speaking in the film became really engaged with the science after meeting the scientist, and was keen to learn more about what was going on inside his body. So it made sense to the artist that he should be the spokesperson for the science, and communicate it in his own words. This also avoided presenting a hierarchical perspective, setting up the viewpoint of the authoritative scientist in contrast with the more subjective viewpoints of the contributors. As with all six films, the desire is to make the film engaging to a non-scientist viewer, and to present an alternate response to the science.

Through the process of developing and producing *Silent Signal* it has been a joy to be involved in conversations between artists and scientists, particularly in group meet ups where the collaborators have been able to give feedback, to challenge, and to offer advice to one another. It will be interesting to revisit these films in a few years' time to see how the ideas being explored have evolved, and there are plans to revisit at least one film five years down the line.

The key to the success of the project was the truly collaborative nature of the partnerships on each project. The scientists who chose to apply to be part of this project all fully embraced the experience, were generous with their time, willing to talk extensively about their work, and keen to be involved in the creative aspects: assisting with scripts, taking part in performances, and even in one case making the music (Professor Oliver made the soundtrack to *Sleepless*). For the artists, being able to work with collaborators from outside their field enabled them to open up their practice and research into areas they might not otherwise have considered. For some it was the first time they had worked in this way, and it has since inspired other collaborative interdisciplinary projects.

More information about each project, including interviews with the contributing artists and scientists, and articles by external artists and scientists, can be found on the project's website silentsignal.org.[20]

---

20 Silent Signal website, https://www.silentsignal.org/ (accessed June 20, 2018).

Ina Conradi (SG/US) | Mark Chavez (US)

Bringing Art to Everyday: Media Art Nexus NTU Singapore in Review 2016–2018

Introduction

"As our cities become more like screens, and we start to expect the same from them as we do from our smart phones, these sites must be treated as a public good and as exhibition spaces for public art that can educate, delight, and challenge our changing identities and cultural practices."[1]

Media architecture, projection mapping, urban screens, and other permanent or temporary interactive media installations support greater community connection between people in their shared public spaces through a field of the interdisciplinary digital place-making.[2]

Media architecture is creating environments for synergy of various disciplines with art practice, influencing city development, creative technologies, and science.[3]

Media Art Nexus (MAN) at Nanyang Technological University (NTU) is the first established noncommercial urban media art platform of its kind in Singapore in that it is dedicated to exclusively showing artistic content. The large public art installation consists of an ultrawide format digital LED screen that measures fifteen by two meters. It is a platform that uses digital animation technology as a medium, showcasing computationally generated artworks along with illustrated and painted animation design (see fig. 1).[4] The large and immersive installation placed in a much-trafficked area by the public at large as well as faculty, students, and other guests of the university viewing the works. In this way, Media Art Nexus (MAN) is an important academic linkage to an artistic practice within the broader field of public art installation.

Art academics often seek modes of teaching and research that integrate topics explored in other disciplines and that investigate artistic ideas that are socially engaging.[5] This project explores the impact of a public media art platform within the university in

---

1 Dave Colangelo, "Urban Media Art: New Directions for Public Art and Cities," www.TheArtfulCity.org (blog), September 15, 2016, https://www.theartfulcity.org/home/2016/9/16/gufjhn9g0hjgwg7bpsgyt23lwula9x (accessed October 3, 2018).

2 Glenn Harding, "What is Digital Peacemaking?" www.urbanscreens.tv (website), February 11, 2011, https://www.urbanscreens.tv/ (accessed October 3, 2018).

3 Susa Pop, "Open Call, Urban Media Art Academy Bangkok, What Urban Media Art Can Do—Why When Where and How, Goethe-Institut Thailand, Jim Thompson House & Bangkok Art and Culture Centre," www. Goethe.de (website), April 1, 2016, https://www.goethe.de/resources/files/pdf120/en_urban-media-art-academy_workshop-call.pdf (accessed December 8, 2018).

4 Ina Conradi and Mark Chavez, "About Media Art Nexus," www.Media Art Nexus (website), July 28, 2017, https://mediaartnexus.com/ (accessed October 3, 2018).

5 Daniel Latorrie and Glenn Harding, "Digital Peacemaking After 6 years: Defining an Emerging Practice," Media Architecture Compendium: Digital Placemaking, edited by Luke Hespanhol, et al., (Stuttgart, 2017), p. 172.

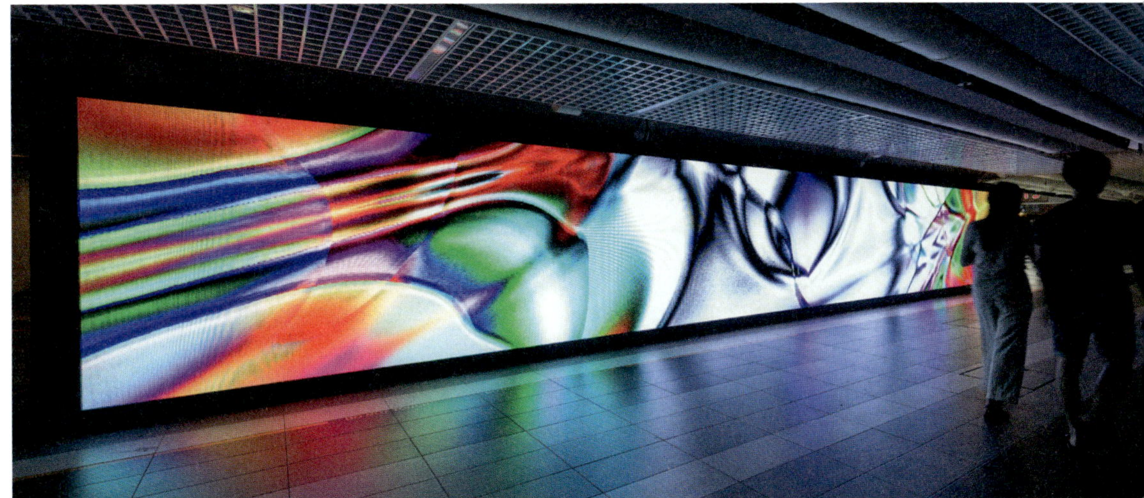

Figure 1: *The Crepuscular Rays of the Moon* by Mark Chavez, playing on a Media Art Nexus LED 15 x 9m, NTU Singapore, Photo Credit: Quek Jia. Liang.

Singapore. We investigate the possibilities and challenges of building community engagement in such transient public spaces. Nanyang Technological University Singapore is the home to a cluster of knowledge as it hosts several colleges devoted to the hard sciences, engineering, humanities, social sciences, and the arts. MAN is the first art installation of its kind on campus that prototypes a rich field experimental media art outside of the classroom walls and traditional gallery spaces. Supported as a public art installation by NTU Singapore Museum, MAN does not have to rely on advertising to earn revenue for maintenance and hardware. Beyond the LED screen alone, MAN brings together a group of student artists who work together to exhibit their artistic ideas. The aim is to promote new media art locally as well as curate internationally-produced media art on this platform. Artists are encouraged to produce work that is more daring, experimental, and cutting edge than traditional outlets for motion-based arts. With the unusual screen and platform, artists are encouraged to express their creative vision without the limitations placed on standard media creation. As a result of this convergence, experimental hybrid methods for animation in Singapore are flourishing.

The Beginning

NTU (Nanyang Technological University) Museum, Singapore, does not have a permanent building. Rather, it is "housed" of public art projects on the NTU Singapore campus. In collaboration with the School of Art, Design and Media (ADM) and Energy Research Institute (ERI@N), the NTU Museum also started a

Renewable Energy Public Art Collection—a collection that is unique to the NTU Museum and not available in other museums in Singapore. The Museum launched an Art on Campus Initiative in 2014 and invited artists to propose memorable and visually bold artwork as focal points for various cite specific locations on campus.

Media Art Nexus was proposed in October of 2015 as a permanent art installation that would be inclusive of the artistic, engineering, and design strengths of the university. The aim of the installation was to bring new media art to 40,000 residents on campus. To ensure the best use of technology and practices, such as benefits for students and other members of the campus community, the following objectives were considered:

- An exclusively artistic installation would integrate works done by students and local and international artists.
- The venue would expand into a curatorial platform for engaging with other universities, cultural institutions, media centers, and new media artists through symposia, exhibitions, and workshops.
- The platform should be easily maintained.

The installation was imagined on a monumental in scale and was planned as a major art installation on the main campus's North Spine Plaza. By the end of the 2015, numerous proposals were considered such as using a flexible OLED form to create multiple sculptural shapes that form an obelisk (see fig. 2). The torqued obelisk would have an ability to reconfigure to form multiple pre-designed shapes. A "walk-inside"

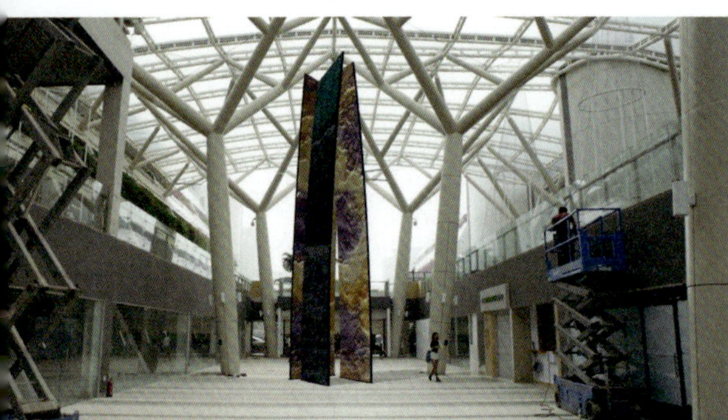

Figure 2: View of the virtual proposal for LED sculpture. Photo Credit: Mark Chavez.

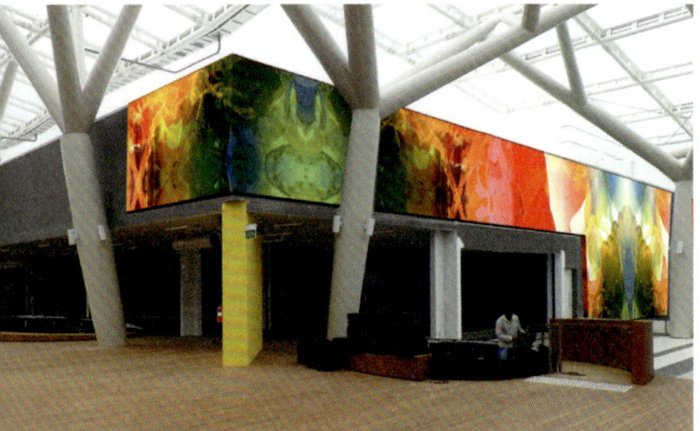

Figure 3: View of virtual proposal for LED marquee. Photo Credit: Mark Chavez.

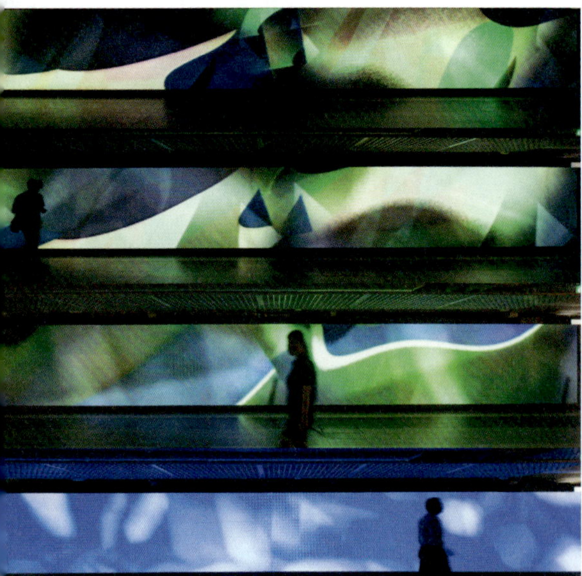

Figure 4: *Emote* by Mark Chavez, MAN. Photo Credit: Q. J. Liang.

space would allow the viewer to engage with the inte grated animated artwork. The second proposal was a tall architectural marquee, (see fig. 3) that would envelope the building above the pedestrian walkway. In August 2016, NTU Singapore Museum approved the final design for a fifteen by two-meter LED screen horizontally oriented along a covered passageway on campus. Its human scale and resulting immersive interaction quickly brought new meaning to the hallway. Since then, MAN's three aims are at the core of its creative mission:

- To co-create concepts and prototypes for urban media artworks locally and internationally.
- To disseminate art content via co-curatorial partnerships between local and international new media institutions, events, labs, and museums.
- To bridge the gap between the formal arts education and academic research programs in the field of art, design, technology, and science on NTU campus.

Art Works Compendium

The number of exhibition opportunities for young emerging artists in Singapore remains quite small. While there have been increasingly more chances for works imported by contemporary international artists to be exhibited, the work of young local artists is still unfortunately undervalued by the Singaporean art world compared to the work of international artists of similar career statuses. Very broadly, this is characteristic of many galleries in Singapore, where it is a risk to promote works from developing artists. For an emerging artist, it is almost impossible to have a venue to show artwork publicly and to be endorsed by the local art scene. For that reason, MAN's main goal is to provide artists the space to experiment and exhibit, allowing them to create artworks that are unique. These works in their unique setting distinguish the artists' portfolios from those of their contemporaries. Artists can test and evaluate art they have produced not only on a semesteral basis alongside other peers but also internationally and alongside established artists. MAN has featured more than 400 artworks done by the community including students and local and international artists and played 3640 hours of original content per year since installation. The work has been showcased at prestigious international venues such as Deep Space 8K at the Ars Electronica Center, the CUBE QUT at the Queensland University of Technology Brisbane, the EPI Center (Expanded Perception & Interaction Centre) at the University New South Wales, the UTV's Federation Square Melbourne, the SG:IO Tokyo, and the Fourteenth Integrated Systems Europe Convention (ISE) Amsterdam.

Experimental Animation

The format of MAN was inclusive to a variety of media from animation, film, and interactive media works. MAN co-organized and curated works coming from joint research with schools at NTU Singapore.

Emote (2017–2018)

The outward goals of science and art seemingly clash: while science is used to extract general rules or principles about the world, art is by its very nature subjective, designed to portray the individual experience and demonstrate what is universal.[6] The following works attempt to investigate artistic and scientific ideas bringing together the disciplines of art and science. Specifically, the *Emote* project brings together aesthetics and neuroscience into the emerging field of neuroesthetics (see fig. 4). Artists working on content for MAN find these new phenomena worth exploring within the context of the artistic educational practice and interdisciplinary environment at NTU Singapore. For the last few years, professors from three different colleges[7] at NTU Singapore have been working on research that combines the arts with neuroscience, creating an artistic interpretation of emotions. Audio reactive music and visuals use technology to evoke emotions.

Emote (2017)[8] is about feelings, brain-waves and real-time experimental audio reactive animation. Using EEG, the brain signals are recorded and analyzed, matching emotional patterns to music. Researchers at the School of Computer Science and Engineering (SCSE) and at the Centre for Research and Development in Learning (CRADLE NTU) using EEG signal analysis confirmed that these twenty musical clips elicited specific emotional responses (happy, exciting, frightening, melancholic) in a sample audience. Artists used the resultant twenty classified music clips to aid in

the generation of audio reactive animation. Emotional states in the brain manifest particular EEG signals. Using machine-learning techniques researchers analyze these patterns and tag them to emotions.[9][10] This analysis can then be used as goalposts for emotion recognition, replicated to generate external stimuli that elicit a desired emotional response. Animated visuals where completed for this project using the Derivative TouchDesigner's reactive audio tool-set.[11] They were numbered and titled one to twenty in sets designed to elicit happy, exciting, frightening, and melancholic emotional responses. In the testing part, (see fig. 5 and fig. 6) a graphic and a music clip related to the recognized emotion are selected and played to the subject. An EEG recording of their neurofeedback

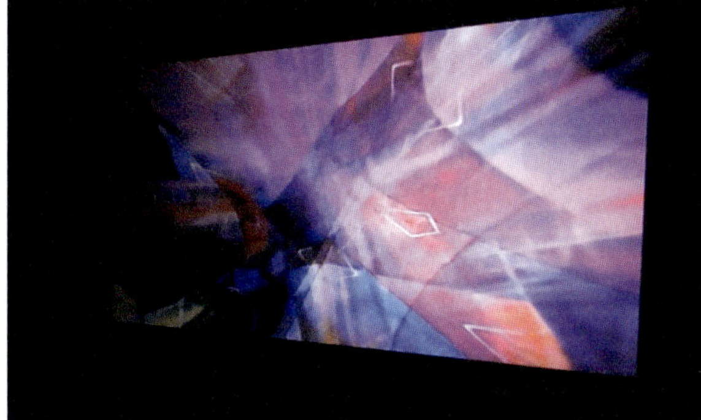

Figure 5: Emote screening during EEG.

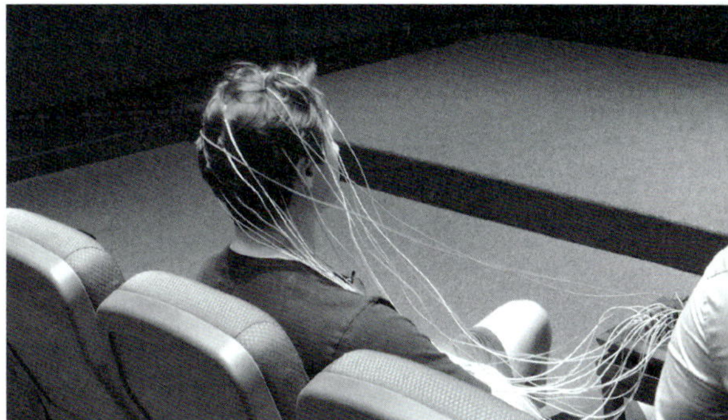

Figure 6: EEG testing. Photo Credit: Ana Chavez.

---

6 Indre V. Viskontas and Suzee E. Lee, "The creation of art on the setting of dementia." *Art, Aesthetics, and the Brain*, edited by M. N. Joseph P. Huston et al., (Oxford, 2015), p. 357.

7 Ina Conradi, School of Art, Design and Media, Annabel Chen, Psychology NTU SINGAPORE School of Social Sciences (SSS), Quek Hiok Chai NTU SINGAPORE School of Computer Science and Engineering, College of Engineering (SCSE).

8 *Emote*. Directed by Mark Chavez, 2017.

9 Sander Koelstra et al., "DEAP: A Database for Emotion Analysis Using Physiological Signals," *IEEE Transactions on Affective Computing*, 2012. Vol. 3(1).

10 Panagiotis C. Petrantonakis et al., "Emotion recognition from EEG using higher order crossings," *IEEE Transactions on Information Technology in Biomedicine* 2010. 14 (2), p. 186.

11 Mark Chavez," Emote Portfolio," www.vimeo.com (website), December 15, 2004 https://vimeopro.com/mchavez/emoteportfolio (accessed October 3, 2018).

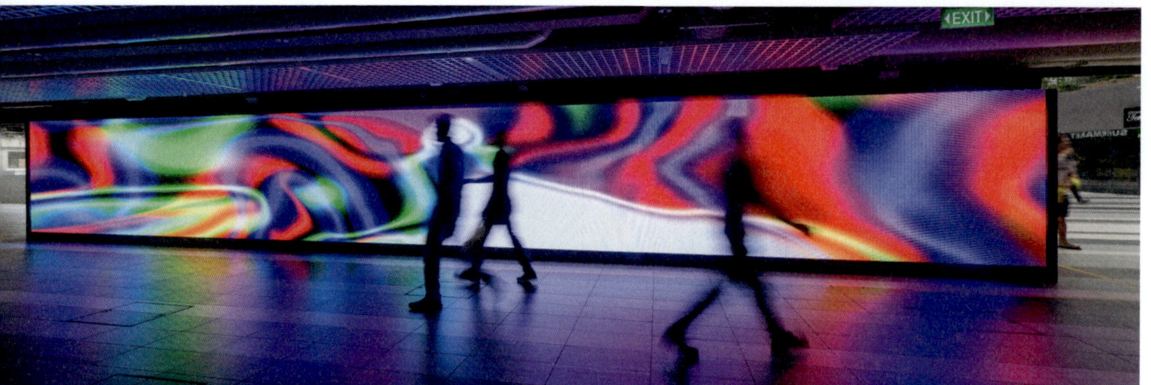

Figure 7: *The Rose* from a series of real-time animation playing on Media Art Nexus Singapore. Photo Credit: Q. J. Liang.

tries to ascertain the subject's emotional state. Then the resulting data is classified and analyzed. The goal of these studies is to create public arts that induce emotional states that help the subject in cognitive functions such as learning, concentration, relaxation, et cetera.

Experimental Series Animated in Real-Time

A permanent exhibition of experimental animation on display daily at the Media Art Nexus consists of a series of six experimental pieces[12] made with audio reactive real-time animation software. *The Rose* was programmed as an animated pin-screen using Claude Debussy's "Clair de Lune" to create an audio reactive painting (see fig. 7 and 8).

Quantonium is audio reactive piece and plays with the idea of mechanical reflections on matter and space. *I wish* (2016) uses Twitter and the search term "I wish", to explore the intimacy of personal commentary through the poetics of social media phenomenon. *NTU Beat* (2016) and *Spheres Visions* (2016) are both responses to sound, the viewer's motion, and colors in

an environment.[13] MAN has exhibited these series of animation locally, in Singapore and internationally.[14] MAN was one of 13 Singaporean (SG) and Japanese (JP) leading contemporary creative talents from performing disciplines and visual arts that took part in the 2017 edition of *Singapore: Inside Out Tokyo* (SG:IO from August 25–27, 2017), organized by the Singapore Tourism Board (STB), in conjunction with the launch of Singapore's new destination brand–*Passion Made Possible*–in Tokyo. *The Crepuscular Rays of the Moon*[15] was created in collaboration with Singaporean fashion designer Josiah Chua and his 2018 capsule collection, titled Hikari (See Fig. 1). The SGIO Tokyo event, at the Bank Gallery, Omotesando district of Tokyo, drew an audience of about 2,000 on the first day of its opening. Joining them were more than 200 key members of the creative trade and media communities.

Supernatural

From 2016 until the end of 2017, MAN organized and integrated seven exhibitions by more than 355 students.[16] Design courses such as *Media Art Nexus* and

---

12 *Series Animated in Real-Time.* Directed by Mark Chavez, 2016.

13 Ina Conradi and Mark Chavez, "Experimental Animation," Media Art Nexus (website), July 28, 2017, https://mediaartnexus.com/ (accessed October 3, 2018).

14 The following is the list of the exhibitions: [1] Exhibition titled *The Double-Slit Experiment*, Conradi Ina+ Mark Chavez, exhibition held at the UCLA Art|Sci Center Gallery, UCLA California NanoSystems Institute (CNSI), Los Angeles, July 19, 2018. [2] Art work titled *The Twelve States of Zodiac* part of the exhibition HOX ZODIAC, Victoria Vesna & Siddharth Ramakrishnan & Marisa Caichiolo, held at the Building Bridges Art Exchange, Bergamot Santa Monica, May 26, 2018. [3] Conference *Visualisation Matters 2017 - Art + Science + Design + Engineering*, held in conjunction with exhibition titled *ON|OFF 100101010 Sydney, Colliding and Surrendering Art Meets Tech*, held at the Expanded Perception and Interaction Centre, (EPICentre), UNSW, November 21–22, 2017. [4] Event titled *An International Symposium and Exhibition ON|OFF 100101010 Singapore*, held at the Media Art Nexus and School of Art, Design and Media at the Nanyang Technological University Singapore, October 11–13, 2017. [5] Exhibition titled *Web3D Art Gallery*, held as part of the WEB 3D 2017, 22nd International Conference, held at the CUBE QUT, Brisbane, June 5–7, 2017. [6] Art Work titled *Emote*, part of permanent collection on Media Art Nexus NTU Singapore, premiered March 01–31, 2017. [7] Premier of *Media Wall Nexus*, at the Deep Space 8K, Ars Electronica Festival 2016, Linz, September 8-12, 2016.

15 *The Crepuscular Rays of the Moon.* Directed and Animated by Mark Chavez, 2017.

16 The following is the list of the seven exhibitions: [1] Exhibition titled *Supernatural-The 7th Month*, with 18 works premiering, November 24–December 1, 2017. [2] Exhibition titled *Beyond the Seas*, with 16 works premiering, November 24–December 12, 2017. [3] *Digital*

Pattern, Art, Design, and Architecture supported students with the conceptual basis and technical insights for the development of one of a kind time-based media. Resulting experimental media such as animation, motion graphics, real time animation and interactive animated works gained international recognition.[17] *Supernatural*[18] offers an overview of emerging talent from these courses. Fantastical myths are the main subject of this series of 144 artworks. Work selected range from Chinese traditional storytelling, history, folklore, and legends from *The Classic of Mountains and Seas* (2015–16), stories of the Southeast Asia Hungry Ghost Festival, (2012–14), Nature and Darwinism (2015), and Daydreaming (2016). MAN team combined and programmed art works into a spectacular digital tapestry for sixteen-meter-wide and nine-meter-high 8K projection in Ars Electronica Center Deep Space (See fig. 9). The digital canvas allowed for a wealth of compositional possibilities in weaving images together. The majestic scale of the Ars Electronica Deep Space 8K enabled audiences to immerse themselves in ancient myths of Southeast Asia and China. The Ars Electronica Festival attracted more than 85,000 visitors to the 2016 festival alone. Media Art Nexus was displaying for the entire duration of the festival alongside giants in the field of new media.[19]

Collaboration

The curating for urban media art makes social and virtual borders disappear. The following collaborations are providing fresh insight into issues of joint curatorial efforts between different locations. These initiatives thrive "on the idea of networking context"[20] which is "enabling art exchange between diverse communities remotely and in real time".[21] These international urban media projects aim to build a sense of community beyond physical space, using art to develop bridge between "social, cultural, and technical differences".[22]

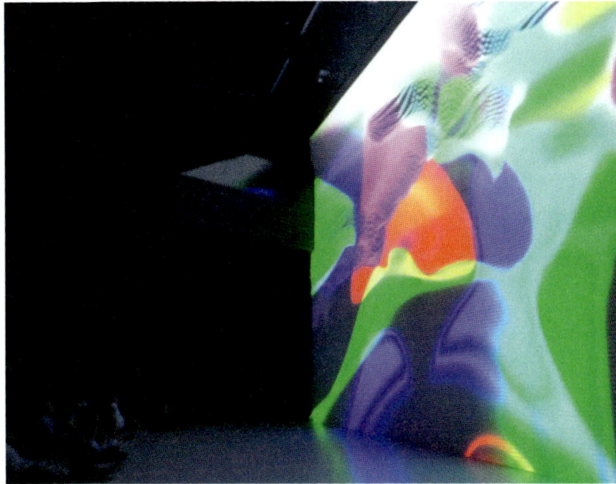

Figure 8: *The Rose* premier at the Deep Space 8k Ars Electronica 2016. Photo Credit: Mark Chavez.

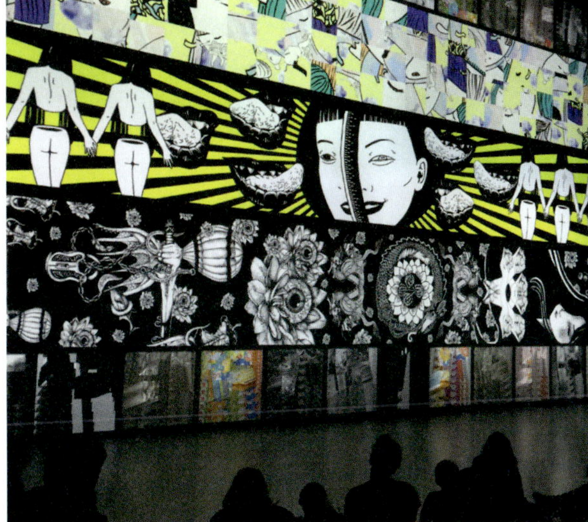

Figure 9: *Supernatural* premier at the Deep Space 8K, Ars Electronica 2016. Photo Credit: Florian Voggeneder.

Murals: dataspaces+ +illusion + play, with 19 works premiering, April 25–May 24, 2017. [4] Exhibition titled *Advice from Caterpillar –Fantastical Fairy Tales*, with 19 works premiering, April 25–May 24, 2017. [5] Exhibition titled *Movie Quotes*, with 673 works by 168 students premiering, January 9–31, 2017. [6] Exhibition titled *Echoes of The City*, premiering 17 works done in collaborated with NTU LKC Medicine, November 18, 2016–January 31, 2017. [7] Exhibition titled *Abstract Thinker*. Works by Ivan Yew, 1.07-17.11.2016

17 Two projects in 2017 have been recognized: [1] *Mapping the Invisible: Transforming Singapore Urban Data into Art through Effective Color Palettes*, directed by Goh Shuhui, was a semifinalists for Adobe Design Achievement Awards, 2017. [2] *The Creature*. Directed by Longfei Zhang, 2017, received *Motion Awards by Motionographer* in category Short Form Experimental.

18 Supernatural, 144 artworks by 98 students premiering, NTU Singapore, School of Art, Design and Media (ADM), class of Pattern, Art, Design and Media. August, 1- September 2016.

19 Ars Electronica 2016, "Exhibition Programme Deep Space 8K, RADICAL ATOMS and the alchemists of our time," ARSELECTRONICA. ART (website), August 01, 2016, https://www.aec.at/radicalatoms/en/deep-space-8k-media-wall-nexus/ (accessed December 29, 2018).

20 Mark Wright, "Collective Curatorial Statement," in What Urban Media Art Can Do: Why When Where and How?, edited by Susa Pop at al., (Stuttgart, 2016), p. 48.

21 Ibid, p. 48.

22 Ibid, p. 48.

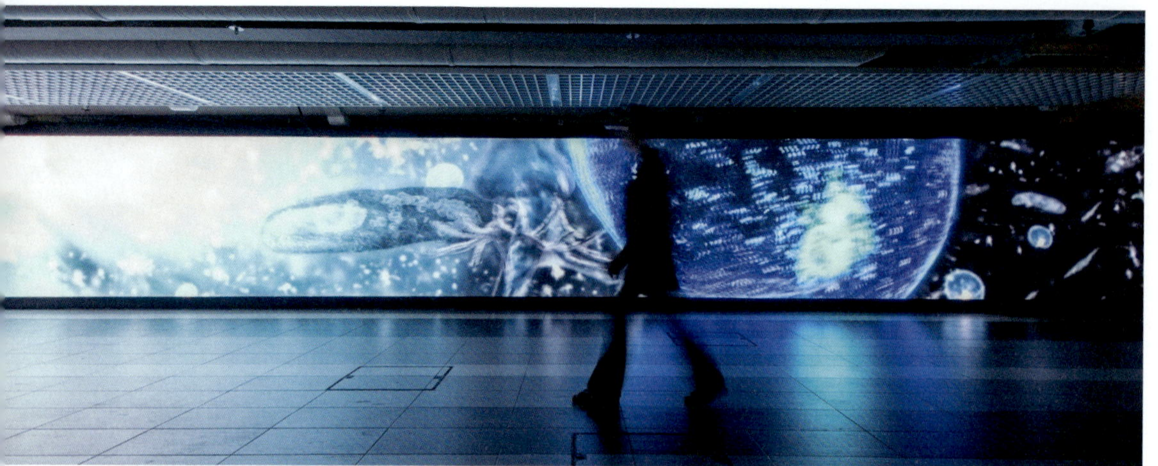

Figure 10: *Noise Aquarium* by Victoria Vesna, one of the highlights of the exhibition On|Off 100101010, playing at the Media Art Nexus NTU Singapore. Photo Credit: Quek Jia Liang.

On|Off 100101010: Colliding and surrendering: chaos and freedom where art and technologies meet, Brisbane, Singapore, Sydney

In the spirit of collaboration and mutual enthusiasm for bringing together art and science, MAN joint efforts with the Web3D consortium[23] [24] and Queensland University of Technology (QUT) Brisbane for the twenty-second Web 3D conference's very first art exhibition titled *Web3D Art Gallery: on|off 100101010, Colliding and Surrendering: chaos and freedom where art and technologies meet*, 5–7 June, 2017.[25] The works premiered at the CUBE QUT, one of the world's largest digital interactive learning and display spaces.[26] The symposium and exhibition in Singapore followed in October 11–28, 2017.[27] Fourteen international research institutions, media labs, and cultural enterprises took part in Singapore event. The three-day symposium and a month-long exhibition in Singapore aimed to present interdisciplinary collaborative art works, which combine fields of art, science, and technology. The international symposium and exhibition examined artistic expressions from visualizations of microscopic plankton to the abstract poetics of a flight pattern database. Curators and artists gave a series of talks about the motivation behind the works and shared their methodologies. In conjunction with the symposium, a media art exhibition with twenty-four projects by twenty-seven international and local artists co-curated and co-produced for the exhibit at the MAN NTU.[28]

The highlight of the art gallery was the spectacular *Noise Aquarium*[29] is a highly interdisciplinary artist-led effort with biologists, chemists, nanotoxicologists, and an animator all working together towards a common goal—to raise consciousness about ocean pollution.[30] (see Fig. 10). In November of 2017 the works

---

23 For the last 22 years, every year the Web3D hosts an annual international conference Web3D. The Web3D Consortium is a member-funded industry consortium committed to the creation and deployment of open, royalty-free standards that enable the communication of real-time 3D across applications, networks, and XML web services

24 Web 3D "About Web3D Consortium," web3d.org (website), November 26, 2007 https://www.web3d.org/about (accessed October 3, 2018).

25 Event Committee Web 3D Art Gallery QUT Brisbane and Visualisation Matters 2017 Sydney, June Kim (UNSW) and Tomasz Bednarz (EPICentre UNSW Art & Design).

26 Queensland University of Technology, "About the Cube," www.aut.edu.au (website), June 12, 2018 https://www.thecube.qut.edu.au/about/ (accessed December 23, 2018).

27 Event Committee for International Symposium and Exhibit on|off 100101010 Singapore, Ina Conradi, (ADM NTU Singapore), Mark Chavez, (MAN NTU Sinagpore) June Kim, (UNSW), Tomasz Bednarz, (EPICentre UNSW Art & Design).

28 Ina Conradi, "On|Off 100101010 International Symposium and Exhibition", ONOFF100101010.COM (website) September 17, 2017, https://onoff100101010.com/ (accessed March 30, 2018).

29 *Noise Aquarium*. Directed by Victoria Vesna (UCLA Art|Sci Center), collaboration with Alfred Vendl Martina Fröschl (University of Applied Arts Vienna, Science Visualization Lab Angewandte).

30 Victoria Vesna, "Noise Aquarium," noiseaquarium.com (website), February 27, 2017, https://noiseaquarium.com (accessed October 3, 2018).

travelled to the Expanded Perception and Interaction Centre, UNSW (EPICentre) Sydney for the occasion of an event titled Visualisation Matters 2017. The event was designed to inspire audiences and demonstrate how art, science, design, and engineering can closely connect through visual creativity.[31]

ELMAN – Collaboration Elbphilharmonie and Media Art Nexus

MAN NTU Singapore hopes to bridge the gap between the formal traditional arts education and use digital media to connect NTU Singapore with other media art programs and cultural institutions locally and internationally. The ELMAN[32] project is the latest effort for establishing creative art exchange between two distant urban media displays, the Elbphilharmonie (Elphi) in Hamburg and the Media Art Nexus (MAN) in Singapore. As a part of the ELMAN University Project 2018, the emerging artists from the University of Applied Sciences Europe, Campus Hamburg, and the NTU Singapore School of Art, Design, and Media have created artworks for both media platforms. Both screens are noncommercial and are valued community assets. The Elbphilharmonie in Hamburg (see fig. 11 and 12) is one of the largest concert halls in the world and plays a pivotal role in providing a platform for creativity and engagement.[33]

The artworks will be connecting these two cities and their citizens through media localities that cannot be more radically different in both the architecture of the space as well as geographically, culturally, and historically. The content was divided into two themes: music for Elphi and Passing By for the long and narrow format of MAN. In that way, the media content thematically and spatially interacted with its surroundings and augmented both venues by a digital layer redefining a public place. Spatial media at both locations interacted with the viewer on an immediate level and it enhanced the narrative by means of light and virtual spaces.[34]

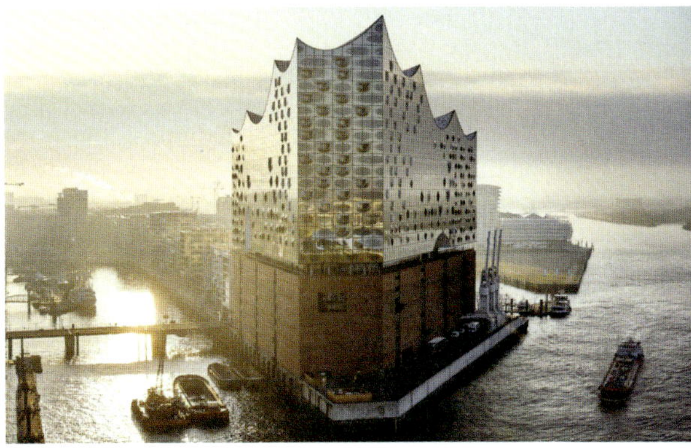

Figure 11: Elbphilharmonie Photo credit Hamburg Marketing GmbH.

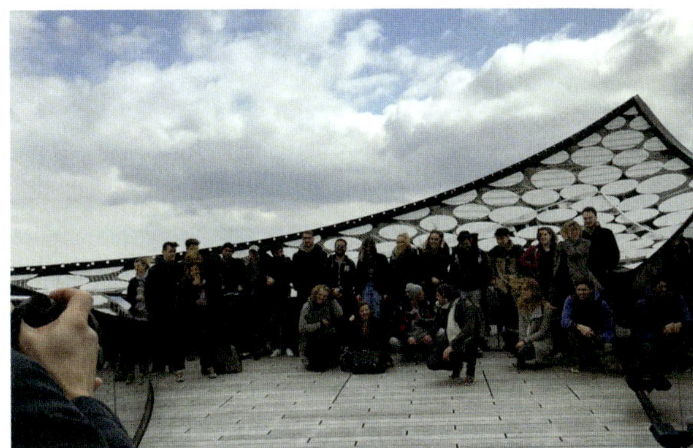

Figure 12. Students from Film and Motion Design Class UE Hamburg on the Elphi's roof top Photo Credit: Julian Conrad.

This collaboration will continue to exist between participants on both continents and will construct a creative educational framework for the urban media art and digital placemaking. The establishment of this co-curatorial partnership is a guarantee for motivating students to learn conceptual and technical skills while circulating their art produced internationally.

---

31 June Kim, VIS MATTERS 2017. www.visualization.matters.today (website), November 11, 2017 https://visualisation.matters.today/2017/#home (accessed March, 2018).

32 *ELMAN*, Project lead Hamburg: Thorsten Bauer (Creative Director Elbphilharmonie Media Wall), Verena Kraemer, (Professor, Head of Program Film and Motion Design, University of Applied Sciences Europe, Department of Art & Design, Campus Hamburg), Project lead Singapore: Ina Conradi (A/P NTU Singapore) Mark Chavez (Giant Monster) and Teh Eng Eng, Faith (Director NTU Singapore Art and Heritage Museum), November 26–December 12, 2018.

33 Elbphilharmonie, "ELBPHILHARMONIE & LAEISZHALLE HAMBURG," www.elbphilharmonie.de. (website), https://www.elbphilharmonie.de/en/ (accessed December 29, 2018).

34 Ina Conradi, "About: Context and Theme," www.elman.online.com (website), November 8, 2018, https://www.elman.online/blank-2 (accessed December 23, 2018).

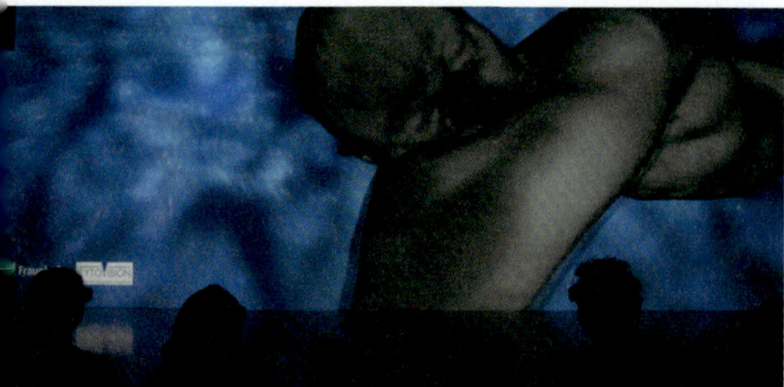

Figure 13: *Before Us Lies EterNERDy*, Stereoscopic 3D animation premier at the Deep Space 8k Ars Electronica Photo Credit: Magdalena Sick-Leitner.

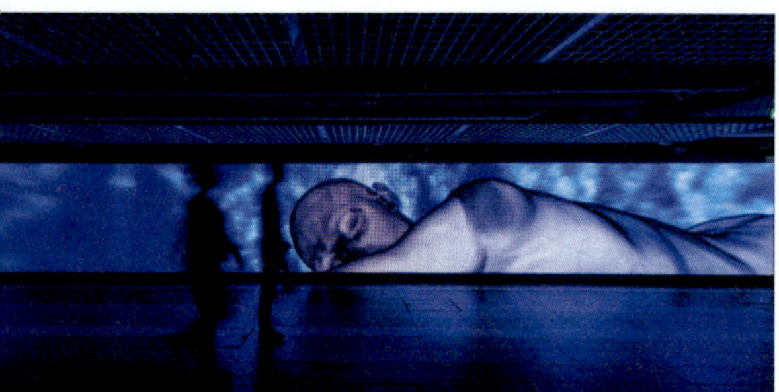

Figure 14: *Before Us Lies EterNERDy* playing at the Media Art Nexus NTU Singapore (SG). Photo Credit: Quek Jia Liang.

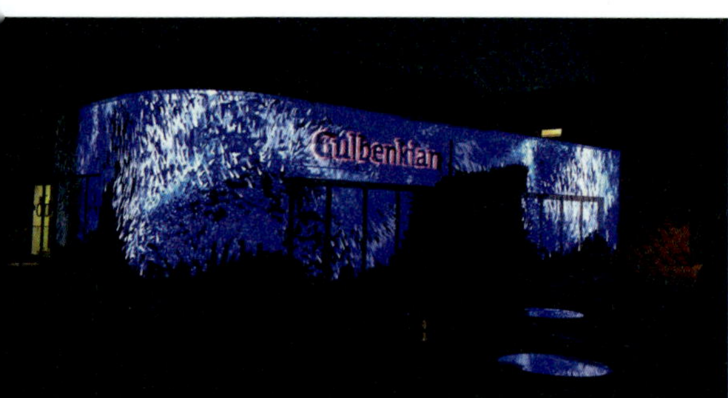

Figure 15: Premier of *WAVES* at the Gulbenkian façade Photo Credit: Rocio Jungenfeld.

Digital Medicine, Arts, and STEAM: "Before Us Lies EterNERDy" Fraunhofer MEVIS: Institute for Digital Medicine + Media Art Nexus NTU Singapore

Digital Medicine, Arts, and STEAM: "Before Us Lies EterNERDy"[35] is a short stereoscopic 3D animation that shows different scales of the human body, from digitized microscopic lymphoma tissue examined with the molecular cytogenetic technique fluorescent in situ hybridization (FISH) to detect abnormal changes in DNA to 3D reconstructions of a liver, as well as a whole-body MRI. The work simultaneous launched at Deep Space 8k during Ars Electronica's Festival (see fig. 13), and at Media Art Nexus NTU Singapore (see fig. 14). The project is the arts' contribution to removing barriers from engagement with severe health topics and as a transdisciplinary approach of innovation in digital medicine. The movie marks the beginning of the cooperation of Media Art Nexus NTU Singapore and Fraunhofer MEVIS: Institute for Digital Medicine, which will provide techniques, tools, scientific expertise, and an educational environment for students from NTU Singapore in Bremen, Germany.[36]

WAVES, Media Art Nexus and Gulbenkian façade Project School of Engineering and Digital Arts (EDA) – University of Kent Canterbury (UKC) England

WAVES[37] delivered two media architecture installations, one at the Gulbenkian Media Façade (GMF,) which is part of the University of Kent's Arts Centre, and one at the Media Art Nexus NTU Singapore (see fig. 15 and 16). The selected artworks were juxtaposed through two themes: one that creates worlds of wonder and another that explores real-life environmental issues, such as the effects of plastic pollution in water.[38]

Conclusion

In short, I suggest that the design of electronically augmented space can be approached as an architectural problem. In other words, architects along with artists can take the next logical step to con-

35 *Before us Lies EterNERDy*. Directed by Bianka Hofmann, David Black, Henning Höfener, André Homeyer, Alexander Köhn, Mathias Neugebauer. Fraunhofer MEVIS: Institute for Digital Medicine in cooperation with Media Art Nexus NTU Singapore Ina Conradi & Mark Chavez, FISH data kindly provided by ZytoVision, September 8-9, 2018.

36 Ars Electronica "Before Us Lies EterNERDy–Error," www.ars.electonica.art (website), September 6, 2018, https://ars.electronica.art/error/en/eternerdy/ (accessed December 29, 2018).

37 *Waves*. Project lead UK: Dr. Rocio von Jungenfeld, (Lecturer Digital Media, School of Engineering and Digital Arts at the University of Kent), Project Lead Singapore: Ina Conradi (A/P NTU Singapore ADM), Mark Chavez (Giant Monster), Teh Eng Eng, Faith (Director NTU Singapore Art and Heritage Museum) August 1-23, 2018.

38 Dr Rocio von Jungenfeld, Ina Conradi and Jayd Alex, "UoK-UK and NTU-Singapore Exhibition," www.xcurrents.gallery.com (website), July 31, 2018, https://xcurrents.gallery/ (accessed December 21, 2018).

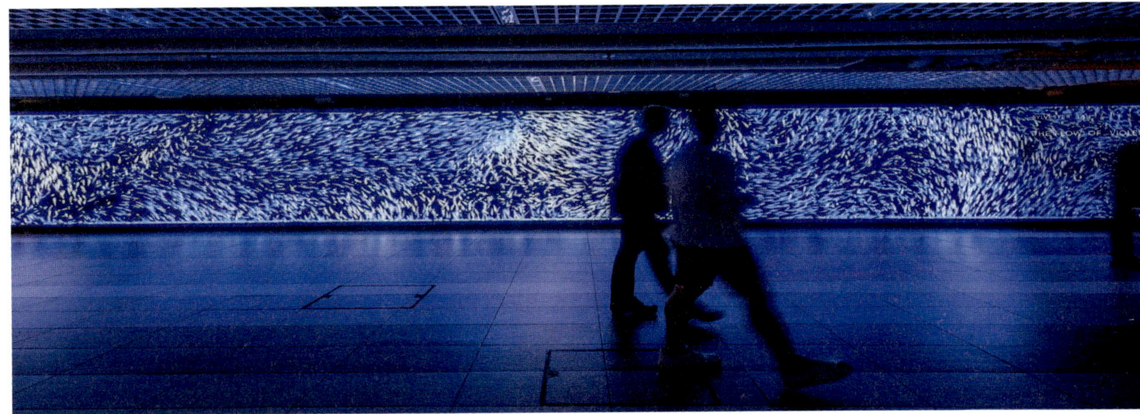

Figure 16: WAVES exhibition playing at MAN NTU Singapore, Photo Credit: Quek Jia Liang.

sider the "invisible" space of electronic data flows as substance rather than just a void—something that needs a structure, a politics, and a poetics.[39]

The first phase of establishing MAN as a public and urban gallery platform has been completed. MAN has successfully organized, hosted, and participated in exhibitions, symposiums, and workshops locally and internationally. The future for this platform would be to explore one-of-a-kind new media art that would integrate art, data visualization, and storytelling within public spaces, while merging the disciplines of fine art and animation.

Acknowledgments

This work is supported by Nanyang Technological University Singapore, NTU SINGAPORE Art & Heritage Museum, College of Humanities, Arts, and Social Sciences, Centre for Liberal Arts and Social Sciences (CLASS), NTU Singapore School of Art, Design and Media (ADM).

---

39 Lev Manovich, The Poetics of Augmented Space: Learning from Prada. 2006. Visual Communication, SAGE Publishing, 2006. Vol. 5(2). doi.org/10.1177/1470357206065527, p. 240.

Bibliography

Manovich, Lev. *The Poetics of Augmented Space: Learning from Prada*. 2006. Visual Communication, SAGE Publishing, 2006. Vol. 5(2). doi.org/10.1177/1470357206065527, pp. 219–240.

Koelstra, Sander, et al. "DEAP: A Database for Emotion Analysis Using Physiological Signals," *IEEE Transactions on Affective Computing* 2012. Vol. 3(1). pp. 18–31.

Latorrie, Daniel, and Glenn Harding. "Digital Peacemaking After 6 years: Defining an Emerging Practice." In *Media Architecture Compendium: Digital Placemaking*, edited by Luke Hespanhol, et al., Stuttgart, 2017, pp.172–175.

Petrantonakis, Panagiotis C., et al. "Emotion recognition from EEG using higher order crossings," *IEEE Transactions on Information Technology in Biomedicine* 2010. 14 (2), pp. 186–197.

Viskontas, Indre V., and Suzee E. Lee, "The creation of art on the setting of dementia." In *Art, Aesthetics, and the Brain*, edited by M. N. Joseph P. Huston, et al., Oxford, 2015, pp. 357–372.

Reinhold Bidner (AT) | Sonja Prlic (AT) | Karl Zechenter (AT)

gold extra: Endeavours in Artistic Diversity

Expanding Dialogues

"Expanded" is derived from the Latin word "expandere" and can be translated as "to open up," "to widen," "to upgrade," or "to develop." Animation is actually expanding into and merging with a wide range of different art fields, diversifying in the process in terms of expansion of usage, of tools, of production, and of access.

We are aiming at a different route to expansion and are attempting to show the workings of this expansion as a form of dialogue between formal, aesthetical, and narrative decisions. Certain art forms are collaborative in kind, rendering discussion, transfers, and exchange of all sorts an essential part of their development, whereas animation—although many people might be working on a project—is, in principle, often a more holistic undertaking. Therefore, this dialogue often remains subconscious or unheard.

To us, as a group of artists working in different fields and contributing to animation works and styles, this has become a very visible process, a process that keeps the definition and the grasp of what animation can or should be constantly fluid. We see the developing, the opening up of animation in our projects as an ongoing process occurring because of necessity as well as an intuitive part of the beauty of animation as an ever-changing working field. We have maintained an equally constant development of definition and redefinition in the nearly 20-year career of the collective gold extra.

gold extra – In Search of the Ever Elusive Art Form

When gold extra started in 1998 in Salzburg, the founding members originally came from theater and performance art. From day one, they felt it was necessary to establish an experimental and also fun edge and bring it to a town famous for its baroque architecture, Mozart, *The Sound of Music*, and classical tourist attractions as well as festivals. There was not necessarily a lot of free space for that kind of goal.

But from early on it was obvious that besides performance art, often cast as interventions in public space, an array of different art disciplines should become part of gold extra's daily production process. To expand over the limitations of a chosen single artform to work in, was the cornerstone of the foundation of the group's collaborative proceedings.

Gold extra "grew up" in a time of constant digital changes, of internationalization, of growing global communications and collaborations. Media art was a less formalized, less canonical area then, with fewer degree programs and diplomas, but with lots of people joining the burgeoning field from different backgrounds. Setting our view on digital arts was an obvious move for us.

In the course of this endeavor artists with a strong background in animation, documentary and media arts joined the group and together became a new formation of gold extra. The six-member core team (Karl Zechenter, Sonja Prlic, Tobias Harnmerle, Georg Hobmeier, Reinhold Bidner, Doris Prlic) has been working together since 2004. Gold extra can look back on projects in digital arts, fine arts, performance, conceptual art, music, hybrid media, animation and games, veering constantly more towards artistic research over the years. An inherent impetus of gold extra works has been engagement in constant research in innovative art forms to create the matching formal environment for new and often unusual ideas, focusing on social and political topics often in the guise of everyday life experiences. We are attempting to translate these interests into new technologies (e.g., environments in augmented reality, virtual reality) and into contexts and art forms that are less well established in the art world, such as games. There are two simple guidelines forming gold extra projects. One is: "How does this relate to me in my private life?" This one often leads to streaks of distinctively silly humor throughout the works. The other motto guides us along the lines of the idea or topic being there first, followed by whatever aesthetic form which may serve that particular idea. These ideas as well as topics often found their complementary form in the digital realm in recent years. Along these lines gold extra members have created a great number of projects that open up and transcend boundaries and that have been presented at countless festivals and exhibitions nationally and internationally.

Works of Reinhold Bidner—Aesthetic Dialogue within the Field of Animation

Animation may at times be perceived as a by-product of gold extra projects, but it is a permanent ingredient and a very necessary one, in one way or another always creeping up, demanding and finding its place: because in all its variety, animation offers an incredible potential for addressing social topics and visualizing their complex interrelations, particularly with new tools and devices coming up and artistic disciplines merging with each other.

Animation can explain and visualize topics in unique ways: it allows us to combine visual layers that do not necessarily fit together at first.

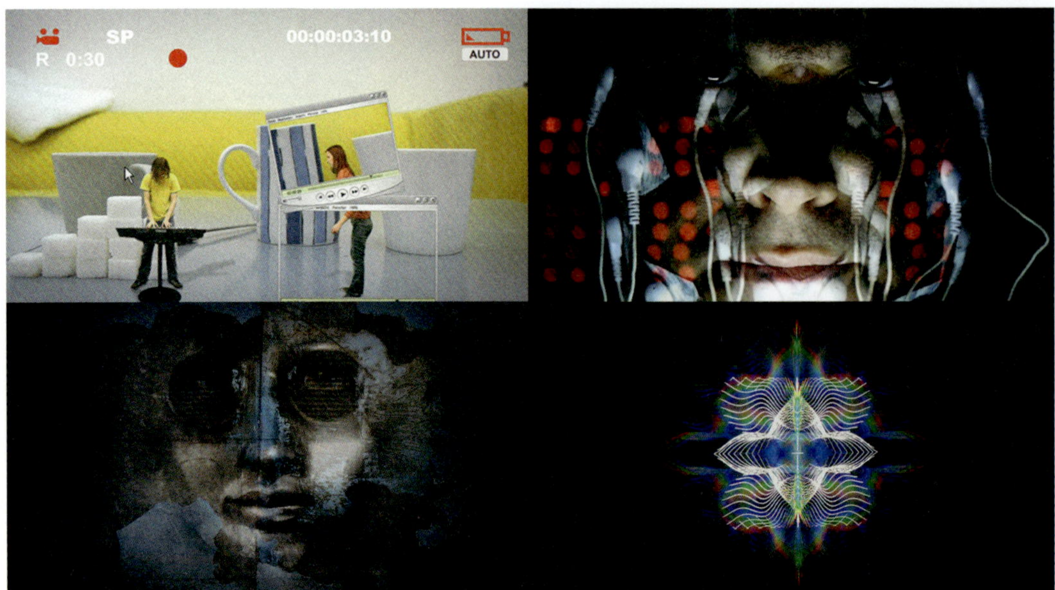

Figure 1: Animation-Experiments by gold extra member Reinhold Bidner: *If we had only tried* (2012), *Impulse* (2013, collaboration with gold extra member Georg Hobmeier), *Ex Terrat* (2016) and *Until we* coleidescape (2017).

Besides being part of the gold extra artist group, Reinhold Bidner, is an animation artist in his own right. Bidner tried to pursue some of the possibilities mentioned above in his individual experimental animations—*If we had only tried* (2012)[1], *Impulse* (2013, collaboration with gold extra member Georg Hobmeier)[2], *Ex Terrat* (2016)[3], and *Until we coleidescape* (2017)[4], to name a few—that are often seen as digital and analog playgrounds in diverse ways.

Taking 2016's *Ex Terrat* as an example, animation for Bidner is not only about visual playgrounds but also to combine its playfulness with questioning and commenting on certain topics in our society in an abstract way that you can only do with the possibilities of experimental animation. Ironically *Ex Terrat* became a rather dark and subconscious animation piece but the beginning of the process for this work was quite light, involving a research journey to Paris in the summertime with the goal of expanding Bidner's individual boundaries in animation. Many kilometers in the streets of Paris were covered; many street scenes, faces, and street art references were depicted. This research material was the basis for a quite uncommon six-minute portrait of Paris that combines various animation fragments in techniques such as 2D-, 3D-, hand drawn-, and stop-motion animation or morphing. In the process it was rather unclear if all these fragments could really fit together, but this multi-layered process simply felt right.

The result allows for different readings: on the one hand, you could simply watch an audiovisual animation about transforming faces, but in relation to all its visual and thematic layers you could also "read" a documentary about a post-*Charlie-Hebdo* Paris that feels dark, insecure, and light all at the same time.

Ex Terrat's "anything is possible" or "anything can be combined" approach is, of course, a blessing and a curse at the same time. It involves the risk of being carried away by all these possibilities, so in general, it may be important to combine your idea or story with a keep-it-simple-approach though things will become complicated anyway. While this remains an inner struggle less visible in the different stages of the production of this artwork, we would like to show examples of transformations of artworks in the process of a dialogue of visual aesthetics and narrative

---

1 *If we had only tried*. Directed by Reinhold Bidner, 2012, YouTube video, 3:09 min., uploaded by "reinoldoo," September 27, 2012, https://www.youtube.com/watch?v=68_K3DgmVDU (accessed April 10, 2019).

2 *Impulse*. Directed by Reinhold Bidner and Georg Hobmeier, 2013, YouTube video, 3:42 min., uploaded by "Wien Energie," May 31, 2013, https://vimeo.com/69462938 (accessed April 10, 2019)

3 *Ex Terrat*. Directed by Reinhold Bidner, 2016.

4 *Until we coleidescape*. Directed by Reinhold Bidner, 2017.

concepts. In the projects *From Darkness*[5] and *Future Rearview*[6] we would like to trace the influence of each part and see how narrative concepts were enabled by visual aesthetic decisions.

From Darkness—Animation as a Guide in Narrative Concepts

Our approach is to take a considerable amount of reflection concerning the formal environments of the artwork. We entered the field of games not as a game design company but as an artist group. Creating a game is therefore an actual rational decision rather than a question of economic viability.

When we entered the field of serious games in 2005/06, the field had a long tradition but was sparsely populated. This has changed a lot in the last ten years and the niche continues to grow and differentiate. The landscape of graphic styles that find acceptance with a wider public became more varied with the breakthrough of the indie scene and mobile gaming. The pursuit of photorealistic games became somewhat diminished by the revival of older graphical styles e.g. pixel aesthetics and game concepts. This is for us especially interesting as it renders a wider range of visual and narrative approaches possible while still maintaining the chance to find interest outside of a dedicated group of art game enthusiasts. Our interest itself shifted to a very special branch of games which might be understood as documentary games. That is to say, games which aim at representing documentary research of actual political or social contexts which are often very complex and mostly contradictory.

Our typical project setup would be to invest a good bit of time on the research of specific topics, then go on research journeys in a style close to ethnological field research and do numerous interviews as well as all kinds of audiovisual recordings. Our documentary game *From Darkness* was released in 2016, but we started working on the project as early as 2011. The game is based on more than forty hours of documentary video material, mostly interviews, which we gathered on a six-week research trip to Kenya and Uganda. In the game the audience can explore in various thematic and visual layers the lives of journalists, shop owners, community workers, priests, nurses, street children, and urban refugees in East Africa. As a documentary game we wanted *From Darkness* to

explore new ways of combining the visual conception of the game with a narration based on documentary material. Most of the material from which we drew consists of video portraits of people telling us their personal experiences with migration, flight, and the complex sociopolitical layers that cause conflicts and force people to leave their homes. We also wanted to highlight the role of a journalist reporting these facts or omitting others.

What we had to deal with at the end of our research period was a vast amount of documentary material containing topics and personal stories which were not easy to explain or to understand, the role of ourselves as journalists or researchers, and a very complex network of worldwide conflicts and geopolitical connections seen from individual perspectives of refugees, social workers, nurses, or street children. How could a game represent this complexity and how could it be transformed into a playable experience? This was the question accompanying our game design process. This is where the dialogue between narrative requirements and approaches to representation started. At first, we attempted a 3D representation, fully equipped with 3D characters and an action storyline, only to walk it back to an abstract labyrinth gameplay which we equally felt did not give the research material enough credit. We did not fully delete the initial strategy but strived to keep the parts of different approaches to design and gameplay concepts which we felt were adequate.

Via the tangent of the representation of background characters, we finally reached a new conceptual perspective for the animation and graphic design of the whole game. *From Darkness* uses a flat aesthetic embedded in a 3D world. Its walls, people (2D characters), and events are mostly two-dimensional layers with varying degrees of transparency in an otherwise familiar 3D environmental setting. The layers themselves are remnants of the different layers of experience of our research journey.

This set another process in motion that brings the dialogue between aesthetic form and narrative approach into play: the visual concept could be interpreted as layers, and layering transformed an erstwhile straightforward storyline. The visual concept gave us a form which made the complexity of the subject accessible. In this way, the visual style, the collage of layers that

---

5 *From Darkness*. Released by "gold extra," October 2016, https://goldextra.com/from-darkness (accessed April 10, 2019).
6 *Future Rearview*. Released by "gold extra," March 23, 2017, https://goldextra.com/future-rearview-ein-rueckblick-in-die-zukunft (accessed April 10, 2019).

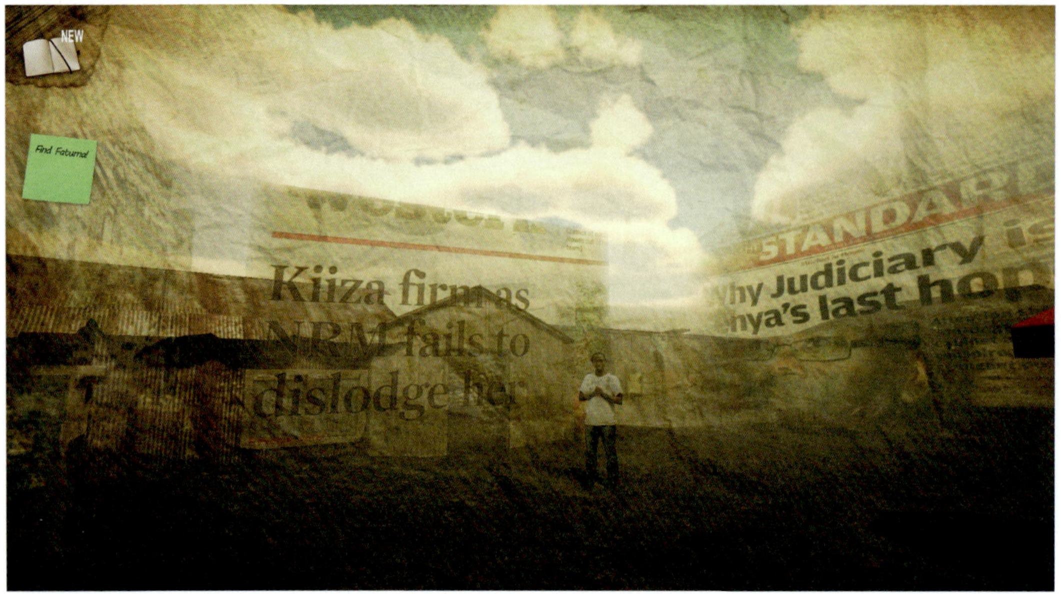

Figure 2: *From Darkness* (2016).

visually defines *From Darkness* became an important storytelling tool with layers representing a link between memories (like pages in a book) and actual events. The layers could represent the act of becoming acquainted with the environment, which is a central motif of the main character in *From Darkness*. The layers and their semi-transparent look open up the possibility for the player to experience different points of time in the same environment and to see the act of making experiences right on the spot as the 3D world becomes more labelled. In this dialogue between aesthetic form and narrative ideas, the animation and visual style have a strong conceptual background allowing for new narrative possibilities.

Future Rearview—A Visual Style to Deal with Narrative Complexity

Future Rearview is a documentary game installation, debuted at the gallery periscope in Salzburg in 2017 as a part of the festival program "Salzburg 2016." In 2014 a research project started focusing on marginalized stories, characters, and perspectives of the city of Salzburg. In a further iteration the research widened its focus to include biographical interviews with a larger number of people in wildly different age groups. The raw data for the future installation were the interviews as audio data, documentary photos, and historical pictures from both public and private archives as well as news media. As an aesthetic spill-over from *From Darkness*, there was the idea of using a game environment as well as the principal idea of abstraction. *Future Rearview* saw significantly fewer iterations than *From Darkness*. Production started in earnest in 2016, and the game debuted eight months later, in 2017. But it is interesting to note from the viewpoint of visual and narrative dialogue that a predecessor research project revolved around the idea of a point-and-click storytelling game and another conceptualized projecting historical pictures on actual buildings. The basic idea of *Future Rearview* backed by a considerable amount of resource data was to show different strata of Salzburg, historical as well societal. It was important to make the complexity of biographical stories and pictures accessible for the audience without overwhelming them and losing their interest in the process. The idea was not to create a shock derived from these complexities but rather to invite the audience to explore these city impressions very individually—on their own terms. The gallery context also demanded nearly immediate establishing of the possibilities of the artwork, ruling out more game-like introductory build-ups offering more time for the audience to get used to the complexity or learn the use of controls to handle them.

Again, it was attempts for the visual concept that prompted a narrative framing of the city experiences. We came up with a dark map lightened only by semi-transparent layers showing pictures from archives when the player moves nearby, thus slowly building up a city following the individual path of the spec-

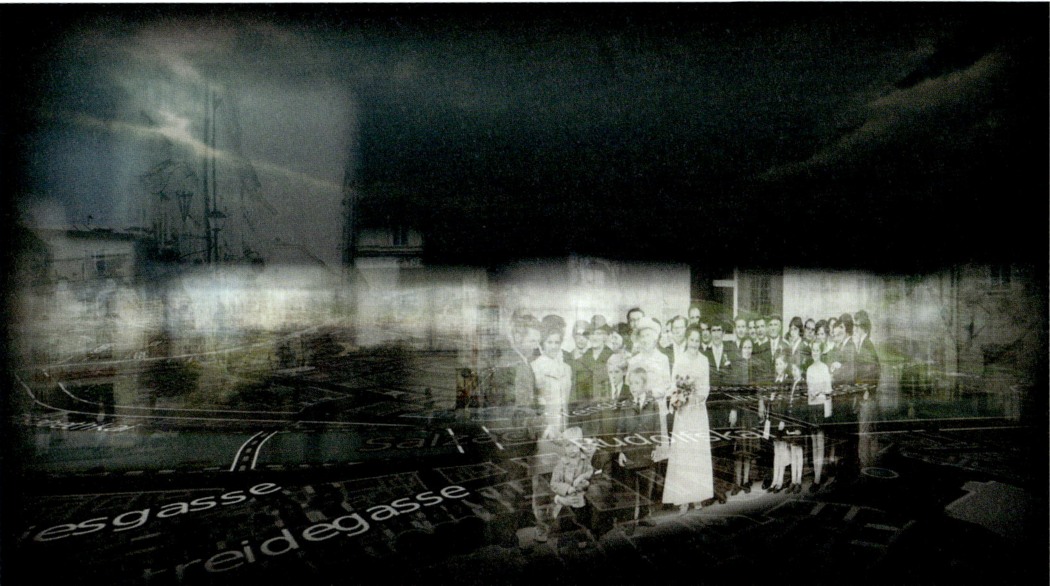

Figure 3: *Future Rearview* (2017).

tator. From here the narrative framework took over and merged the pictures with the audio-data and provided a gameplay system. The gameplay lets the player switch on or off different topical sets expressing the four guidelines of our Salzburg research: "to come and to leave," "beauty and ugliness," "the beginning of things," and "disappear and forget." In the finished game installation, the player "walks" on the map, seen on a number of monitors, using keyboard controls. Interviews appear on certain spots on the map connected with pictures, while the player can choose the grade of complexity he or she wants to experience. The player may either follow only one theme or get lost in the density of all interviews being displayed at once. Here the visual style and animation significantly and visibly establish the expansion of storytelling. While an audio-walk might deal mainly with the consonance or dissonance of the audio commentary versus the visual perception, *Future Rearview* allows for an experience selected by the player offering different layers of association to follow on different spots in the map. The path the spectator chooses plays a role: either follow one line or jump between topical lines that touch each other on certain locations on the map. In total *Future Rearview* ended up offering three levels of storytelling: topological storytelling, associative storytelling, and stories from different points in time, all linked through the grades of complexity the player chose. The interviewees' stories related to different times across the topological or thematical order.

In these intersections new associations continue to appear and reappear. The collage forms a synchronicity of information, which is especially interesting for a documentary art project focusing on the developments through different times, helping to bring the material in a more dimensional order.

Take Your Time

We have seen in our works the great value of experimenting with an exchange between aesthetic forms and narrative concepts, both complimenting themselves and finally enhancing the projects significantly. These processes take some time—which is well invested—and require sensitivity to bridge different approaches in collaborative creation strategies. In this manner the dialogue between visual and narrative concepts may become heard and visible and over time, a truly expanded animation, a truly expanded artwork, develops.

Anezka Sebek (DE/ES)

Now You Touch it, Now You Don't: Experiments in Virtual Interfaces

Introduction

Three years have passed since my experiments in interfaces talk at the Ars Electronica Festival's Expanded Animation. Meanwhile, the global industry media inventions continue to emerge, evolve, transform, and push our students to create imaginative realities, stories, simulations, and applications. The high pitch of the virtual reality buzz since 2015 has cooled a bit, primarily because of the lack of VR's generalized adoption. At the time, I applauded Google Cardboard's delivery of immersive journalism on smartphones and making the 360 surround medium available as a mass medium for the first time since our industry experiments with Virtual Reality Modeling or Markup Language (VRML). At the beginning of my talk, I mentioned Palmer Luckey because he was indeed a very lucky "baby billionaire" who capitalized on making VR the medium of the masses with his garage tinkering success of the Oculus head-mounted display (HMD). *Time* magazine elevated Luckey to the status of an angel hanging with bare feet on its front cover.

In this general climate of giddiness about the promise of VR, the moment was perfect to show the Parsons students' projects. Previous iterations of VR technology took interactors through the stages of early adopter love, then mass-market temperance, then disappointment, and eventual demise of each successive version. The Evans and Sutherland *Sword of Damocles* was VR 1.0.[1] Arcade rides of the eighties and nineties represented VR 2.0. Now, fueled by decades of momentum from the booming video game industry, we have VR 3.0 with the Oculus, HTC Vive, and Cardboard. However, the technology is still not light, comfortable, or cheap enough, nor is the content compelling enough to consider VR a mature medium.

If we must believe the current market-hyped verdict on VR, this iteration is yet another phase that will live a short life in the medium's maturation process. Some say that VR was not worth the $2 billion that Zuckerberg paid Luckey to kick off the VR 3.0 mania. Some say that we are still in early days for VR because the lack of viable data speeds delivered by current technology. There is hope, however. By 2020, most developed nations will deploy 5G wireless broadband (1,000 times faster than 4G). Higher data transmission rates will mean access to higher quality images and fast delivery of interaction (low latency), which will mean more

---

1 Ivan Sutherland, "A head-mounted three dimensional display," Fall Joint Computer Conference (Fall 1968), pp. 757–764.

comfortable uninterrupted delivery of bandwidth-demanding VR experiences. HMDs and other emerging technology from industry giants such as Apple, Google, and Facebook (Oculus) are ready to deploy product pipelines that may add full body VR experiences.

In 2015, I presented eight projects that each challenged some or all of virtual reality constraints and limitations. The 2015 graduating students of the MFA in design and technology at Parsons, as well as some of the first-year students, explored the many aspects of interface design with their projects. In this article, I review six projects because the students allowed me to feature them. They provided me with the writing and research they did for their projects. I present them here as small case studies of projects that demonstrated physically tangible interfaces for control by the interactor (Henry Lam, Geyao Zhang, Madhav Tankha) or a linear emotional experience that affected interactors physically (Alec McClure, Sultan Barodawala, Lucy Bonner).

Expanding Animation into Virtual Worlds

Despite ebbs and flows of VR invention, adoption, and demise, our students pushed further and tinkered with tangible interfaces such as motion bases, spatial interaction, and crude rigs that attempted to simulate flying. The imminent promise of these advances will make the projects I showed in 2015 all the more prescient. In that same year, the New School was in the process of sorting and separating the animation and experience design programs to distinguish animation technologies in a variety of media and applications. The two-dimensional practices and stop motion animation were shepherded into the illustration program. Interactivity on the web and motion graphics became the shared domain of the communication design and design and technology (DT) programs. The DT Program pushed the expansion of three-dimensional computer animation into games, virtual, augmented realities, coded realities, installation and physical/performance experimentation. Expanding animation for the DT program is exploring the implications of space, tactility, and the use of digital agents and artificial intelligence the ever-advancing technological, computer-based practices. Our program encourages thinking ahead of emerging technology. At the same time, students are reminded that they must lead their inquiry in design and technology with questions that are rooted in meaning- making. Stories, characters, conflict, and messaging all find their way into the expansion of animation in virtual spaces. The challenge remains the delivery of experiments through a variety of often

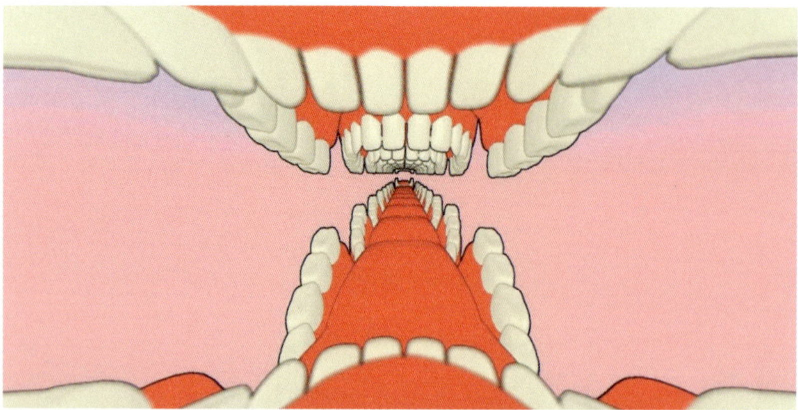

Figure 1: *Oral Perspectives*. The mouth point-of-view as an interface between the body and food.

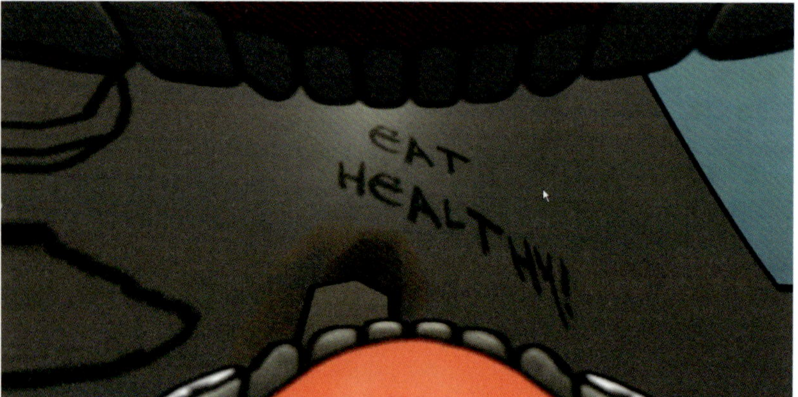

Figure 2: *Oral Perspectives*. POV of the mouth "perceiving" admonitions about how to "eat healthy".

kludged-together technologies in our program.

In 2015, The New School Curriculum designers were attempting to codify and sort out the differences of the VR medium from other media. I used Myron Krueger's constraints as my guide. I recognize that other practitioners in communication technologies were creating important distinctions and taxonomies in the early days of synthetic media.[2][3] In recognition of Myron Krueger's pioneering career accomplishments in this domain, the focus here is on Krueger's short article entitled "Responsive Environments".[4] He proposed five ideas for this new visual interactive computer-based artform. He said: "Interactive [computer] art is potentially a richly composable medium quite distinct from the concerns of sculpture, graphic art or music."[5] As a demonstration of how far we have come in close to thirty years, the 2015 experiments by my students advance some or all of Krueger's arguments. As a computer scientist, Krueger posited (paraphrased—my comments are in parentheses):[6]

1. In order to respond intelligently, the computer should perceive as much as possible about the participant's behavior (artificially intelligent responsive systems).

2. Only small numbers of people should be allowed in the interaction at one time to *limit the experience to the responsive environment* and not as participants to

---

2 Paul Milgram and Fumio Kishino, "A Taxonomy of Mixed Reality Visual Displays," IEICE Trans. Information Systems, Vol. E77-D, No. 12, (December 1994), pp. 1321–1329.

3 Warren Robinett, "Synthetic Experience: A Proposed Taxonomy." Presence: Teleoperators in Virtual Environments 1, 2 (January 1992), pp. 229–247.

4 Myron Krueger, "Responsive Environments," Association for Computing Machinery, National Computer Conference (June 1977).

5 Juno A. McClure, "Depth Perception." 2015, https://alecmcclure.com/post/119923239838/depthperception (accessed October 4, 2018).

6 Myron Krueger, "Responsive Environments," Association for Computing Machinery, National Computer Conference (June 1977).

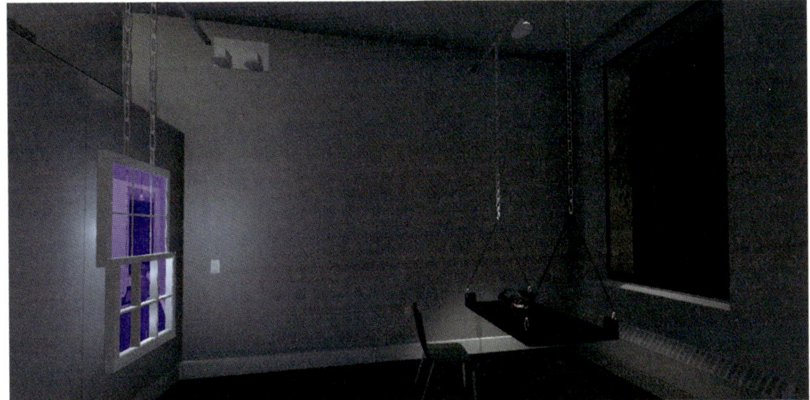

Figure 3: *Depth Perception*. "Realistic" computer-generated rendering of a physical space.

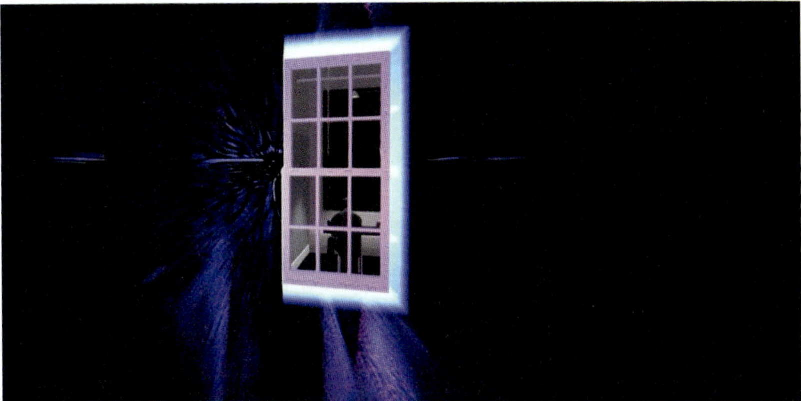

Figure 4: *Depth Perception*. The window as a gateway between physical and virtual realities.

each other. (I disagree. The environment can become responsive to a larger number of people via networks. The environment can address many people in the same digital space. Networked technologies and the web were still about a decade away in 1977.)

3. Participants should be aware of how the environment is responding to them. (Feedback to users is the most critical aspect of user experience design.)

4. Sound and visual response *systems* should convey a wide variety of conceptual relationships. (This is critical in the design of any engaging experience.)

5. Visual responses should not be judged as art nor sounds as music. *The aesthetic concern should focus on the quality of the interaction.* (This is a quality often overlooked by interaction designers and requiring interaction tests with a target audience.)

In addition to Krueger's responsive environment constraints, four decades later, several of the MFA DT students in this article, argue that haptic touch and tangible interfaces should update the current version of virtual experiences whether projected or in an HMD. I also point out that the VR experience is distinct from other forms of screen-based media because of several experiential distinctions. Some of the examples of student work in this article address these distinctions.

The viewer as auteur. Headset controls lead the viewer of the VR in the direction they choose by their head movement (by tracking technology). The auteur producer of an environment invites the participant into the experience, but each participant can experience that reality on their own terms and according to the level of comfort and agility they have with the user interface (see projects by McClure, Lam, Tanka, Zhang).

More accessible technology. The experience varies greatly with the many different delivery methods for HMDs. The cardboard viewers still need a phone that can produce the VR experience, so cardboards are, in fact, still expensive. The HMDs on the market require an investment that many people cannot afford. Other media don't need complex delivery systems, and

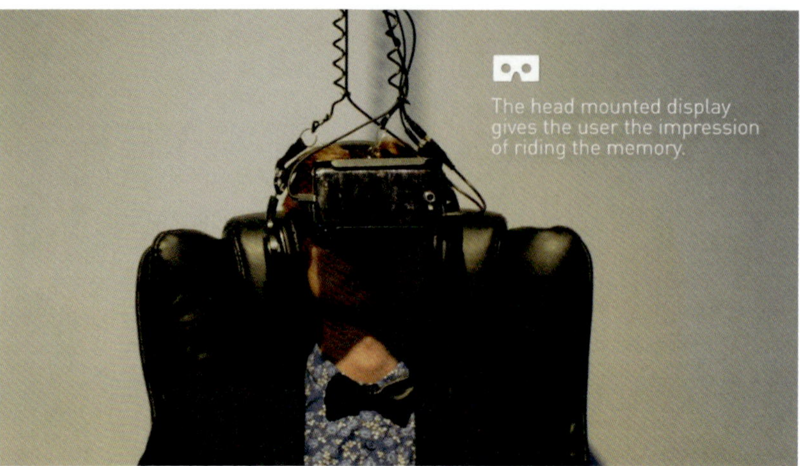

Figure 5: *The Memory of Aden Walker.* The HMD coupled with a narrative experience in a motion-base chair.

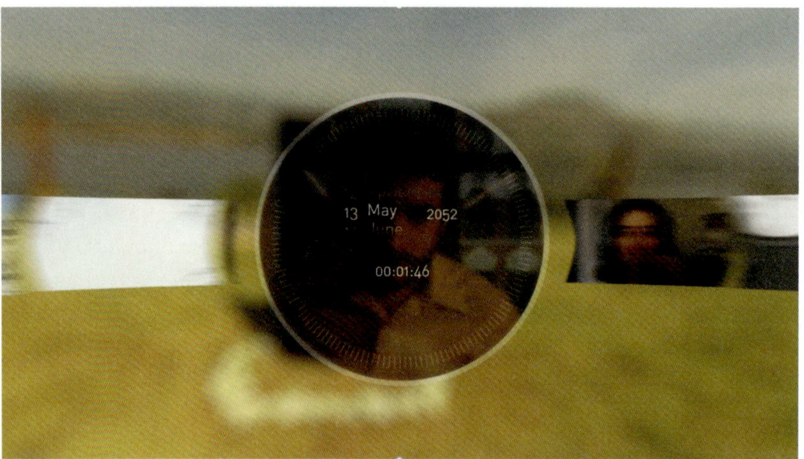

Figure 6: *The Memory of Aden Walker.* Graphical user-interface to call up memories at critical times in the narrative.

audio is often left as an add-on where it is given lots of attention in other film and video- screened media (see project by Bonner).

Controllers have a learning curve. Rather than a passive experience, VR requires new attention because there is more viewing area. Controllers that activate the nodes of interaction are often a challenge for first-time users (see Lam, Zhang).

VR experiences are limited by a time constraint. Most viewers do not want to wear an often increasingly-hot viewing device for more than ten to twenty minutes. The experience must sustain interaction and engagement whether delivered by an HMD or an environmental projection. (All projects in this article were shorter than seven minutes.)

The MFA in Design and Technology Project Summaries

The first four projects I review here did not accomplish Krueger's criteria for responsive environments. They are linear narratives presented in head-mounted virtual reality displays. The narrative leads the viewer into compelling questions about virtual submersion or immersion where a lack of control is one of the story elements. The second set of three projects uses physical interfaces to control various narrative experiences from a dreamscape to a first-person shooter to an interactive painting. The last three projects are experiments in the visceral interaction between the image and the interactor and the meaning that emerges from the physical effects of the interactor's action. These are true responsive ways to create effects in

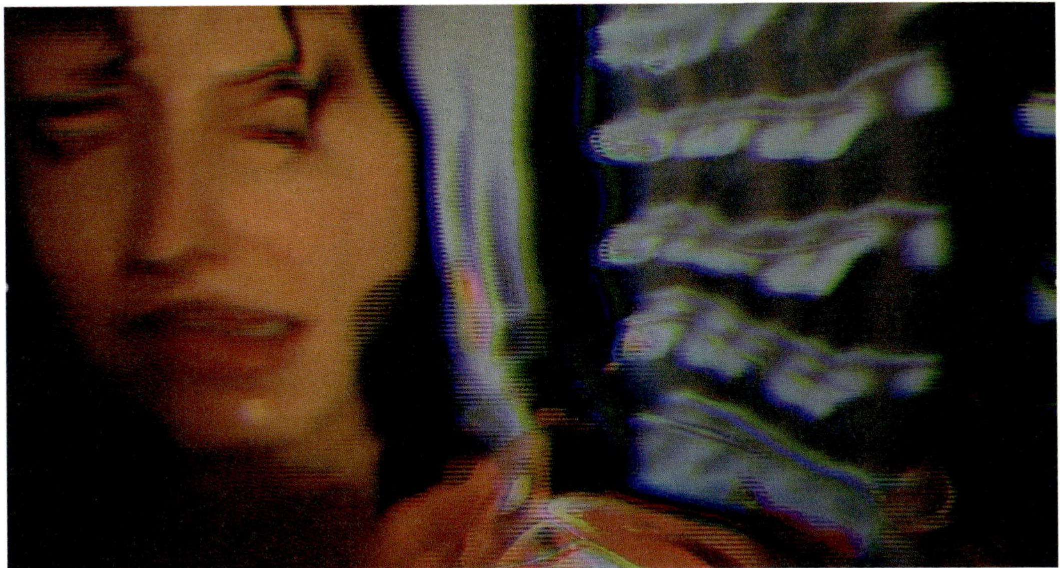

Figure 7: Aden Walker's memory from an unpleasant past.

the virtual environment. Especially in the last project, "Penumbra" by Madhav Tahnka, the projected image is the computer and human interaction generates the image. The human hand creates the abstraction in tandem with the images generated and authored by the computer. The experiment is a nod to Krueger's criteria for responsive environments and, it is also the only project in this group that is a projected experience rather than an experience in an HMD.

Alec (Juno) McClure – *Oral Perspectives*

Oral Perspectives[7] in the Recursive Reality Studio was taught by Robert Yang and Kyle (Kan Yang) Li. McClure produced a virtual experience at the mouth level rather than the eye level. "This primarily passive experience takes place from a visually, aurally, and kinesthetically shifted perspective a few inches lower than the natural position, inside the user's oral cavity."[8] McClure asked: what is the experience of being a mouth? How does food come toward the dental structure, and how do we look at the teeth being brushed and pieces of food that are meant to be chewed and swallowed? The reactions of the interactors were sometimes extreme.

Alec (Juno) McClure – Depth Perception

In McClure's thesis project, Depth Perception[9], McClure created a physical space and a duplicated virtual environment where there are two viewpoints possible. Interactors are challenged by the relationship of the self in virtual and physical spaces. The project emerged from a William Gibson quote "None of this was real, but cold was cold" (1984).[10]

Utilizing immersive multimedia tools, such as VR, for their impressive resolution of representation and effectiveness in bringing these questions to light, this project aims to evoke a confused verisimilitude, suggesting a "hyperreal" nature of existence, along with the arbitrariness and sentimentality with which we attribute authenticity to the perceived. The form of this project is that of a multimodal experiential installation, with the intention of creating a disconnect between the user and their environment. This installation takes place between an infinite number of room pairs, each room serving as a loose reflection of its counterpart adjoined through a common window, with a shifting relationship.[11]

---

7 Juno A. McClure, "Oral Perspectives" a Recursive Realities Studio Project, 2015, https://junomorrow.itch.io/oral-perspectives (accessed October 4, 2018).

8 Ibid.

9 Juno A. McClure, "Depth Perception," Recursive Realities Studio Project 2015, https://alecmcclure.com/post/119923239838/depth-perception (accessed October 4, 2018).

10 Gibson, William, *Neuromancer* (New York, 1984), p. 227.

11 Juno A. McClure, *Depth Perception*, Master's Thesis (Master of Fine Art in Design and Technology, The New School, Parsons, 2015), p. 3.

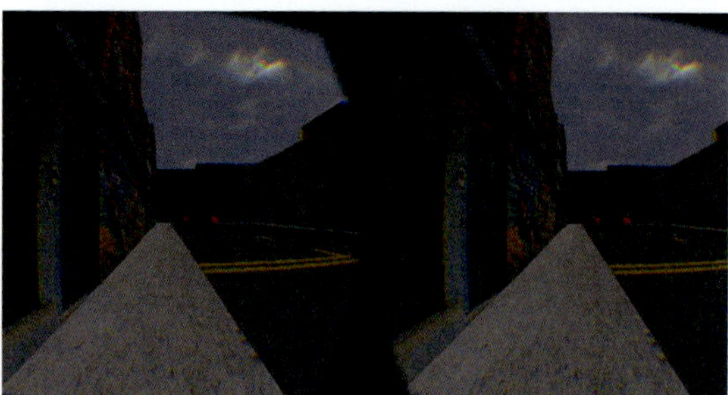

Figure 8: *Not A Compliment*. Urban environments from the Unity 3D store to help set the gritty mood.

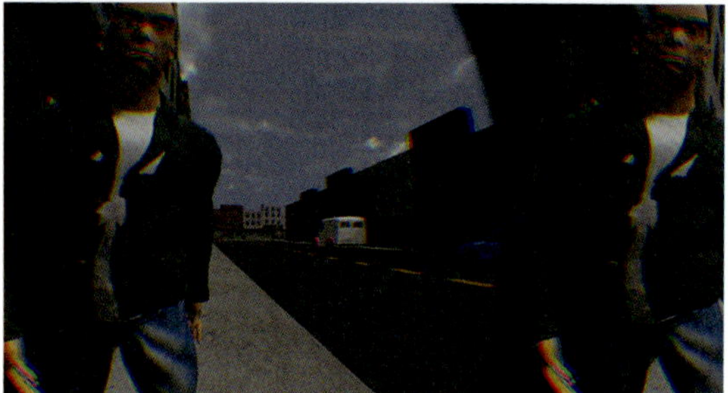

Figure 9: *Not A Compliment*. Threatening men call out to the helpless interactor.

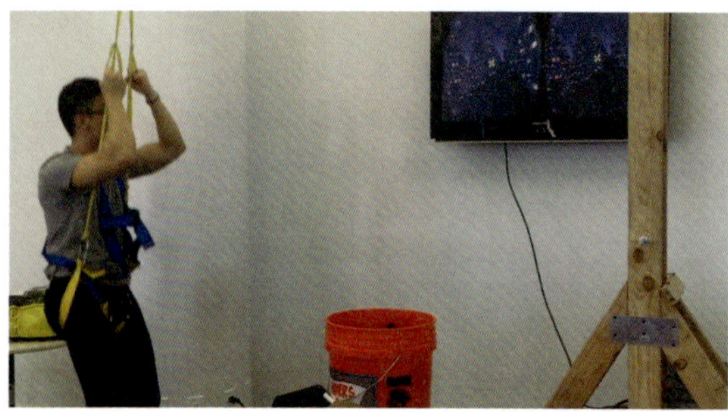

Figure 10: *Unequal Paired Cooperative Controls*. The Carrier.

Throughout the making and creation of the project, McClure asked: "Surrounded by technological media and inescapable imagery, does the object imaged possess a true location or essence? And can a computer-mediated reality experience destabilize our assumptions about the nature of reality, inspiring a 'confused verisimilitude?'"[12] The staging of the project was in a large open space that was duplicated in virtual reality. A window served as a gateway between the virtual and the physical. Space was thus a very important component in the experience that was mediated by computer-animated images (created in Blender). Sound cues alert the interactor to where the playable attention-getting elements are located in the space. Doubt is created by the experience as to what is "real" and what is not. McClure's thesis document is available upon request for a deeper understanding of her project. I argue that in-situ installations like *Depth Perception* aim squarely at demonstrating the integration of the virtual in space, a kind of blended reality. Using Krueger's responsive environment qualities, McClure was able to lead the interactor through a linear experience with sound cues. The rest of the conflict between what is real and not was created through the level of abstraction in the imagery. The possibility of furthering the visual meshing of fantasy with tactile reality is the contribution this project makes.

Sultanali Barodawala – *The Memory of Aden Walker* – An Immersive Experience of a Memory of the Future, MFA DT thesis 2015

Sultan Barodawala created a fully immersive experience in a motion-base activated chair that synchronized movement with the content in the film about a fictitious character, Aden Walker.[13] The obsessive recording of Barodawala's own life from the time he was a young teenager was an important impetus for this project. He writes:

> I have been documenting memories for a long time, but I've always been faced with the same conflict: capturing the memory verses being part of the memory. We often see people capturing moments rather than experiencing them. Take a simple music concert, for example. Most of today's generation has a phone in their hand recording parts of the concert rather than expe-

---

12 Ibid., p. 3.
13 Sultanali Barodawala, *The Memory of Aden Walker*, YouTube video, 7:17 min., uploaded by "Barodawala, Sultanali," October 31, 2015, https://www.youtube.com/watch?v=u9pOd5z6Gdc (accessed October 4, 2018).

148

riencing it a hundred percent. With the advent of wearable computing, will we in the future be able to seamlessly record our memories and experiences without a physical device? How will that change the way we see and remember our lives? The question that fascinated me the most was how we would experience memories in the future.[14]

Barodawala's fascination led him to investigate the sociocultural and psychological effects of memory deeply. He created a narrative where everyone's memory is a commodity served up by large cloud storage farms. In his project documentation, he inquired about a future "with new technologies inventing different ways to look at the virtual, the way we see and remember will completely change." The resulting experience is a linear narrative displayed in a head mounted display rigged into a motion-base driven chair with haptic signals occurring at emotionally heightened moments. We travel on Aden's memory flow. Aden's memory is like a roller coaster ride. The soundtrack was, according to Barodawala, almost as important as the live-action 360 narrative with actors shot in New York, Puerto Rico, and Mumbai, India. The entire experience needed a graphical user interface that delivered the points of the mysterious narrative about the demise of a loved one.

Barodawala, an accomplished cinematographer and visual effects artist, personally created the transitions and other necessary effects to maintain the viewer's orientation on the narrative. The controlled memory provides an unpleasant look back at a relationship gone wrong and an unhealthy, addictive adherence to nostalgia and pain of the past. Reinforced by a surround sound track and physical stimuli help the immersion deliver an emotional effect.

Here, Barodawala offers a critical experience of our relentless recording of present reality; and, how a corporation might usurp a memory for sale in the future. The linear VR experience was limited to a window of about a ninety-degree view. Being strapped into a vibrating chair and enclosed in an HMD limits the interactor's ability to move and emphasizes the claustrophobic experience of living inside another person's point of view. What would Krueger think of this experience? I think, like McClure's experience, that the success is in delivering a message but not an

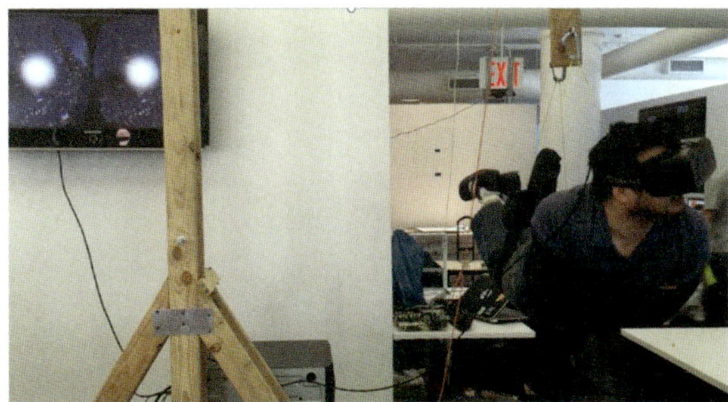

Figure 11: *Unequal Paired Cooperative Controls.* The Rider.

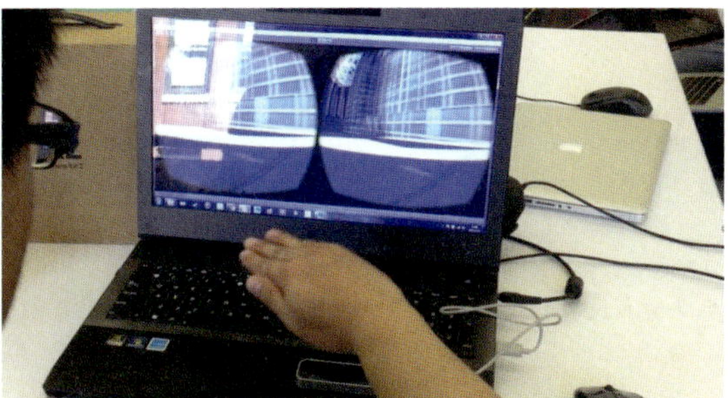

Figure 12: *Dreamscape.* Hand gestures make leaping and turning intuitive

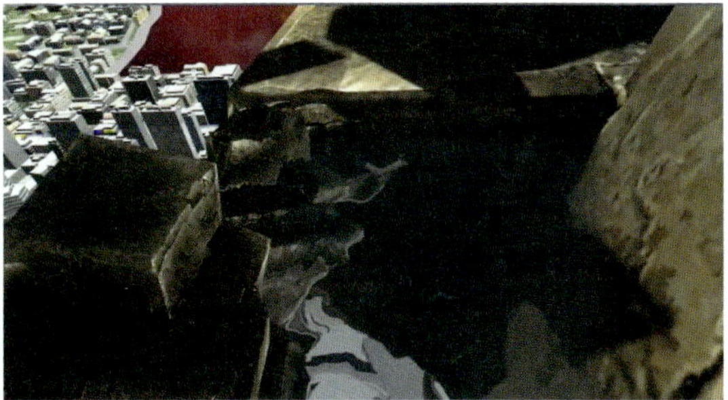

Figure 13: *Dreamscape.* A leap into a dreamscape with an exact mirror on the other side of the reflecting pool

---

14 Sultanali Barodawala, *The Memory of Aden Walker,* Master's Thesis (Master of Fine Art in Design and Technology, The New School, Parsons, 2015), p. 4.

Figure 14: *Penumbra*. The hand of the painter obscured by the computer-generated version of the painting.

interactive one. The linear narrative is a journey that delivers an abstracted critique of systems that control us even with today's technology. The environment is not responsive as Krueger would like us to experience, but it is provocative and evocative. In seven minutes, it does deliver meaning and commentary.

Lucy Bonner – *Not A Compliment*

I included Lucy Bonner's *Not A Compliment*[15] because she found, that the visceral, physical effects of confrontation by catcallers on dark and gloomy urban streets are very effective in virtual reality.

> When I moved to New York, I was suddenly confronted by the overwhelming amount of street harassment and its ensuing emotional effect. While in Houston I was sheltered from it for the most part—I have a theory about the protective bubble of cars—but on Broadway, in my Bushwick neighborhood, I was hit full-force on a daily basis. When attempting to explain why the harassment upset me, [especially] to those who had not experienced it for themselves ... Some people simply had no idea what it was like and were unwilling to give it much credence. Men were surprised by the regularity, pervasiveness, and severity of my experiences with street harassment, but did not really understand the repercussions of it or how street harassment supports and is a symptom of, the dominant patriarchal system in which we live .... I realized that I could use my daily experience and my anger at continued disbelief to craft a project exemplifying the 'compliment' of street harassment.[16]

Bonner created the project in her first core MFA DT Major Studio when she did not yet know Unity 3D. Her novice level use of the medium still drove home the intended message of the experience, however. For example, she dealt with the aesthetic issues of pre-modeled and rigged human characters and character rigs. Nevertheless, the concept and the execution of the first-person point-of-view in a linear, non-interactive experience held up to deliver a message especially for men who were not aware of the effects of catcalling on women. The reality unfolded without having the power to do anything to change it. Again, sound played a critical part.

Most palpable were lascivious and disturbing catcalls the interactors experience as they walked down the street. Bonner's tests with both male and female viewers demonstrated the success of the virtual experience. The simulation demonstrates the painful attack

15 Lucy Bonner, *Not A Compliment*, Vimeo video, 2:20 min., uploaded by "Bonner Lucy" September 30, 2015, https://vimeo.com/140943705 (accessed October 4, 2018).
16 Lucy Bonner, *Not A Compliment*, Major Studio 1 Project (Master of Fine Art in Design and Technology, The New School, Parsons, 2014), p. 1.

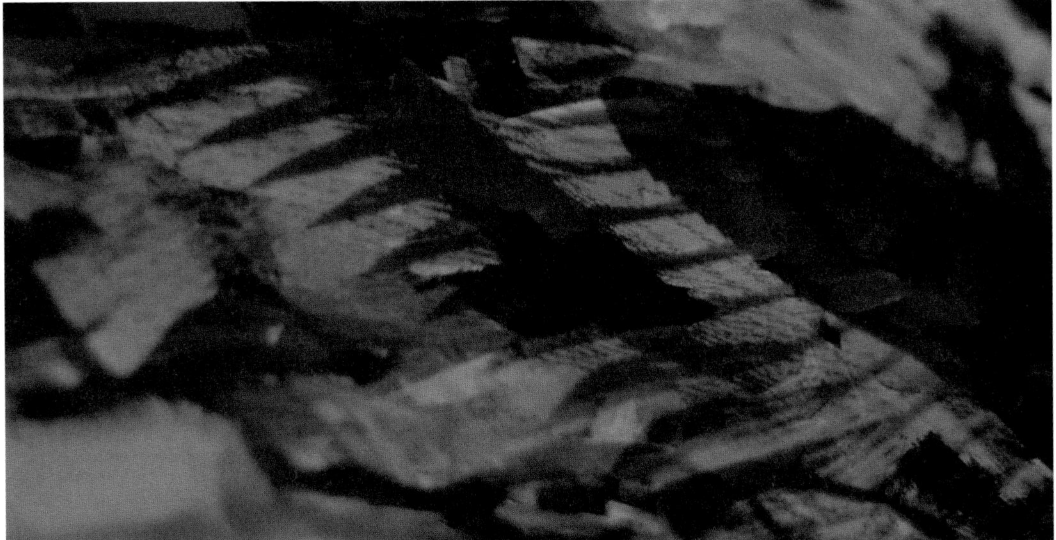

Figure 15: *Penumbra*. Painting pattern created by the computer.

of language on the psyche. The effect of walking down the street to receive the barrage of insults is visceral, particularly for men who are rarely subjected to this reality.

Henry Lam – *Unequal Paired Cooperative Controls Motion Simulation for Use with Oculus Rift*

Henry Lam involved the physical and psychological concentration of the interactor in a two-player video game where one player (the Carrier) is controlling the motion of another player (the Rider) who is shouting commands to shoot at hostiles firing on him.

> I am studying compliance and defiance in a cooperative gaming environment because I want to find out how attempts at control and authority can be exhibited, in order to understand unequal peer relationships. I am more interested in exploring the user interaction than the biomechanical functions of this piece. Although both users are tied to the same overall experience, the two users have two completely different roles in the interactions and sensory inputs with the device. Because certain sensory inputs and mechanical controls are exclusive to each user, attempts at commanding the other user emerge. This establishment or conflict of authority will highlight the unequal

nature of the two users. Although the Rider seemingly has the most engaging experience, the Carrier has the ability and choice to guide, disturb, or cooperate with the Rider.[17]

Lam created a human-sized jib made out of two-by-four struts where one of the collaborative team participants is suspended and attached to the long end of the lever arm. Lam calls this participant, the Carrier. On the other end of the rig, the Rider experiences the actions of the Carrier with an HMD displaying a game (built in Unity) that simulates flight over a large city. In his production paper, Lam describes: "The Carrier's range of motion will be jumping, standing, kneeling, and crouching in place ... the opposite vertical motion for the Rider, who is lying prone in a sling harness set, [translates] to a drop in elevation when the Carrier jumps and a rise in elevation when the Carrier crouches."

Exploration of interfaces that cause collaborative play is both fun and evocative. Whether the Carrier decides to listen to the Rider's shouting instructions or whether the Rider feels they are at the mercy of the Carrier are emotional states that we experience in our journeys through life. A game that helps us experience this simulation might give us clues to decisions we make in collaborative teams. A new experiment in sociopsychology awaits!

---

17 Henry Lam, *Unequal Paired Cooperative Controls: Motion Simulation for use with Oculus Rift*, Major Studio 2 Project (Master of Fine Arts, The New School, Parsons, 2015). p. 3.

When considering Krueger's criteria, these kinds of interfaces go well beyond what was possible in the nineteen-seventies. The synchronization of the effect of the jib on the person experiencing the world in the HMD effectively demonstrates the importance of a full-body haptic experience.

Geyao Zhang – *Dreamscape*

In his second MFA in design and technology studio, entitled *Dreamscape*,[18] Yang challenged the limitations of controllers and joysticks to control the experience. We find ourselves navigating through a large city of skyscrapers. The interface is a Leap Motion interface that tracks the child-like finger puppet motions that Yao makes in this dreamscape. The interactor can leap up to the height of the buildings. We soon discover a land beyond the top of the skyscraper that is an exact mirror of the original world. According to his project paper, Zhang's target audience is adventurous and wants to try new interfaces to play games. They are interested in science fiction and other kinds of realities, like dreams. In Virtual Reality, Zhang created an experience of flying. To give the audience complete navigation control, he chose specific gestures like finger "walking" that can invoke childhood memories of navigating the world of the imagination. Simple gestures above the Leap Motion sensor help us walk forward, leap, and turn. This project was a simple translation of hand gestures into an off-the-shelf software development kit (SDK) to create a compelling, nostalgic, and childlike interactive experience. The hand gestures were simple to learn because they reminded interactors of their own childhood imaginary journeys through dream spaces.

Madhav Tankha – *Penumbra* – Interactive painting MFA DT Thesis 2015

With *Penumbra*[19], Madhav Tankha achieved a different immersive experience objective than telling a traditional story. In his project document, he describes "*Penumbra* [a]s a ceaseless exchange between a physical painting and a digital image, each evolving in response to the other. Black and white, geometry and organicity, space and time, the human and the computer, converse to form an endless, ever-transforming cycle of echoes upon echoes."[20]

Tankha was the solo interactor as he created a performance with the layers of projections of black and white imagery that the computer created and the marks on the canvas that he made himself. He struggled to understand the materiality of paint on a surface versus the digital light patterns from a computer program. He concludes that painting and sculpture are generally static, but they can represent things like time and narrative in ways that are often more impactful precisely because of their static nature. The digital image, in contrast, is immaterial and eminently changeable. Bringing the two together and manipulating the relationship between these qualities … can produce interesting aesthetic and narrative effects. In *Penumbra*, the painter must try and capture the essence of a moving and shifting digital projection. Different transformational states of the projected images are depicted in simultaneity, replacing linear temporal progression with one where the reading of time becomes a more ambiguous task. This ambiguity can perhaps lend the image an air of timelessness and eternity.[21]

Conclusion

The projects presented here addressed challenges of meaning creation in virtual realms, whether being involuntarily subjected to catcalling insults on a dark street (Bonner) or having the interactive power to leap from one building to the next in a dream-like interactive experience (Zhang). Beginning the analysis and inquiry into the effects of these experiences and comparing them to the standards that were set by pioneers like Myron Krueger is what I attempted to do with this summary of my 2015 talk. With the advances in 5G networks and faster CPU and GPU processing, virtual and mixed realities will continue to mature in delivery methods such as less cumbersome head-mounted displays coupled with full-body engagement gear. Content that is successful in virtual space remains the biggest challenge. As Jonathan Gottschall[22] tells us, our minds organize stories into meaningful experiences no matter what the input: stories make us human. By extension, the interface experiments of the MFA DT students featured here further challenged the way media makers create visual as well as embodied meaning.

18 Geyao Zhang, *Dreamscape*, Major Studio 2 Project (Master of Fine Arts in Design and Technology, The New School, Parsons, 2015).
19 Madhav Tankha, *Penumbra*, master's thesis (Master of Fine Art in Design and Technology, The New School, Parsons, 2015).
20 Ibid., p. 1.
21 Ibid., p. 4.
22 Jonathan Gottschall, *The Storytelling Animal: How Stories Make Us Human* (Boston, 2012).

Lower-end access such as mobile phones and cardboard interfaces and production resources and their distribution on internet channels such as Google's YouTube 360 have made virtual, augmented, and mixed reality experiences ubiquitous. Work in both theory and practice is awaiting us to study the impact of these new mass media and our ability to deliver compelling stories and meaning.

Bibliography

Gibson, William. *Neuromancer*. New York,1984.

Gottschall, Jonathan. *The Storytelling Animal: How Stories Make Us Human*. Boston, MA, 2012.

Kreuger, Myron. "Responsive Environments." National Computer Conference. New York: Association for Computing Machinery (June 1977).

Milgram, Paul, and Fumio Kishino. "A Taxonomy of Mixed Reality Visual Displays," Tokyo, Japan: Institute of Electronics, Information and Communications Engineers. Information Systems, Trans:Vol. E77–D, No. 12 (December 1994), pp. 1321–1329,.

Robinett, Warren. "Synthetic Experience: A Proposed Taxonomy." *Presence: Teleoperators in Virtual Environments* 1, 2 (January 1992), pp. 229–247.

Sutherland, Ivan. "A head-mounted three dimensional display." University of Minnesota, Minneapolis: American Federation of Information Processing Societies (Fall 1968).

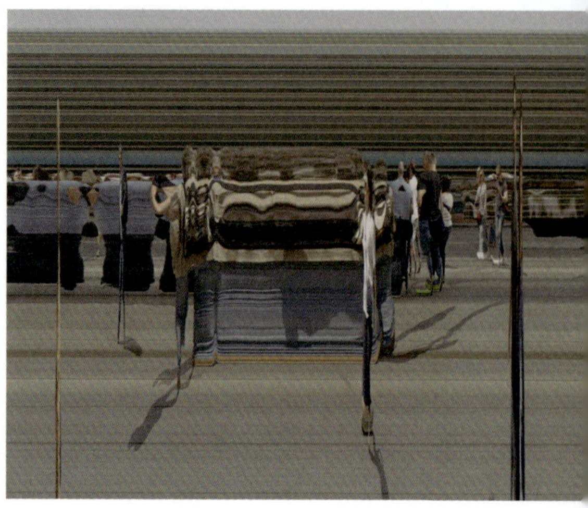

Virgil Widrich (AT)

Images between Digital Realism and Analog Believability

Analog film techniques, with which previously unseen moving images were created for more than a century, have almost completely disappeared in recent years. They have been replaced by digitally generated images, which are essentially created with a small number of market-dominating tools and, despite their seemingly infinite possibilities, they have become surprisingly similar. Instead of just looking ahead and further optimizing the software animation of moving hair and exploding fireballs, it is also worth taking a look back: the combination of analog and digital techniques, the multiple "in" and "out" of analog and digital, is a considerable, unexplored treasure to create entirely different images that do not pretend realism but become credible precisely through their abstraction.

The fifty-year-olds today are the generation that has experienced the disruptive change from analog to digital photo and film technology during their own lives. There will never again be filmmakers who, without knowing the digital possibilities ahead, have had years of personal experience with Super 8 or sixteen millimeter film, Steenbeck editing tables, film glue, or the exciting waiting time between the exposure of

negative film and its first screening. The change of the entire film production pipeline imposed by the industry has long since been completed, most analog film devices have only museum value and the cinemas can no longer screen thirty-five millimeter film—once one of the very few formats of worldwide standardization. While the possibilities of film creation are expanding, however, there are also losses to complain about, like the art of not showing something but instead leaving it to the imagination of the audience. This art was born out of technical limitations and because many effects could not be produced with the help of pure mechanical and chemical film tricks: the slow transformation of Fredric March in *Dr. Jekyll and Mr. Hyde* (1931)[1] was seen in a scene that focused not on his face, but on his hands. The monster from *Alien* (1979)[2] similarly exposed only a few details. The first time director Ridley Scott showed the whole monster was the moment it died: the beast lost its power through the revelation of its form.

Nor does the digital world seem to be concerned with filming a CGI scene as if it had really happened. We see cameras that follow the fast gliding *Spider-Man*

---

1 *Dr. Jekyll and Mr. Hyde*. Directed by Rouben Mamoulian, screenplay by Samuel Hoffenstein and Percy Heath, based on the novel by Robert Louis Stevenson, 1931.
2 *Alien*. Directed by Ridley Scott, screenplay by Dan O'Bannon and Ronald Shusett, 1979.

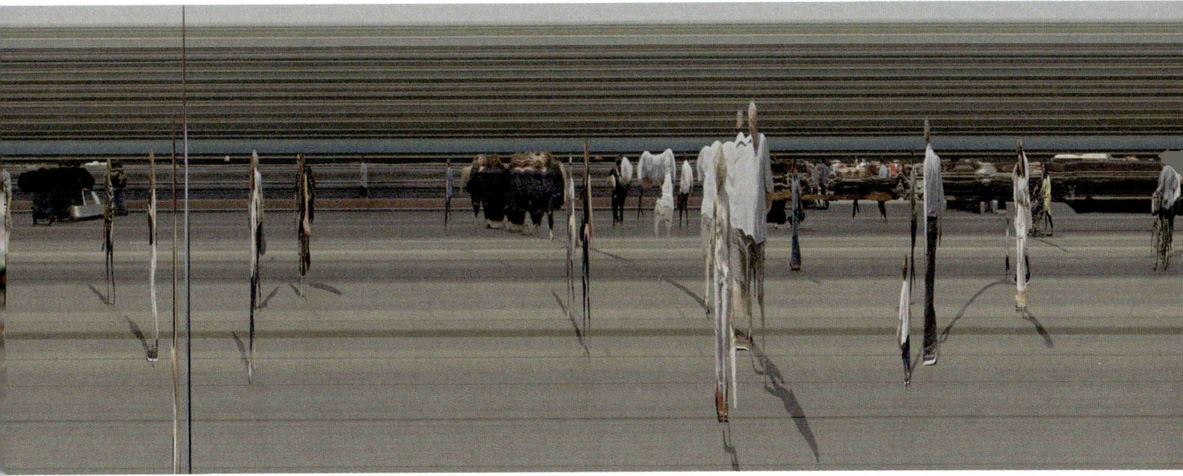

Figure 1: Test for new *tx-transformations* in 2018. Camera: Martin Putz.

(2003)[3] right around the curves, but this is not a real camera with a certain mass and controlled by a person who first has to react to the action. It is the omniscient camera from a video game that does not follow the action, but rather dictates it and thus deprives the viewers' gaze. However, since no medium in the history of the media has ever been completely replaced by a new one, small resistance groups are sprouting up in many cities in which a new generation of artists are engaged in analog film techniques.

Instead of either cheering on progress or regretting the loss of film grain and playing off "analog" and "digital," old and new, against each other, it is worth taking a look at some personal examples of artistic possibilities that the combination of these two worlds offers.

In the 1990s, analogous thinking gave Austrian film-maker and inventor Martin Reinhart the idea of regarding film as a paper flipbook and thus as an "information block." He wondered what would happen if you did not look at this block from the front, page by page, but across time, as if you were cutting a book into slices and looking at the pictures at the cut edges. He named this new technology *tx-transform*[4]: normally each indi-

vidual frame of film depicts the entire space but only a moment in time (1/24 second). With tx-transformed films, it is just the opposite: each frame shows the entire time, but only a tiny portion of space–the left portion of the picture turns into the "the before," the right one into "the after." With *tx-transform*, sequences can be produced in which filmic representation is no longer fixed exclusively through the spatial presence of an object; rather, its form depends upon a complex interplay of relative motions. Accordingly, an object on film is no longer defined as the likeness of a concrete form of existence but as a condition over time resulting in a series of astounding visual effects: heads grow out of themselves, moving trains become shorter and shorter with increasing speed, and fixed objects, like houses, start to disappear–which is like the opposite of the beginning of photography itself: some of the first images taken by Louis Daguerre in the 1840s showed completely empty cities. The reason was the very long exposure time which made all moving persons and vehicles simply disappear.

Martin Reinhart first began cutting a series of physical photos of a moving Viennese tram into strips and

---

3 *Spider-Man*. Directed by Sam Raimi, screenplay by David Koepp, based on the Marvel comic book by Stan Lee and Steve Ditko, 2002.
4 Martin Reinhart, "tx-transform," (website), https://www.tx-transform.com/ (accessed October 4, 2018).

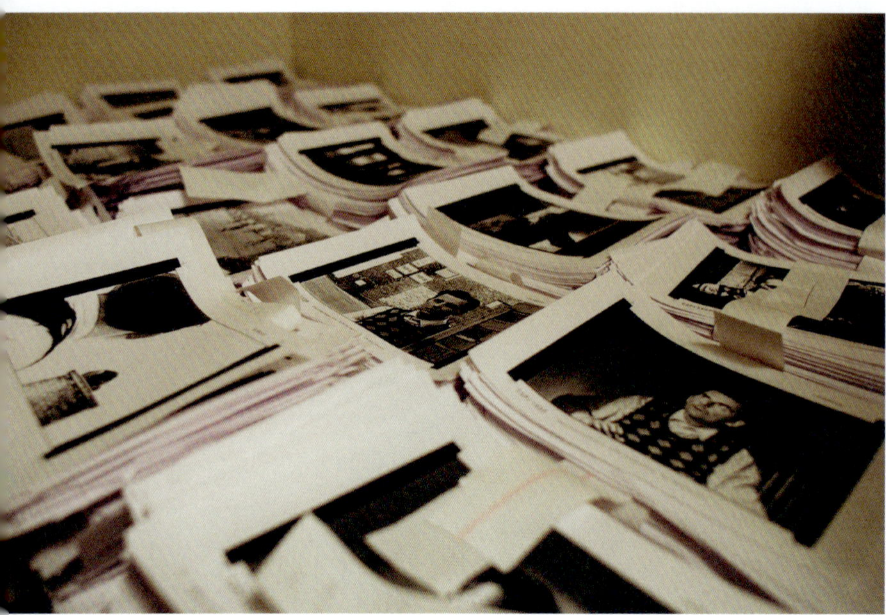

Figure 2: Paper with the film frames ready for the animation table for *Copy Shop* (2001).

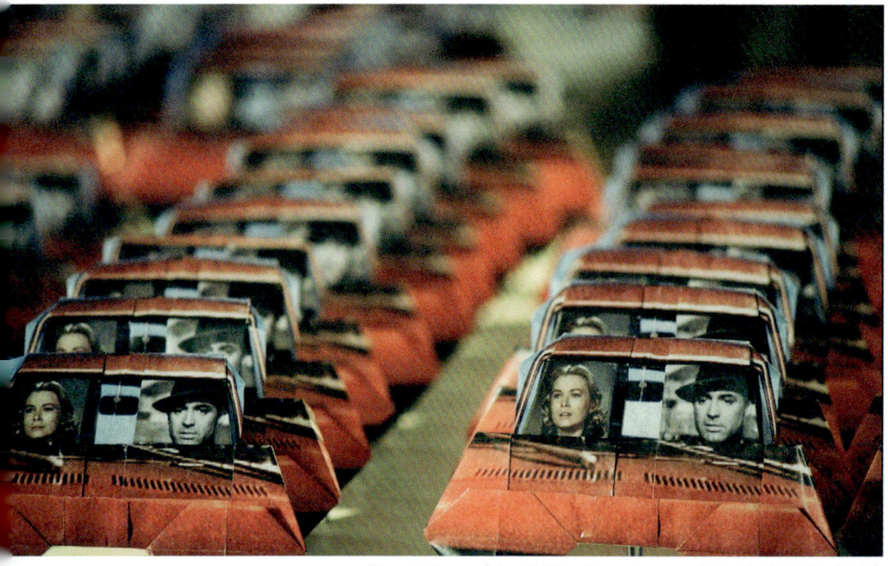

Figure 3: Some of the 60,000 objects that were folded for *Fast Film* (2003).

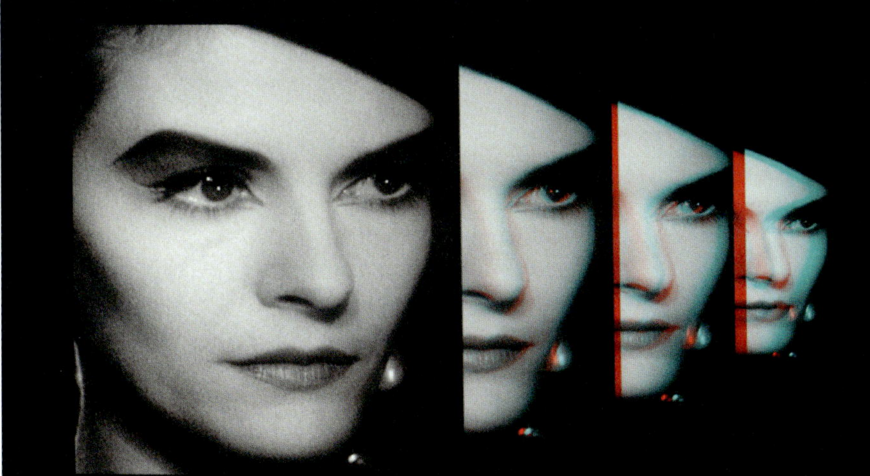

Figure 4: Still from *back track* (2015).

glued them together again. In 1998, the short film *tx-transform* (1998, 5 minutes)[5] was finally made, not with the help of knives, but with computer technology. It illustrated a parable of Bertrand Russell on the theory of relativity and was presented at Ars Electronica in Linz in the same year and subsequently at international media festivals. However, the hardware and software options at that time only allowed images to be calculated in PAL resolution (720 by 576 pixels).

In 2018, on behalf of ZKM—Zentrum für Kunst und Medien Karlsruhe—a real-time extension of *tx-transform* with the now available higher resolution, and a 360 degree installation was filmed with the OmniCam of the Fraunhofer Institute Berlin.[6]

Copy Shop (2001, 12 minutes)[7] is another example of mixing analog and digital film techniques: The film, about a man who reproduces himself until the whole world consists only of him, was first shot digitally with DV video cameras. The compositing of the doppelgangers was done in the AfterEffects program, but the finished digital film frames were printed out on paper and photographed again on a thirty-five millimeter animation table. Several unplanned disturbances (shadows caused by the overheated drum of the printer, stripes caused by uneven or fading toner,

tremors, cracks, and movements of the paper on the animation table) were not corrected but permitted as an artistic means. The idea of viewing paper as both an information carrier and as an object was further developed in 2003 in the animated short movie *Fast Film:*[8] while *Copy Shop* still had flat images, *Fast Film* turned folded paper objects printed with film classics into a chase of origami horses, railways, and airplanes. The reduction of the action sequences to paper format took away the original violence from the scenes and allowed a game with the interchangeability of standardized multiple heroes. Could this film have been made with a computer? Yes, every image, including all paper folds and tears, could have been produced digitally—but in such a work process completely different ideas would have emerged than with the use of real paper and thus the result would be different.

Can one remix old 2D movies into a new 3D movie? The short film *back track* (2015, 7 minutes)[9] tried the experiment and projected excerpts from twenty-five feature films onto screens, which were then photographed in 3D frame by frame. Filmmaker Peter Tscherkassky on *back track*:

---

5 *tx-transform*. Directed by Martin Reinhart, Virgil Widrich, 1998.
6 Martin Reinhart, Virgil Widrich "tx-reverse-360°," https://zkm.de/de/ausstellung/2018/10/tx-reverse-360deg (accessed October 4, 2018).
7 *Copy Shop*. Directed by Virgil Widrich, 2002.
8 *Fast Film*. Directed by Virgil Widrich, 2003.
9 *back track*. Directed by Virgil Widrich, 2015.

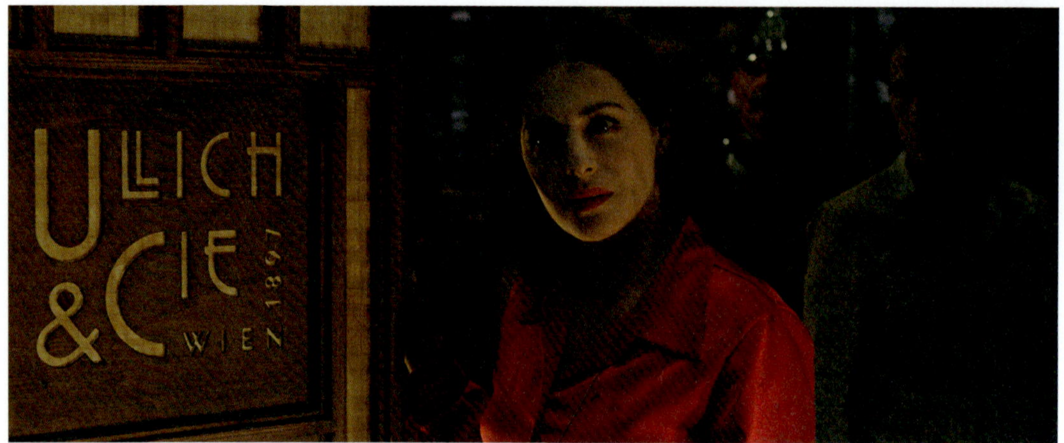

Figure 5: Amira Casar in *Night of a 1000 Hours* (2016), directed by Virgil Widrich, DOP Christian Berger.

Various found footage scenes are projected onto as many as seven movable, semi-transparent panes of glass at once, while a computer-guided camera photographs them frame by frame and translates the imagery into a three-dimensional spectacle. At the same time, a host of lovingly constructed props introduce analog components that flit through this digitally Burroughsian cut-up cosmos of Widrich's conjuring. The plot is seamlessly interwoven, narrated by an off-screen voice entirely in keeping with the film noir tradition to which 'back track' is evidently deeply committed: a woman; several men (a writer, a womanizer, a criminal?), each hopelessly under the spell of the siren-like lady. Ultimately they all meet in a house full of mirrors where time seems to stand still, the scene culminating in a showdown that leaves three dead and the storyteller perplexed: "The more you look, the less you really know."[10]

In a way, *back track* was an artistic and technical preparation for the feature film *Night of a 1000 Hours* (2016, 90 minutes)[11]. The story of a family haunted by all their deceased ancestors takes place entirely in a Viennese palace. However, the palace is not a real place but the memory of its present and former inhabitants of their domicile at different times. Consequently, the building should not allow exact orientation and should not adhere to objective building standards in its viewing directions. Since the palace changes dramatically over the course of the film and is destroyed in the end, original locations or complete studio replicas were dispensed with and the entire film was realized instead on a six by six meter studio stage with rear projections behind it. The walls, the rooms, the furniture in the background, the views through the windows to the outside were created digitally in advance according to templates and played on the set as rear projections on two screens; at the same time the movable props in the foreground, doors, furniture, beds, et cetera were placed in the studio and illuminated in such a way that digital and real light sources could no longer be separated. Thus the digital moonlight illuminated real faces through projected windows or real objects (e.g., candles) cast back their glow or shadows onto virtual wallpaper walls. The perspective of the virtual backgrounds had been adjusted for each camera perspective setting. It is only through the montage that the credible impression of a real three-dimensional space emerges in the minds of the audience, which is the memory of a house that never existed in this way. By pre-visualizing the palace as a 3D model with the real-time-machinima engine *Moviestorm*[12] and projecting interactively changeable content on set, *Night of a 1000 Hours* represents a new combination of virtual reality and linear cinema. The whole project created enormous technical and artistic challenges for the selective lighting of the set with the help of reflectors, using the CRLS (Cine Reflect Lighting System)[13]

10 Peter Tscherkassky, "back track," Sixpackfilm (website), https://sixpackfilm.com/en/catalogue/show/2239 (accessed December 5, 2018).

11 *Night of a 1000 Hours*. Directed by Virgil Widrich, 2016.

12 *Moviestorm*. Software developed by Moviestorm Ltd. https://www.moviestorm.co.uk/ (accessed October 4, 2018).

13 Christian Berger, "CRLS – Cine Reflect Lighting System," Christian Berger (website), https://www.christianberger.at/crls/ (accessed

developed by cameraman Christian Berger. After the many "flicker films" by Peter Kubelka,[14] Tony Conrad,[15] Paul Sharits,[16] and others from the 1950s to 1970s, the perfect digital film technology offers the potential to study pure perceptual effects. *Light Matter,*[17] an experimental work from 2018 leaves any contamination and creation of (apparent) film grain only to the eyes and the brains of its viewers trying to process the information. Continuously brightening flashes of light, initially black on black and barely perceptible, increase in intensity over the course of five minutes to such an extent that, depending on the viewer and the technical screening situation, astonishing effects are produced by rapid alternation of light and black film frames. Although the film is black and white, the flashes trigger the perception of pseudocolors in blue, orange, or yellow in many viewers due to the over-irritation of the optic nerve. In some parts of the film, abrupt cuts can occur due to a reversal of the brightness, which in reality does not exist at all but is due to the fact that, depending on the contrast between the images, the electronic structure of brightness takes place faster than its deletion. *Light Matter* takes advantage of a physiological phenomenon that was described by Gustav Theodor Fechner and Hermann von Helmholtz

as early as the middle of the 19th century but has not yet been satisfactorily explained scientifically. Around the turn of the century, the effect was finally marketed as an optical toy and has since been named after its inventor, the English toymaker Charles Benham. The rapid change from light to dark triggers a subjective perception of color in the brain without the detour via the receptors of color vision in the eye. *Light Matter* was made without a camera and goes straight to the brain.

These subjective examples from my own work demonstrated some possibilities to create other kinds of images using the process of digital "in" and "out." But what will become of the camera, which thanks to digital technology now floats through any story free of its physical body, masseless and omniscient? Which is not bound to a human angle of vision, but can have a 360 degree panoramic view? Are traditional editing and narrative techniques still appropriate for this camera? Shouldn't such a camera also think completely differently and have a different kind of "brain"? The question "who is the camera?" which is as old as the cinema itself, will be answered by future filmmakers in completely new ways.

October 4, 2018).
14 *Arnulf Rainer*. Directed by Peter Kubelka, 1960.
15 *The Flicker*. Directed by Tony Conrad, 1965.
16 *Ray Gun Virus*, Directed by Paul Sharits, 1966.
17 *Light Matter*. Directed by Virgil Widrich, 2018.

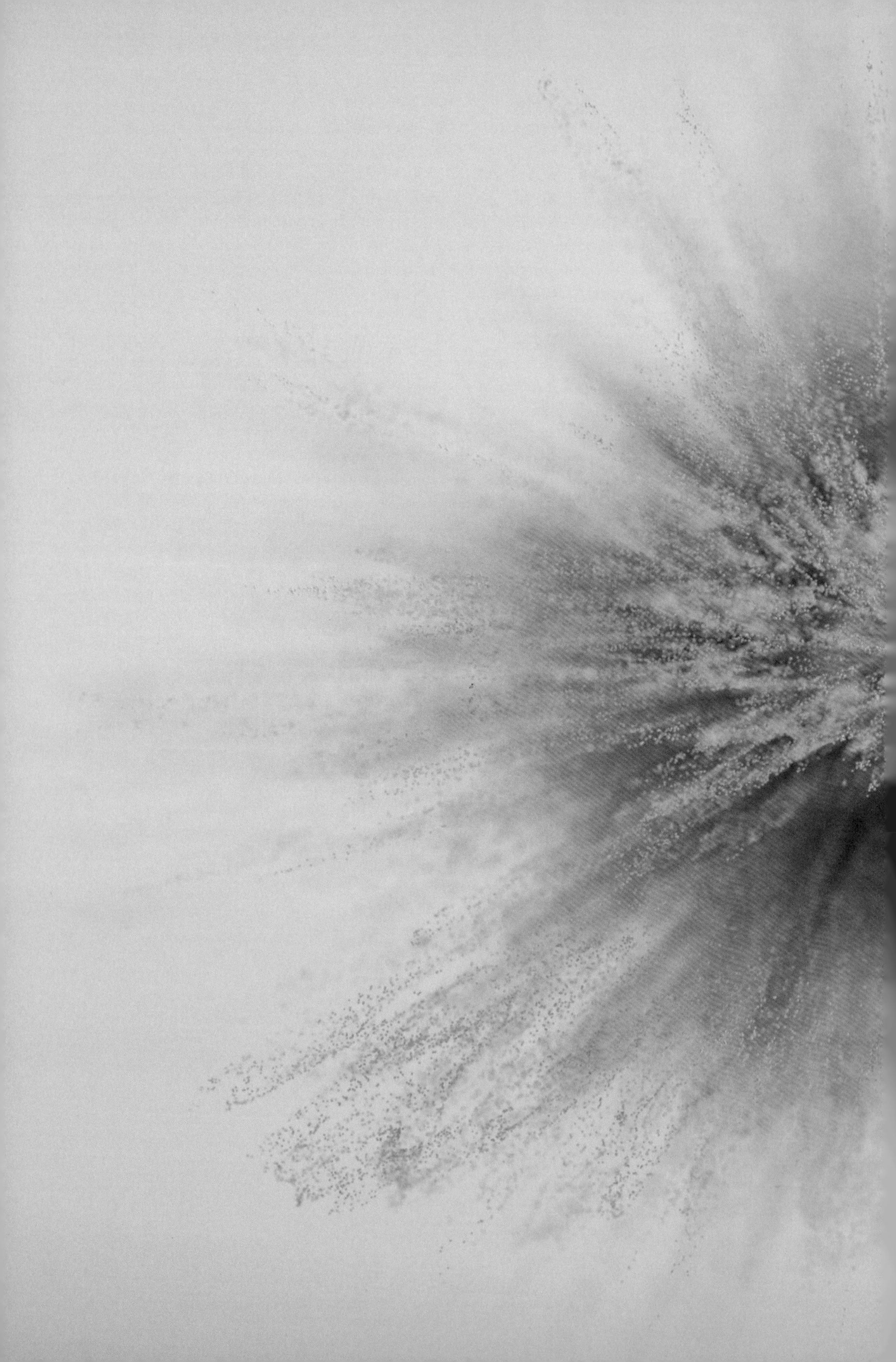

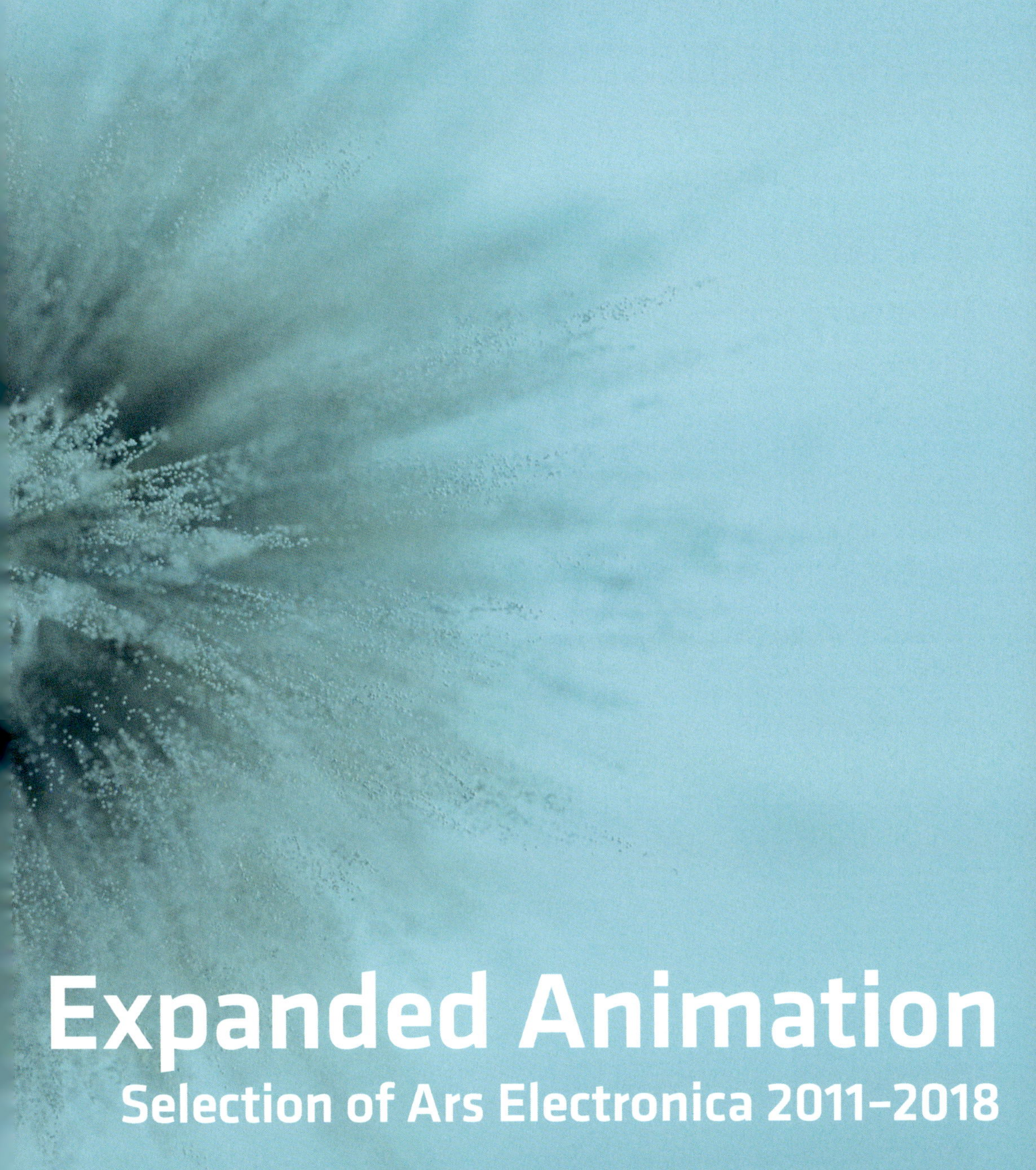

Expanded Animation

Selection of Ars Electronica 2011–2018

Black Rain

Black Rain is a moving-image work made in collaboration with scientists, using data from the Heliospheric Imager (HI). HI is a pair of hi-tech cameras that are observing the space between the sun and the earth from two vantage points in space on the Stereo mission satellites, investigating the structure and propagation of CMEs (coronal mass ejections) as they travel into space from the sun's surface.

We worked directly with the scientists to acquire the individual images, which we turned into a time-lapse sequence. We were able to work with the raw data and had the luxury of asking for the images to be processed to reveal specific information for our requirements. Scientists routinely clean up their data to remove unwanted visual noise which interferes with their scientific objectives. We wanted to encourage these "visual anomalies" in the image processing so that we could reference the technology being used, which emphasizes the presence of a human observer looking out on the universe and trying to understand their place in it. We often use technology signatures in this way to suggest the presence of a watcher.

We explore the nature of the physical world, how we experience it and create an understanding of it, often mediated through the tools of science. We are interested in the matter we see in the data, how the technology reveals these things to us that would otherwise go undetected with the limits of human perception. The way we are observing it comes to the forefront when we see the noise it introduces in the capturing process, as well as cosmic ray flecks impacting the camera's CCD and other interesting material affects on the capturing process, it also includes many visual anomalies introduced to the image through the capturing technology.

There are three versions of this work, single screen, installation and a live performance.

Single channel + installation
A Semiconductor work by Ruth Jarman and Joe Gerhardt

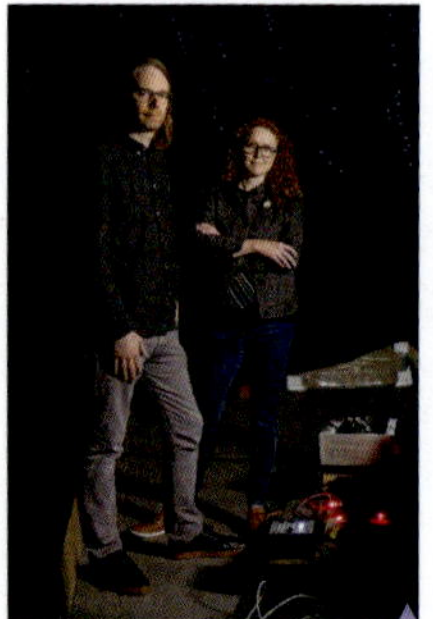

Semiconductor (GB) is the artist duo Ruth Jarman and Joe Gerhardt. Through moving image works, sound and multi-media installations they explore the material nature of our physical world and how we experience it. They have worked together for twelve years developing a unique approach to working with the computer as a sculptural tool. Through self-developed techniques of manipulation, generation and observation they create first-person experiences of the material world around us, beyond the limits of our perception.

Website

https://semiconductorfilms.com/

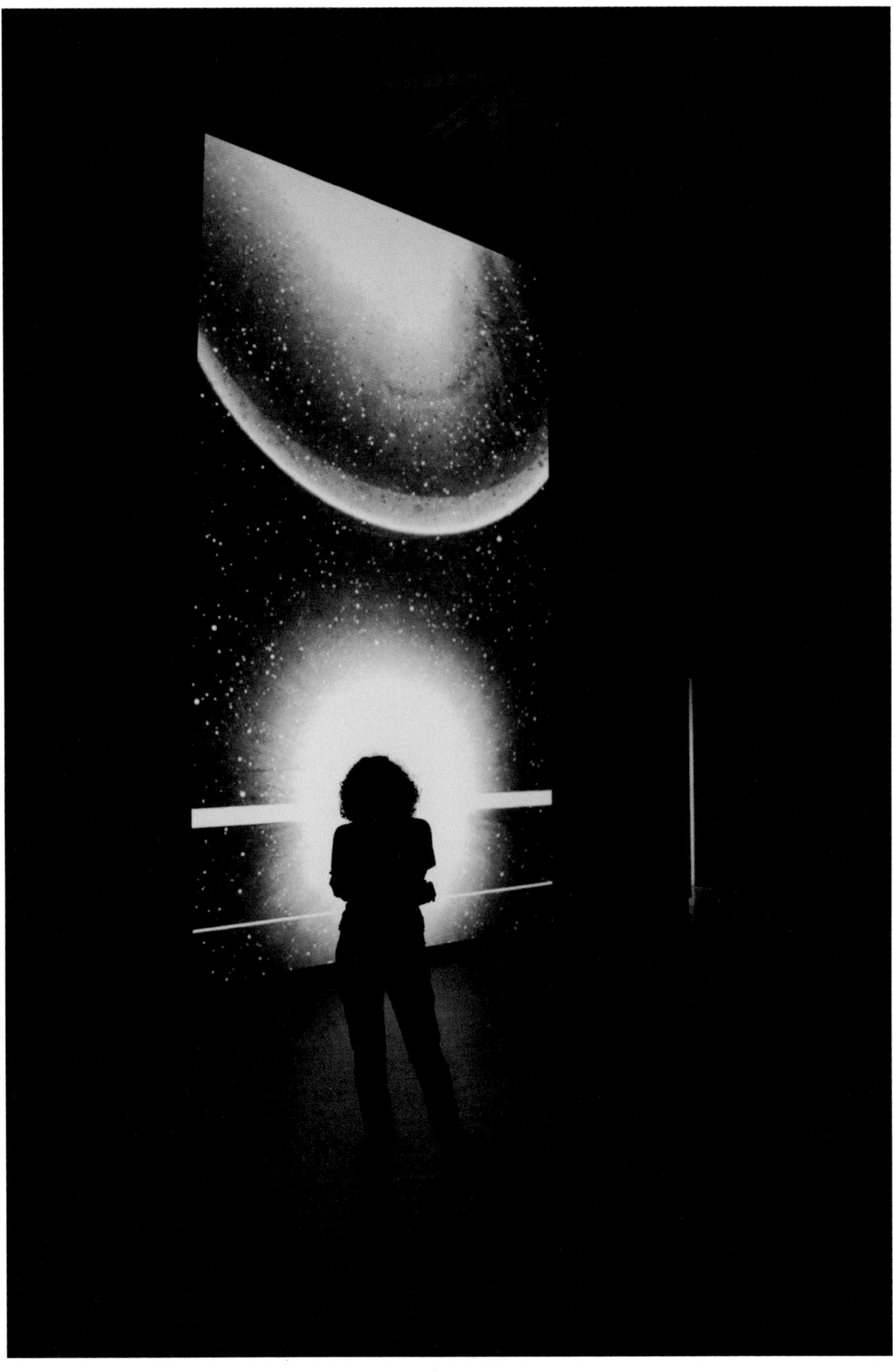

Black Rain

Flux

Candaş Şişman's video installation *Flux* is dedicated to famous sculptor Ilhan Koman. *Flux* can be defined as a digital animation inspired by the structural features of some of Ilhan Koman's works like *Pi*, *3D Moebius*, *Whirlpool* and *To Infinity...* A red circle, colored in reference to the red radiators of *Ogre*, is traced in a morphological transformation that re-interprets the formal approach of Koman's works.

In Flux, Koman's design process in the making of the *Pi* series has been treated as the emerging of a sphere from a two-dimensional circle by the principle of increasing the surface, and that simple direction is re-interpreted in digital medium. Thanks to this, in the digital animation an entirely different form serial, which does not resemble *Pi* yet remains its design principle, can be followed through the flow of a circle to the sphere. As a conscious attitude of the artist, this work is not designed in a direct visual analogy with Koman's works. During the animation, none of the moments of the transforming form look like *Pi* or *3D Moebius*, but the subjective reading of Koman's approach can be observed.

With the integration of the sounds of various materials—which Koman used in his sculptures—*Flux* turns into an impressive spatial experience.

Video and sound design: Candaş Şişman
Commissioned by: Plato Art Space (Plato collage of higher education), www.platosanat.org.tr

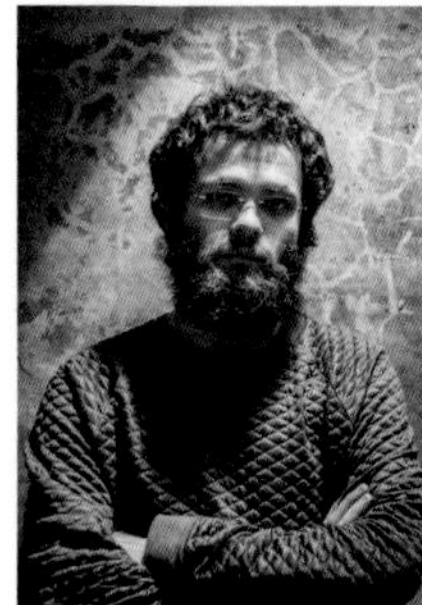

Candaş Şişman (1985, Izmir-Turkey) studied fine arts in high school and graduated from the Animation department of Eskişehir Anadolu University. He spent one year at university in the Netherlands, studying multimedia design. In 2011 he co-founded Nohlab, a studio producing interdisciplinary experiences around art, design & technology. He is also a member of NOS Visuals, which is a collaborative platform that creates real-time, sound-reactive audiovisual performances. For the last five years, he gives lectures on the interaction between sound and visuals in university. Candaş Şişman has received several awards since 2007, among which is an Honorary Mention from Prix ARS Electronica Computer Animation/Film/VFX and Jury Selection Award in Art Division from 18th Japan Media Arts Festival. He participated in many exhibition and festival, such as Venice Architecture Biennale, TED X, Ars Electronica, Todaysart Festival and Japan Media Arts Festival. Candaş Şişman recently exhibited Sonicfield-01 Sound Installation in Venice Architecture Biennale and *Flux* audiovisual installation among İlhan Koman Hulda festival in Istanbul.

Candaş Şişman aims to manipulate our notion of time, space and motion by his work, using digital and mechanical technologies. Taking the natural sciences and universe as his reference point, the artist combines physical forms with digitally produced images. Thus a bridge between the physical world and the digital world becomes visible. The works of Şişman build on complex bases, but the forms are simple, allowing the audience to engage in intellectual interaction with the artwork, in which the "process" is the utmost important structural element.

The artist lives and works in Istanbul, and is represented by PG Art gallery in Turkey.

Selected Exhibitions

2015 | Borders and Boundaries, Mixer – Istanbul, Turkey

2015 | Weltschmertz, PG Art Gallery, Maslak Art Space – Istanbul, Turkey

2015 | Waves exhibition, BlokArt Space – Istanbul, Turkey

2014 | Histories of the Post-Digital: 1960s and 1970s Media Art Snapshots, Akbank Art Space – İstanbul, Turkey

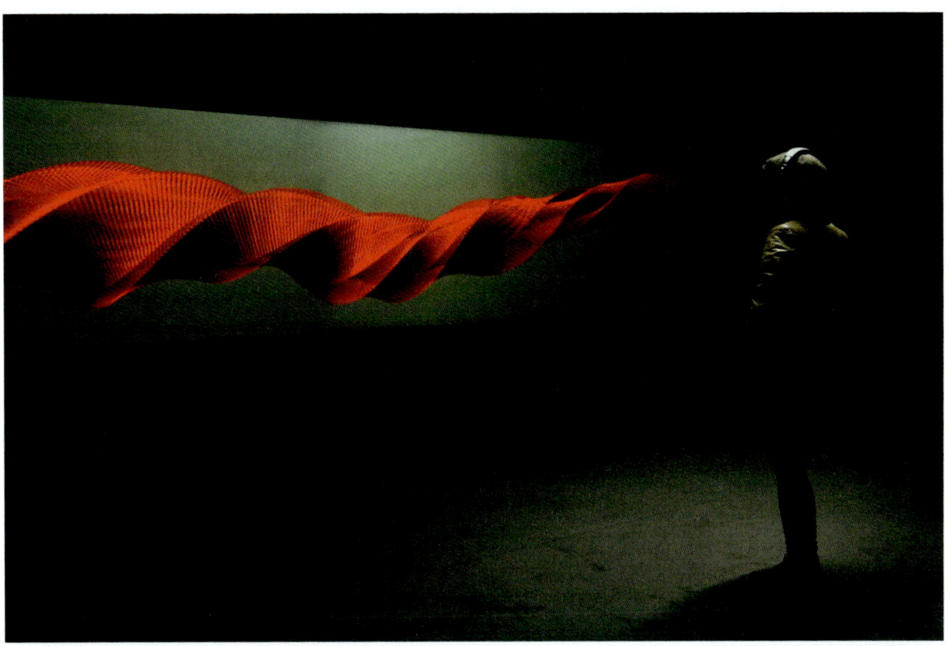

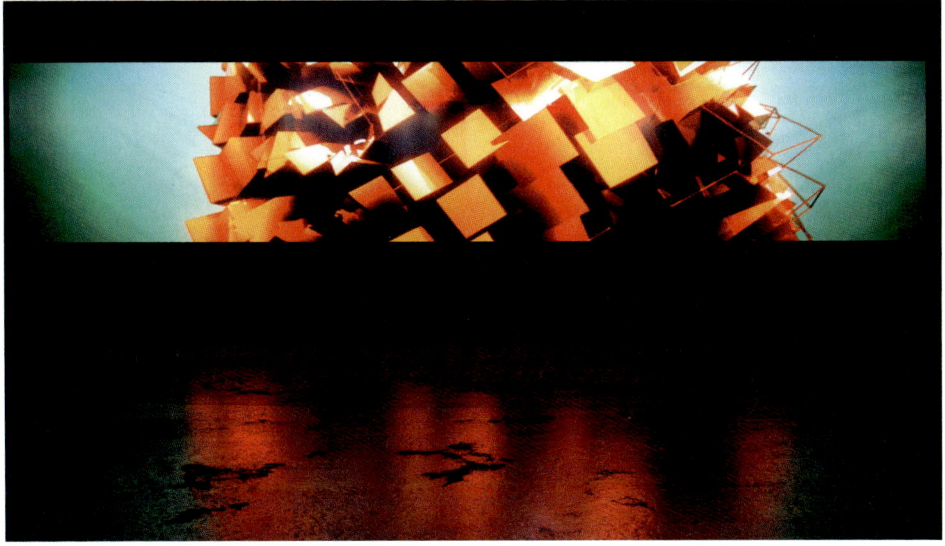

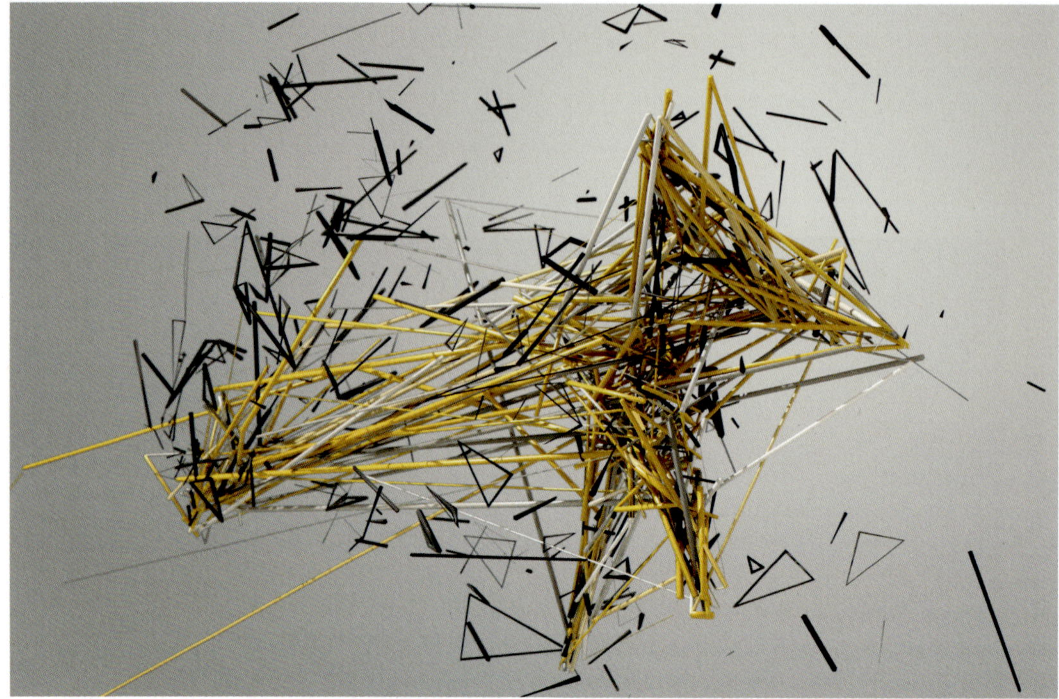

Memo Akten (TR) | Quayola (IT) | 2012

Forms

Forms is a collaboration between the visual artists Quayola and Memo Akten. A series of studies on human motion and its reverberations through space and time.

It is inspired by the works of Eadweard Muybridge, Harold Edgerton Étienne-Jules Marey as well as by similarly inspired cubist works such as Marcel Duchamp's *Nude Descending a Staircase No.2*. Rather than focusing on observable trajectories, it explores techniques of extrapolation to sculpt abstract forms, visualizing unseen relationships—power, balance, grace and conflict—between the body and its surroundings.

The project investigates athletes pushing their bodies to their extreme capabilities, their movements shaped by an evolutionary process targeting a winning performance. Traditionally a form of entertainment in today's society with an overpowering competitive edge, the disciplines are deconstructed and interrogated from an exclusively mechanical and aesthetic point of view, concentrating on the invisible forces generated by and influencing the movement. The source for the study is footage from the Commonwealth Games. The process of transformation from live footage to abstract forms is exposed as part of the interactive multi-screen artwork to provide an insight into the evolution of the specially crafted world in which the athletes were placed.

Quayola & Memo Akten – Artists
Nexus Interactive Arts – Production Company
Beccy McCray – Producer
Jo Bierton – Production Manager
Matthias Kispert – Sound design
Maxime Causeret – Houdini Developer
Raffael F J Ziegler (AKA Moco) – 3D Animator
Katie Parnell – 3D Tracker
Eoin Coughlan – 3D Tracker
Mark Davies – 3D Tracking Supervisor

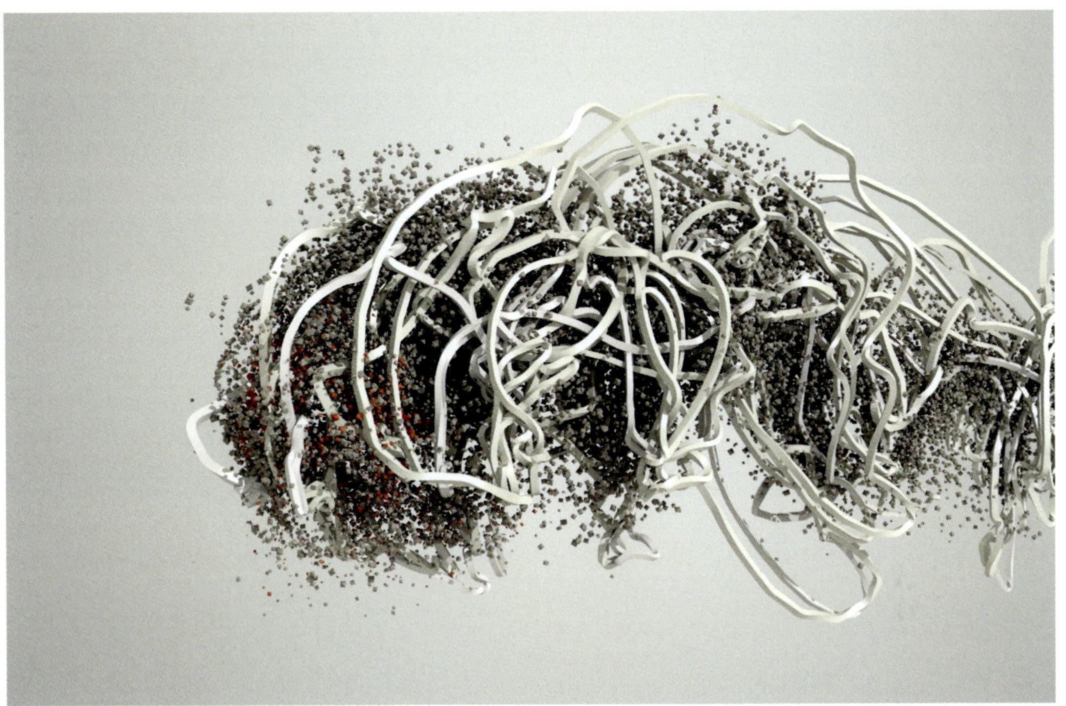

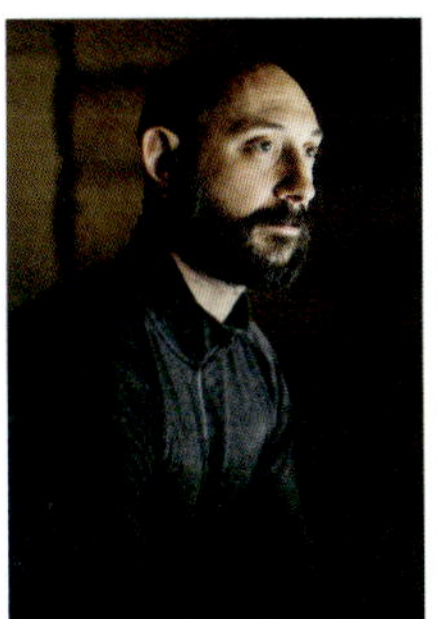

Quayola (IT). Regarded for his enigmatic video installations, Quayola creates hybrid spaces of animated painting and sculpture. Engaging a practice of audiovisual performance, drawing, photography and software programming, he explores a fine boundary between the real and the artificial. Special institutional commissions of Quayola's work have allowed him exceptionally rare access to the art and architecture of churches, theaters and museums in Europe, such as Notre Dame and the Vatican. In his work, original masterpieces and collections become raw canvas, as Quayola anchors a video-based exploration in a conversation about archives, collage, intellectual property and the appreciation of an object.

Website

https://www.quayola.com/

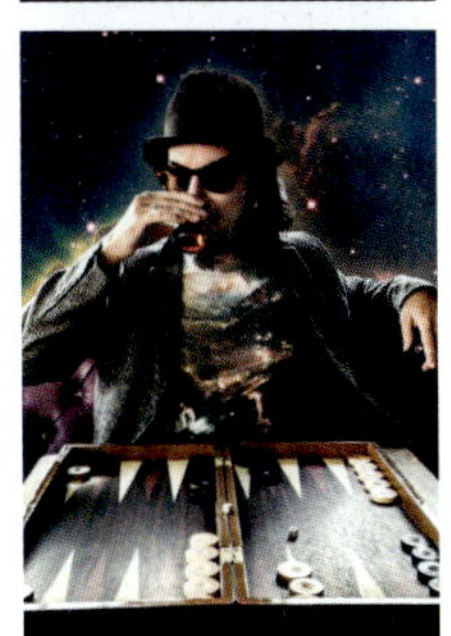

Memo Akten (TK) is an artist, researcher and philomath from Istanbul, Turkey, working with computation as medium, inspired by the intersections of science and spirituality; and collisions between nature, science, technology, ethics, ritual, tradition and religion. Combining critical and conceptual approaches with investigations into form, movement and sound; he works with computational systems and algorithms, designing behavioural abstractions and data dramatizations of natural and anthropogenic processes, to create (interactive, non-interactive or responsive) moving images; video, sound and light installations and performances. Alongside his practice, he is currently working towards a PhD at Goldsmiths University of London in artificial intelligence and expressive human-machine interaction, to enable collaborative creativity between humans and machines. Fascinated by trying to understand the world and human nature, he draws inspiration from fields such as physics, molecular & evolutionary biology, ecology, abiogenesis, neuroscience, anthropology, sociology and philosophy.

Akten received the Prix Ars Electronica Golden Nica in 2013 for his collaboration with Quayola, *Forms*. Since 2009 his works *Body Paint* and *Gold* have toured with the Victoria & Albert Museum's *Decode* exhibition. In 2014 his work as Marshmallow Laser Feast *Laser Forest* was part of the Barbican's *Digital Revolutions* exhibition. Exhibitions and performances include the Grand Palais (Paris FR), Royal Opera House (London UK), Moscow Museum of Modern Art (Moscow RU), Holon Museum (Tel Aviv IL), EYE Film Institute (Amsterdam NL) and Lisbon Architecture Triennale (Lisbon PT).

Website

https://www.memo.tv/

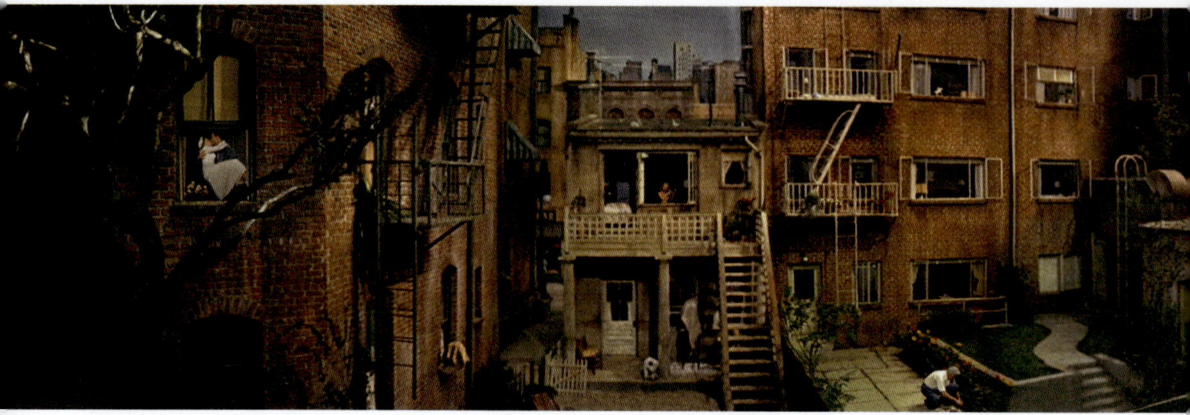

Jeff Desom (US) | 2012

Rear Window Loop

By most accounts, Alfred Hitchcock's 1954 classic *Rear Window* is as perfectly constructed a film as any the medium has ever produced. It is a "purely cinematic film," as Hitchcock later described it, whose obvious spatial handicaps both exploited and negated one of the camera's pre-eminent virtues, its effortless ability to navigate between the proximal and distal. The plot is well-known: world-weary photographer, wheelchair-bound Jeff (Jimmy Stewart) is confined to recuperative leave in his Greenwich Village apartment with only (or mostly) a panorama of the encompassing tenement complex beyond as his company. But as Jean-Luc Godard commented, one never recalls the particulars of any of Hitchcock's narratives but, rather, only the shots that framed them. In the case of *Rear Window*, however, neither specific scenes nor shots prove more memorable than the architecture and spatial configuration of the famed courtyard set. These have been analyzed to the point of exhaustion, with the chief exegetic points being well familiar to any casual student of cinema, but never have they been seen before like this video time-lapse.

Meticulously assembled by Jeff Desom, using just After Effects and Photoshop, the video condenses Hitchcock's masterwork into three breathtaking minutes in which the entirety of the film's events—sans the dramatic, personal scenes between the protagonists—play out before Jeff's gaze. Desom's collage is completely comprised of footage from the film, with the iconic window panorama being neatly tailored and augmented with various photographic effects (tilt-shift, stabilization, "rain") so as to achieve verisimilitude with the original and to re-create the environmental changes that propel the narrative along. "Since everything was filmed from pretty much the same angle," Desom writes, "I was able to match them into a single panoramic view of the entire backyard without any greater distortions."
(Text: Samuel Medina)

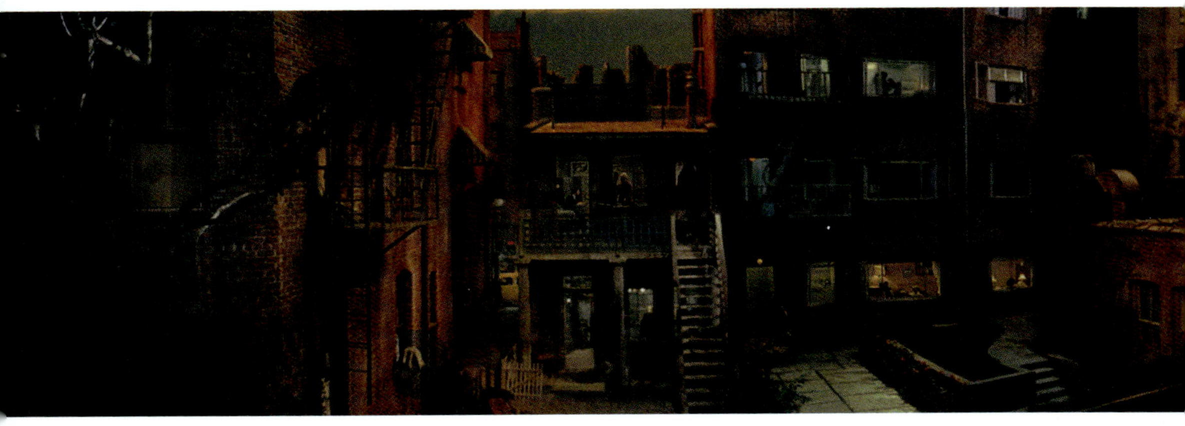

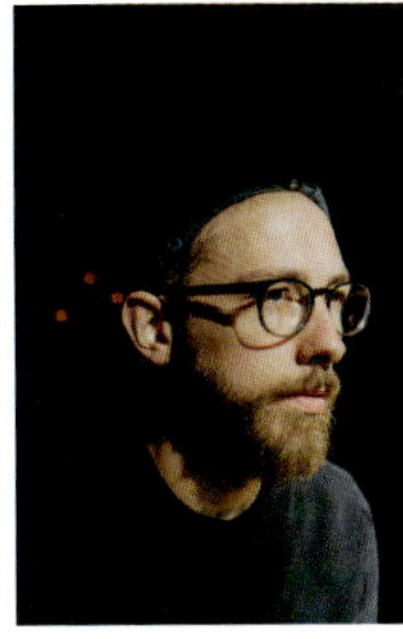

Jeff Desom is a writer, director and visual artist. Combining live-action, found footage and digital effects, his work has been selected and awarded at festivals and museums around the world. In 2007 he graduated from the Arts University College at Bournemouth, England where he specialized in directing. His graduation film Bloksky (2007) was awarded at the Akira Kurosawa Memorial Short Film Competition.

His 2009 short film X on a Map starring Sean Biggerstaff (Harry Potter) and Vicky Krieps (Phantom Thread) premiered at the Moscow International Film Festival. In 2009, the curators of the PlazaPlus Festival in Eindhoven approached Jeff to produce an audiovisual live show with Hauschka. The result was Ghost Piano, a stage piece that blends Hauschka's improvised music with projection map- ping and an ancient theatre illusion known as Pepper's Ghost. The piece went on to be staged at the Philharmonie Luxembourg and marked Jeff's first step outside the film industry. Inspired by his experiments with unique projection sur- faces, Jeff developed Rear Window Loop as a commissioned piece for CarréRotondes, Exit07, supported by the Luxembourg Ministry of Culture. For this he dissected the entirety of Hitchcock's 1950s original and stitched it back together as a single panorama depicting all of the sub-plots in one continuous shot and in chronological order. The work has gone on to win the Golden Nica at Ars Electronica 2012, as well the 2012 Vimeo Award for best remix. The work continues to be exhibited in museums around the world, including at this year's Greater Taipei Biennial of Contemporary Arts and in Mexico City at the Cineteca Nacional. In 2012 the Creators Project offered Jeff the chance to direct a music video for an American band Health and their track entitled Tears. The clip was produced by Roman Coppola's company, The Directors Bureau, and has since been selected for South by Southwest Festival as well as the Los Angeles Film Festival.

Jeff's first solo exhibition was commissioned by the Luxembourg Film Festival and the Robert Schuman award in 2014. Inspired by the great tradition of optical theatres, he recreated a series of iconic film sets as miniatures and brought them to life using holographic projections (Holorama). In 2014 Jeff was also awarded the Edward Steichen Residency in New York. This allowed him to further establish himself as a filmmaker and artist in the United States. His first US group exhibition took place at the Museum of the Moving Image in New York alongside works from artists such as Jean-Luc Godard, Michel Gondry, Gregory Crewdson and Guy Maddin. His most recent credits include a music video for Father John Misty, a science fiction television pilot, and a documentary mini-series for Stranger Things on Netflix. Jeff currently resides and works in Los Angeles.

Website

https://jeffdesom.com/

Daniel Franke (DE) | Cedric Kiefer (DE) | 2012

unnamed soundsculpture

The basic idea of the project *unnamed soundsculpture* is built upon the consideration of creating a moving sound sculpture from the recorded motion data of a real person. For our work we asked a Laura Keil, a Berlin-based dancer to interpret a musical piece—Kreukeltape by Machinefabriek—as closely as possible with the movement of her own body. She was recorded by three depth cameras (Kinect), in which the intersection of the images was later put together to a three-dimensional volume (3D point cloud), which made it possible to use the collected data throughout the rest of the process. The three-dimensional image allowed us a completely free handling of the digital camera, without limitations on the perspective. The camera also reacts to the sound and supports the physical imitation of the musical piece by the performer. She moves to a noise field where a simple modification of the random seed can constantly create new versions of the video, each offering a different composition of the recorded performance. The multi-dimensionality of the sound sculpture is already contained in every movement of the dancer, as the camera footage allows any imaginable perspective.

Dancer: Laura Keil und Music: Machinefabriek "Kreukeltape"
www.onformative.com / www.daniel-franke.com

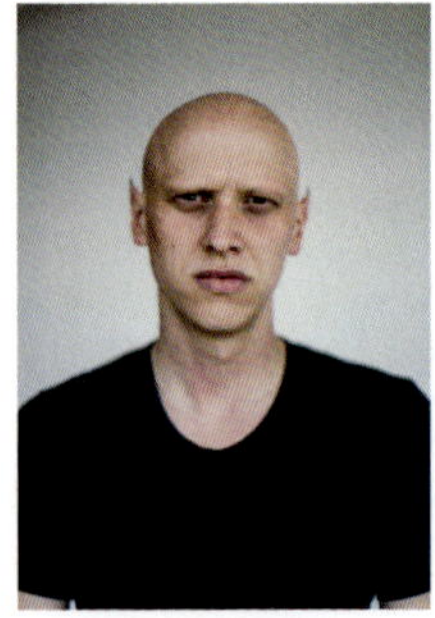

Daniel Franke (b. 06.09.1982) is an artist, curator and researcher living and working in Berlin. He studied Visual Communication and Media Art at the University of the Arts, Berlin completing his master thesis studying under Prof. Siegfried Zielinski in 2009 and achieved his Meisterschüler under Prof. Joachim Sauter and Prof. Alberto DeCampo in 2011. Currently he is artistic associate in the Media-Art Department at Hochschule für Gestaltung, Karlsruhe (HfG) and PhD candidate at the Bauhaus University, Weimar, both in Germany. He is also one of the founders of LEAP (Lab for Electronic Arts and Performance), a non-profit interdisciplinary project for emerging, digital media arts and performance that aimed to initiate the dialogue between art, science and technology. In his own work he challenges our understanding of the digital, aiming to view it in the context of a physical perception at the transformation process of algorithmic thinking into the real. He thereby transforms practises known from classical animation into tangible expressions in the "real", factual and bodily world to explore and visualise complex coherences.

Website

https://www.daniel-franke.com/

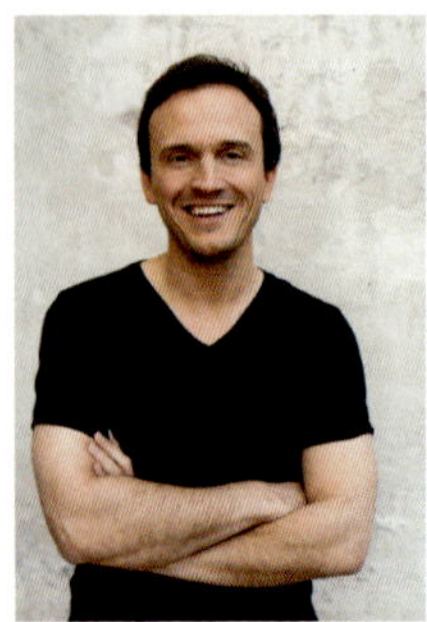

Cedric Kiefer is an artist and designer from Berlin. In 2010 together with Julia Laub, he founded onformative; a studio specialized in digital art and design. As the creative lead, Cedric develops and directs projects to define the creative vision of the studio.

onformative is a Berlin-based studio constantly searching for new forms of creative expression. Observations of their surroundings inspire them to explore the possibilities that lie between analog and digital fields to examine the relationship of humans and technology. They develop innovativeprojects across media that range from interactive installations and generative design to dynamic visuals and data-driven narratives.

Website

https://www.onformative.com/

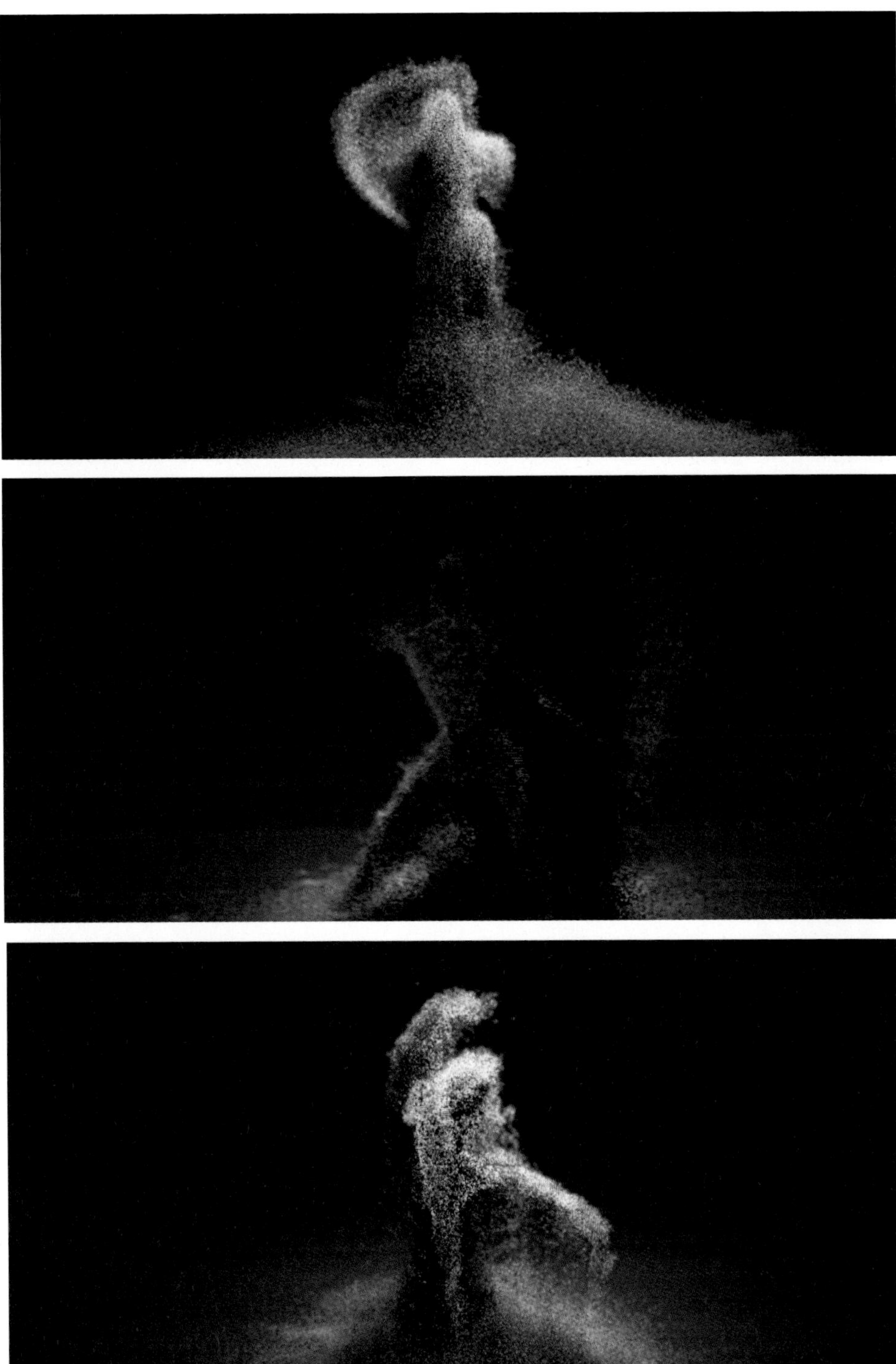

The Ark

The Ark is an ephemeral, site-specific audiovisual installation that took place in the ethnobotanical garden of Oaxaca, Mexico, during the first edition of Proyecta Oaxaca, a new festival dedicated to digital art. Exceptionally, the garden was open at night, and the visitors were invited to walk down the narrow paths that led to the cactus grove standing at its very heart. In a poetic approach, The Ark gives voice to the plants which are turned into abstract characters: an unpredictable choir, and the beating heart of the garden. Telling their story and revealing their imaginary nature, The Ark is a mise en abîme of the course.

Loosely inspired by the myth of the Great Flood, this audiovisual installation in three parts unfolds like a movie projected into space, where the spectator's motion serves as a camera.

Installation by Romain Tardy
Music by Loran Delforge
Production: Proyecta Oaxaca
Coordination & project management: ANTIVJ
Ethnobotanical garden, Oaxaca, Mexico, May 2013

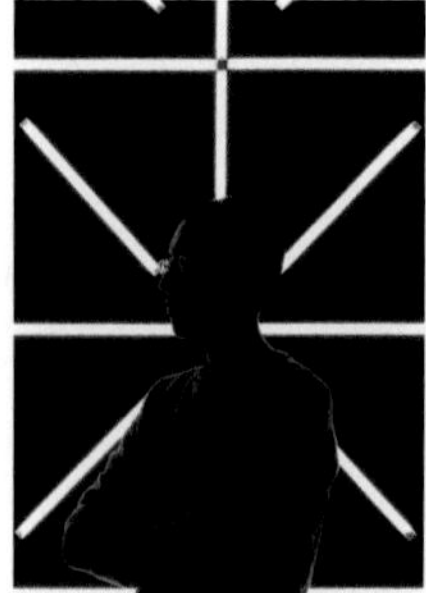

Romain Tardy (FR) is a visual artist, and focuses his work primarily in new media. Born on September 23, 1984, in Paris, he studied at the École des Beaux-Arts before working for various animation and post-production studios in Paris. He also worked as a VJ at numerous events in France and across Europe, which led him to further examine the complex connections between sound and image. With this experience, Tardy, along with three other artists, created the European visual label Antivj in 2008, which formed the base of his research and work on projected light and its influence on perception. He remained one of the label's main artists until late 2013. His installations, which often use the technique of videomapping, are conceived as tangible experiences in situ and use light as a way to enhance existing architecture or original structures. By examining our relationship to reality as we are confronted by computer imagery and the social changes that it triggers, as well as the way that digital technology is situated in public space, Tardy's installations seek to evoke these current issues through a poetic approach. His work has been exhibited in more than 15 countries, including France, Sweden, The Netherlands, Poland, Switzerland, UK, Czech Republic, Belgium, China, South Korea, Japan, Mexico, USA (New York), Cuba ...

Website

https://www.romaintardy.com/

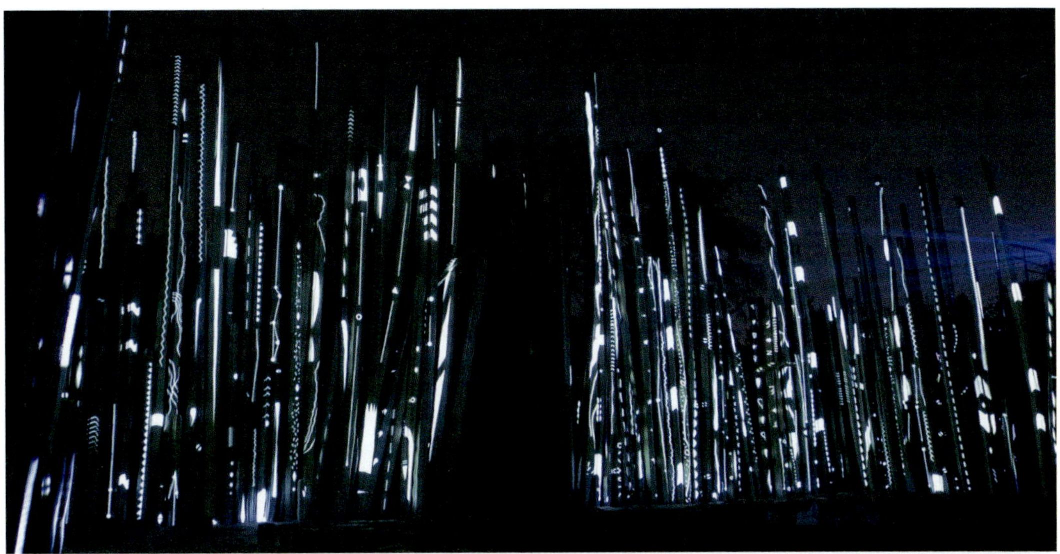

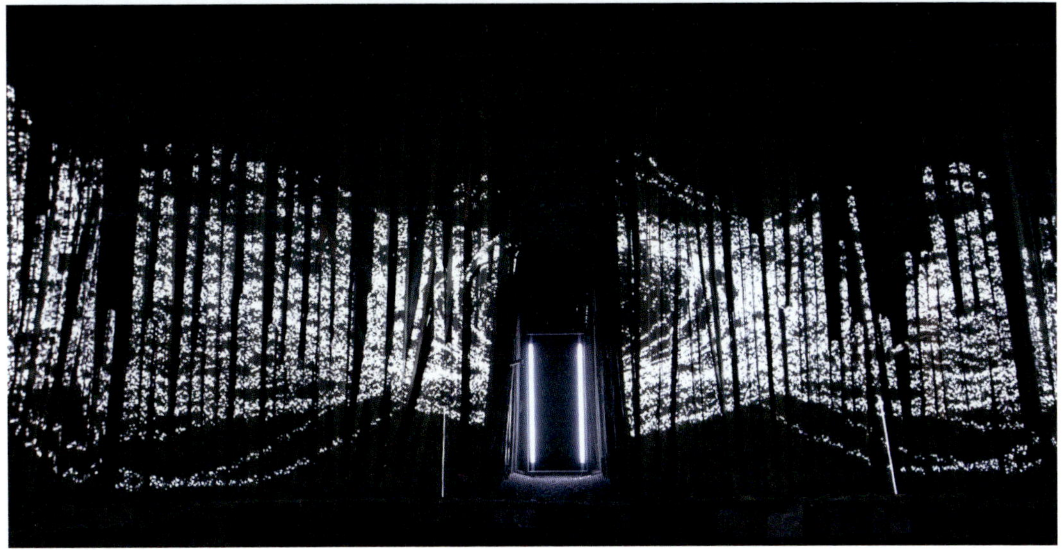

Sebastian Buerkner (DE/GB) | 2013

The Chimera of M.

At its core the digital animation *The Chimera of M.* attempts to wed its physical constitution to its narrative ambition. Viewers find themselves behind the eyes of an unseen and distinctly unreliable protagonist, so evasive that he and his motives can hardly be identified. He moves through the old haunts, seemingly attempting to re-engage with two abandoned relationships, one with a man, one with a woman. The very fractured and expressive manifestation of the three-dimensional space in this stereoscopic film, combined with the protagonist's point of view, puts the viewers inside these contorted relationships. The spatial and visual ambiguity of the film seems to evade definition and induces a personal investment by the viewer in unraveling the perceived imagery.In contrast to camera-shot 3D film, where space tends to be hyperdefined and "sculpted," in *The Chimera of M.* the animation, objects and places have been dismantled and redistributed in space to fit their expressive purpose in the visual landscape. All the elements were initially animated in 2D through multitudes of transparent layers and later suspended in space. This process amplified the fertile interplay between the visual appearance and its representation.

Credits:
Director, animator: Sebastian Buerkner
Script: Sebastian Buerkner, John Moseley
Sound edit and mix: Gernot Fuhrmann
Voices: James French, Martina Schmücker, Micheal Grime
Additional animation: Peter Caires, Timothy Divall, Natalie Rose Young
Motion capture performers: Nissa Nishikawa, Junya Ishii

Sebastian Buerkner (DE/GB) is an artist working predominately in moving image based in London. His experimental works focus on specific phenomena of visual or audible perception and explore the subjectivity of experience. For over a decade his practice was based exclusively in animation but recently also includes live-action. His films and installations are exhibited at art galleries and film festivals internationally, where they have won several awards.
Recent solo shows include Kunsthaus im KunstkulturQuartier Nuremberg, Germany; Tramway, Glasgow; Sketch, London; The Showroom Gallery, London; Whitechapel Project Space; London and LUX at Lounge Gallery, London; Art on the Underground, Screen at Canary Wharf, London. He has also participated in group shows and screenings at Tate Britain, Tate Modern, London; Tate Liverpool; Site Gallery, Sheffield; Barbican, Whitechapel Gallery, South London Gallery, London and Kunsthalle Wien, Vienna. His films "Purple Grey", "Tosse not my Soule" and "Rhinoceros" were broadcast Channel 4 in the UK. He currently is a film practice research fellow at the Queen Mary University London. He currently is a film practice research fellow at the Queen Mary University London.

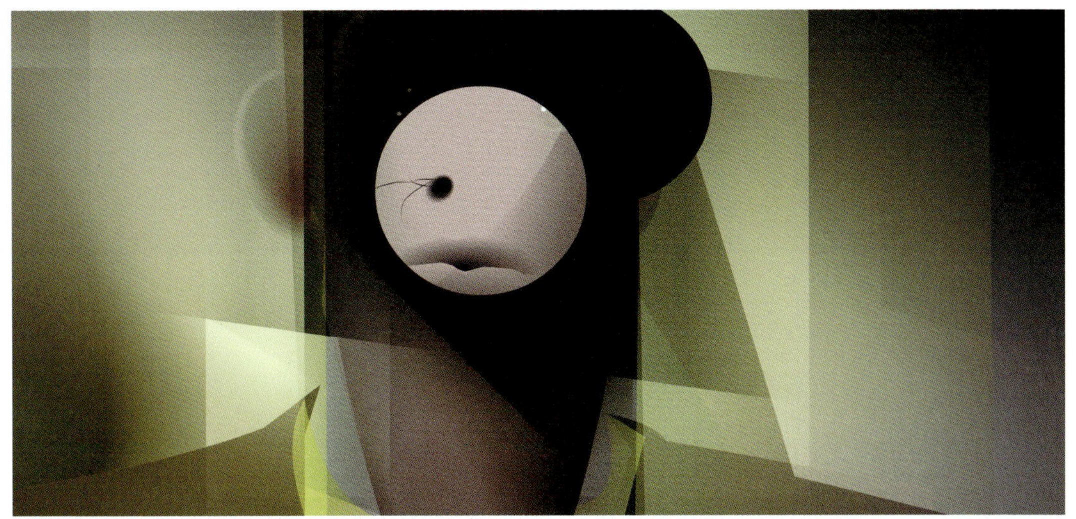

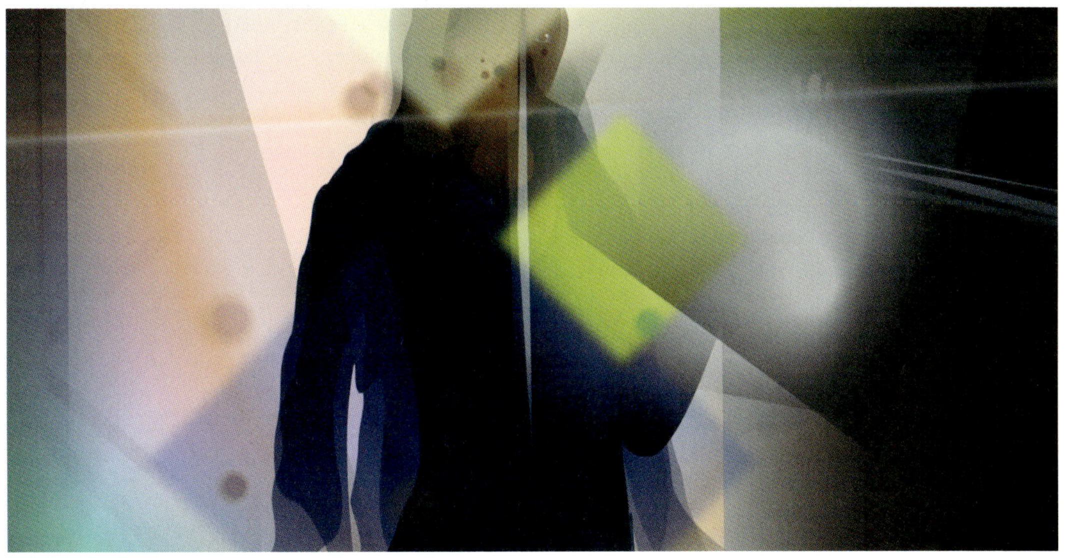

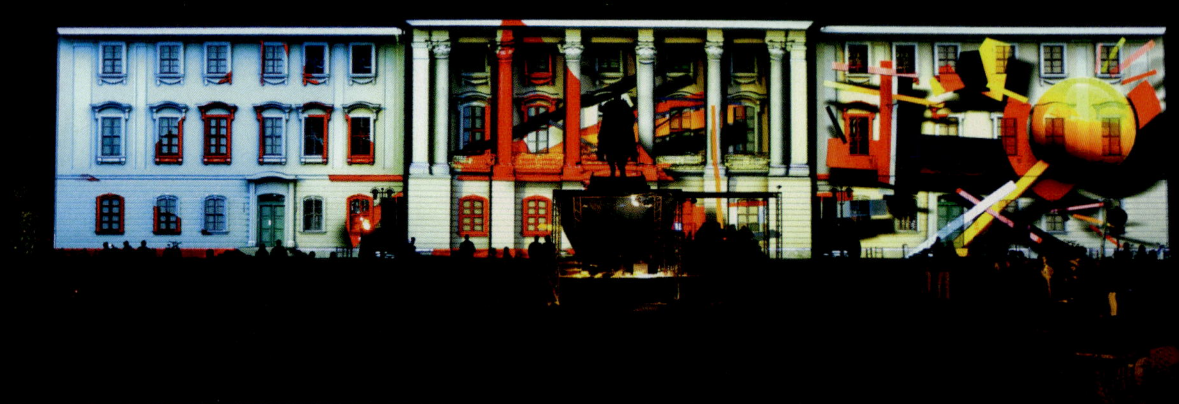

Under An Alias

Under An Alias is the big new fairytale of Nerdworking, a digital historical expression. This time our story takes place in the small German town of Weimar. Weimar is a meeting and creation point for eminent intellectuals of our times. This is the town where Goethe wrote his masterpieces, where the music of Franz Liszt could be heard. This is where the German Republic was founded in 1919, whose legacy was subsequently marred by the establishment of a Nazi concentration camp here in 1937. Weimar, a city that currently merges art and architecture in the Bauhaus university, has many untold stories.

Although difficult, telling Weimar's story was incredibly educational for an Istanbul-based group of artists. It gave an opportunity for Nerdworking to illustrate a story from another perspective. Dozens of people spent long hours immersing themselves the rich cultural background, while taking into consideration the opinions of previous researchers.

Under An Alias, created through the collaboration of international artists and working completely in cyberspace, made its debut as the main act of the Genius Loci Festival. *Under An Alias* was exhibited from 10 to 12 August 2013 at the Fürstenhaus, Franz Liszt Conservatory, every night several times a night from 8 pm until the early hours. We decided that there could be nothing more appropriate, than projecting the analogy onto this iconic building. The initial section of this tribute to the legacy of Weimar is the spirit, then the muscles then the skin. The story was based on the linear history of the city.

Producer: Nerdworking
Design and Art Direction: NOHlab (Candaş Şişman – Deniz Kader)
Motion Design and Animation Teams: Fehmican Gözüm, Gökalp Gönen, Saygın Soher, Sinan Büyükbaş, Ouchhh
Creative Director: Ferdi Alıcı
3D Artists & Designers: Çağlar Özen, Emre Önol, Ferdi Alıcı
2D Artists & Designers: Dilan Tanrıkulu Regal, Harun Kerem Köse, Yusuf Emre Kucur
Compositing: Ferdi Alıcı
Robotika
CG Supervisor: Coşku Özdemir
3D Artists & Designers : Davut Toy, Vikram Puttanna
Sound Design: Alp Coksoyluer, Giray Gürkal, Görkem Şen
Architectural 3D Modelling: Kerem Asfuroğlu
Storyboard Artist: İsmail Anıl Güzeliş
Documentation: Cansu Turan
Project Management: Nerdworking (Erdem Dilbaz)

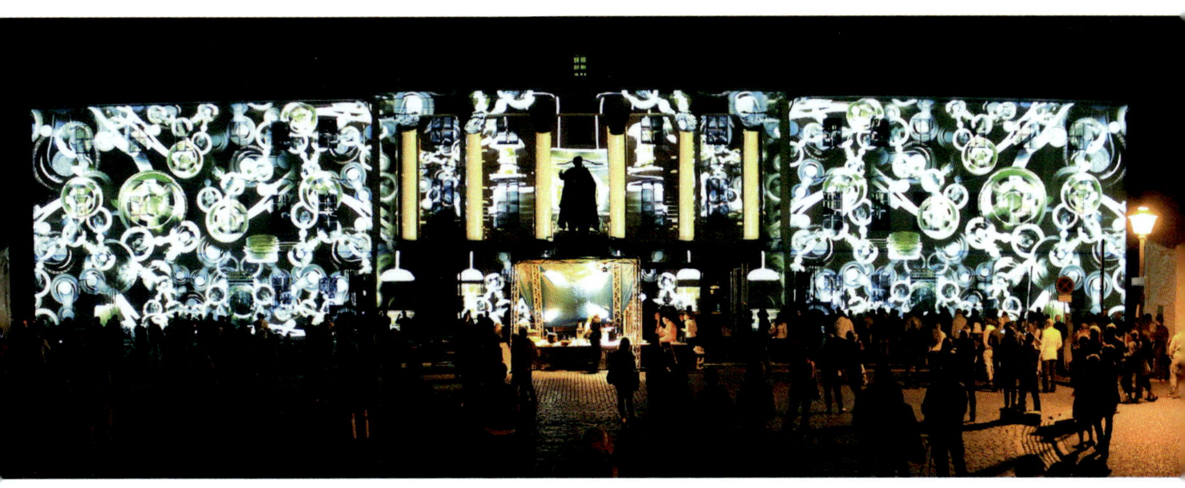

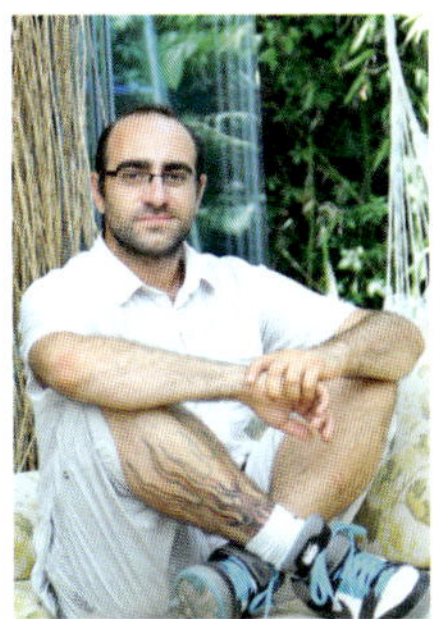

Nerdworking (TR) is a network project (founded in 2009) focused on research and development to provide unique tools for artistic, commercial and interactive media projects for public spaces.
Erdem Dilbaz is Founder & Producer at *Nerdworking*, Istanbul / Berlin. Experienced about designing a mixture of digital and classic stage and public performances for 8 years, managing creative businesses for 12 years, being a part of culture industry for over 15 years. Wrote an award winning economical model for creative minds to work without physical boundaries. Produced and managed 60 stage shows and performances. Very creative about creating a production in a holistic way from scratch to realization with all components such as conceptualization, technical needs, interaction design, scenography and even organizational backbone.

Andy Lomas (GB) | 2014

Cellular Forms

Cellular Forms uses a simplified biological model of morphogenesis, with three-dimensional structures generated out of interconnected particles to represent cells.

Each form starts with a small initial ball of cells which is incrementally developed over time by adding iterative layers of complexity to the structure. The aim is to create forms emergently: exploring generic similarities between many different shapes in nature rather than emulating any particular organism, revealing universal archetypal forms that can come from growth-like processes rather than top-down externally engineered design.

Cell division is controlled by accumulated nutrient levels. When the level in a cell exceeds a given threshold the cell divides, and various parameters control how both the parent and daughter cells re-connect to their immediate neighbors. Rules can also be adjusted for how nutrient is created, such as by being randomly uniformly created by each cell, or by incident light rays creating nutrient in cells hit by photons. Nutrient can also be allowed to flow to adjacent cells. The simulation process is repeated over thousands of iterations and millions of particles, with typical final structures having over fifty million cells.

A number of internal forces affect the structures, including linear and torsion spring forces between connected cells. Additional forces repel cells that are in close proximity but are not directly connected.

Many different complex organic structures are seen to arise from subtle variations to the rules governing the systems, with selection of forms based on aesthetic considerations rather than optimizing a conventional fitness function.

All the software used to run the simulations and render the resulting images was written and designed by the artist and implemented using C++ and CUDA.

Software and Visuals: Andy Lomas, (UK)
Music: Max Cooper, (UK)

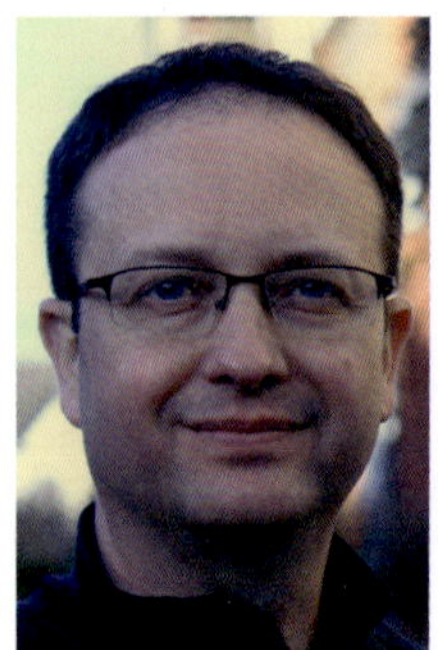

Andy Lomas (GB) is a computational artist and Emmy award winning supervisor of computer generated effects. He lives in London, and for a number of years has been developing Morphogenetic Creations: a series of artworks that explores how complex intricate organic structures, such as those seen in nature, can be the emergent generative products of growth processes.

Selected Exhibitions

2018 | Chance and Control: Art in the Age of Computers. V&A

2018 | MUTATIONS / CRÉATIONS 2: Coder le monde, Pompidou Centre, Paris

2018 | Great Exhibition of the North, Newcastle upon Tyne

2017–2019 | Open Codes I and II, ZKM, Karlsruhe

Website

https://www.andylomas.com/

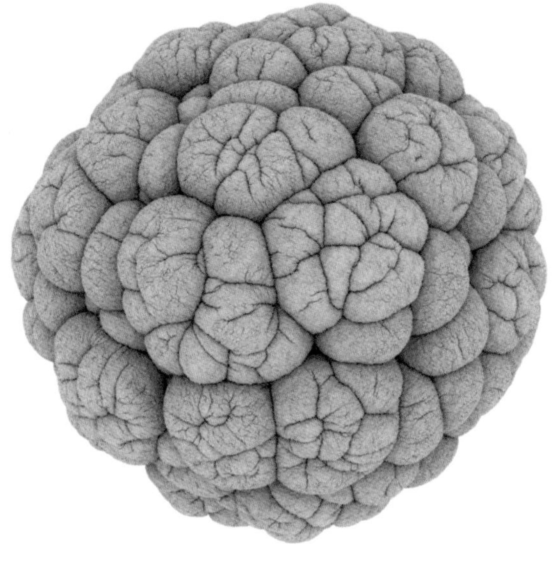

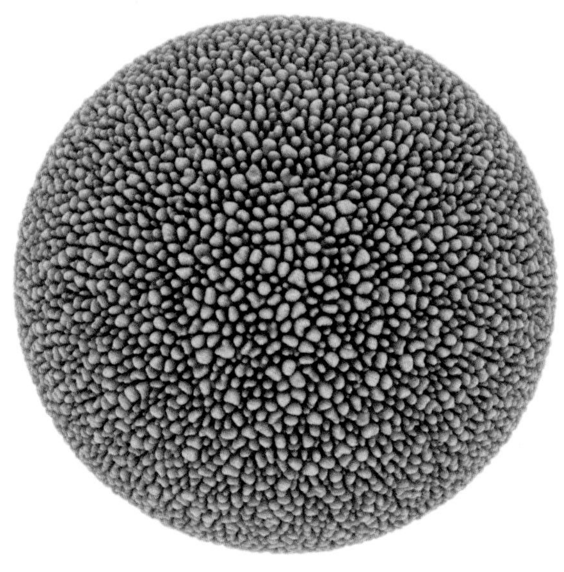

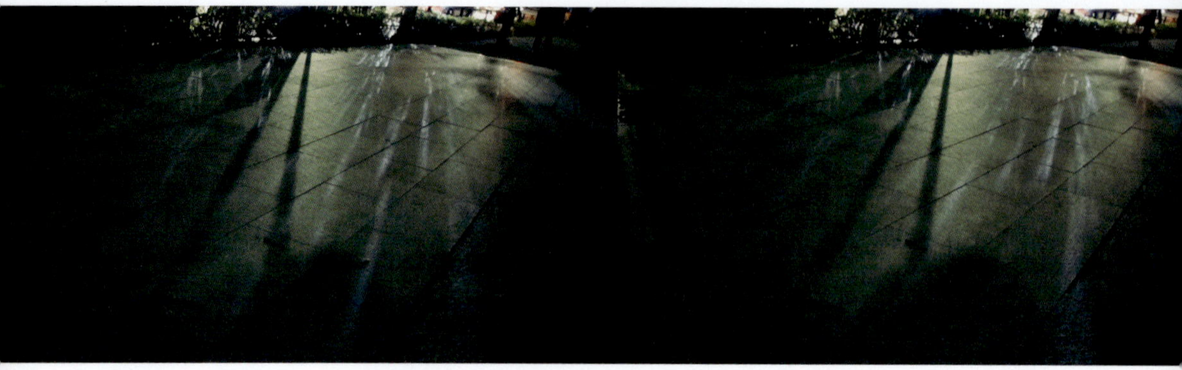

Kazuhiro Goshima (GB) | 2014

Shadowland

This is a 3D (stereoscopic) film shot with one DSLR camera. Only the shadows become 3D, without any digital special effects.

"Shadows" are cast on the streets by the headlights of cars driving through the city. These are another substance in the streets. Every night, the city itself is overwritten like a retina thousands of times, and no one can decipher its memories. One of the themes of my works is to express a feeling that cannot be there. The 3D shadow can have peculiar presence simply because it has neither color nor texture.

3D films using one SLR camera

I have made three 3D films since 2010—all of them shot with a traditional 2D camera, for example a Pentax K7, a Sony HDR-CX700V or a Canon EOS Kiss X5 (D600). The essential factor of 3D vision is binocular parallax. I derive parallax from the slight time lag between the movies projected onto the right and left eyes. There are no digital special effects. I show the same movies to each eye, but there is slight time lag (1-5 frames). If the object in the footage moves sideways (or the movement of the object has a horizontal element), the parallax is produced. It is like the "Pulfrich illusion." In the first 3D film, *Tokyo Three Dimensional Suite*, I moved the camera position horizontally by walking (i.e., stop-motion animation). Because of the delay between the image for left eye from that for right eye, the distance moved becomes the parallax. In the second film, *t2z*, the camera was moved on a handmade

motorized dolly. In this film I shot close-up 3D vision, which is difficult with a twin-lens 3D camera.

The mechanism of 3D shadows

In *Shadowland*, I shot footage using one fixed camera. The moving element as the source of parallax is the car headlights. The moving lights draw the shadows on the wall in the night-time city. The shadows move dynamically as the cars drive down road. The parallax arises from the horizontal movement of the shadows. The extent of parallax is influenced by many factors. The shadow moves faster according to the speed of the car, if it is close to the wall, if the object is near the car or if the object is far from the wall. The depth of the shadow is inverted by the direction of movement. There are many cars on the road and many objects throw shadows on the wall. This all gives rise to the complex 3D harmony.

Technical details

In general, processing of images for this work is very simple. I shot the footage with a Canon EOS Kiss X5 (D600). The format is 720p/50fps, because of slow motion and to reduce AC flicker. Although it seems bright to the eye, in a large town at night the light is insufficient to shoot a movie. The limits of my equipment were F1.4-1.8 stop, 1/50 sec. and ISO1600. I searched for a place without unnecessary light. Car headlights are designed to illuminate the ground, they seldom shine upwards. So I looked for a wall on a slight

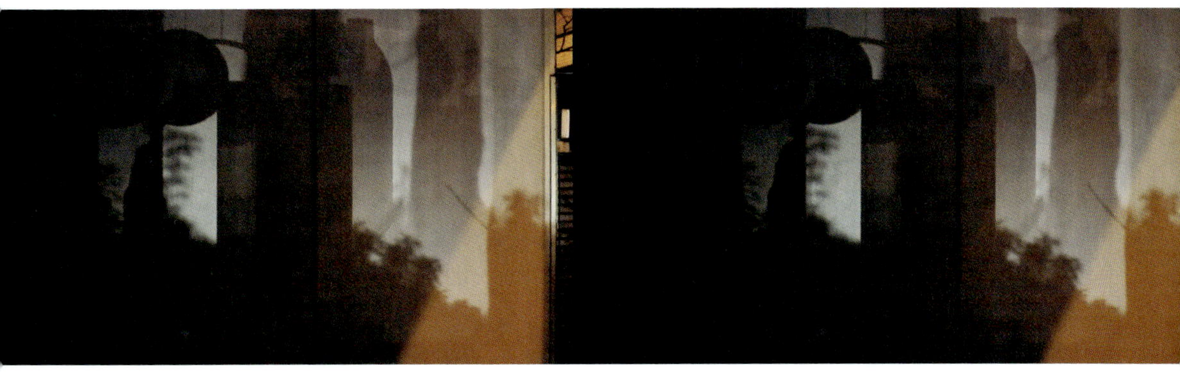

uphill slope. It was difficult to find an ideal place, and it took more time than expected. The footage lasts 20 hours or more.

The converted movies run at 24fps (half speed). After noise reduction, I adjusted the soundtrack. The shadow contrast is sometimes very low and sometimes very sharp. If the contrast is too low, it is hard to feel a 3D illusion. There are also elements apart from a shadow in a frame where I carefully emphasize contrast. The tone-adjusted movies are copied to the right and left eyes as a parallel 3D format. After this, I can process and edit in stereoscopic view, sending the 3D video preview of After Effects and Final Cut Pro 7 to Sony 3DTV.

In ex-3D work, I adjusted the depth of field to a screen by fine tuning the horizontal position of right and left images. An image looks large if it is far away from a screen. But in *Shadowland* it is important that elements apart from shadow are visible in 2D, because the 3D illusion of shadows is very sensitive. It will easily break down if other 3D elements are shown on screen. It is important that only the shadow is a solid. Finally, the 3D shadow is completed by attaching a brief time lag to images on either side.

Finally, I adjust the time lag between images on either side to optimum 3D viewing and edit the movie timeline at the same time.

Music: "Dusk" by Frank Bridge
Piano: Sachiko Kawakita
Music producer: stravinsky ensemble
Support: Masaru Fuchigami, Jun Nito, Yumi Goshima

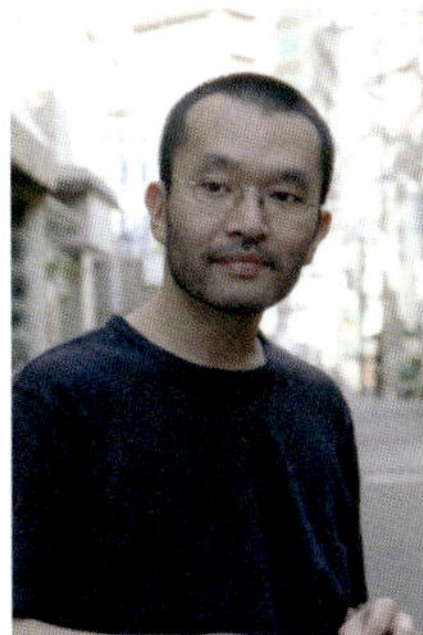

Kazuhiro Goshima (JP), a visual creator, produces videos and multimedia content. His 3DCG work, *Fade into White #2* (2000), won the grand prix at the 2001 Image Forum Festival. *Fade into White #3* (2001) received an award at the Annecy International Animation Film Festival and also won the excellence award at the Japan Media Arts Festival. A number of his visual works have also been highly regarded at film festivals abroad.

Selected Works

2018 | the Absence of the Painter

2017 | I might not have been what I am

2016 | BUMPY

2015 | Looking and Listening

2014 | THIS MAY NOT BE A MOVIE

Website

https://www.goshiman.com/

Universal Everything (GB) | 2014

Walking City

Walking City is a continuation of Universal Everything's artistic line of enquiry, investigating human movement, emotional design, architecture and sound. It is inspired by the sense of walking through a city, how absorbing your surroundings alters sensation and emotion. How you become part of the fabric of the city, a man-made eco system.

Referencing the utopian visions of 1960s architecture practice Archigram, *Walking City* is a slowly evolving video sculpture. The language of materials and patterns seen in radical architecture transform as the nomadic city endlessly walks, adapting to the environments it encounters.

What appears as a 3D person, shrouded in a digital costume, shifts and breaks, reshapes and endlessly evolves into a video sculpture continuously walking in the center of the screen: creating an artificial form whose movement feels alive, not synthetic.

It explores the structural processes found in modern architecture, which have led to a multitude of aesthetic outcomes. From Buckminster Fuller's domes to Richard Rogers's inside out buildings, Daniel Liebskind's angular public museums to Future Systems' biomorphic structures.

Created using Houdini, *Walking City* utilizes a procedural process to seamlessly change into different costumes—moving from faceted shapes, through contours and brutalism—as the walk cycle anchors the piece.

Creative Director: Matt Pyke
Animation: Chris Perry
Sound design: Simon Pyke (Freefarm)

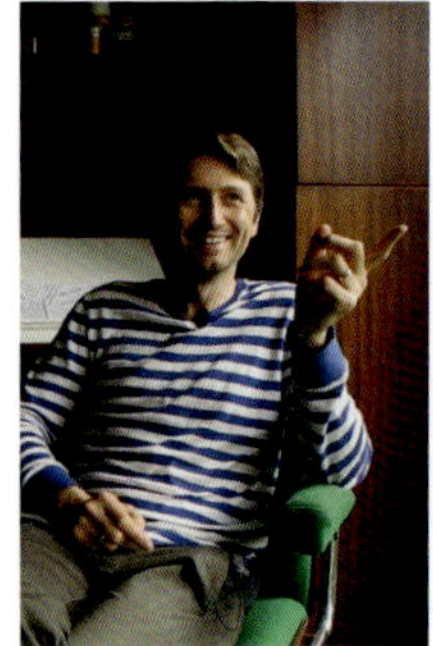

Universal Everything is a global collective of digital artists, designers, animators, musicians and developers. Founded in 2004 by creative director Matt Pyke, the collective create video artworks for iconic architecture, invent immersive multi-sensory experiences and direct new forms of moving image for the screens of the future.

Universal Everything's work explores the future of human expression and collaboration, brought to life using emerging display technologies.It has played a central role in launch events for pioneering brands, illuminating iconic architecture and exhibitions at leading cultural institutions worldwide. Past collaborators include Apple, Samsung and Zaha Hadid Architects, Radiohead, and Sydney Opera House.

Website

https://universaleverything.com/

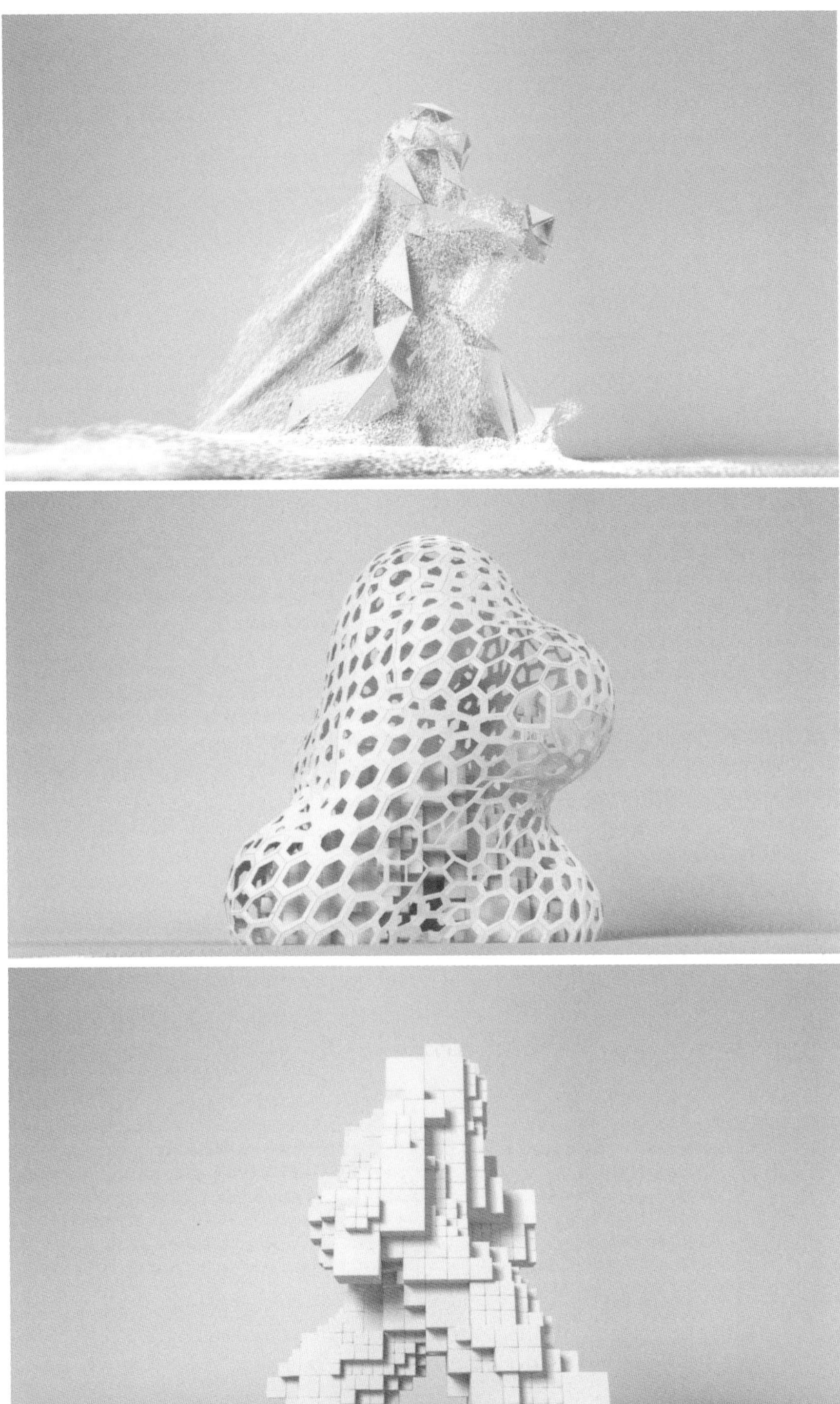

The Reflection of Power

This film is a rare glimpse into one of the most reclusive places of the world, Pyongyang, the capital of North Korea. Slowly, an unknown anomaly devours this strange city. But the city's atmosphere of eternal celebration never changes no matter how obvious the approaching end. The people keep absurdly demonstrating the same preset patriotic behavior. The visual poetry of the film rests upon metaphoric relations being created between architectural objects, including symbols of the North-Korean regime, and the natural phenomena sent to dissolve them. The film supposes history to be a chain of situations that seem to be unshakable until they are gone forever.

Director: Mihai Grecu
Production: Bathysphère Productions
Producer: Nicolas Anthomé
Script: Mihai Grecu
Camera: Mu-jin
Editing: Mihai Grecu, Seto Momoko, Clémence Diard
Sound editing: Mihai Grecu, Guiz Maubert
Sound design: Mihai Grecu, François Martig, Yann Leguay
Mixing: Simon Apostolou
Animation and special effects: Mihai Grecu, Manea "Dexter" Alexandru

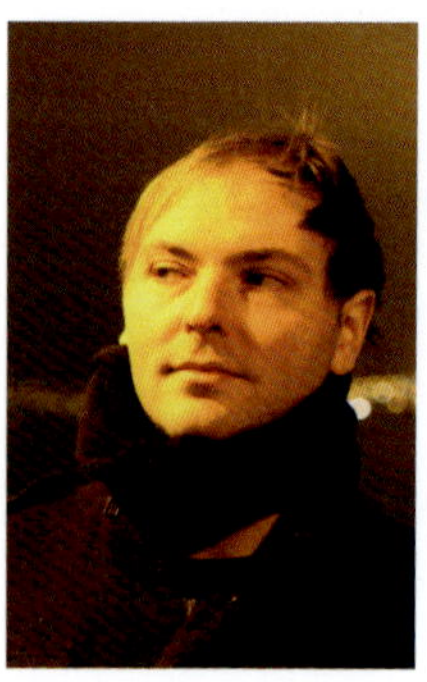

Mihai Grecu (HU/RO) is a Romanian born artist and experimental filmmaker. His works challenge the viewer's perception by mixing hyper-real visions of mysterious alternate realities with contemporary imagery. Topics such as environmental crisis, absurd hybridations, the sublime and catastrophes articulate this multifaceted universe. His works have constantly been shown in numerous film festivals (Locarno, Rotterdam, Festival of New Cinema in Montreal, et cetera), digital art festivals and events (Ars Electronica, Elektra Montréal, Transmediale) and contemporary art exhibitions ("Dans la nuit, des images" at the Grand Palais, "Labyrinth of my mind" at the Cube, "Video Short list: the Dream Machine" at the Passage du Retz).

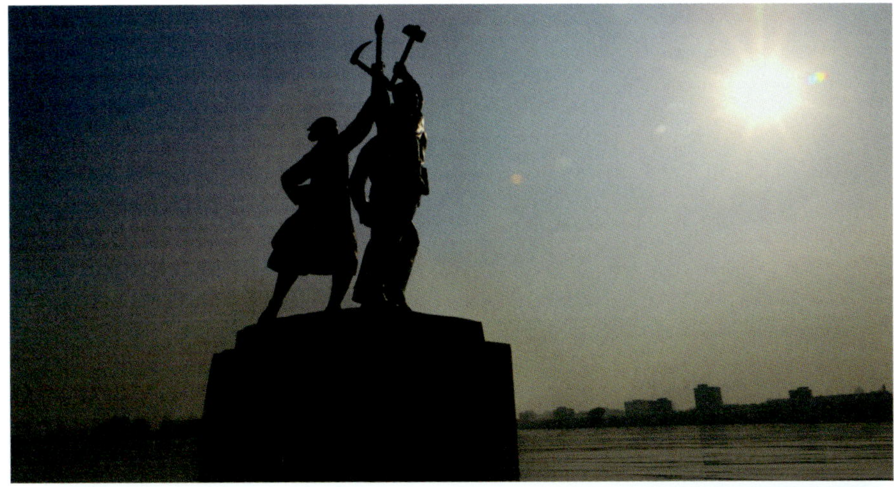

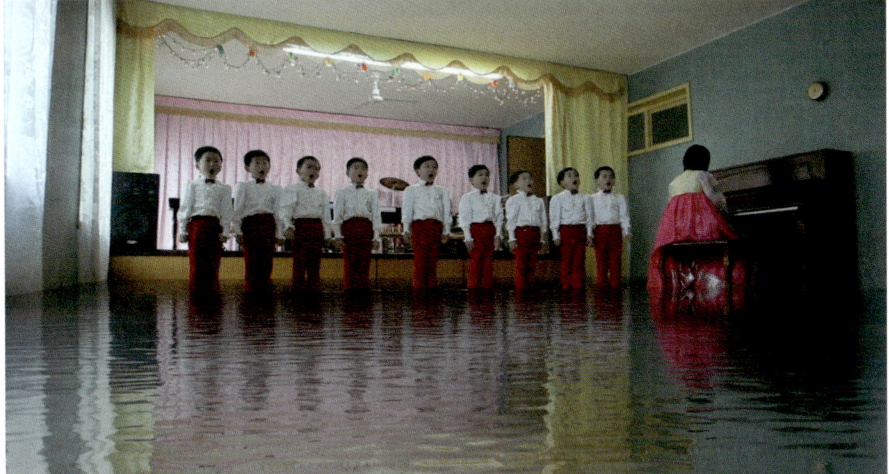

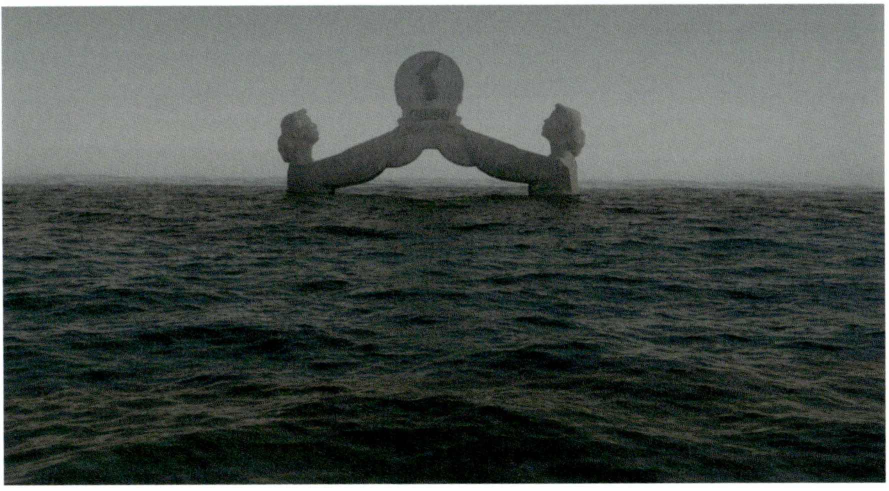

The Reflection of Power

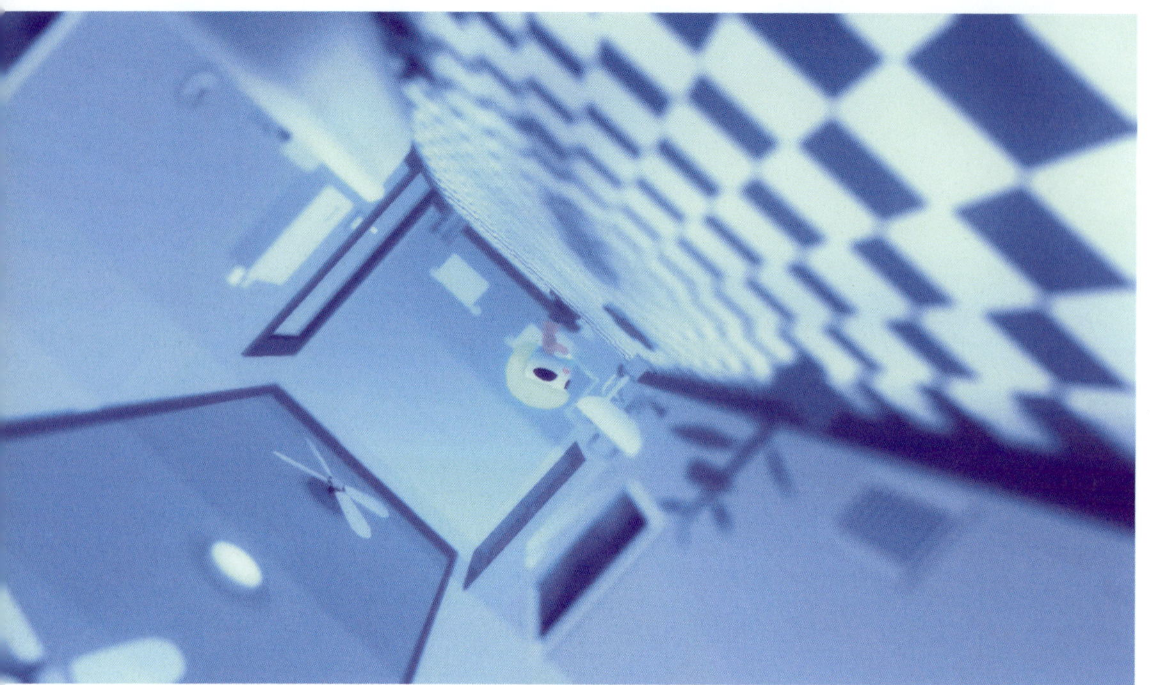

10964579043769284765O

10964579043769284765O is a collection of absurdist short films, strewn across the internet as the meandering dreams of a dying AI.

https://www.davidoreilly.com/#/10964579043769284765O/

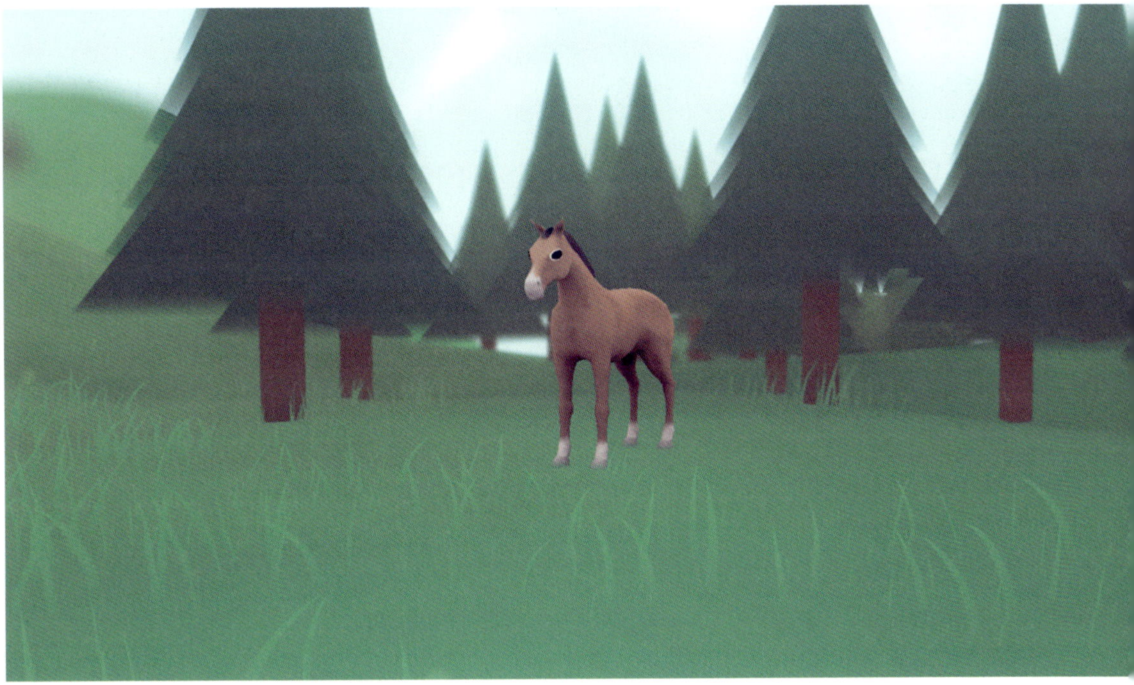

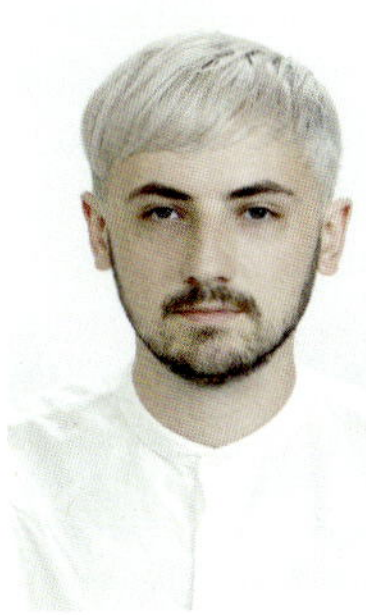

David OReilly (b. Ireland, 1985) is an artist based in Tokyo, Japan. Starting out as an independent animator, he created numerous award winning short films, pioneering the use of low poly and glitch aesthetics. He has written for TV shows such as Adventure Time & South Park and created fictional video games in Spike Jonze's Academy Award winning film *Her*. Creator of the iconic game *Mountain* and the universe simulation game *Everything*, narrated by Alan Watts.

Selected Exhibitions

2018 | David Lynch's Festival Of Disruption, US

2018 | Roleplay Reality at FACT, GB

2018 | Unwanted Stories at Edith-Russ-Haus, DE

2017 | La Roche Sur Yon solo, FR

Selected Works

2018 | Eye of the Dream, interactive simulation

2017 | Everything, interactive simulation

2014 | Mountain, interactive simulation

Website

https://davidoreilly.com/

Golan Levin (US) | Kyle McDonald (US) | Chris Sugrue (US) | 2015

Augmented Hand Series

The *Augmented Hand Series* is a real-time interactive software system that presents playful, dreamlike, and uncanny transformations of its visitors' hands. Conceived as a tool for muddling embodied cognition, the installation consists of a box into which a visitor inserts their hand, and a display that shows their "reimagined" hand, altered by various dynamic and structural transformations.

The system uses the real-time posture of the participant's real hand as the moment-to-moment baseline for its transformations. Participants are free to use either of their hands and, within certain limits, the system works properly even with visitors who wiggle their fingers, or who move and turn their hand.

Critically, the project's transformations operate within the logical space of the hand itself. That is to say: the artwork performs "hand-aware" visualizations that alter the deep structure of how the hand appears— unlike, say, a funhouse mirror, which simply distorts the entire field of view.

The hand is a critical interface to the world, allowing the use of tools, the intimate sense of touch, and a vast range of communicative gestures. Yet we frequently take our hands for granted, thinking with them, or through them, but hardly ever about them. Our investigation takes a position of exploration and wonder. Can real-time alterations of the hand's appearance bring about a new perception of the body as a plastic, variable, unstable medium? Can such an interaction instill feelings of defamiliarization, prompt a heightened awareness of our own bodies, or incite a reexamination of our physical identities? Can we provoke simple wonder about the fact that we have any control at all over such a complex structure as the hand?

About twenty different transformations have been developed. Some of these perform structural edits to the hand's archetypal form, cutting-and-pasting the visitor's digital body; others endow the hand with new dimensions of plasticity; and others imbue the hand with a kind of autonomy, whose resulting behavior is a dynamic negotiation between visitor and algorithm. These scenes include:

Plus One: The hand obtains an additional finger.
Minus One: The hand has one finger omitted.
Extra Knuckle: Each finger has an extra phalange.
One Knuckle Fewer: Each finger has a phalange omitted.
Two Thumbs: The thumb is copy-pasted to the other side of the hand.
Transposed Thumb: The thumb is relocated to the other side of the hand.
Fractal Hand: Each finger terminates in a small hand.
Throbbing Fingers: The fingers appear to throb, as with a heartbeat.
Variable Finger Length: The fingers' length changes over time.
Meandering Fingers: The fingers take on a life of their own.
Procrustes: All fingers are made the same length.
Lissajous: The palm is warped in a periodic way.
Breathing Palm: The palm inflates and deflates.
Vulcan Salute: The third and fourth fingers are cleaved.
Angular Exaggeration: Finger adduction and abduction angles are amplified.
Springers: Finger movements are exaggerated by bouncy simulated physics.

The Augmented Hand Series was conceived and developed by Golan Levin, Chris Sugrue, and Kyle McDonald, with additional software assistance from Dan Wilcox, Bryce Summers, Erica Lazrus, and Zachary Rispoli. The project was commissioned by the Cinekid Festival, with support from the Mondriaan Fund, and developed at the Frank-Ratchye STUDIO for Creative Inquiry at Carnegie Mellon University.

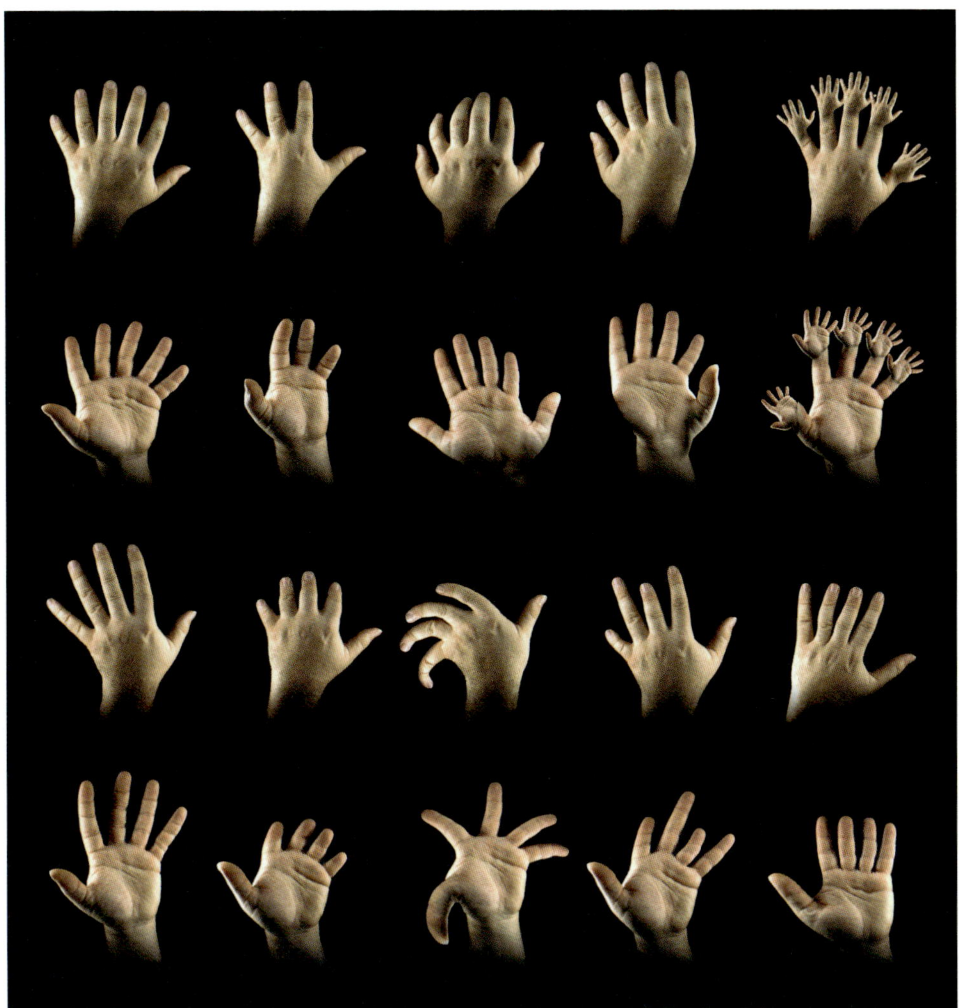

Golan Levin (US) explores the intersection of abstract communication and interactivity. Blending equal measures of the whimsical, the provocative and the sublime in a wide variety of media, Levin applies creative twists to digital technologies that highlight our relationship with machines, expand the vocabulary of human action and awaken participants to their own potential as creative actors. At Carnegie Mellon University, he is Professor of Electronic Art and serves as Director of the Frank-Ratchye STUDIO for Creative Inquiry, a laboratory dedicated to supporting atypical, anti-disciplinary and inter-institutional research projects across the arts, science, technology and culture.

Chris Sugrue (US) is an artist and engineer who develops interactive installations, audio-visual performances and experimental interfaces. Her works experiment with technology in playful and curious ways and investigate topics such as artificial life, gestural performance and optical illusions. She has exhibited internationally in such festivals and galleries as Sónar Festival, Pixel Gallery, Matadero Madrid, and La Noche En Blanco Madrid. As an educator, Sugrue has taught workshops on interactivity, visual programming and design, at institutions such as the School of Machines, Making and Make-Believe; Medialab-Prado; and the Parsons School of Design in Paris.

Kyle McDonald (US) works with sounds and codes, exploring translation, contextualization, and similarity. With a background in philosophy and computer science, he strives to integrate intricate processes and structures with accessible, playful realizations that often have a do-it-yourself, open-source aesthetic. He enjoys creatively subverting networked communication and computation, exploring glitch and embedded biases, and extending these concepts to the reversal of everything from personal identity to work habits. Kyle has been an adjunct professor at NYU's ITP, and a member of F.A.T. Lab, community manager for openFrameworks, and artist in residence at YCAM in Japan.

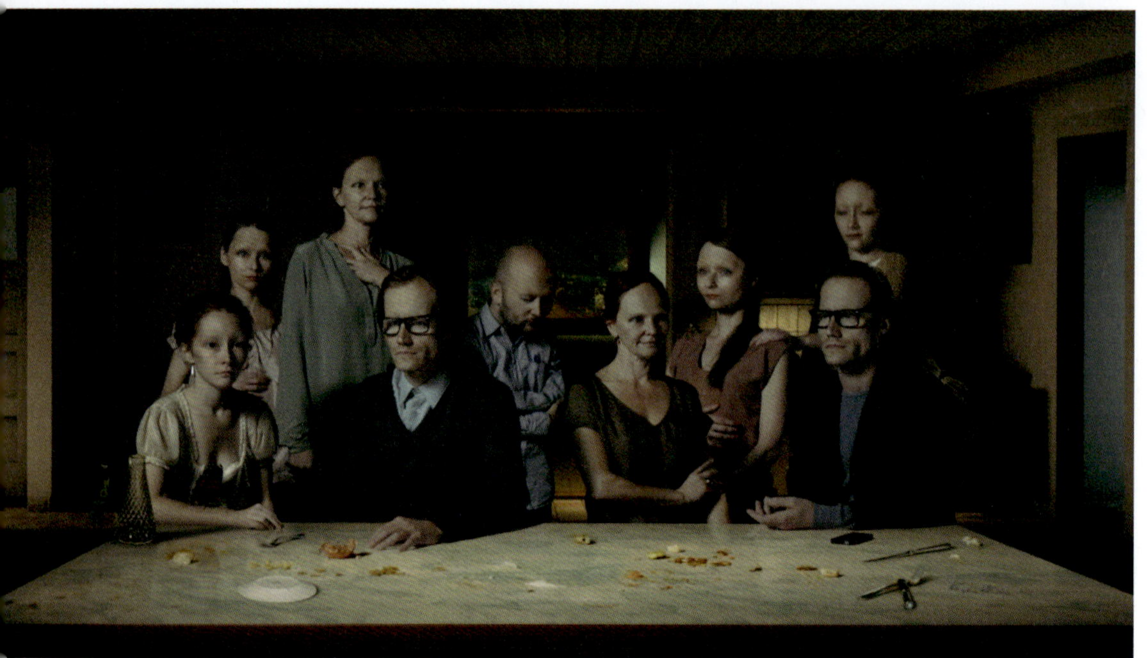

Alex Verhaest (BE) | 2015

Temp Morts / Idle Times

Alex Verhaest's works are visual explorations and investigations of the nature and boundaries of language, communication and social conventions and the potential of contemporary storytelling. The basis of each project is a narrative script, existing or newly written, around which she creates a body of standalone works by analyzing its storyline and exploring the limits of what constitutes communicable language. Her highly pictorial work operates by the juxtaposition of painting, video and contemporary technology.

The script of *Idle Times / Temps Mort* operates as the narrative backbone for a series of works on the suicide and character assassination of an absent *pater familias*, and the incapacity of the family members to communicate about, and to deal with this tragic event. The protagonists of *Idle Times/ Temps Mort*, the "mourning" relatives (Hélène, Dolores, Peter, and Madeleine) and the storyteller (Angelo) are introduced via a series of five Character Studies: a series of portraits that visualize the internal emotional struggle and inability of the surviving relatives to adopt an adequate attitude. Hélène is about to cry but she

doesn't. Is she trying to cry because she needs to, or because society expects her to do so? Dolores is pregnant and about to give birth to the first grandchild of the deceased father. Her portrait suggests a mental state which balances between salvation, expectation and disappointment and fear.

The character studies also operate as standalone works that investigate the pictorial, historical and psychological potential of portraiture. On the one hand the protagonists seem to operate in a timeless or even futuristic and parallel universe, on the other hand the aesthetics of the works refer to old master paintings (e.g., Cranach the Elder) and contrast with the technology and data carriers (Ipads) used for these works. The combination of these temporal aspects gives the works a universal and timeless yet very contemporary dimension.

This art historical dimension of the character studies is also present in another series of five works: the Table Props. Each character study corresponds with a so-called Table Prop. At first sight, these works remind us of classic still lives of Pieter Claesz and

Willem Claesz Heda. A broken plate, a fallen glass, bread crumbs and leftovers suggest a hasty departure, or memento mori. Upon closer inspection, each Table Prop is literally a *tableau vivant*, a very subtle video loop without beginning or end. Table Props operate as allegoric representations of the protagonists of *Idle Times* and their mental states. Again, the combination of contemporary technology and classic themes results in an alienating visual anachronism.

Idle Times / Temps Mort also includes two interactive works, which engage the direct participation of the viewer and explore another aspect of Alex Verhaest's work. Indeed, the title *Temps Mort / Idle Times* is derived from the feeling of missing out when using (or not using) a networked device, such as a smartphone or laptop. Verhaest feels that using a networked appliance generates a sort of buffered time zone, where her sense of time is suspended between physical presence in her environment at a particular moment and the time in which others send an e-mail or update their Facebook status. This caused her to reflect about layers in time, about our ever-failing relationship with it and the depth perception of memory as a container of the past and present.

The View is a life-size interactive animation loop. As the title of the work suggests, visitors are welcomed by a view: the view from an apartment located in an unknown city. Upon closer inspection the viewer is however confronted with (the reflection of) another person: Hélène, one of the protagonists of *Idle Times / Temps Mort*. Even though The View is not intended to deliver a specific ethical or philosophical message, it irrevocably questions the duality and relation between the Other and the Self and the concept of intersubjectivity.

The Dinner scene brings together all protagonists of *Idle Times*. The composition and setting of the work refer to a *Last Supper* scene. The relatives are represented twice, on the left and right of Angelo, the storyteller. The relatives are depicted before and after the suicide of the absent father. When the visitors call Peter (via a phone number given on a business card handed out during exhibitions), they activate a conversation, or at least a series of monologues between / of the family members. The relatives do not communicate or interact, they are making small talk to break the awkward silence. Even though Alex Verhaest takes a neutral stance on the usage of social media or networked devices, *Dinner Scene* does illustrate the discrepancy between the multitude of means to communicate and social platforms (which only allow for a binary state of mind: like/dislike) on the one hand and our inability to communicate and interact on complex state of minds and tragic events on the other.

Direction, writing, CGI and post-production: Alex Verhaest
Senior post-production assistance and compositing: Dustin Kershaw
Overall assistance: Sam Monballiu
Interaction design advisor: Bas Withagen
Recoding to html: Jean Joskin & Present Plus
Sound: Sonogents & Wouter Verhulst

Actors:
Hélène Devos
Mieke Versyp
Dolores Bouckaert
Angelo Tijssens
Pieter Genard

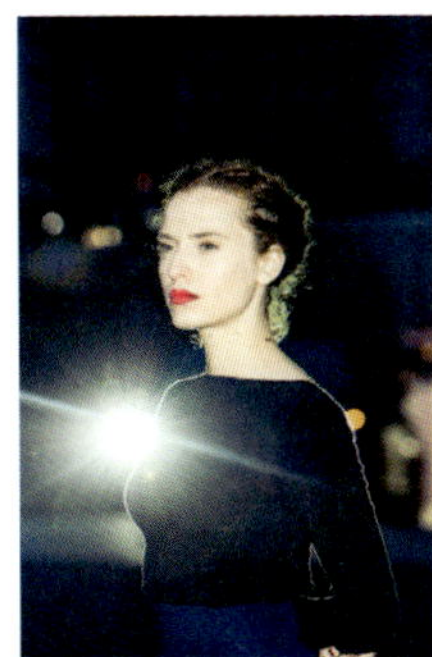

Alex Verhaest (BE) is a filmmaker investigating the possibilities of interactivity and responsivity within cinematic arts. The basis of each film is a highly narrative script, existing or newly written, around which she creates a cinematic installation consisting of objects, videos and interactive videos. In September of 2013, her debut solo Temps Mort/Idle Times opened at Grimm Gallery, Amsterdam. Her work has been selected by several arts and new media festivals and competitions; i.e., the FILE electronic language festival in Sao Paolo, the New Technology Art Award in Gent, TAZ Oostende and Arts Festival Watou, and her work is featured in the Akzo Nobel Collection. She won the New Face Award at the Japan Media arts Festival and the Golden Nica at the Prix Ars Electronica 2015.

Selected Exhibitions

2018 | Art dans la Ville/Lumen #3 | Le Musée des arts de la Marionnette | Tournai

2017 | Tendencies | BOZAR | Brussels

2017 | No maps for these territories (Solo exhibition) | Centre des Arts Numeriques | Enghien les Bains

2016 | a la folie / To Insanity (Solo exhibition) | Dauwens & Beernaert Gallery | Brussels

Website

https://www.dauwensbeernaert.com/artists/alex-verhaest/

VOID – Bahadir Dağdelen (TK) | Yusuf Emre Kucur (TK) | 2016

Bio-Inspire FullDome Performance

Bio-Inspire is an inspired A/V 3D dome performance which has screened in the Institute of American Indian Arts (New Mexico) and Fiske Planetarium – University of Colorado Boulder (Colorado).

Two A/V artists and two sound designers worked for the project. It is a five minute long mapping video that took three months to be completed. Red, white, and black fractal patterns flutter across the screen. A show of abstract webs and networks of connected organisms visualize artificial neuron connections and the growth & gradual sophistication of neural networks. This is *Bio-Inspire*.

It is mainly inspired by Artificial Neural Networks, which is a widely used method in machine learning and cognitive science. They are human-made versions of biological neural networks, namely the neural system of the animals. The ANNs are composed of several nodes, layers, and connections which simulate to some extent the message exchange and processing through a biological neural network. Each function is specific to the learned data according to which the form of the ANN is shaped.

As the quantity of layers, nodes, and connections in an artificial neural network increase, the structure gets more complex. Getting the inspiration from the structure of an ANN, our aim was to redefine the complexity of a neural network using abstract objects and sound referring to its natural form.

All visuals are made by using C4D, Softimage and ICE.

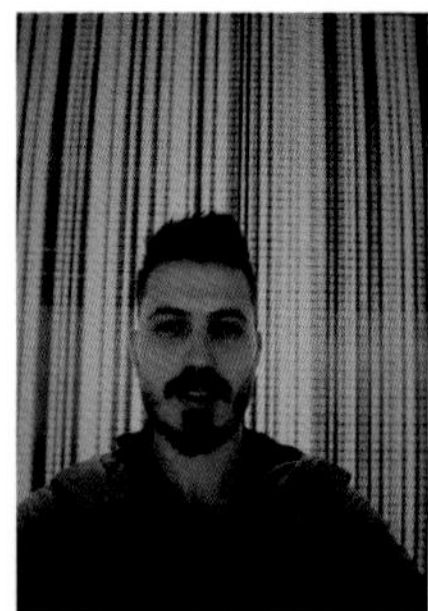

Bahadir Dağdelen (TK) is a 30 years old multidisciplinary new media artist based in Istanbul. He met street art and graffiti at his early age and involved in several national and international festivals with his graffiti paintings. He always had an interest in digital art and media during this time. In 2009, he was accepted to study Visual Communication Design (VCD) in Istanbul Bilgi University (IBU). He kept growing on computer graphics and 3D while studying. He took parts in significant national & international projects and got numerous awards and published in significant artistic websites and magazines. His A/V performances were exhibited in substantial platforms around the globe such as; Walt Disney Concert Hall in Los Angeles, Burning Man Festival (USA), CERN Particle Physics Laboratory, Society For Arts And Technology [SAT], The Institute of American Indian Arts, WIRED, Fubiz, Vimeo (Staff Pick), Prix Ars Electronica, 350 Mission in San Francisco and the second largest building of the world; The Palace of Parliament in Bucharest. Since 2015, he continues his works as designer and co-founder of VOID.

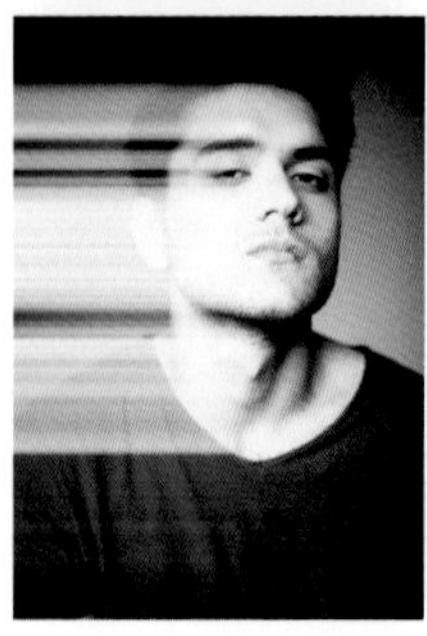

Yusuf Emre Kucur (TK) is 27 years-old multidisciplinary designer, living in Istanbul, Turkey. In his teenage years, he has been curious about the new internet technologies; accordingly started to learn more on some basic web coding such as HTML, CSS, Javascript and made his first trials for web designs. His curiosity which was not satisfied by his earlier works on web design directed him to participate in graphic design education in a private institute; where he decided to continue his career on this path. In 2009, following his career plans, he was accepted to study Visual Communication Design (VCD) in Istanbul Bilgi University (IBU). In addition to his academic studies, he took part in various design projects in the university. In 2011, he started to work as a freelancer in different agencies and involved in significant art festivals. His audio/visual works were displayed in several national and international festivals, received numerous awards and got published in significant artistic websites and magazines. His A/V performances were exhibited in substantial platforms around the globe such as; Walt Disney Concert Hall in Los Angeles, Burning Man Festival (USA), WIRED, Fubiz, Vimeo (Staff Pick), Prix Ars Electronica, 350 Mission in San Francisco and the second largest building of the world; The Palace of Parliament in Bucharest. Since 2015, he continues his works as an artist and co-founder of VOID.

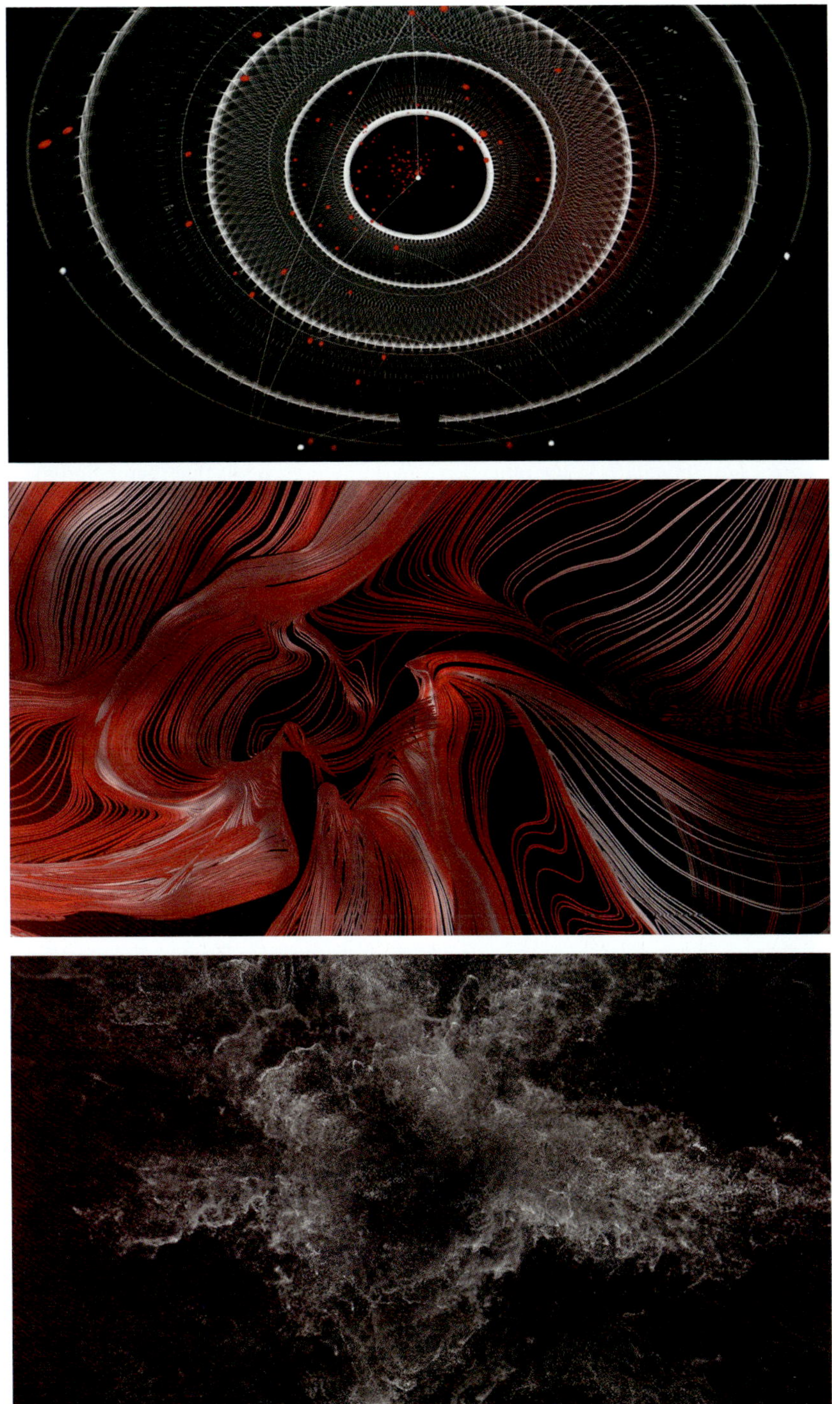

Bio-Inspire FullDome Performance

Die Gegenwart sucht ihren Mund in der Spiegelung der Suppe

The present searches for its mouth in the reflection of the soup, an artistic intervention in the depot of a Museum of Ethnology, 36 projections and 80 objects in wood or textile.

This playful synaptic prelude intensifies in the dark depot of the Museum Rietberg—an exuberant place of foreign artifacts—into an opulent genuine static, which is manifested in the osculation point of nothing less then birth, life, death, religion, and cult. In this, one finds once more Netzhammer's central theme of assemblage—be it bodily, linguistically, or culturally.

The 36 video works that seem effortlessly and yet very precisely integrated, become just as much an integral part of the visible depot as the innumerable geometrical miniature sculptures which are formally a counterpoint to his opulent formal world. Netzhammer turns us into explorers of our contact with the foreign. And makes us conscious of the fact that the innumerable artifacts that are assembled here have been carefully created by hand in another region and another time. He succeeds in all this with dazzling intensity, gentle irony, and immense empathy.

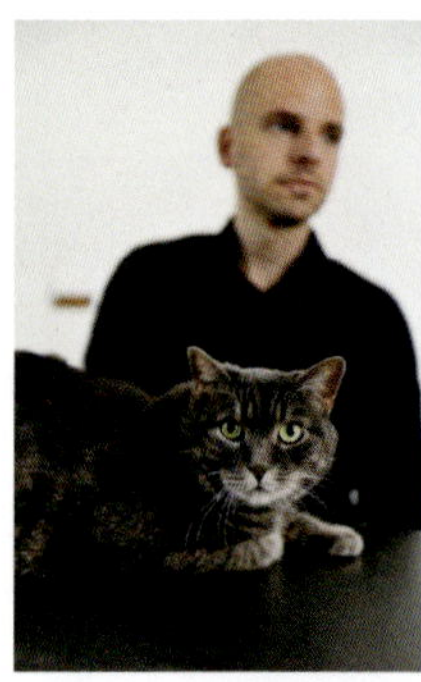

Yves Netzhammer (CH), born in 1970, studied Visual Design at Zurich College of Art and Design. Since 1997 he has been working on a widely ramified, poetic cosmos of imagery. His video installations, objects, slide shows, and drawings fascinate through their bodily charisma and their formal clarity. Solo exhibitions include LWL, Münster (2016), Kiev Biennale, Kiev (2015), MONA, Tasmania (2013), Minsheng Art Museum Shanghai (2013), and many others. Yves Netzhammer lives and works in Zurich.

Selected Solo Exhibitions

2018 | „Biografische Versprecher", Museum zu Allerheiligen Schaffhausen

2018 | „Die Pflege der Argumente", Galerie Mark Müller, Zürich

2017 | Refurnishing Thoughts, FOSUN Foundation, Shanghai

2017 | „Gesichtsüberwachungsschnecken", Kunst und Bau, U-Bahn „Altes Landgut", Wien

Selected Group Shows

2018 | „Métamorphoses" Goethe Institut Paris

2017 | „Revolution in Rotgelbblau", Marta Herford, Deutschland

2017 | Independent Animation Biennale Shenzhen, China

Website

https://netzhammer.com/

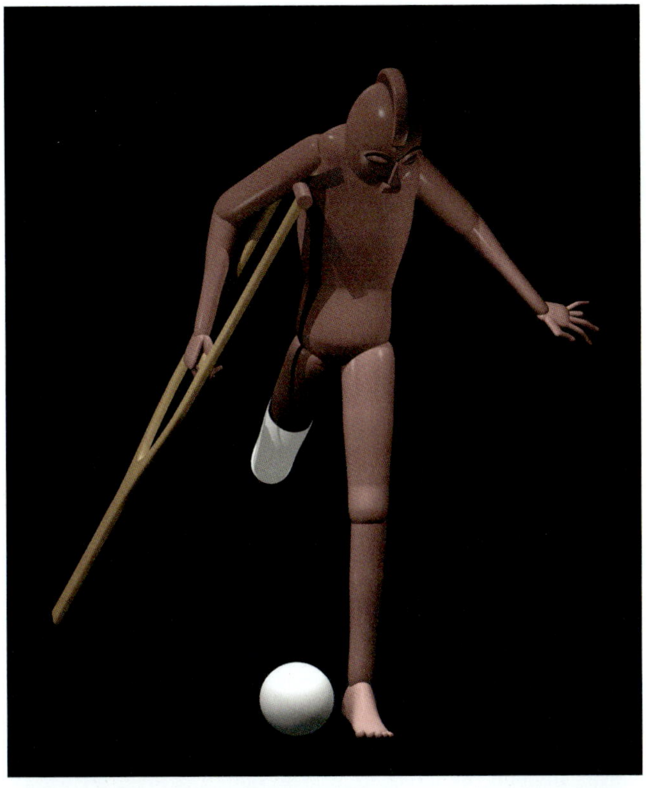

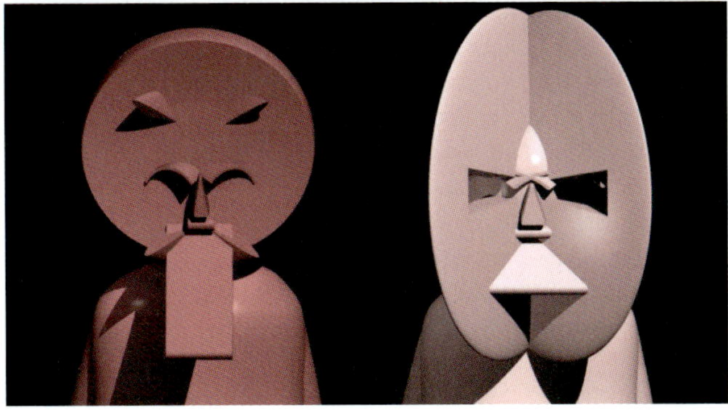

Die Gegenwart sucht ihren Mund in der Spiegelung der Suppe

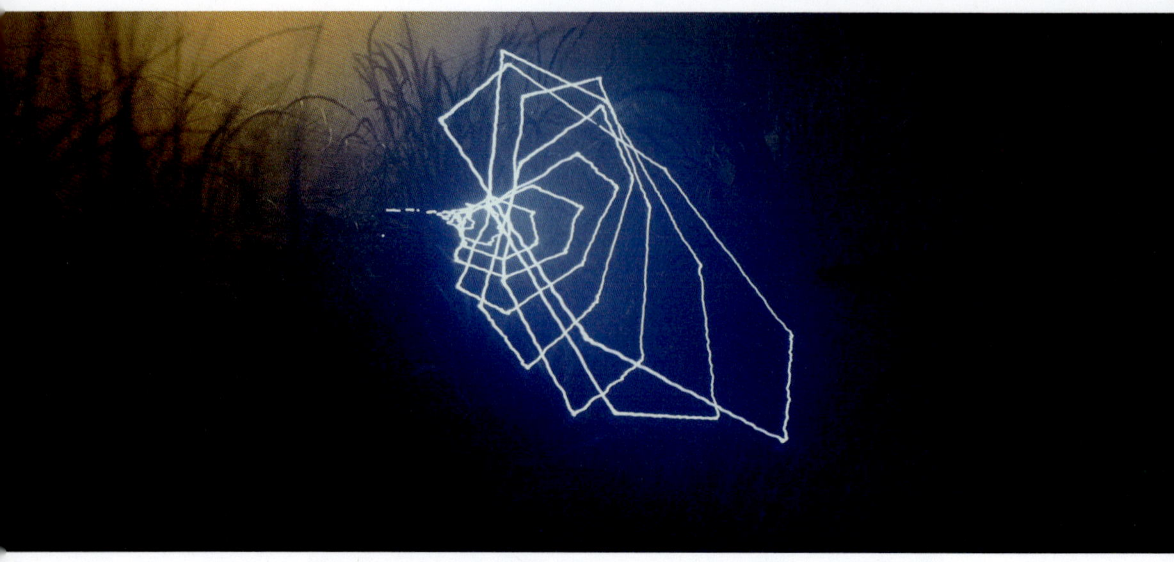

Hamill Industries – Pablo Barquín (ES) | Anna Diaz (ES) | 2016

Floating Points – Silhouettes

The experimental music video for Floating Points (the name under which English musician and neuroscientist Sam Shepherd performs), portrays an abstract oscillating light that evolves through the music in different life forms. All lights are in-camera produced effects that are made by a self-developed light paint machine. We've created a piece that, both in content and in its implementation, speaks of an analogue universe. Technique and form merge to bring out the geometry of Floating Points's sound, which, as a living being, mutates and creates a particular ecosystem. We invented a light-painting machine capable of reproducing light forms in motion, allowing us to film it with a camera, without the need of postproduction.

The machine was also capable of controlling other aspects such as camera shutter release, lights and fog machines, and a self-built motion control system. We wanted to make a video that involved a technical challenge and allowed us to conceptually explore the artistic complexity of Floating Points's sound, so we could reflect its music in a visual way. It took us 6 months of work divided between development and shooting (outdoors and indoors).

Direction: Junior Martínez, Hamill Industries (Pablo Barquín & Anna Diaz)
Director of Photography: Nathan Grimes
Music by Floating Points

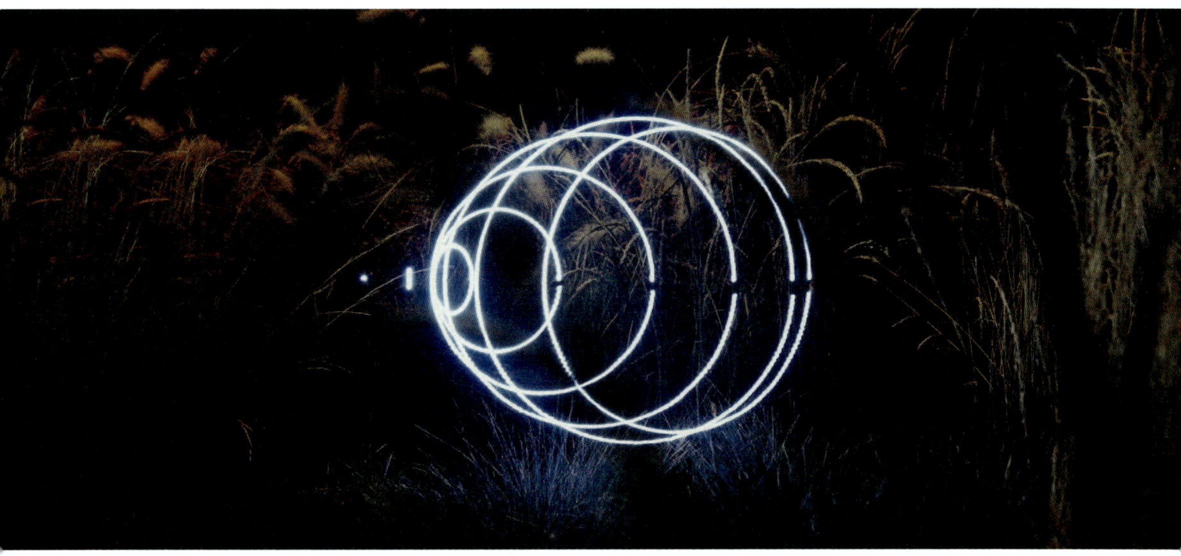

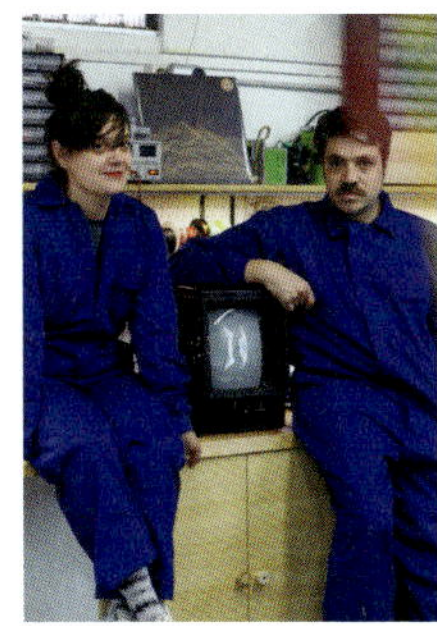

Hamill Industries (ES) is a creative studio partnership composed of skilled film directors, inventors and mix-media artists Pablo Barquín and Anna Diaz. Their body of work focuses on marrying computerised, robotic and video techniques to explore concepts from nature, the cosmos and the laws of physics. Deeply influenced by their practice as filmmakers, the duo carry out artistic and technological research in the field of visual arts and the visualisation of sound, combining new media and ground breaking experimental technologies with mechanical inventions and inspired by the world of early avant-garde cinema and sci-fi movies. Hamill Industries has become an inspirational place to realise ambitious visual artwork and to expand artistic practice into new creative dimensions, achieving poetic and playful visualexperiences by combining digital and analogue technologies with craftsmanship to offer each client a unique and personalised experience. Hamill Industries works across multiple mediums including film (TV, advertising, music videos), art installations and live performance. Their pieces have gained international recognition with publications in industry media (Motionographer, Deezen, The Creators Project) and awards including *Laus Gold 15* and top 10 for the *Startz Prize EU Award 2016*. Since 2015 they have been touring together with Floating Points creating his mesmerising visual shows, and recently have directed his visual album *Reflections – Mojave Desert*. They have presented their work at internationally recognised festivals such as *Ars Electronica* and worked for institutions and brands including Converse, Diesel, MTV, Barcelona Football Club or the Contemporary Arts Museum of Barcelona (MACBA).

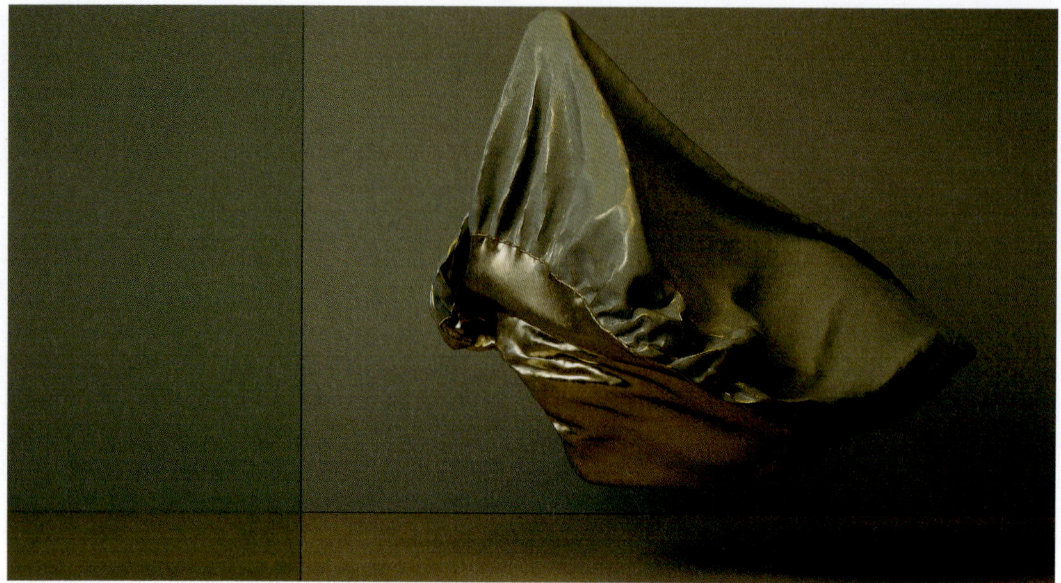

geist.xyz

On January 6, 2016, ZEITGUISED released *geist.xyz*, a different kind of fashion project: what looks at first glance like an eccentric tangle of simulated dance and a color-coordinated tumblr exploration turns out to be a study of handcrafted algorithmic textiles and procedural surfaces presented in and for exquisite realities. A synthetic ghost shifts simulated textiles from passive matter to live organisms. They behave like apparitions in an artificial choreography, with movements that are imaginary, yet familiar. Like a constant metamorphosis, the same sequence gets transformed over and over again. At each step, all aspects of the designs are modified, from algorithmic pattern to color scheme to fabric behavior. The results are meandering layers of style changes. To highlight the open nature of this process we took samples and present them in two forms: one is a grid of moving images on *geist.xyz* that visualizes our conceptual approach. The other is a linear montage showing the intricate details in 4K resolution. Shuffled layers of metronomic sounds emphasize the transformation fluctuating in and out of sync.

We have a background in sculpture and fashion design, and wanted to make this design project for years. We felt that algorithmic design is underrepresented in fashion still, due to approaches that are either too

nerdy or executions that don't work. We wanted to change that, and bring more design thinking to making patterns with algorithms. We also want to see these patterns being worn, and wear them ourselves—even if self-transforming textiles don't exist yet to the extent that we show. We just simply didn't want to wait for it. Our focus on algorithmic design stems from an interest in the rules that shape things and how designers can work with a feedback loop of the design intention into emergent results of synthetic processes.

We were infatuated with the idea of algorithm-driven design in general and particularly fabrics and prints for a while. At some point we realized that it will take a while for the current textile technologies to be developed to a state where they are usable in products or even artwork. Visualizing them first in the most enticing way would maybe be a valid precursor of ideas to take shape soon after.

Switching around the initial brief of algorithm-driven design that we used was a choice that presented itself when we thought about textile design. Design-driven algorithms and processes were now the goal. The concept for the final piece was to document and exhibit the process itself—displaying the layered technique of feeding back the results into a design process that is

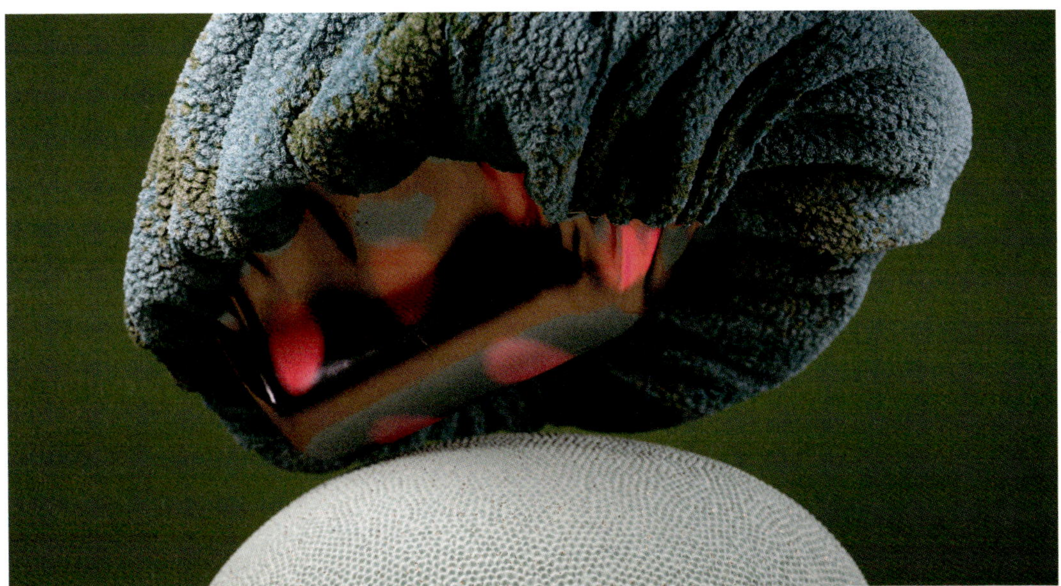

not bound by authenticity and could therefore bear unexpected transformations. We tried to keep it subtle by adhering to a color scheme that we used to guide the manic layered shuffling of design elements.

In terms of aesthetics, the resulting sequence bears quite a few moods, from bright to contrasty to dark, from elegant to exuberant, but the flow between those moods was the decisive point we wanted to make, on a micro and a macro level.

On a technical level, we worked with many software packages like Marvellous Designer for the fabric simulations and Houdini for the procedural surfaces and algorithm-driven patterns, and Substance Designer for additional procedural surfaces. It was all put together in Cinema 4D and rendered in Octane in full 4K resolution.

The most challenging part was curbing the sprawling complexity of possibilities. At some point we had oodles of movements, shapes, patterns, and textures that we had to sift through, declutter and recombine in ways that we couldn't have preconceived.

All conceptual, design and production work: ZEITGUISED
Sound track: *geist.xyz* by Superimposed Void
Production outtakes on: instagram/zeitguised

ZEITGUISED (DE) is a studio for consultancy for synthetic art and design with inhouse creative direction and production. The exquisite realities of ZEITGUISED are crafted as a unique blend of tantalizing design, handmade algorithms and bespoke generative processes. ZEITGUISED was initially founded by Henrik Mauler (DE) and Jamie Raap (US) as a collective of artists, designers, and technologists. Their work has been presented in numerous international new media festivals and selected work has also been shown in galleries and art shows around the world. Their collective is based in Berlin.

Website

https://www.zeitguised.com/

ELEVENPLAY (JP) | Daito Manabe (JP) | MIKIKO (JP) | Rhizomatiks Research (JP) | TAKCOM (JP) | 2016

Nosaj Thing / Cold Stares ft. Chance The Rapper + The O'My's

This is a music video of "Cold Stares", a collaboration between Los Angeles-based artist and beatmaker Nosaj Thing, who is actively working around the world, and rapper Chance The Rapper. A dance piece by two dancers was produced to express the message in the lyrics—their mental situation and conflict, searching for reason of being and memories, wandering along the border between reality and illusion. This dance has been shown in two ways: the real world performed by people and the delusional world of CG.

A plug-in has been developed to link a drone equipped with a camera for synthesizing video images, drone control, image synthesizing software, and existing CG software (e.g., Maya). While controlling with a program the position and angle of the drone and the camera using the motion capture technology, the camera data for synthesizing CG are recorded at the same time. The significant reduction of the process has been realized by using the acquired data at the time of shooting on the existing CG software. Dancers in the real world are shot by cameras set on six drones. Dancers in the world of illusion are shot by 48 cameras. Using technology for restoring 3D models from plural 2D data, 3D models with a high quality of texture can be achieved.

Camera motions used for the two worlds of reality and fantasy are identical. It is usually difficult to move a camera motion for the real world as freely as a camera motion for CG due to many restrictions. In this project, however, a system to move drones according to a camera motion created by CG software has been developed. Using this system, we can move drones accurately and freely like a CG camera. What's more, we could achieve a smooth transition between live action and CG.

Rhizomatiks Research: Daito Manabe, Motoi Ishibashi, Yuya Hanai, Katsuhiko Harada, Momoko Nishimoto, Youichi Sakamoto, Tomoaki Yanagisawa
ELEVENPLAY: MIKIKO, Kaori Yasukawa, Erisa Wakisaka
TAKCOM
P.I.C.S.: Takahiko Kajima, Syuhei Harada
McRAY: Akira Miwa, Kohki Okuyama, Akira Iio
Crescent,inc.
Yae-pon

Daito Manabe (JP) is a media artist, DJ and programmer. Daito founded Rhizomatiks in 2006, and since 2015 he has worked with Motoi Ishibashi on Rhizomatiks Research, which conducts projects for the purpose of R&D.

Rhizomatiks Research (JP), researching into the relationship between human beings and technology, is an organization which introduces to the world, art and entertainment projects through collaborating with creators including artists, researchers, graphic designers, athletes, dancers, choreographers, directors, musicians, and engineers.

MIKIKO (JP) is a stage director/choreographer, the artistic director and choreographer of world-famous Japanese artists, and choreographer/director of the dance company ELEVENPLAY.

ELEVENPLAY (JP) was founded by MIKIKO in 2009 in hopes of creating dancers who possess highly artistic sense and creativity on top of exquisite techniques, body and spirit.

TAKCOM (JP) is a director of the moving image and an artist, based in Tokyo. He has garnered acclaim worldwide with gallery exhibitions and art festivals. From art gallery to advertising, he takes pleasure in pursuing artistic expression in all mediums and forms.

Website

https://rzm-research.com/works/coldstares/

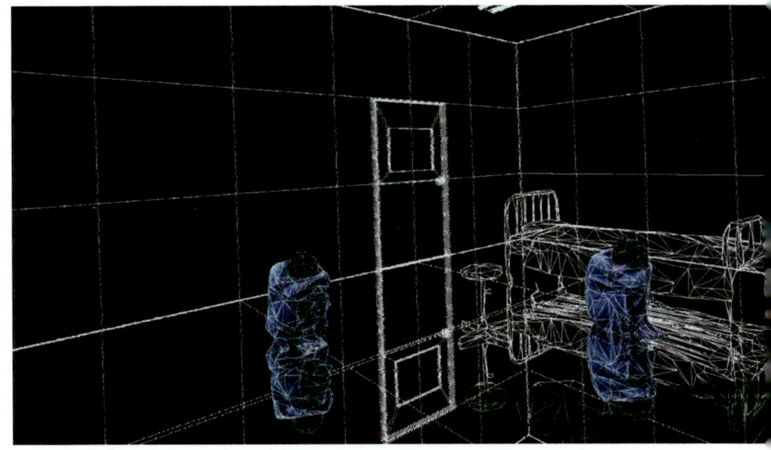

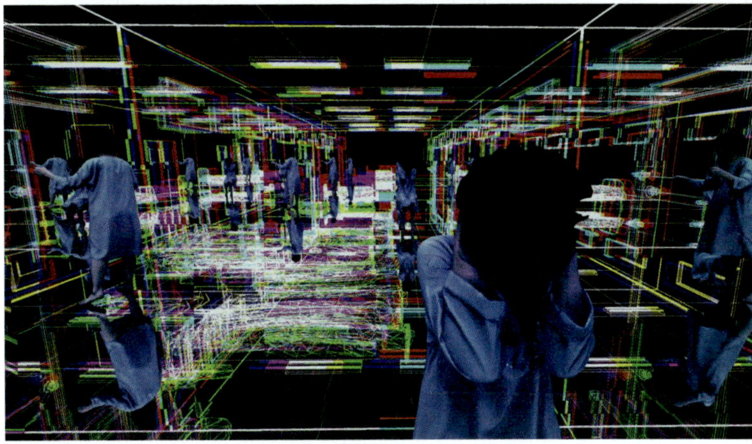

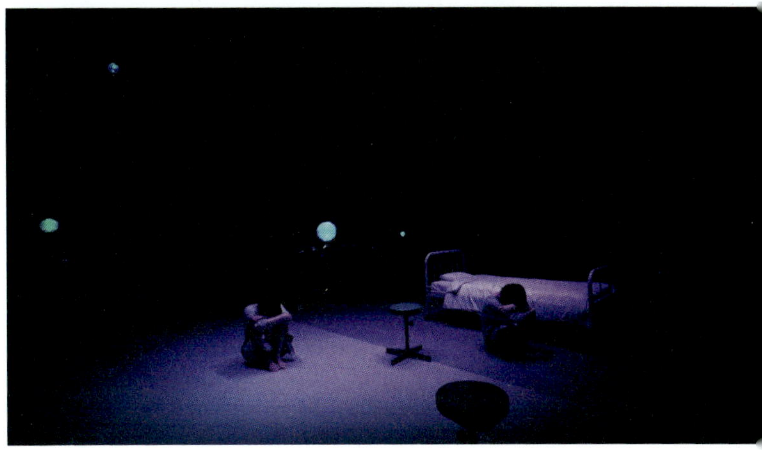

Nosaj Thing / Cold Stares ft. Chance The Rapper + The O'My's

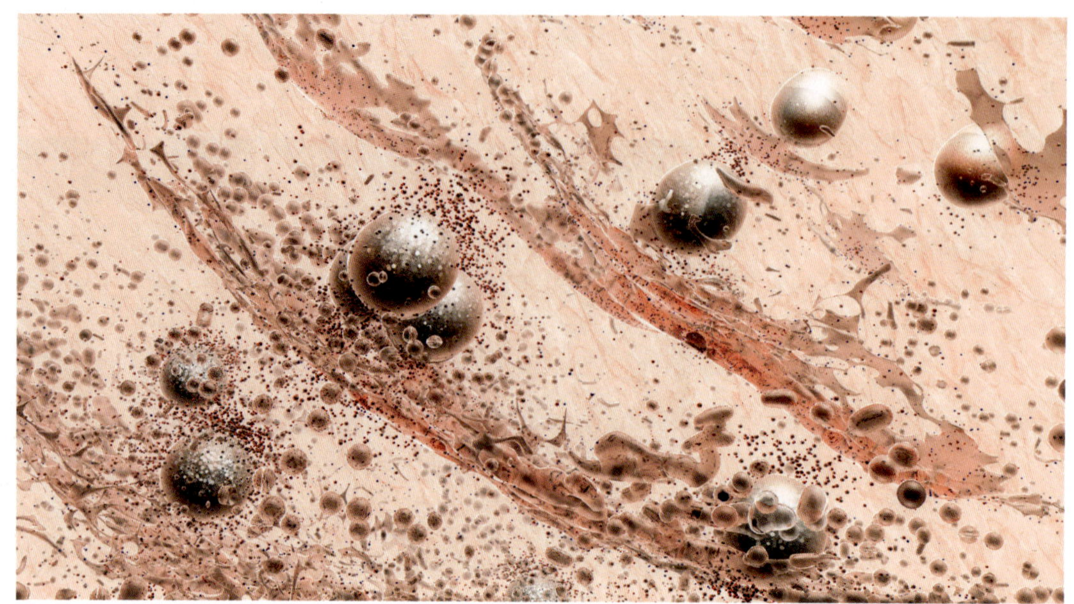

Markos Kay (GB) | 2016

Quantum Fluctuations

Made as a series of virtual experiments, *Quantum Fluctuations* shows the complexity and transient nature of the most fundamental aspect of reality, the quantum world, which is impossible to observe directly. In the laboratory, elementary particles are observed by measuring the spoils of a proton collision and comparing the findings with data collected from supercomputer simulations. It is perhaps the most indirect method of observation imaginable, a non-representational form of observation mediated by computer simulations.

In *Quantum Fluctuations*, particle simulations are used as the brush and paint to create abstract moving paintings that visualize the events that happen during a proton collision. In these virtual experiments millions of virtual particles interact to create stochastic structures and patterns that allude to quantum properties such as wave-particle duality, superposition, entanglement, and indeterminacy. Using simulations as an artistic tool can be likened to abstract art methods. There is no control over the way events unfold, however there is some control over initial parameters. It involves setting initial conditions such as the physical forces, properties, and entities of a virtual environment, and then the simulation evolves on its own with no intervention. This mirrors the simulation methods used at the CERN but also physical reality itself.

The film begins with the underlying quantum fluctuations and interactions that occur in the background of a collision. It shows the intricate structure of the proton beams that collide to create an outflow of particle showers which create composite particles that eventually decay. These visualizations were created with input from scientists working on the Large Hadron Collider at the CERN, Geneva. By using computer simulations as an artistic tool, this conceptual reimagining of quantum theory aims to challenge our ideas of how scientific observation and knowledge are formed. Science is able to profoundly change the way we understand the universe but also our societies and our minds. From an artistic perspective, science is an extremely powerful metanarrative and is therefore a subject that needs to be deconstructed through art. The scientific method itself can be seen as an artistic process—it aims to answer questions about how

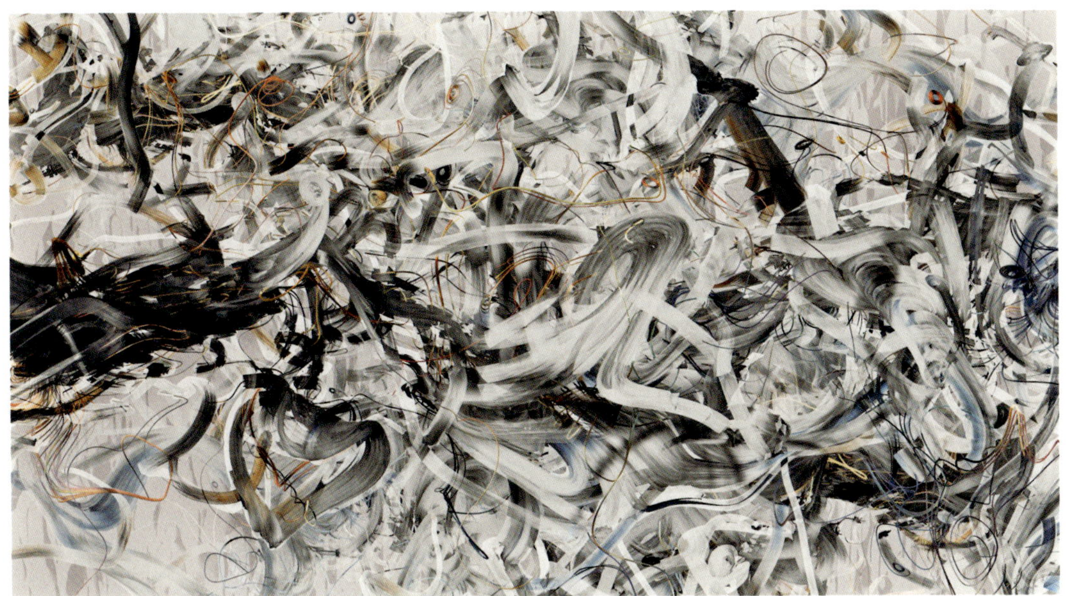

the world works but more importantly it creates more questions about reality. It deconstructs and reconstructs knowledge and it uncovers beauty, complexity, and simplicity just like art.

Produced by Epoche.io

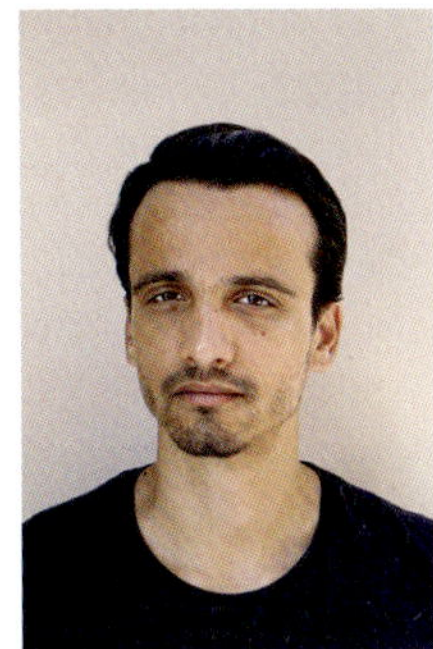

Markos Kay (GB) is a visual artist, director and lecturer with a focus in art & science, digital abstraction and computational art. He is best known for his video art experiment aDiatomea (2008), exhibited at Ernst Haeckel's Phyletic Museum, the conceptual visualisation The Flow (2011) and Quantum Fluctuations (2016), a visual interpretation of particle collisions. His work can be described as an ongoing investigation of the relationship between the digital and the physical through the use of computationally generative methods. The resulting experiments explore the emergence and complexity of nature and the digital sublime. His art and design practice ranges from screen-based media, to projection and print and has been featured worldwide in museums, exhibitions, film festivals and art publications.

Selected Exhibitions

2018 | All Possible Paths: The Extraordinary Life of Richard Feynman exhibition, ArtScience Museum, Singapore

2018 | Punto Y Raya Festival, CeTA Audivisual Technology Centre, Poland

2018 | Digital Intersections exhibition, San Martino di Lupari, Italy

2018 | STARTS exhibition, Prix Ars Electronica, Honorary Mention, Austria

Website

https://www.mrkism.com/

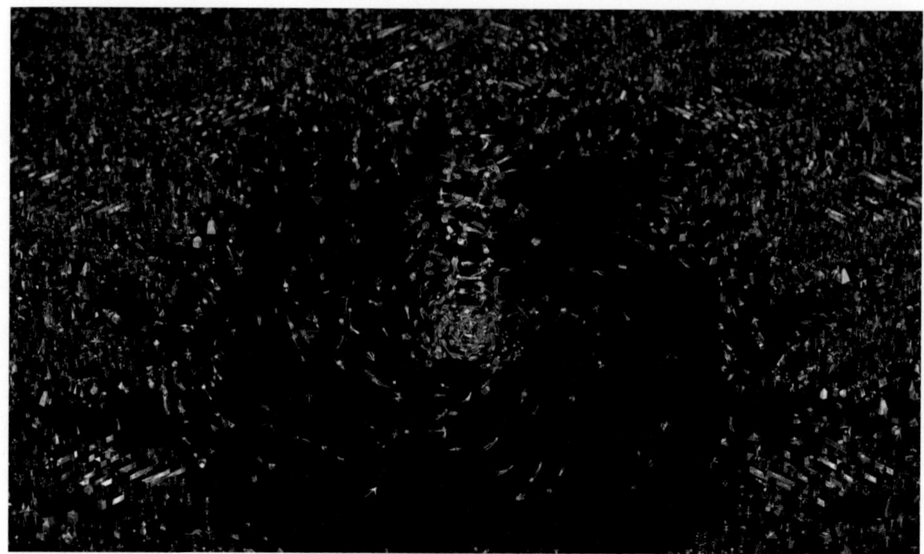

Boris Labbé (FR) | 2016

RHIZOME

"Unlike trees or their roots, the rhizome connects any point to any other point, and its traits are not necessarily linked to traits of the same nature; it brings into play very different regimes of signs, and even nonsign states. ... It is composed not of units but of dimensions, or rather directions in motion. It has neither beginning nor end, but always a middle (milieu) from which it grows and which it overspills. ... What is at question in the rhizome is a relation to sexuality, but also to the animal, the vegetal, the world, politics, the book, things natural and artificial, that is totally different from the arborescent relation: all manner of 'becomings'."

Extract from *A Thousand Plateaus* by Gilles Deleuze and Félix Guattari (translation by Brian Massumi).

RHIZOME is an experimental animated short film that has its foundation in the homonymous philosophical concept, coined and developed by Gilles Deleuze and Félix Gattari, involving research that is close to Steve Reich's repetitive music, Escher's mathematical art work, Bruegel and Bosch's paintings and different scientific theories about the development of life, genetics, the infinitely small and the infinitely large.

The film propels us from the beginning to a big zoom over a dimension that is not accessible for us until now, infinitely small or infinitely far away. There, we attend the birth of an unknown form of life. By repetition, connection, or metamorphosis the organism experiences very fast evolution, giving shape to three big ways of evolution: organic, vegetable and mineral. Really fast, by connection, contact, or mixing, these organisms hybridize and metamorphose until they create a whole society made out of unknown plants, peculiar animals, and archetypal architectures. This scene develops until it creates a constellation, a great ensemble in movement, a wave that spreads towards emptiness. Then the system itself starts a huge revolution: the elements converge in a central point and destroy themselves in order to renew themselves, through pure color and on spiral upward movements to a series of air circles. Finally, we leave this world in a large zoom out, which first seems infinite, huge, but as the distance increases, it becomes microscopic, disappearing from itself again.

RHIZOME was made by a small team of artists and technicians and directed by Boris Labbé. The animation of animated sequences consists of Indian ink and watercolor drawings on paper (21 x 30 cm and 60 x 84 cm). Approximately 2,300 original drawings were needed to create the whole film, with between 1 to 80 elements in each drawing.

The principle of animation runs on a system of loops,

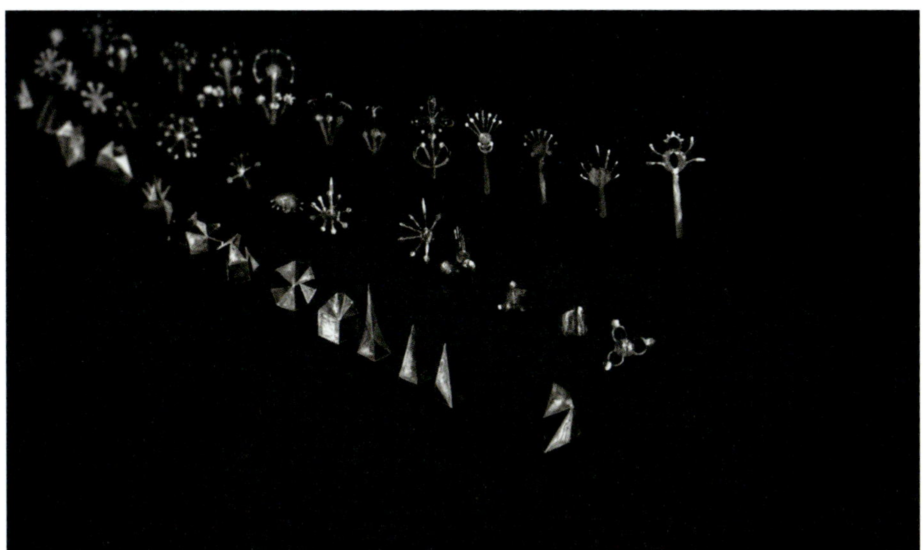

which are organized like a canon: modules with multiple inputs and outputs which have the ability to connect with other modules. The drawings were progressively photographed or scanned. Then, a digital treatment of the animation was done (cleaning the images, setting negative, et cetera) and the film got its shape due to the work of compositing on the After Effects software (camera animation, compositing image, et cetera).

The musical composition was created by Brazilian composer Aurélio Edler-Copes from a series of musical motives analogously recorded from the electric guitar and followed by digital compositing work on the computer (editing, treatment and transformation of the sound). The haunting rhythmic base, acute and repetitive, forms the word R-H-I-Z-O-M-E in Morse code. This pattern is submitted to progressive acceleration and deceleration towards the bass and treble, increasing then the sound spectrum. The ensemble creates an expanding sound constellation that finds its climax with the arrival of the final spiral and the gradual emergence of color.

Produced in France by Sacrebleu Productions, the film received support from the Agence Culturelle d'Alsace during a two-month pre-production residency and from the CICLIC Région Centre during 8 months on a production residency in 2014. The film also received financial support from SACEM, CNC, France Television and PROCIREP – ANGOA.

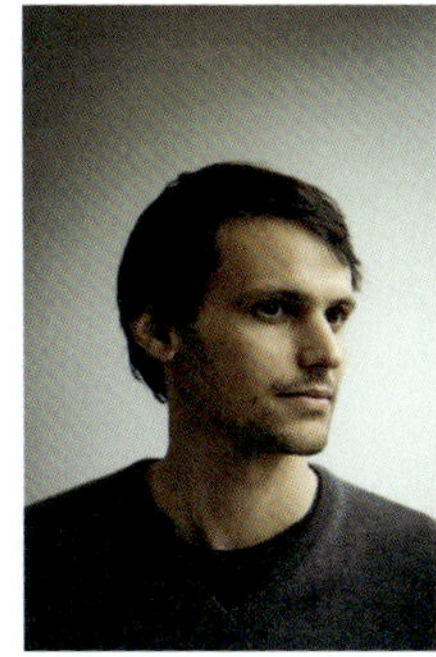

Boris Labbé (FR). After obtaining a DNAP (National Diploma in Visual Arts) at l'Ecole supérieure d'art et de céramique de Tarbes, Boris Labbé continued his studies at the EMCA of Angoulême (Ecole des métiers du cinéma d'animation). At the EMCA, he produced *Kyrielle*, his final film project, which was awarded the Special Jury's prize for Graduation Films at the Annecy International Animated Film Festival in 2012. Simultaneously, he developed an artistic work that is both visual and plastic. He spent a year at the Casa de Velázquez in Madrid. *RHIZOME* is his first professional film.

Selected Solo Exhibitions

2016 | Rhizome, Millennium Point, Flatpack Film Festival, Birmingham, GB

2016 | Animation Cabin 2, Au Praxinoscope, Tokyo, JP

2016 | Danse macabre, Cinémathèque Québécoise, Montréal, CA

Selected Group Exhibitions

2018 | Immortality! "Do you want infinite lives?", Overkill Festival, Enschede, NL

2018 | Multivision, Erarta Museum of contemporary art, Saint Petersburg, RU

2018 | Cyberarts exhibition, OK Center for Contemporary Art, Festival Ars Electronica, Linz, AT

Website

https://www.borislabbe.com/

489 Years

489 Years shows an animated landscape of the Demilitarized Zone between North and South Korea, based on the narration of a former soldier who had entered the DMZ—one of the most dangerous and heavily armed places in the world. Since only authorized personnel can enter the DMZ, Hayoun Kwon uses animation as a medium to reconstruct the space that plays on the fiction and the fantasy of a forbidden territory, providing an indrect experience for the viewer.

The former soldier featured in *489 Years* tells Hayoun Kwon various stories of his experiences in the DMZ. Among his many accounts, the artist was touched by his story of the landmines and flowers, realizing that she wanted the viewer to experience the DMZ as a paradoxical place where intense anxiety and subliminal beauty coexist. In creating her imagined landscape, Hayoun Kwon addresses the geopolitical realities of the peninsular division, its violence and projected images of this mythical space.

Originally shown through a Virtual Reality device, artificial interventions and fictional constructions enable the artist to film what cannot otherwise be shown. Animation affords her the freedom to theatricalize, exaggerate, and push the frontiers of representation, and even to exploit the fantasmatic potential of her subjects. Reflecting on identity and the notion of the border, Hayoun Kwon interrogates the construction of individual and historical memory, as well as the ambiguous relationship of both to reality and fiction. Offering the viewer an entrance into the DMZ, Hayoun Kwon's work leads the viewer to experience the DMZ through human emotions of anxiety and wonder.

Director: Hayoun Kwon
Level designer: Fabrice Gaston
Tech artist/Animation: Guillaume Bertinet
3D Modeler: Laurent Raynaud
Sound designer: Sylvain Buffet
Composer: Pierre Desprats
Consultant: Balthazar Auxietre

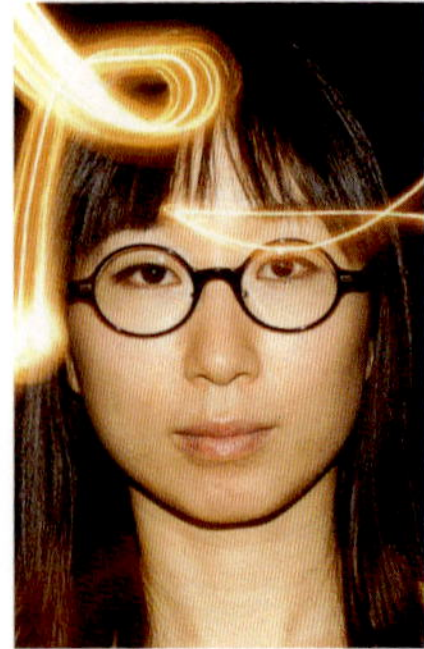

Hayoun Kwon (KR), born in 1981, is a multimedia artist and documentary director. She graduated from Le Fresnoy – Studio national des arts contemporains in 2011 and she lives and works in France and in Korea. Her films Village Model (2014) and 489 Years (2016) have received several awards and been shown at a number of film festivals including Ars Electronica 2018. The reflection on identity and borders is central to her previous works. She has focused more specifically on the construction of historical and individual memory and their ambivalent relationship to reality and fiction.

Selected Exhibitions

2019 | DOOSAN Gallery, New York, US (solo)

2019 | BIENNALE DE LYON, Lyon, FR

2019 | LEVITATION, Arario Gallery, Shanghai, ZH (solo)

2018 | LEVITATION, DOOSAN Gallery, Seoul, KR (solo)

2018 | I Suddenly Hear the Flap of Wings, galerie Sator, Paris FR (solo)

2018 | NO MAN'S LAND, Musée d'Art Moderne Grand-Duc Jean MUDAM, Luxembourg LU

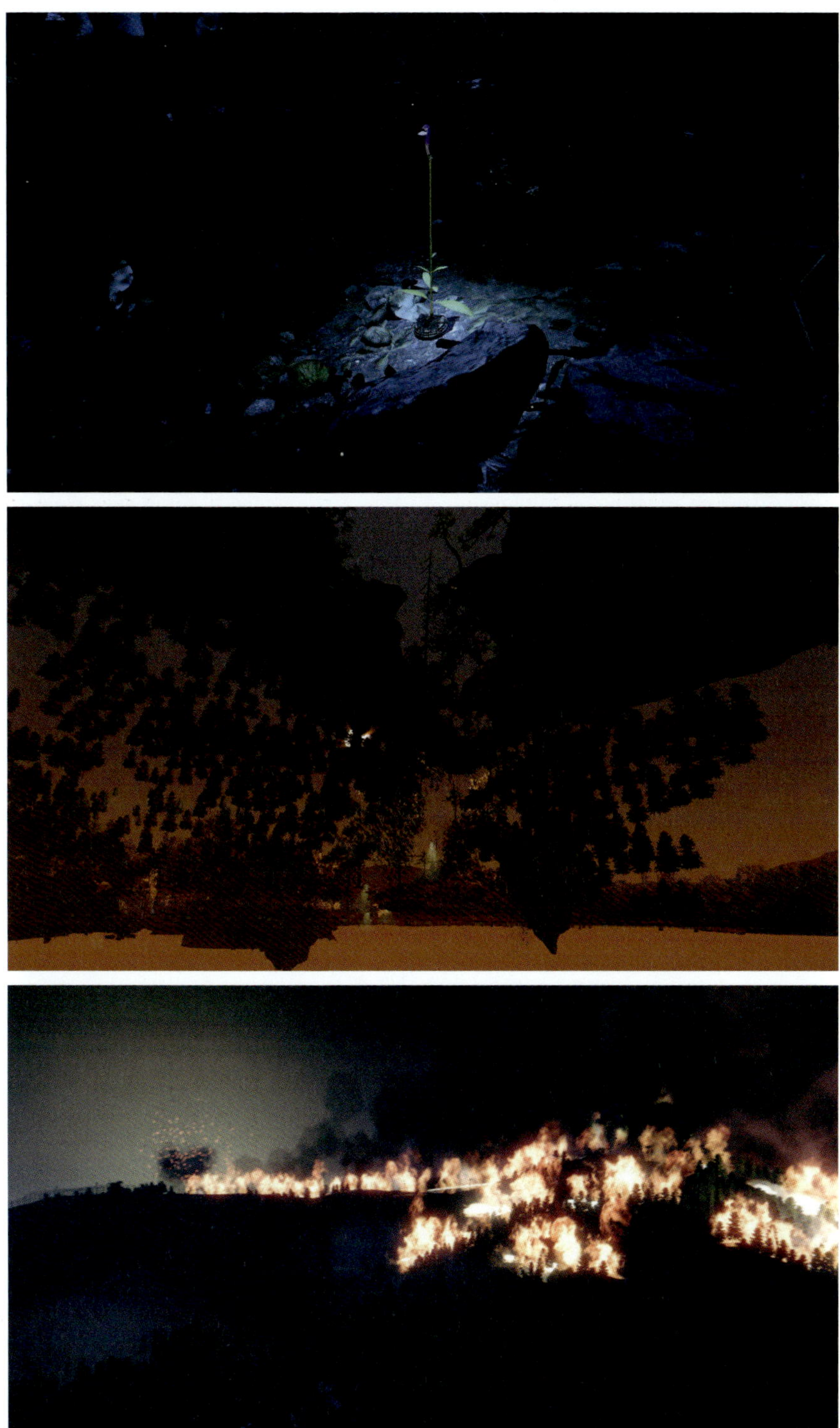

489 Years

Blade Runner–Autoencoded

Blade Runner–Autoencoded is a film made by training an autoencoder—a type of generative neural network—to recreate frames from the 1982 film *Blade Runner*. The Autoencoder learns to model images by trying to copy them through a very narrow information bottleneck, being optimized to create images that are as similar as possible to the original images. The network was trained on all the frames from the *Blade Runner* 20 times. After training, the autoencoder reinterprets each frame from the film in order, and the reconstructed frames are then resequenced back to create a reconstruction of the film. The resulting sequence is very dreamlike, drifting in and out of recognition between static scenes that the model remembers well, to fleeting sequences—usually with a lot of movement—that the model barely comprehends.

The film *Blade Runner* is adapted from Philip K. Dicks novel *Do Androids Dream of Electric Sheep?*. Set in a post-apocalyptic dystopian future, Rick Deckard is a bounty hunter who makes a living hunting down and killing replicants, artificial humans that are so well engineered that they are physically indistinguishable from human beings. Because replicants are indistinguishable from humans, Deckard has to issue the Voight-Kampff empathy test in order to determine whether they are humans or not. The technological advances of the Nexus-6 replicants makes it increasingly difficult for Deckard to determine what is human and what is not, and Deckard himself has the growing suspicion that he himself may not be human.

By reinterpreting *Blade Runner* with the autoencoder's memory of the film, *Blade Runner–Autoencoded* seeks to emphasize the ambiguous boundary in the film between replicant and human, or in the case of the reconstructed film, between our memory of the film and the neural networks. Aspects of the flaws in its visual reconstruction are reminiscent of the deficiencies of our own, especially regarding memories of dreams. By examining this imperfect reconstruction of *Blade Runner*, the gaze of a disembodied machine, it becomes easier to acknowledge the flaws in our own internal representation of the world and easier to imagine the potential of other, substantially different systems that have their own internal representations.

Carried out on the Msci Creative Computing course at the Department of Computing, Goldsmiths, University of London under the supervision of Mick Grierson.

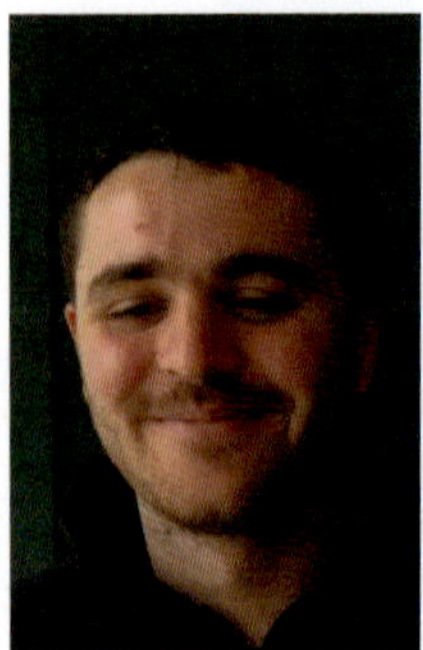

Terence Broad (GB) is an artist and machine learning researcher based in London. He works at the forefront of technological developments in machine learning, exploring both the perceptual capabilities and limitations of these techniques. He graduated in 2016 from the Creative Computing Masters programme at Goldsmiths, University of London. His work has been exhibited internationally at venues including The Whitney Museum of American Art, Art Center NABI, and The Barbican.

Selected Exhibitions

2018 | IAM, Garage Museum For Contemporary Art, Moscow, Russia.

2017–2018 | All these Moments will be lost in Time like Tears in Rain, Médiathèque du Fonds d'art contemporain de la Ville de Genève (FMAC), Geneva, Switzerland.

Website

https://terencebroad.com

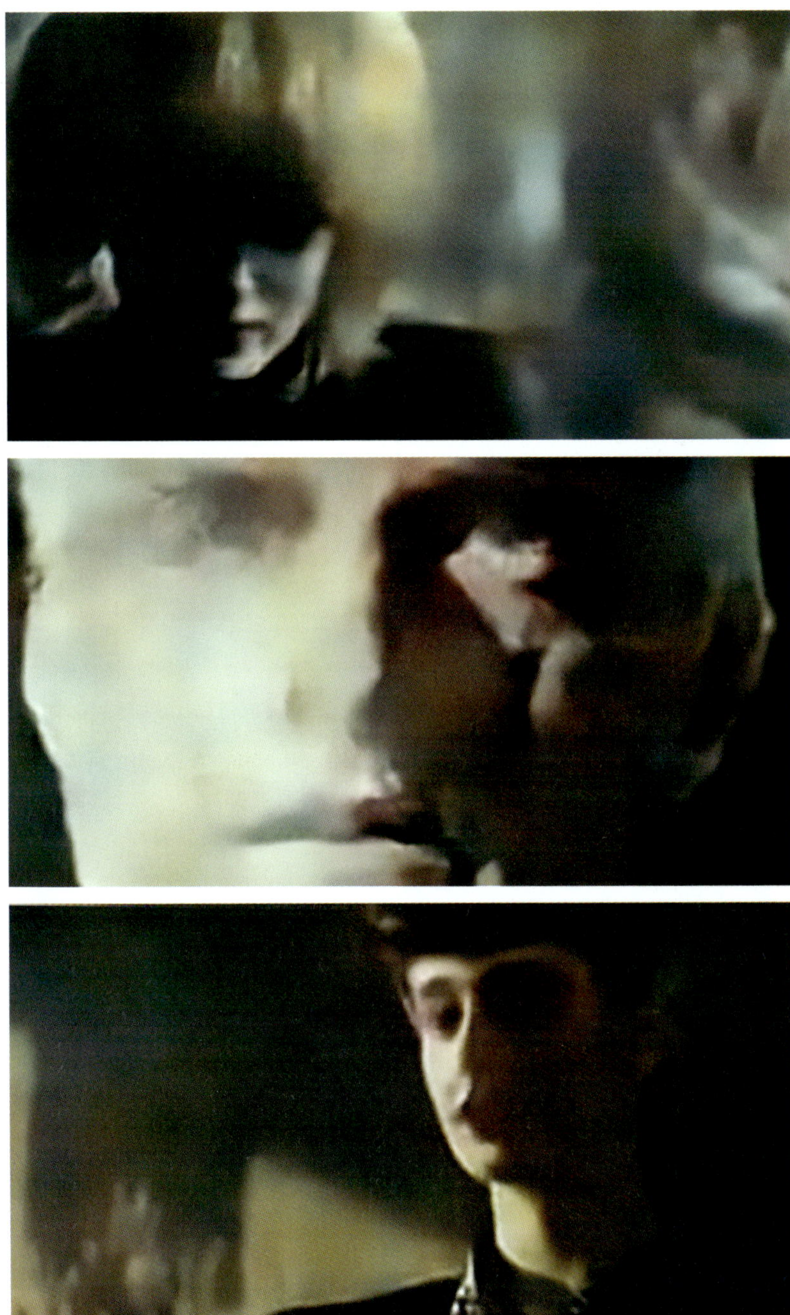

Blade Runner – Autoencoded

Max Hattler (DE/HK) | 2017

Divisional Articulations

Repetition and distortion drive this audiovisual collaboration between composer Lux Prima and visual artist Max Hattler, where fuzzy analogue music and geometric digital animation collide in an electronic feedback loop, and spawn arrays of divisional articulations in time and space.

Director: Max Hattler
Music: Lux Prima
Animation: King Lam Chan, Po Yi Chan, Hinyi Cheuk, Ka Man Chow, Cheuk Hei Kai, Tsz Ching Kwan, Hau Ying Lui, Ka Man Luk, Ngai Wan Ma, Cheuk Lam Mui, Kam Ian Sio, Susan Sun, Qi Yu Teo, Ka Yiu Wong, Crystal Yip, Ka Man Yu, Max Hattler
Code: Sune Petersen

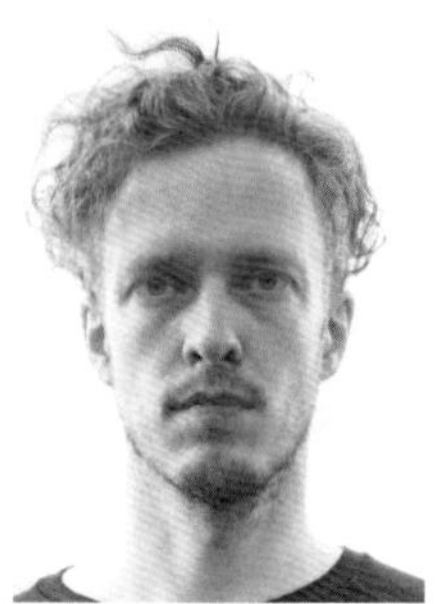

Max Hattler (DE/HK) is an artist and academic who works with abstract animation, video installation and audiovisual performance. He holds a master's degree from the Royal College of Art and a Doctorate in Fine Art from the University of East London. Max has lectured at CalArts, USC, Goldsmiths, KASK and many more. His work has been shown at festivals and institutions such as Resonate, Ars Electronica, ZKM Center for Art and Media, MOCA Taipei and Beijing Minsheng Museum. Awards include Supernova, Cannes Lions, Bradford Animation Festival and several Visual Music Awards. Max has performed live around the world including at Playgrounds Festival, Re-New Copenhagen, Expo Milan, Seoul Museum of Art and the European Media Art Festival. He lives in Hong Kong where he is an Assistant Professor at School of Creative Media, City University of Hong Kong. Max's current research focuses on synaesthetic experience and visual music, the narrative potential of abstract animation, and expanded artistic approaches to binocular vision.

Website

https://www.maxhattler.com/

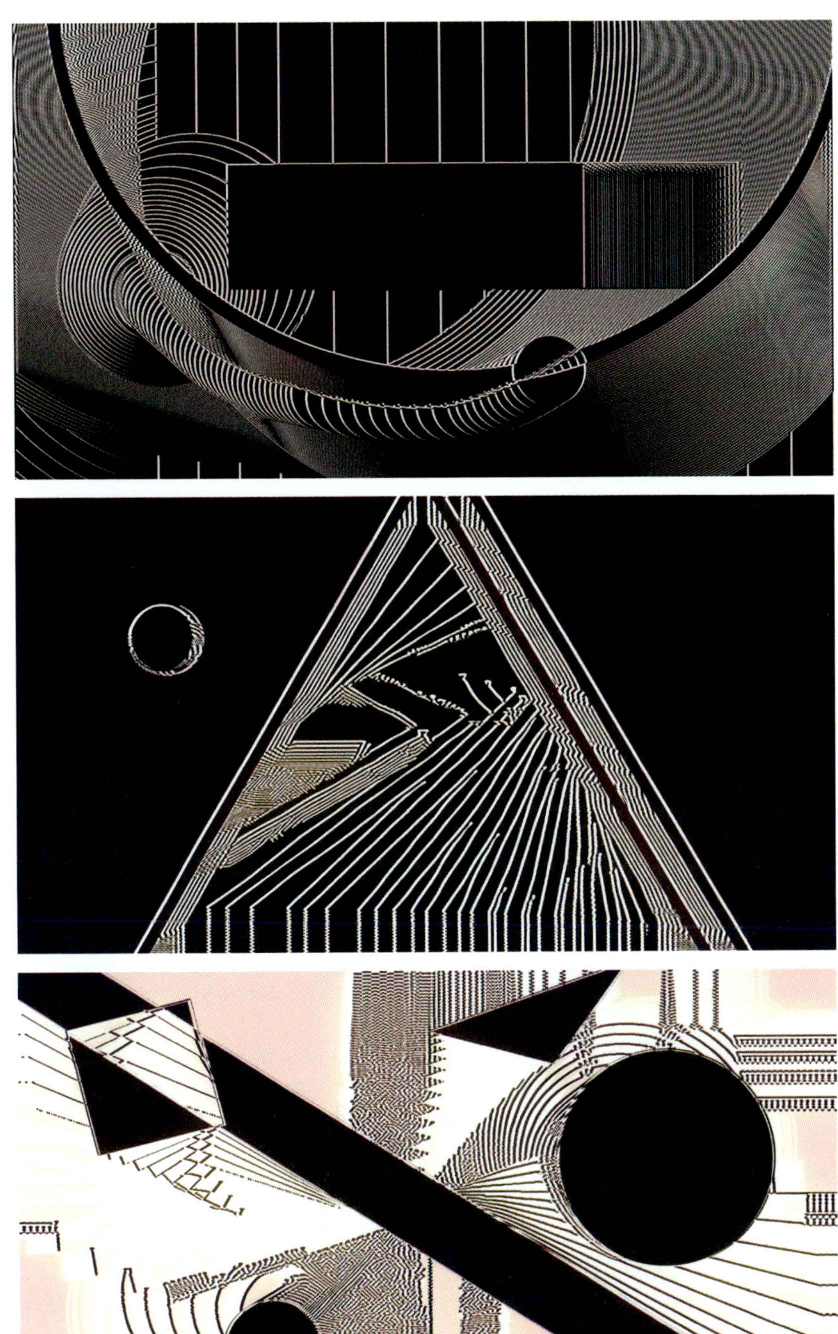

Divisional Articulations

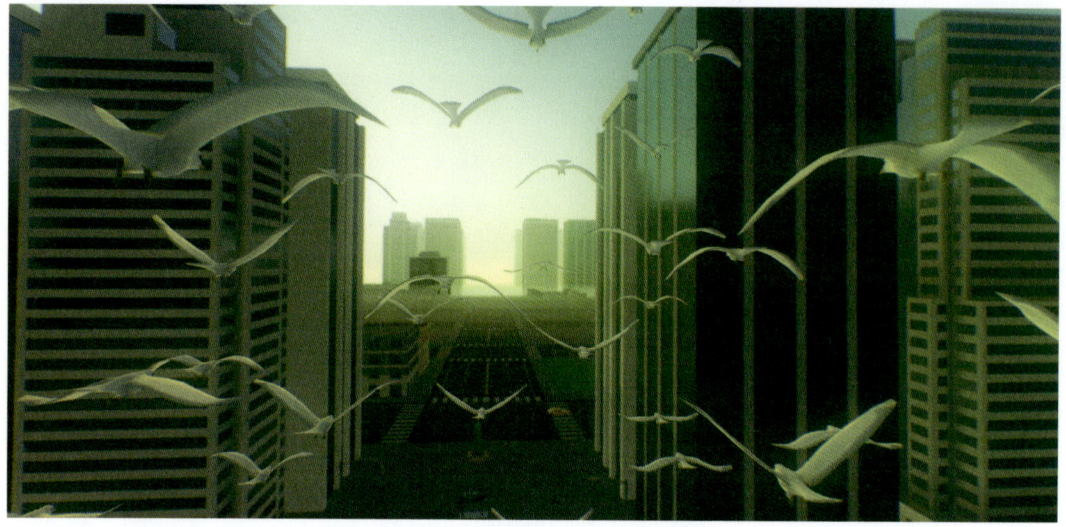

David OReilly (IE) | 2017

Everything

Everything is an interactive experience where everything you see is a thing you can be—from animals to
planets to galaxies and beyond. The player can travel
between outer and inner space, and explore a vast,
interconnected universe of things without enforced
goals, scores, or tasks to complete. Playing *Everything*
involves traveling through the Universe and seeing it
from different points of view—it has elements of role
playing games, sandbox & simulation. The systems
connecting the game are designed to create moments
of peace, beauty, sadness, and joy—and allow the
player to do whatever they want. There is no right or
wrong way to play, and each person's game will be different. Things are the basic unit of *Everything*, and the
entirety of the game is designed to be playable. Levels
can be characters and vice versa. The game's universe
is designed to let you travel freely in any direction, and
intuitively find things when and where you'd expect
them to be. Continued exploration will lead you to
unseen environments, containing new sights, sounds,
things, thoughts, and abilities.

Everything requires no player input—it will play automatically if left unattended. This "Autoplay" function
can be tweaked by the player to produce particular
results over time. The game also acts as a kind of 3D,
living encyclopedia—where thousands of things are
discovered—and each has an associated data entry.

The player/user will discover hundreds of existing spe-
cies and objects in a play-through. The persistent universe featured in *Everything* can be both explored and
used as a creative canvas. The game is fundamentally
changed by player input, meaning you can create and
design levels when you're inside them. Each part of
the world allows complete freedom to create your own
images, worlds, scenes, and experiences using things
instead of pixels or polygons.

Everything presents a philosophy about life which
takes several forms—in its mechanics, narration, content, structure, and design. *Everything's* philosophy
is designed to be experienced in all of its parts rather
than read linearly, it is created to reflect life and not
impose a singular framework on it, and above all to be
playful, entertaining, and helpful. The philosophy of
Everything is not easy to categorize as it does not sat-
isfy any existing school or canon. It is not based on any
one source and is not advocating any particular way of
thinking. It is both serious and funny, silly and sincere,
rational and absurd. It intentionally contradicts itself
and criticizes itself for it.

Everything contains narration in the form of recordings
of the late philosopher Alan Watts. These recordings
are an optional part of the experience and offer a ver-
bal framework for interpreting the game and life itself.
There are hours of material—dealing with subjects such

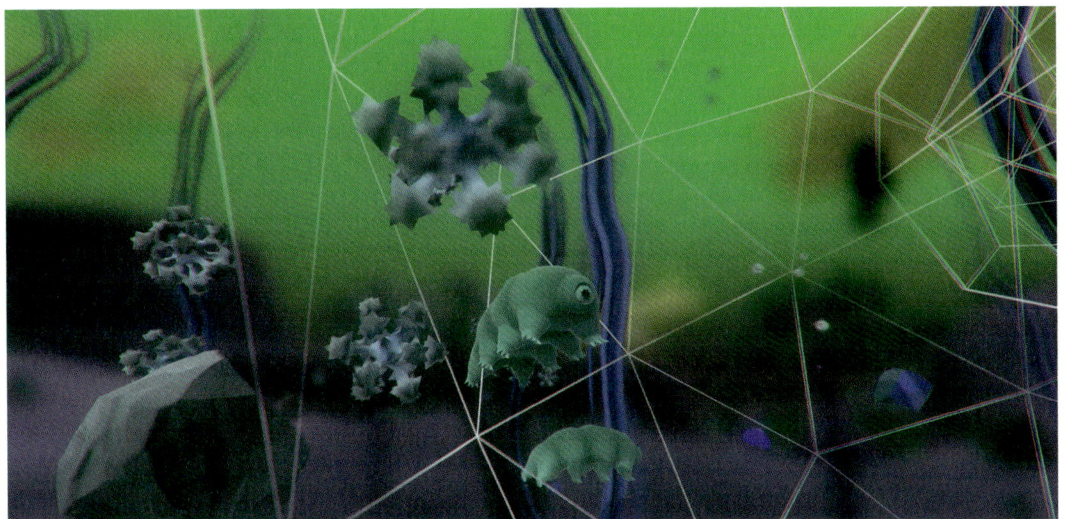

as perception, how our brains interpret the world, the structure of the universe, physics, biology, ideas of self vs. other, and more. Many written thoughts in the game are taken from continental philosophers, such as Schopenhauer or the Roman stoics, Marcus Aurelius and Seneca. There are hundreds of these thoughts embedded into the game, rewritten and edited for length, and integrated into the game's thought system. *Everything* seeks to revive these ideas, liberate them from their texts, and bring them to a new audience.

Everything features a beautiful score by composer Ben Lukas Boysen and world-class cellist Sebastian Plano. Over 3 hours of original music were composed—with each track corresponding to a particular kind of ecosystem observed at a particular scale. *Everything* was produced and self-funded by David OReilly, who is Irish and currently based in Los Angeles. The entirety of the game's production was distributed worldwide, with contributors based in Texas, New York, Brighton, and Berlin.

Creator, Designer, Producer: David OReilly
Programmer: Damien Di Fede
Music: Ben Lukas Boysen & Sebastian Plano
Sound: Eduardo Ortiz Frau
Additional 3d Design: Anne Yang
Additional Sound design: Ryan Collins
Narration: Written & Performed by Alan Watts
Concept Art: 30000fps & Elle Michalka
Publisher: Greg Rice

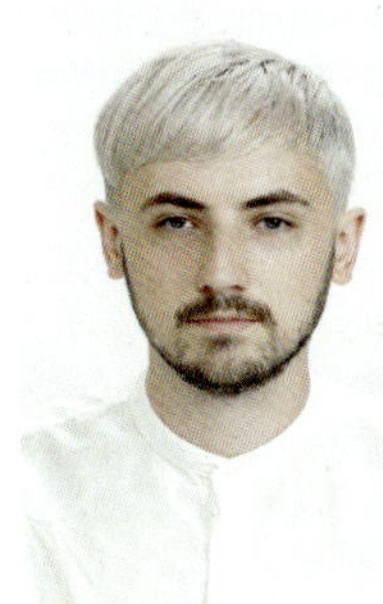

David OReilly (b. Ireland, 1985) is an artist based in Tokyo, Japan. Starting out as an independent animator, he created numerous award winning short films, pioneering the use of low poly and glitch aesthetics. He has written for TV shows such as Adventure Time & South Park and created fictional video games in Spike Jonze's Academy Award winning film *Her*. Creator of the iconic game *Mountain* and the universe simulation game *Everything*, narrated by Alan Watts.

Selected Exhibitions

2018 | David Lynch's Festival Of Disruption, US

2018 | Roleplay Reality at FACT, GB

2018 | Unwanted Stories at Edith-Russ-Haus, DE

2017 | La Roche Sur Yon solo, FR

Selected Works

2018 | Eye of the Dream, interactive simulation

2017 | Everything, interactive simulation

2014 | Mountain, interactive simulation

Website

https://davidoreilly.com/

Depart – Leonhard Lass (AT) | Gregor Ladenhauf (AT) | 2017

Lacuna Shifts

"The Lacuna Shifts" is a spatio-poetic VR Experience (5-8min). It opens a volatile room that keeps changing around its guest—shifting in scale and mutating its architectural features—while revealing traces of poetic narratives.

Loosely inspired by Lewis Carroll's Alice books "The Lacuna Shifts" combines sound, text and imagery into an alternate surreality. Disembodied, the viewer's gaze becomes the only instrument of connecting to this space—it leaves traces, activates and builds structures. Instead of traveling through a world the world shifts around the spectator—at times covertly behind the back, sometimes in plain sight. It rejects its passive role as a trusted, immutable shelter and permits a physically impossible experience of poetic space and a reflection about the fragile relation of the beholder to her/his environment. Lacuna's unstable architecture is based on a parametric wall system that enables ever changing spatial configurations. Thus, one cannot enter the same room twice. Each viewer will experience a different "journey", manifesting different aspects based on her/his behavior and the world's own erratic character.

Instead of a linear story, it unfolds as a modular, hyperpoetic system, which consists of text (spoken and written), wall graffiti, symbolic objects, animations, and the architecture itself.

Commissioned by sound:frame in cooperation with O.K. – Offenes Kulturhaus OÖ and Metro Kino Wien

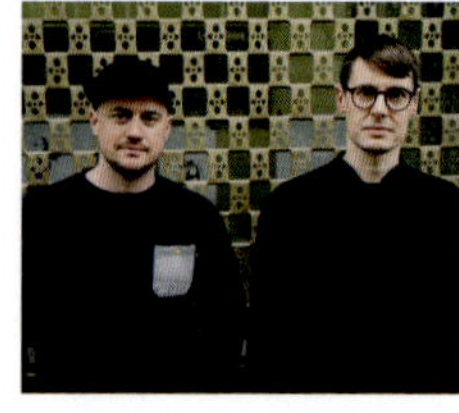

Leonhard Lass (b. 1978) and Gregor Ladenhauf (b. 1978) are Depart. Their core endeavor is the conception of poetic, individual experiences. They construct audiovisual worlds as dynamic systems. These transitory sandboxes of synchronicities border on the surreal and enable the unexpected by means of cross-modal emergence. Deeply rooted in the digital, they explore the ritualistic character of algorithms and venture deliberately into the uncanny – creating unique moments that are coined by formally rigorous and profound aesthetics. In their almost 20 years of collaboration they have produced award-winning work that has been internationally exhibited (USA, China, UK, Germany, Spain, Russia, Netherlands, Switzerland, ...). Depart is based in Vienna, Austria.

Website:

https://www.depart.at/

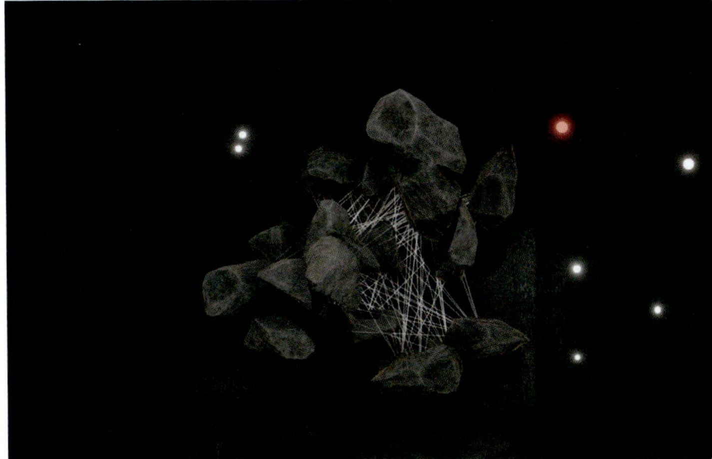

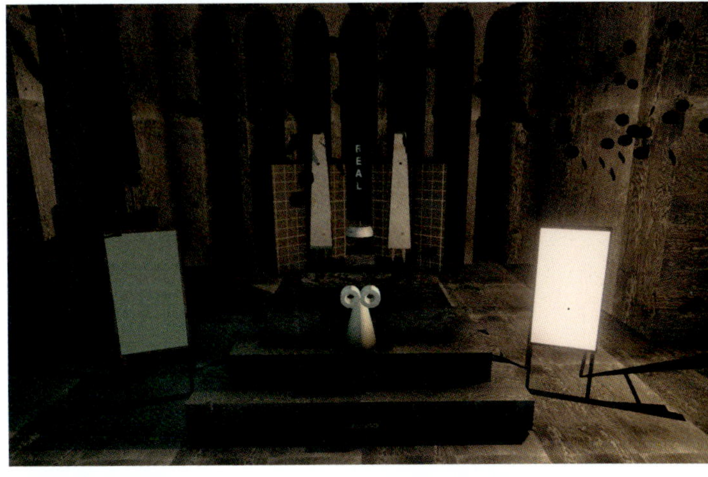

F
E
A
L

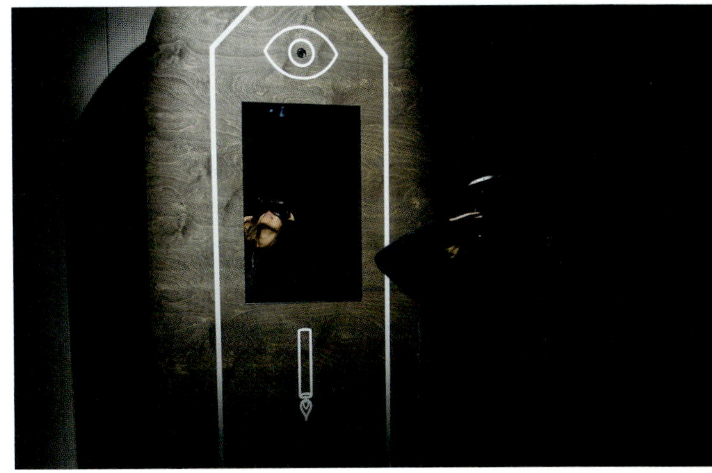

Light Barrier 3rd Edition

The Light Barrier series by studio Kimchi and Chips creates volumetric drawings in the air using hundreds of calibrated video projections. These light projections merge in a field of fog to create graphic objects that animate through physical space as they do in time.

The installations present a semi-material mode of existence, materializing objects from light. The third edition continues to exploit the confusion and non-conformities at the boundary between materials and non-materials, reality and illusion, and existence and absence. The viewer is presented with a surreal vision that advances the human instinct of duration and space. The name refers to the light barrier in relativistic physics, which separates things that are material from things that are light, and since 1983 has been used to specify the exact meaning of the metric system of spatial measure.

The 6-minute sequence employs the motif of the circle to travel through themes of birth, death, and rebirth, helping shift the audience into the new mode of existence. The artists use the circle often in their works to evoke the fundamentals of materials and the external connection between life and death.

The artists are interested in how impressionist painters were inspired by the introduction of photography to create "viewer-less images". The installation allows images to arise from the canvas, creating painting outside of perspective. It is a direct approach to the artists' theme of "drawing in the air'"

In this third edition, 8 architectural video projectors are split into 630 sub-projectors using an apparatus of concave mirrors designed by artificial nature. Each mirror and its backing structure are computationally generated to create a group that collaborates to form the single image in the air. By measuring the path of each of the 16,000,000 pixel beams individually, light beams can be calibrated to merge in the haze to draw in the air. 40 channels of audio are then used to build a field of sound that solidifies the projected phenomena in the audience's senses.

The third edition of Light Barrier was commissioned by the Asia Culture Center in Gwangju. The technology is enabled by Rulr, an open source graphical toolkit for calibrating spatial devices, created by Kimchi and Chips.

Artist: Kimchi and Chips (Mimi Son and Elliot Woods)
Engineering: Chung Youngjae, Studio Sungshin
Sound Design: Pi Junghun
In collaboration with Arts & Creative Technology Center
Commissioned by Asia Culture Center

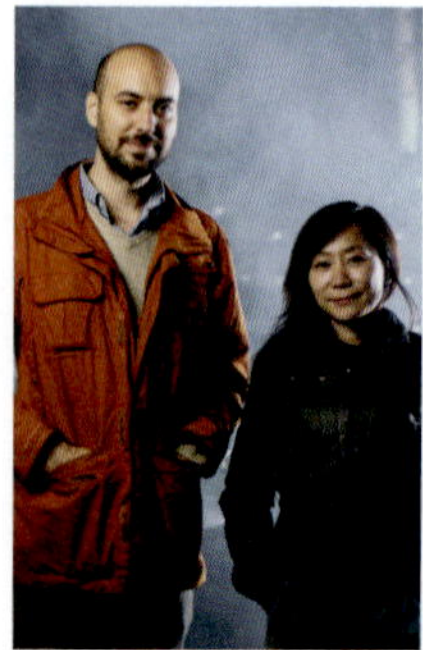

Mimi Son (KR) was born and works in Seoul. In her childhood she was fascinated by her father's painting and music that led her into experimenting with materials and drawing. An obsession with geometry and Buddhist philosophy inspires her to articulate space and time from alternative perspectives. These continuous experiments aim to depict an intersection of material and immaterial, real and virtual, presence and absence.

Elliot Woods (UK) is a digital media artist from Manchester. He tests possible futures between humans and visual design technologies (e.g., cameras, projectors, computation). Towards this goal, Elliot co-founded Kimchi and Chips, an experimental art studio based in Seoul with Mimi Son. He applies his academic studies in physics to produce sense-able phenomena from abstract systems.

Website

https://kimchiandchips.com/

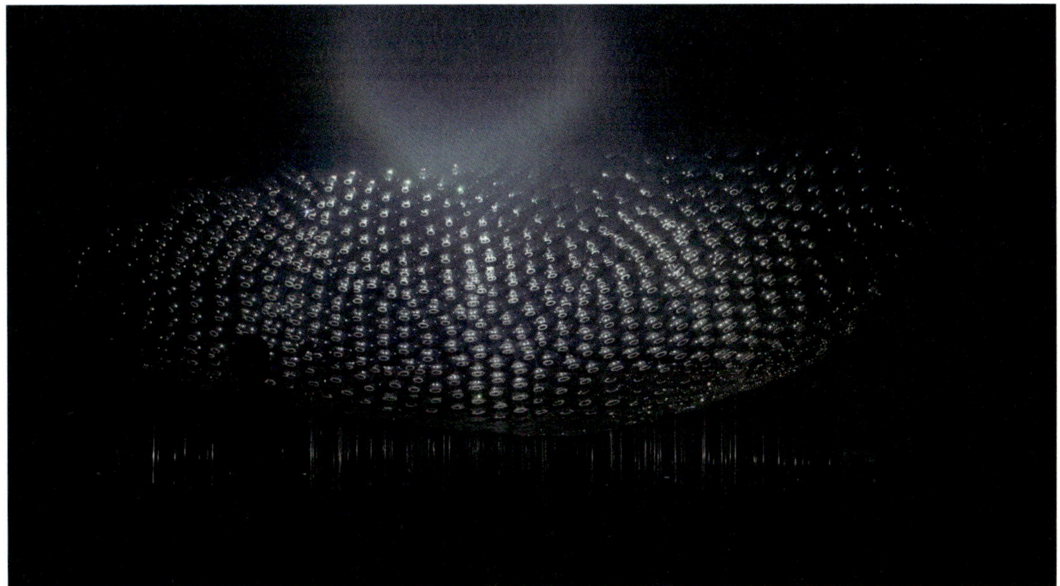

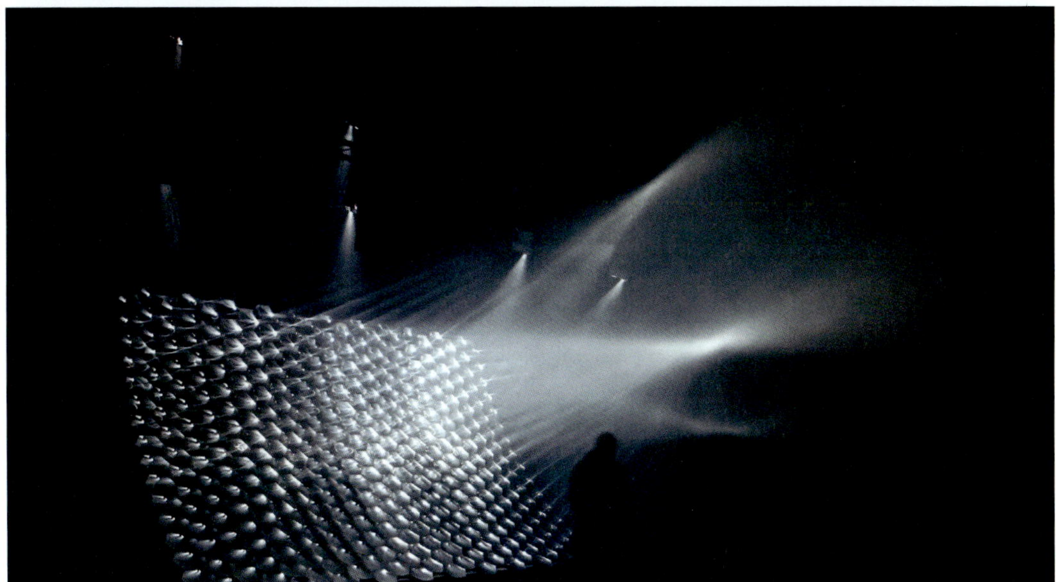

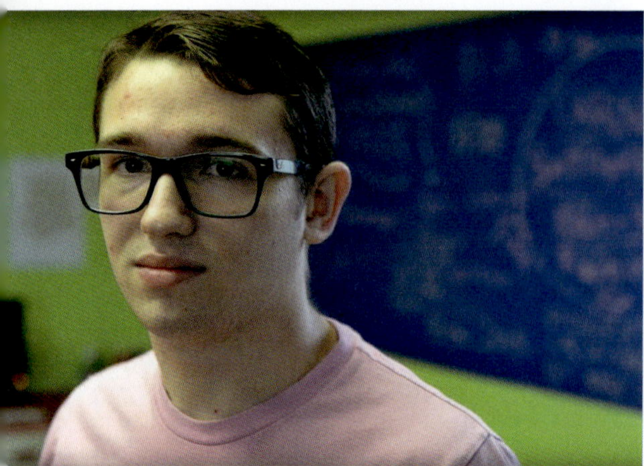

Emblematic Group – Nonny de la Peña (US) | 2017

Out of Exile

When Daniel Ashley Pierce is confronted about his sexual orientation by his family in a "religious intervention," the scene turns startlingly dramatic and violent. Using real audio combined with walk around virtual reality that puts the audience inside the story, *Out of Exile* is a powerful parable of the kind of hostility faced by so many in the LGBTQ community. With 40% of homeless youth in America identifying LGBTQ, the piece shines light on this terrible statistic and further reveals that the majority of those facing homelessness come from communities of color. The audio that Daniel recorded was so powerful and is what made the piece compelling for a VR experience. Just listening to the audio puts you at the scene when everything is happening around you.

Out of Exile was first commissioned by Tony Award© winner, Sara Ramirez, who is best known as orthopedic surgeon Dr. Callie Torres on ABC's top rated television drama Grey's Anatomy. It was created in collaboration with Emblematic Group, True Colors Fund, and Atrevida Productions. The True Colors Fund is working to end homelessness among lesbian, gay, bisexual, and transgender youth, creating a world in which all young people can be their true selves.

A two-part series, *Out of Exile*, places the viewer immediately in Daniel's living room right before the conflict unfolds. Surrounded by Daniel's family, the user joins Daniel as a witness to the event. Designed for the HTC Vive, the user is given flexibility to survey their environment.

Out of Exile also used the radical new technique of videogrammetry to create holograms of the central character and his peers, which allowed the user to walk around a video hologram of a person. Emblematic Group's partner, 8i, built a Unity Plug-in tool to bring human holograms into volumetric VR experiences. As we move beyond the flat screen, and increasingly consume content on immersive platforms like VR and AR, volumetric 3D holograms enable us to experience human content and each other in the most realistic way. The format presents the unrivaled quality standard for volumetric capture and holographic video of real humans—including accurate representation of skin, hair, hands, facial movement, and color. Holograms eliminate the uncanny valley effect of CG humans, giving you unprecedented sense of presence like you're in the same room with the person you're watching.

The animated characters were brought to life by first placing actors in motion capture suits. These suits

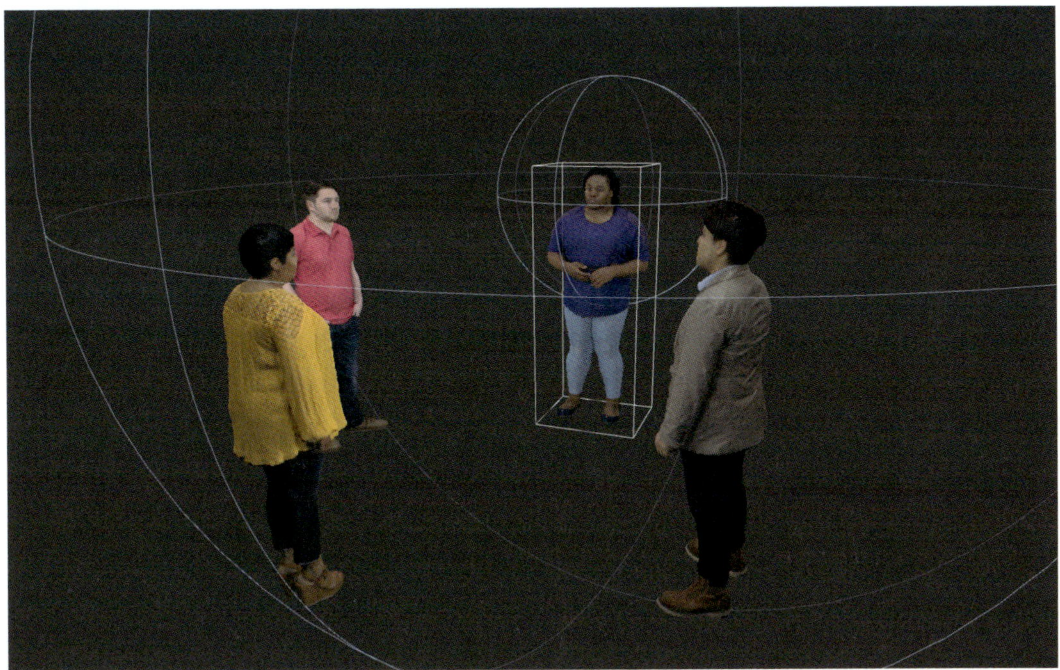

recorded actions and movements that were used by animators to create 3D characters. The source material for this experience was taken from Daniel who secretly recorded the altercation. Following the incident he posted the recording on YouTube, and within two days, the video garnered nearly 850,000 views.

Out of Exile is a 13-minute room scale experience that is viewable on the HTC Vive. It accommodates one viewer at a time. Space must be assigned in the installation set-up to allow viewers to walk through and interact with the experience for maximum impact.

Lead Artist: Nonny de la Peña, Emblematic Group
Producer: Julie Young
Executive Producers: Sara Ramirez, Michael Licht
VR Technical Director: Jonathan Yomayuza
Developer: Alex Batty
Composer: Gingger Shankar
Narrator: Sara Ramirez
Associate Producers: Ivana Coleman, Eren Aksu, Cedric Gamelin;
Actors: Kyle Wills, Julene Renee, Deborah Cartwright, Ed Mehler, Rudy Whitcomb, Donna Callaway

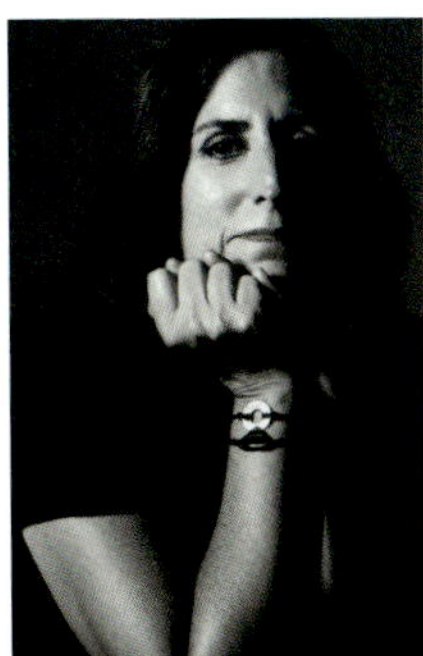

Nonny de la Peña (US) is CEO & Founder of award-winning innovation company Emblematic Group. Often acknowledged as "The Godmother of Virtual Reality," she is a pioneer of virtual, augmented, and mixed reality who is widely credited with inventing the genre of immersive journalism. In 2012, her piece "Hunger in Los Angeles" debuted at the Sundance Film Festival, marking its place in history as the first VR experience to be shown at the festival, and since then her work has continued to elicit global recognition at institutions and events such as the Victoria and Albert Museum, Brooklyn Museum, World Economic Forum and Venice International Film Festival. Under her leadership, Emblematic has built a critically acclaimed body of work that includes tracking the chaos of the Syrian civil war to working with AT&T on projects that leverage the future of 5G technologies. Her newest breakthrough is Emblematic's WebVR platform REACH which creates scalable distribution in the medium, democratizes content authorship and empowers new voices to share their stories.

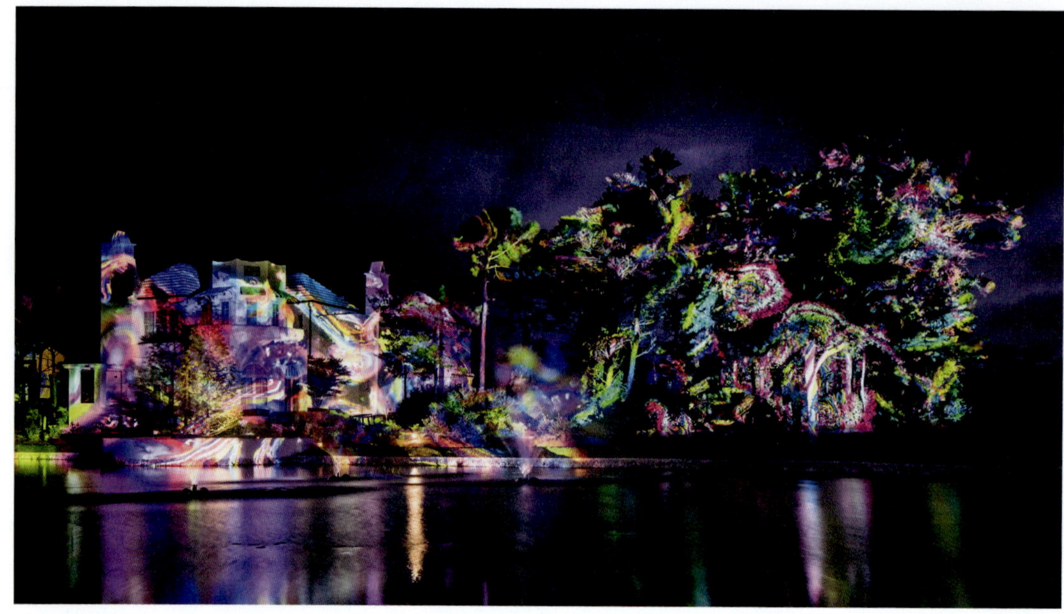

Robert Seidel (DE) | 2017

Tempest

tempest is an environmental video installation commissioned for the 10th anniversary of Digital Graffiti Festival. The work combines abstract video projections and immersive soundscapes with choreographed artificial fog and water fountains. In doing so, the artwork literally repaints the lake, woods and architecture of Alys Beach, Florida.

In a melancholic restaging of the sublime, *tempest* invites spectators to experience the awe of nature, yet also a sense of loss at a nature bred and cultured in the accelerated convergence of our digitalized lives. Through chimerical colors and equivocal gestures, it magnifies the ever-changing possibilities of the unfiltered physical world.

The piece's speculative geo-engineering melds distinct scales of location, artwork and audience into one another. The theatrical cascade of smoldering images is interrupted by static drawings that visualize the intricate airflow of the lake, in turn becoming erratic spectral experiments where high-frequency color patterns are scattered through water, fog and vegetation. Nikolai von Sallwitz's vivid music and sound further refract the scalar differences, mixing ethereal voices and protruding noises into the stochastic humming of the flora and fauna.

Two years prior to the complex installation the artist's personal experience of the unstable climate conditions alongside the Gulf of Mexico became a long-lasting memory. A gentle evening suddenly turned into a pageant rainstorm, later sparking the title *tempest* and the concept to technically heighten the local climate, combining it organically with the unpredictable weather conditions. Almost on cue, toward the end of the festival a storm approached, melting the artwork with real rain and lightning, extending the speculative tableaux into reality.

Installation by Robert Seidel
Music by Nikolai von Sallwitz

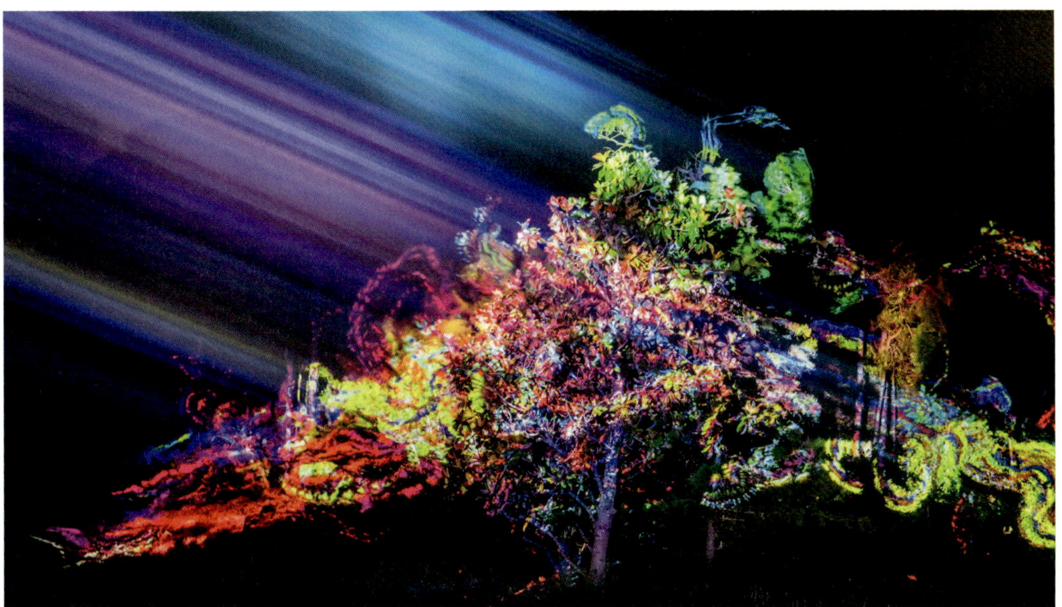

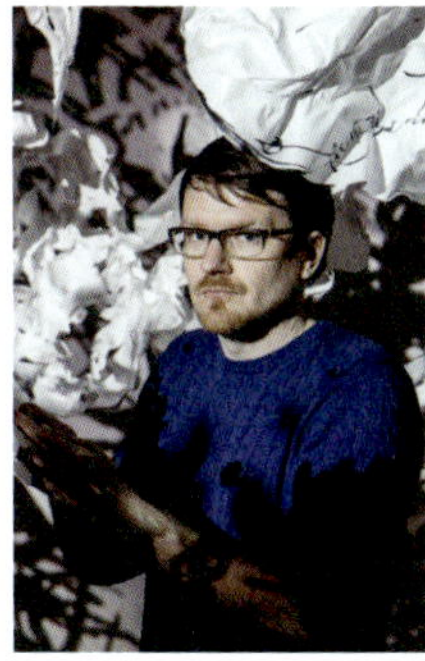

Robert Seidel (DE) began his studies in biology before transferring to the Bauhaus University Weimar to complete his degree in media design. His projections, installations and experimental films have been shown in numerous international festivals, as well as at galleries and museums such as the Palais des Beaux-Arts Lille, ZKM Karlsruhe, Art Center Nabi Seoul, Young Projects Los Angeles, Museum of Image and Sound São Paulo and MOCA Taipei. His works have been honoured with various prizes, including the KunstFilmBiennale Honorary Award and the Visual Music Award Frankfurt.

In his work Seidel is interested in pushing the boundaries of abstracted beauty through cinematographic approaches, as well as ones drawn from science. By the organic interplay of various structural, spatial and temporal concepts, he creates a continuously evolving complexity. Out of this multifaceted perspective emerges a narrative skeleton, through which viewers connects to the artwork on an evolutionary-derived and phylogenetic-fixated symbolic level.

Selected Works

2018 | *sfumato* – series of slow-motion videos postulating a future of painting in the digital age

2015 | *magnitude* – environmental laser drawings in the San Andreas Fault area

2011–2013 | *black mirror*, *tearing shadows* and *grapheme* – series of laser-cut projection sculptures based on the artist's drawings, expanding video into fragmented space

2011 | *scrape* – media façade artwork creating a hypnotic contrast to Seoul's pulsating city life

2009 | *vellum* – slices of a large-scale virtual sculpture, that is revealed in an LED façade and multiple screens distributed throughout a high-rise building in Seoul

2008 | *processes: living painting*s – projection on the façade of Ernst Haeckel's Phyletic Museum

2004 | *_grau* – award-winning experimental film melting drawings, paintings, 3d models and scans as well as MRI, X-Ray and Motion Capture data into painterly tableaux vivants

Website

https://robertseidel.com/

Nikita Diakur (DE/RU) | 2017

Ugly

Inspired by the story *Ugly the Cat* found on a website featuring wisdom quotes and sad stories, *Ugly* is a broken simulated short film about a Native American chief and an ugly cat trying to find peace in an evil neighborhood.

Starting as a part-time research for alternative animation methods, *Ugly* developed into a series of experiments and the above film was partially supported via German film funding (FFA), a Kickstarter campaign, and the help of many creatives who joined the team during the 4-year production period.

Restrictions of all sorts played a huge part during the development of project. Due to a limited budget and to save time the team had to find shortcuts and alternative working methods, many of which contributed to the final look.

The animation in *Ugly* is a combination of puppeteering and dynamic computer simulation and varies between physically accurate and broken. The *Ugly* characters are ragdolls built from connected dynamic body parts that can collide with the environment.

Traditional animation is non-linear. The animator can tweak and adjust everything by going back and forth between different states of the animation. Thus, he is always in control of the outcome. Contrary, when simulating, the animator gives up control by outsourcing a number of tasks to the computer. The computer executes these tasks based on calculations/algorithms and outputs a linear simulation result. Here, the animator can control the outcome only to a ce tain degree. A typical ragdoll test includes a character tumbling down a staircase in a realistic fashion. Unlike most YouTube references, the first *Ugly* staircase ragdoll test produced unexpected results: instead of tumbling to the bottom of the stairs, the character got stuck in the middle, started trembling, and later exploded into the air. This happened due to initial inexperience with dynamics and inaccuracy or low sampling in the simulation. The result was partly realistic, partly broken, which pretty much suited the *Ugly* concept, and was taken to the next level during the later production of the film.

In order to enable the characters to interact with the environment, with objects or with each other, the *Ugly* characters are constructed similar to marionettes. Each dynamic body part is connected to animated controllers via simulated strings. By keyframing or recording the movement of the controllers, it is possible to evoke a specific action.

Animating like this feels like real-life filmmaking—the animator sets the direction and the simulated characters interpret the action similar to real actors. Accordingly, the focus shifts from outcome to process. The animator is left with the challenge to find the right balance between staying in control and leaving enough room for randomness. This means experimenting and being ready to deal with unpredictable or broken results. When animating towards a specific goal, this can be very frustrating. At the same time, the loss of control is liberating and the outcome is spontaneous and always unique.

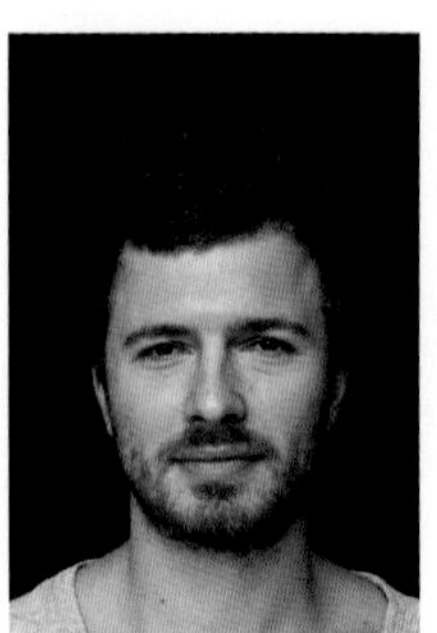

Nikita Diakur (DE/RU) is a Russian-born filmmaker based in Germany. His most distinguished projects "Ugly" and "Fest" have received multiple awards and screened at film festivals around the world. The signature technique used in his films is dynamic computer simulation, which embraces spontaneity, randomness and mistakes. Diakur is regularly giving talks and workshops at Festivals and Universities, has been artist in residence at Q21 in Vienna and is a member of the European Film Academy.

Website

https://www.ugly-film.com/

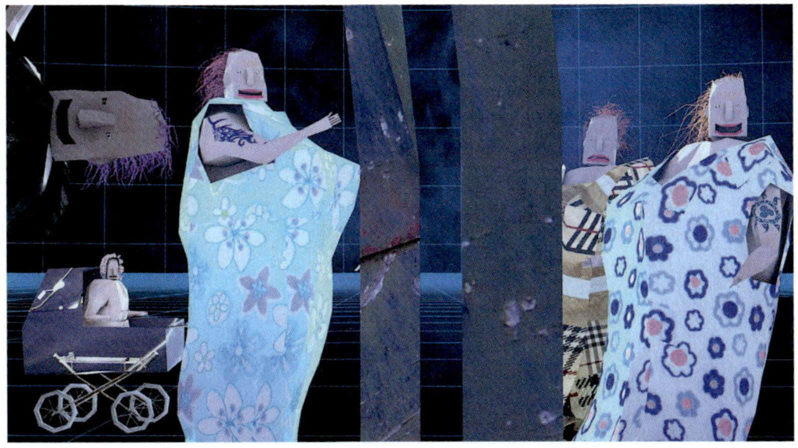

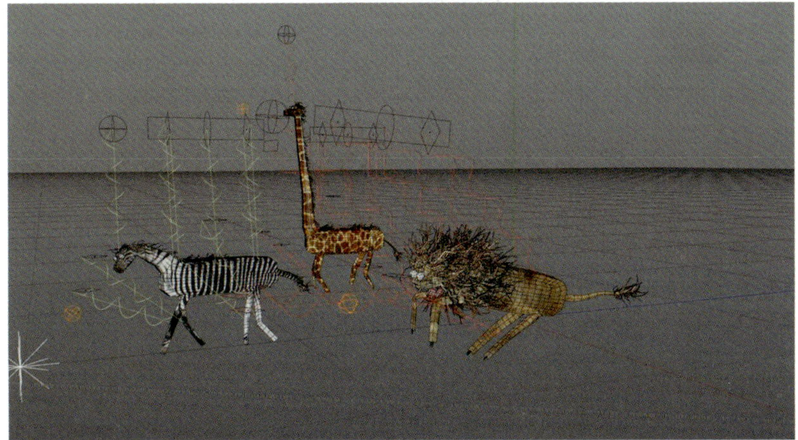

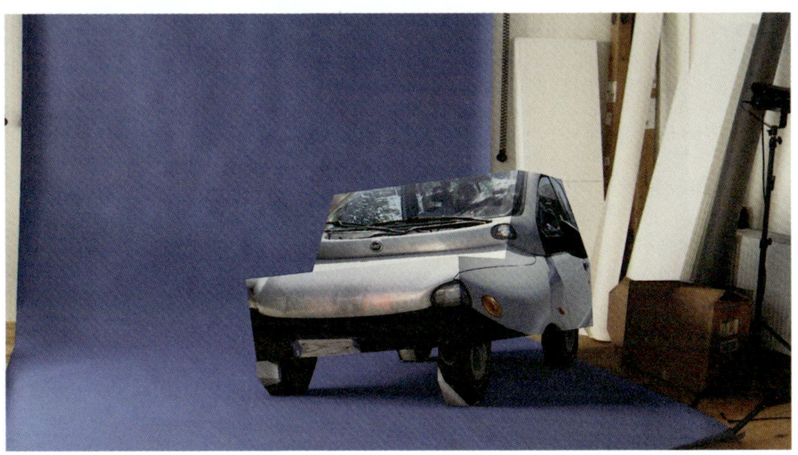

John Gerrard (IE) | 2017

Western Flag (Spindletop, Texas) 2017

Western Flag (Spindletop, Texas) 2017 depicts the site of the "Lucas Gusher"—the world's first major oil find—in Spindletop, Texas in 1901, now barren and exhausted. The site is recreated as a digital simulation and placed at its center is a flagpole bearing a flag of perpetually-renewing pressurized black smoke.

The computer-generated Spindletop runs in exact parallel with the real site in Texas throughout the year: the sun rising at the appropriate times and the days getting longer and shorter according to the seasons. The simulation is non-durational (having no beginning or end) and is run live by software that is calculating each frame of the animation in real time as it is needed.

Producer: Werner Poetzelberger
Programmer: Helmut Bressler
Modelers: Max Loegler, Philipp Marcks
Game Engine: Unigine
Installation development: Jakob Illera / Inseq Design

From April 21–27 2017 *Western Flag* displayed on the the Edmond j. Safra Fountain Court at Somerset House, WC2R 1LA London.

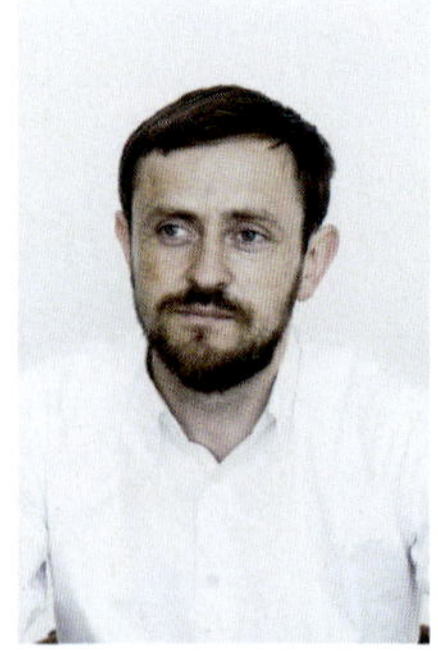

John Gerrard (IE), born in 1974, is widely regarded as a key contemporary figure in the development of digital media. Deceptively looking like film or video, his works are simulations—virtual worlds, made using real-time computer graphics, a technology developed by the military and now used extensively in the gaming industry. John Gerrard received a BFA from Oxford University in 1997 and an MFA from the School of the Art Institute of Chicago in 2000. He lives and works in Dublin and Vienna. Gerrard's work is in the collection of Tate, London; MoMA, New York; SF Moma, San Francisco; LACMA, Los Angeles; Hirshhorn Museum and Sculpture Garden, Washington; Kistefos Collection, Norway; IMMA, Dublin; Borusan Contemporary, Istanbul, and many private collections internationally.

Website

https://www.johngerrard.net/

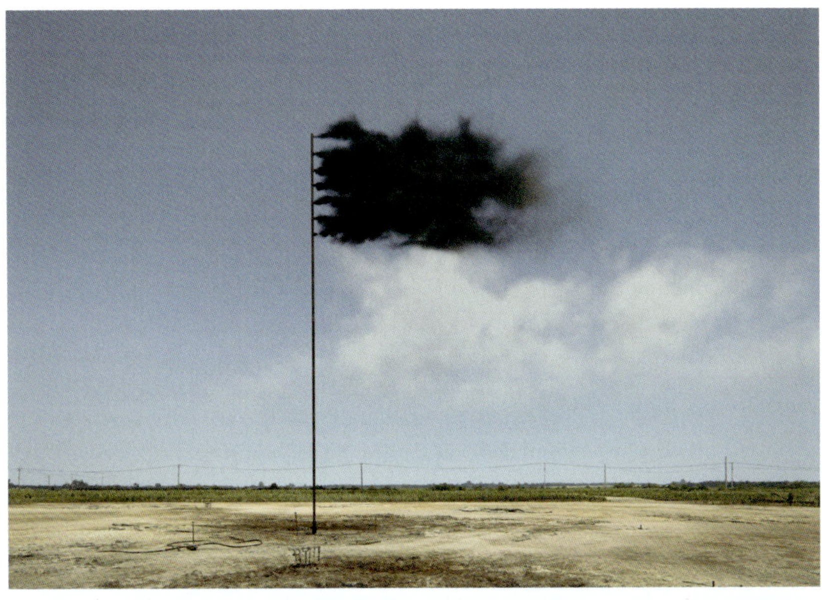

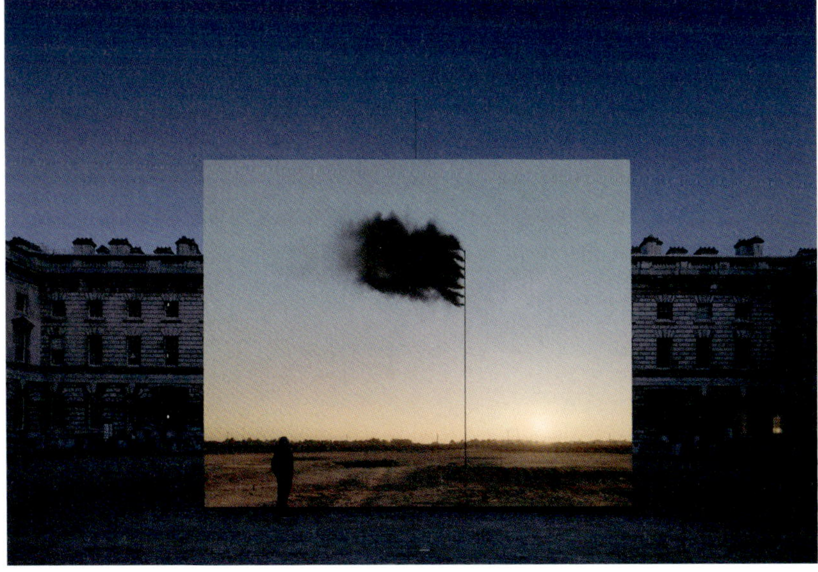

Western Flag (Spindletop, Texas) 2017

Scatter – Yasmin Elayat (US) | James George (US) | Alexander Porter (US) | Mei-Ling Wong (US) | Elie Zananiri (US) | 2017

Zero Days VR

Zero Days VR is a virtual reality documentary telling the story of Stuxnet—the first cyber weapon known to cause physical destruction. Stuxnet is a self-replicating computer virus created by the US and Israel to sabotage an underground Iranian nuclear facility. *Zero Days VR* illustrates the journey of Stuxnet, from the perspective of the virus itself. As a viewer you are guided through a series of immersive virtual world—from the NSA headquarters where you hear the testimony of an informant, into the underground nuclear facility infected by the virus. You witness the counterattack from Iran's newly minted cyber army and finally travel into the heart of the virus itself as it calculates its attack on the facility. In the final scene, the viewer finds themself face to face with the informant for a final reveal—seeing themselves represented as a live 3D hologram immersed in the virtual space.

Created using a real time game engine and optimized for "six-degrees of freedom" positional tracking, *Zero Days VR* pushes forward the cinematic medium of virtual reality. The experience combines real-time generative visualizations alongside live-action volumetric video filmed with our own 3D filmmaking system, DepthKit. This hybrid format allows for interactivity while staying true to the project's purpose as a documentary conveying true events.

Based on the Participant Media documentary *Zero Days* directed by Alex Gibney, *Zero Days VR* is an original adaptation of the feature film. Our adaptation takes an entirely different approach to the Stuxnet story. Our immersive virtual spaces, original illustrated graphics of the virus' processes, and the juxtaposition of news-breaking reveals from the informant with public news archives makes the experience native to virtual reality. *Zero Days VR* places audiences inside the invisible world of computer viruses and allows them to experience and understand the high stakes of cyber warfare.

Zero Days runs on the Oculus Rift Virtual Reality display. Viewers are captured using an Intel RealSense R200 camera during the experience and implicated in the story during the final scene in a surprising reveal.

Director: Yasmin Elayat
Technology Director: Elie Zananiri
Executive Producers: Alex Gibney, Sarah Dowland, Alexander Porter, James George
Producers: Mei-Ling Wong, Yasmin Elayat, Alexander Porter
Writers: Yasmin Elayat, Alexander Porter
Design Director: Bradley Munkowitz

scatter

Scatter (US) is an award-winning, next-generation creative company. Scatter is recognized for pioneering the emerging language of Volumetric Filmmaking through its original volumetric film productions and its AR/VR creativity tools. Scatter's first product Depthkit is the most widely used toolkit for accessible volumetric video capture. Scatter's first virtual reality title Zero Days VR (Sundance 2017) a documentary about cyber warfare and the Stuxnet virus recently won the Emmy for Original Approaches: Documentary.

Website

https://scatter.nyc/

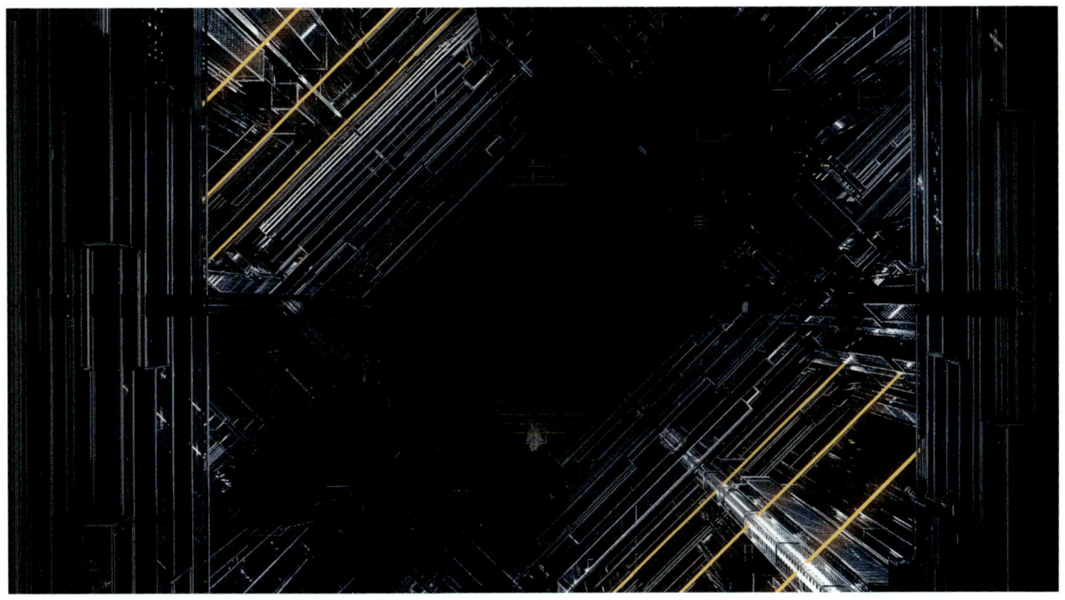

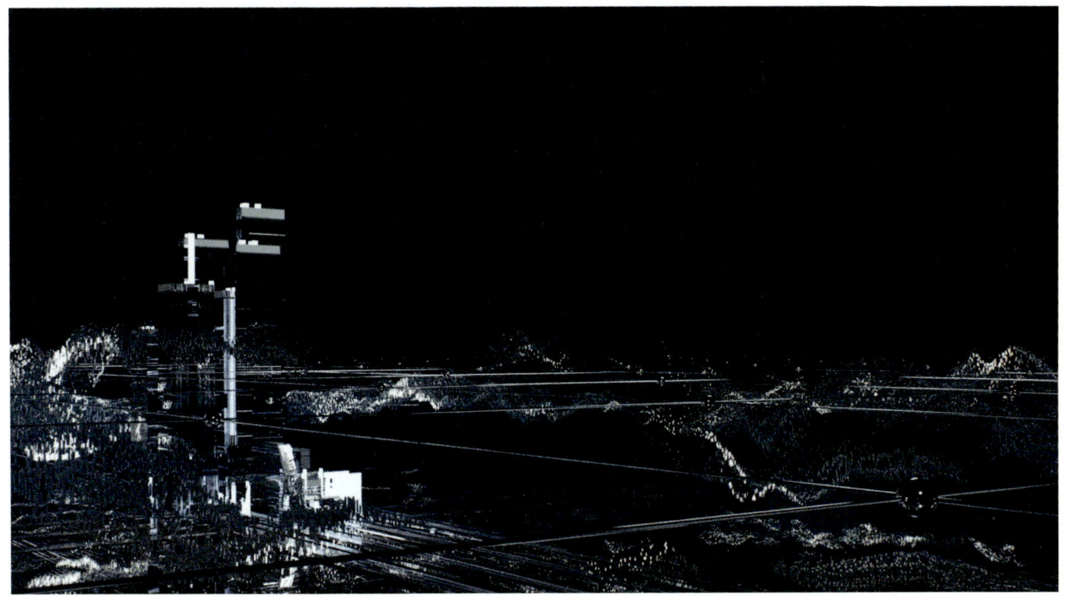

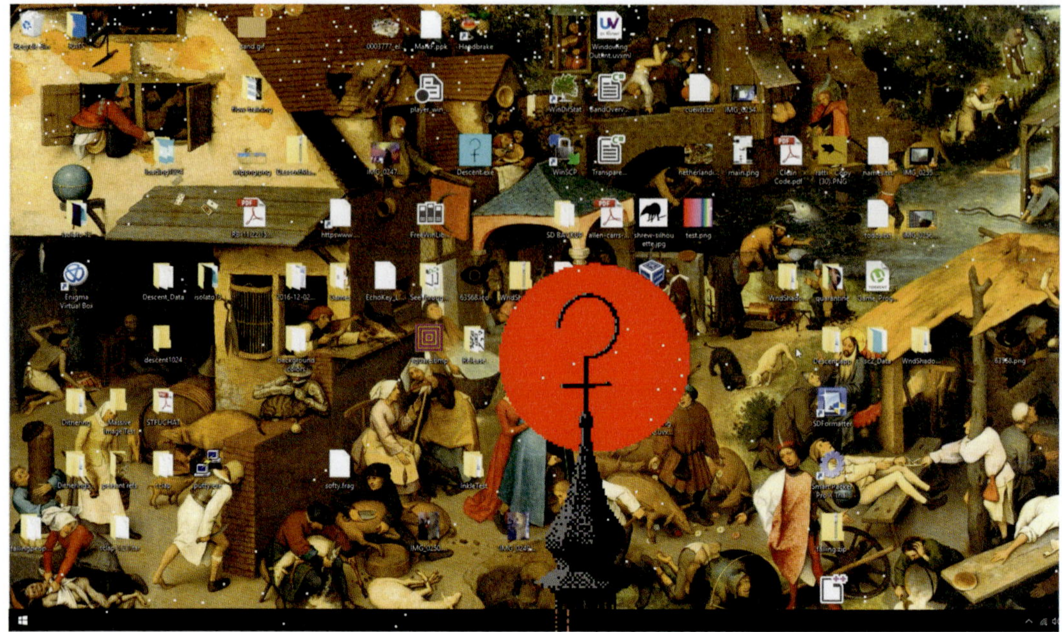

Peter Burr (US) | Mark Fingerhut (US) | FORMA (US) | 2017

Descent

In 1562, Flemish artist Pieter Bruegel the Elder completed a painting called *The Triumph of Death*. In this panoramic landscape the sky is blotted out by black smoke; ships and dead fish litter the ocean shore; and an army of skeletons experiment with myriad death techniques. The living are badly outnumbered and the variety of fated tortures seems endless. There is little room for whimsy in this tableaux.

Over 200 years earlier, a nasty plague, commonly known as the Black Death, left a cruel and massive mark on European civilization, wiping out half of Europe's total population. This was a quiet pervasion of death—an invisible pathogen carried by herds of tired rats. This plague triggered a series of social and economic upheavals with profound effects on the his-tory of medieval Europe, guiding its survivors into the sort of self-inflicted darkness pictured by the Elder Bruegel.

Looking back at this historical trajectory, Peter Burr, Mark Fingerhut, and Forma have created a spiraling inter-dimensional narrative aptly titled *Descent*—a meditation on one of humanity's blackest hours. Taking the form of a desktop application, descent. exe gives the user a brief glimpse of a world descending into darkness—an unrelenting plague indifferent to the struggles of the user. There is a silver lining, however, tucked into the software's final sweep. An equanimous watcher, reduced to a single eye, looks on as the plague of rats that has infested your desktop destroys itself.

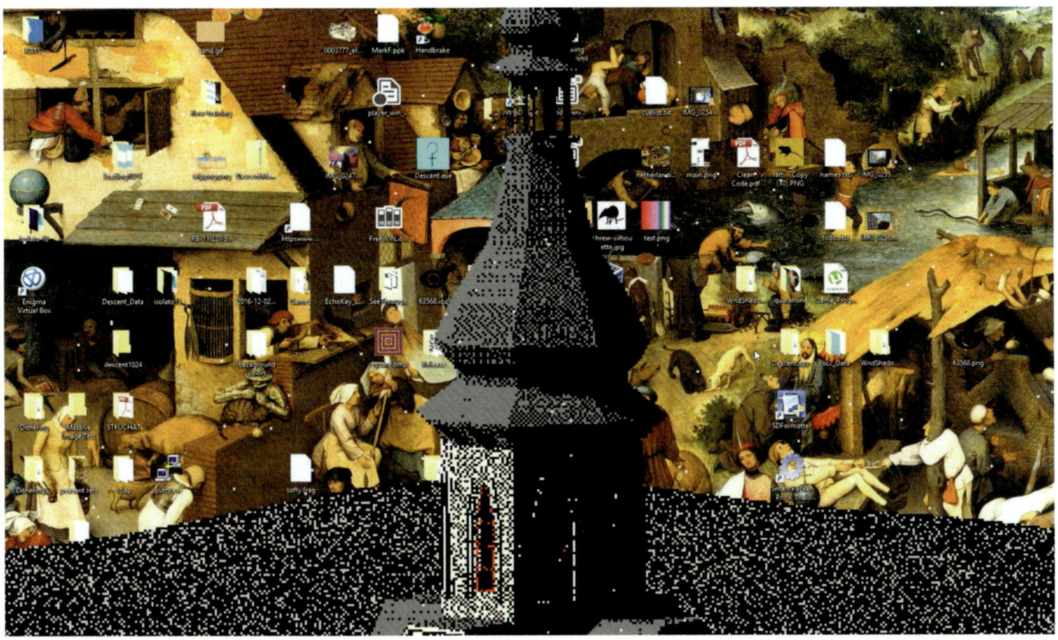

Peter Burr (US) is an artist from Brooklyn, NY. A master of computer animation with a gift for creating images and environments that hover on the boundary between abstraction and figuration, Burr has in recent years devoted himself to exploring the concept of an endlessly mutating labyrinth. His practice often engages with tools of the video game industry in the form of immersive cinematic artworks, which have been presented internationally. His practice has been recognized through grants and awards including a Guggenheim Fellowship (2018), Creative Capital Grant (2016), and a Sundance New Frontier Fellowship (2016).

Mark Fingerhut (US) is an artist and programmer who is primarily interested in the potential of desktop computer usage as performance. Using a handmade suite of software, malware, and virus-like programs called "artdisks" he transforms his desktop computer environment into a theatrical stage of potential where anything is possible and the rules of the OS are bent and broken.

FORMA is a musical trio formed in 2010 in Brooklyn, NY, currently consisting of members Mark Dwinell, George Bennett and John Also Bennett. FORMA's mixture of minimalism, ambient explorations, kosmische, and frenetic rhythm has captivated the international experimental music community since their 2011 self-titled debut on John Elliott's influential Spectrum Spools label. *Physicalist* (2016), their debut recording for Kranky, was a shift in a new direction for the group–their first recording to utilize acoustic instrumentation alongside their formidable electronic arsenal.

La Chute / The Fall

As celestial beings descend to Earth vitiating its population, the world's order unbalances. Initiated by these terms, a tragic fall leads to the parturition of crucial opposites: Hell and Heaven's circles.

Boris Labbé got the inspiration for his film from reading Dante's *Divine Comedy*, but it isn't an adaptation. In fact, the work gives a sensation of being an amplified imaginary creation that draws upon art, myths, and the history of mankind. The artist was clearly influenced by Bosch's *The Garden of Earthly Delights*, Bruegel's *The Fall of the Rebel Angels*, Botticelli's illustration of Dante, Goya's *The Disasters of War* and Henry Darger's *In the Realms of the Unreal*. With *La Chute* Boris Labbé continues his experimental research with a new sense of narrative, and pursues his work around loops, metamorphoses, and the intertwined processes of degeneration and regeneration.

The artist uses traditional techniques combined with computer composition editing. The animated sequences consist of Indian ink and watercolor drawings on paper (21 x 30 cm), approximately 4,000 original drawings were needed to create the whole film. The multilayered compositing as well as the camera movements were made with After Effects during the process. Boris Labbé works with a small team of artists, technicians, and animation students who help him to assume this laborious and non-conventional working process. Parallel to the animation process, the musical composition was created by the Italian composer Daniele Ghisi. He's worked with database existing music, mainly string quartets, edited digitally in a complex multilayered electronic music composition.

Director: Boris Labbé
Music: Daniele Ghisi, www.danieleghisi.com
Producer: Sacrebleu Productions, Ron Dyens
Animation: Boris Labbé, Armelle Mercat, Hugo Bravo, Capucine Latrace
Animation trainees: Claire Boireau, Edgar Collin, Johann Etrillard, Jean Gégout, Alexis Godard, María José Suárez
Compositing: Boris Labbé, Sami Guellaï
Calibration: Yves Brua
Mixing: Régis Diebold

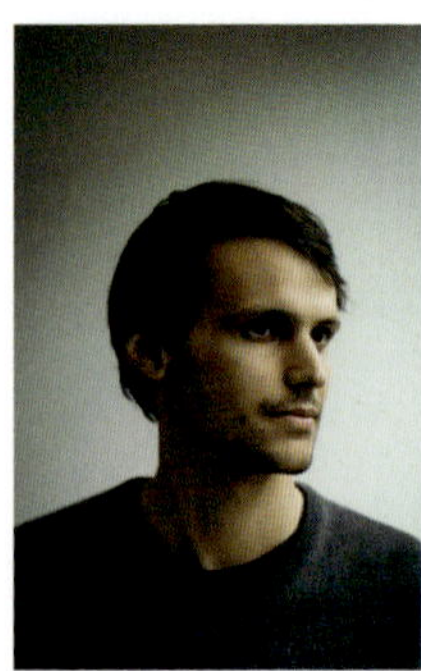

Boris Labbé (FR). After obtaining a DNAP (National Diploma in Visual Arts) at l'Ecole supérieure d'art et de céramique de Tarbes, Boris Labbé continued his studies at the EMCA of Angoulême (Ecole des métiers du cinéma d'animation). At the EMCA, he produced *Kyrielle*, his final film project, which was awarded the Special Jury's prize for Graduation Films at the Annecy International Animated Film Festival in 2012. Simultaneously, he developed an artistic work that is both visual and plastic. He spent a year at the Casa de Velázquez in Madrid. *RHIZOME* is his first professional film.

Selected Solo Exhibitions

2016 | Rhizome, Millennium Point, Flatpack Film Festival, Birmingham, GB

2016 | Animation Cabin 2, Au Praxinoscope, Tokyo, JP

2016 | Danse macabre, Cinémathèque Québécoise, Montréal, CA

Selected Group Exhibitions

2018 | Immortality! "Do you want infinite lives?", Overkill Festival, Enschede, NL

2018 | Multivision, Erarta Museum of contemporary art, Saint Petersburg, RU

2018 | Cyberarts exhibition, OK Center for Contemporary Art, Festival Ars Electronica, Linz, AT

Website

https://www.borislabbe.com/

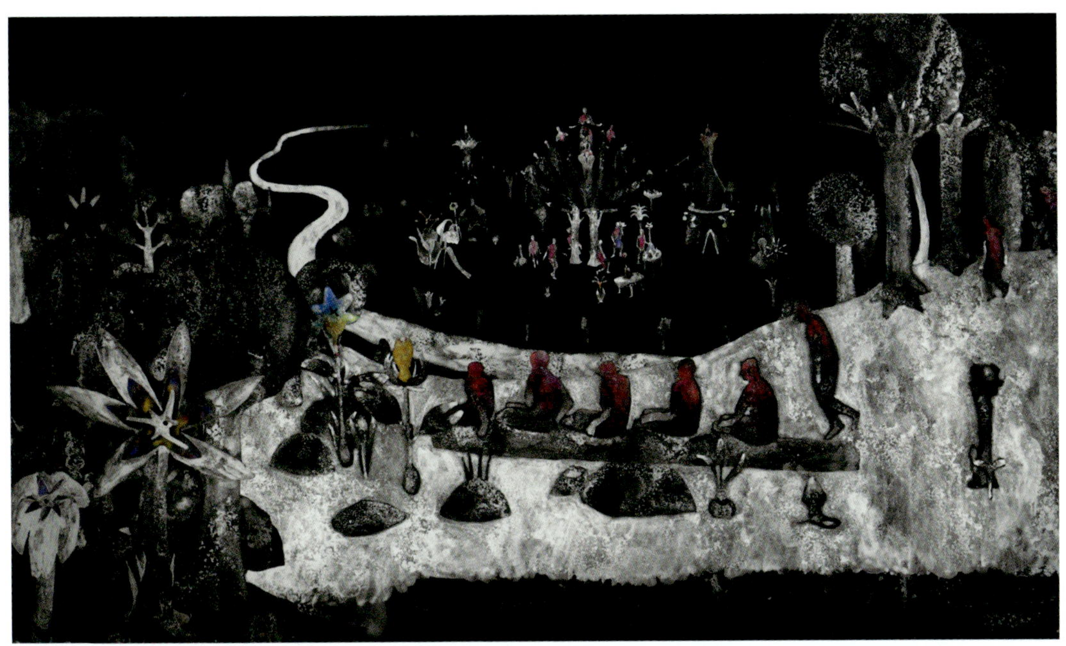

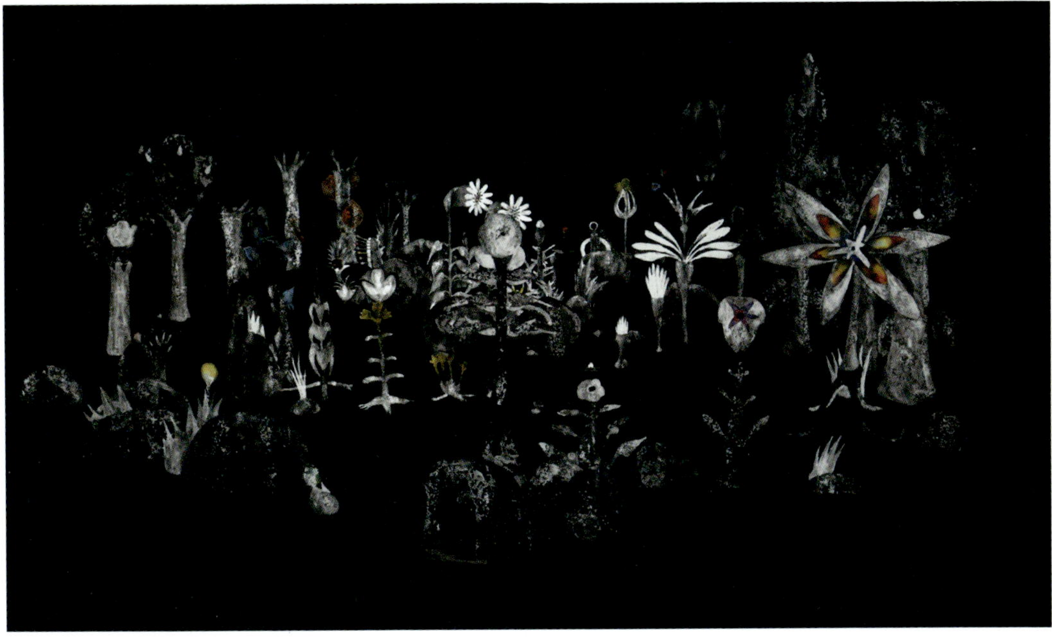

La Chute / The Fall

Rainer Kohlberger (AT) | 2018

more than everything

In a certain way, the stereoscopic image produced here, of abstract, moving information, is a remarkable test for perception. Since there is no distinct body in the space, also no object fixation takes place; our habitual seeing becomes inadequate. Already the first cut—a demonstratively implemented ubiquitous static—allows the moving picture to lift from the screen; there is no longer any dependence on the projection's carrier surface, all visual data vibrate at a certain distance, an in between. Whereas narrative 3D cinema presumes the perceptual difference of a stable background and the depths of the bodies lifted out from it; here, an emancipation from natural object perception takes place. This stream of ambiguous visual material's ontological status is somewhere between gas- and water-shaped. Rainer Kohlberger programs both channels differently, places a visual incoherence at the origin of the images, provokes a "binocular rivalry." Our perception apparatus no longer applies a statistically calculable synthesis, does not generate a powerful third element (the "depth") but instead produces, as the title also heralds, a capricious "more" from the structural ambivalence. A more that generates restlessness, even the geometric figures no longer create certainty for the order of the space. All attempts fail to locate these images interpretively. The demand for a uniform-coherent form (of the nation state, the everyday objects, or images) is rejected with the indication that coherence should always be a readiness to admit every interregnum of form, no matter how unknown or strange. (Marc Ries)

This is a dance between your brain and the world. A hallucinatory figure of information that speaks on the threshold of being. We are bathed in interferences from sensual data to what might be out there. We will go to another land, we will try another sea. One plus one equals three. (Rainer Kohlberger)

Humans and other animals that have their eyes attached towards the front of their bodies see the world with binocular vision. Stereoscopic seeing enables a precise perception of depth. This film challenges this perceptual apparatus that interacts with the brain to generate a coherent image of the surroundings. In more than everything, I use stereoscopic technology that was experimented with in early and pre-cinema by Münsterberg et al. and became installed in digital cinema in the last ten years due to the popular culture of 3D movies.

Here different images for the left and the right eye were generated that are blended to a third image in the

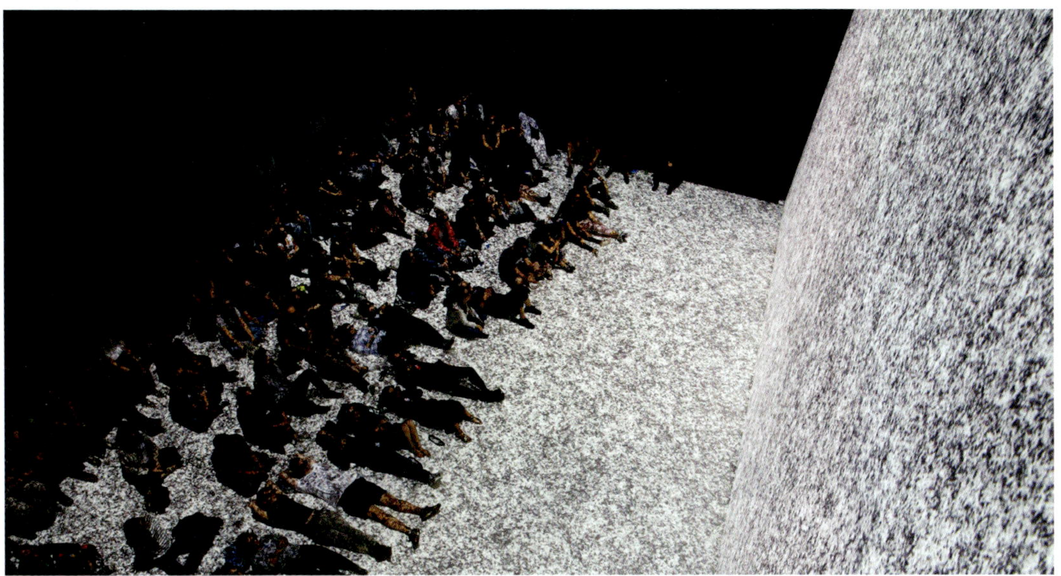

spectators brain. We have the tendency to prefer visual input from one eye to the other, a phenomenon called *Ocular dominance*. Approximately two-thirds of the population is right-eye dominant and one-third left-eye dominant (some don't have a preference). If the perceptual apparatus has to deal with different inputs for each eye, instead of superimposing the image in the brain it alternates between the two images, something called *Binocular rivalry*. In this cinematic endeavour, the characterised physical phenomena above are incorporated in its artistic formulas. According to the visual preference of the viewer for one eye or the other, the film will be perceived quite differently. Other parts give the same importance to both channels where an oscillation between left and right will occur.

Due to its nature, the film has to be presented with stereoscopic technology, there's no other version of it. Still, if someone in the cinema does not want to wear glasses (or only has one eye), I took care in the artistic process that it is still possible to watch another consistent version of the film. (production note)

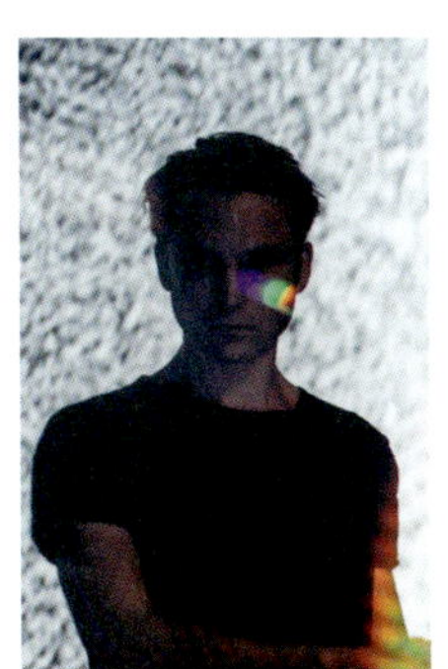

Rainer Kohlberger (AT) is an Austrian born freelance visual artist / film maker living in Berlin. His work is primarily based on algorithmic compositions with reductionistic aesthetics influenced by flatness, drones and interference. Within his works there always lies a layer of noise, that fascinates him as a sense of the infinite, which is both the ultimate abstraction and inveterately fuzzy. In his films, installations and live performances maximum forms of intensities come into play. His work has won several prizes internationally.

Website

https://www.kohlberger.net/

Norman

In 2017 I created a custom animation tool—for myself. A tool to enable and facilitate my imagination and flow. Norman is the animation tool I've always wanted. Named after Norman McLaren, a visionary Canadian animator, the tool is built in JavaScript, runs in a web browser, and lets me animate naturally in 3D using VR controllers. The project, initially funded by Google Creative Lab, is available as an open-source tool. This enables everyone to peek into the inner workings, see how it's made, and/or adapt it for their own purposes.

It makes the process of animating more like playing a musical instrument. For instance, one mode automatically creates new frames and advances through the timeline each time you make a mark. The user can get completely lost in the process of drawing through time and space, without having to manually control the time-line. Norman is an experiment in building a medium and using that medium to create concrete works, at the same time.

James Paterson (CA) is an artist and creative technologist whose work hangs out at the intersection of drawing, animation, and code. Each of these mediums offers limitless room for exploration, but when braided together they can open up wormholes of creative possibility. Weaned on books like *Neuromancer* and *Snow Crash*, James has been daydreaming about the emergence of spatial computing since childhood. Over the past few years he's finally gotten a chance to explore creative tools popping up in this new space, and experiment with building his own tools from scratch like *Norman*—an open source VR animation sketchbook which runs in the browser. Since 1999 Paterson has exhibited his work at galleries and museums all over the world.

Website

https://normanvr.com/

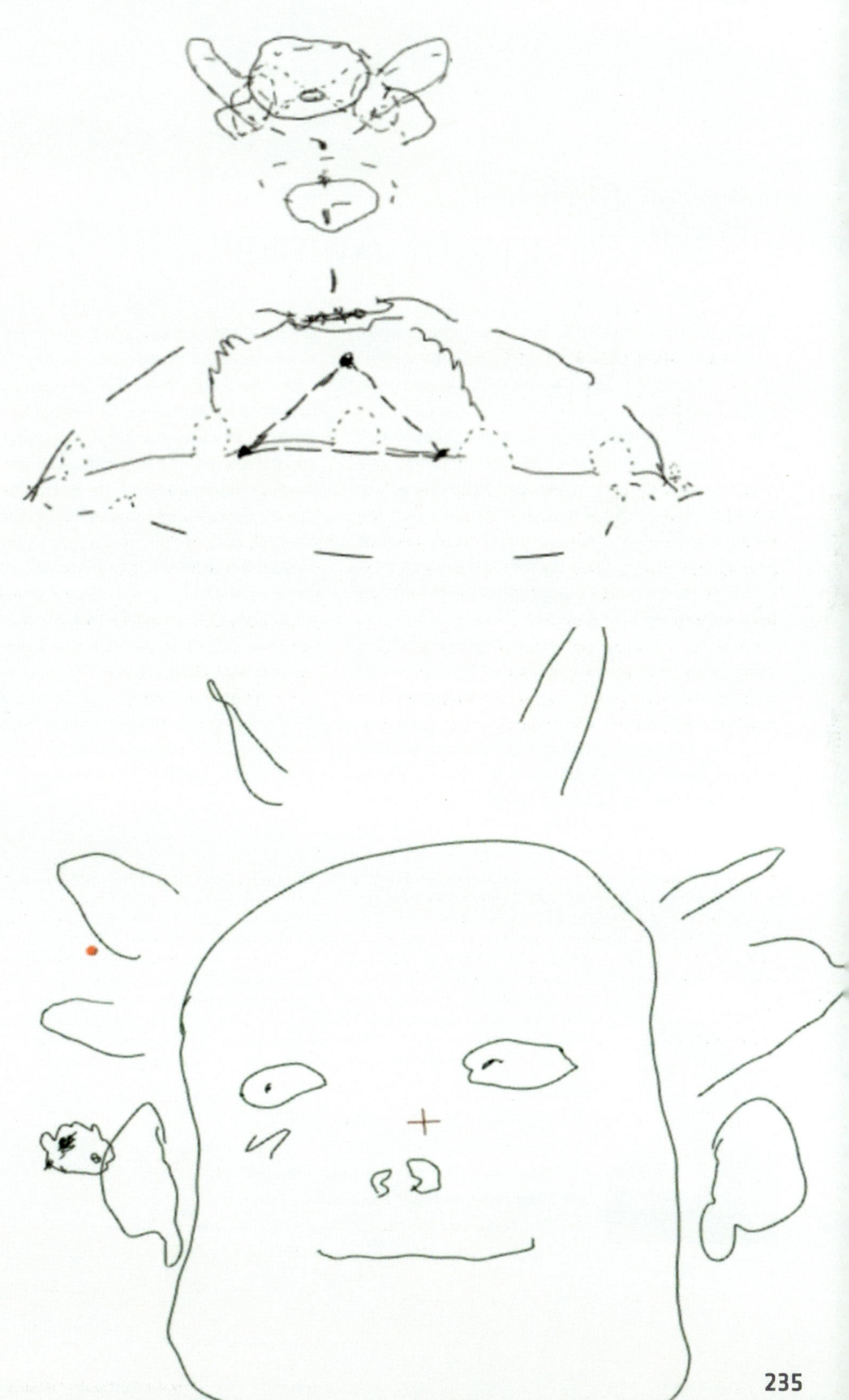

Rediscovery of Anima

The aim of this project is to discover "anima," which could have existed, but did not exist. The word "anima" means "life" or "soul" in Latin, and the word animation stems from anima.

This project is derived from the "toki-"series, which I have long been creating using a 3D printer to give shape to time through movement. When I was creating the "toki-"series, I realized that it was not the advent of modern technologies that made this method possible; rather, if one had the idea and the insight, it could have been created a long time ago in the distant past. Consequently I decided to completely abandon the digital technologies that I had previously been using, relying only on techniques that existed around the time of the birth of cinema in the 19th century to produce a work entirely from wood.

If a method to generate anima had existed in the 19th century, when movies were born, it is possible that methods of playing and recording footage would be different from how they are today. In my research, I learnt that there is a theory that cave paintings from around 30,000 years ago might have represented movement with frames, like in animation. So I went back even further than the 19th century and decided to make a work using stone, tree branches, hemp, and sunlight, in a way that could have existed in ancient times. This method is constructed so that when an image is exposed to the sunlight streaming through the slit between the stones, it will appear as if the person is moving.

This project attempts to rediscover "anima" through primitive methods using sunlight. While exploring how society might have interacted with these "anima" if they had been discovered at the time these primitive methods were available, the project also aims to show people anew the sheer joy and admiration of the illusion of movement in an age where technological advancements have made it possible to consume visual media in many different situations.

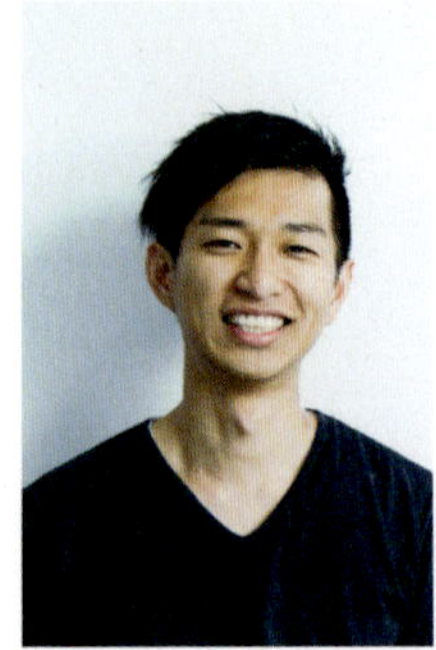

Akinori Goto (JP), born in Gifu in 1984, is an artist. He graduated from Musashino Art University, Department of Visual Communication Design. His works, capturing invisible connections and relationships by combining cutting edge technology with methods and media that existed long ago, are now on exhibition. The main exhibitions in which he recently participated include Ars Electronica Festival 2017, SXSW ART PROGRAM 2017, and STOP LICHT exhibition 2017. His works are being publicly collected by the National Media Museum in the UK.

Selected Exhibitions

2018 | "Gyoen Night Art Walk" Shinjuku Gyoen, Tokyo

2018 | "Prix Ars Electronica Exhibition" OK Center, Linz, Austria

2018 | "Japan Media Arts Festival Overseas Promotion" Annecy, France

2018 | "Media Ambtion Tokyo" Roppongi Hills, Tokyo

2017 | "The Doraemon Exhibition 2017" Mori Arts Center Gallegy, Tokyo

2017 | "GLOW SPECIAL:STOP LICHT" Van Abbemuseum, Eindhoven, Netherlands

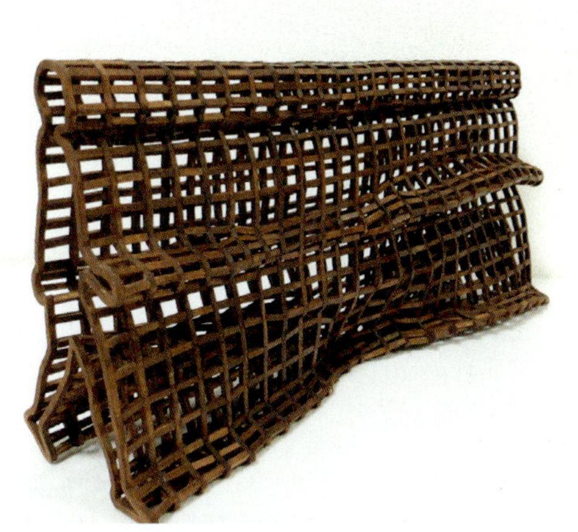

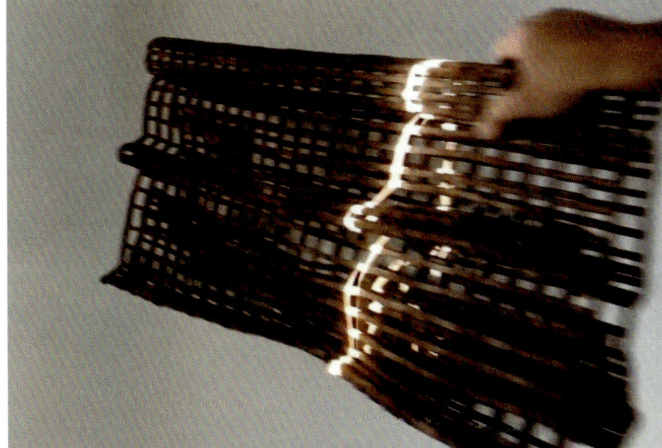

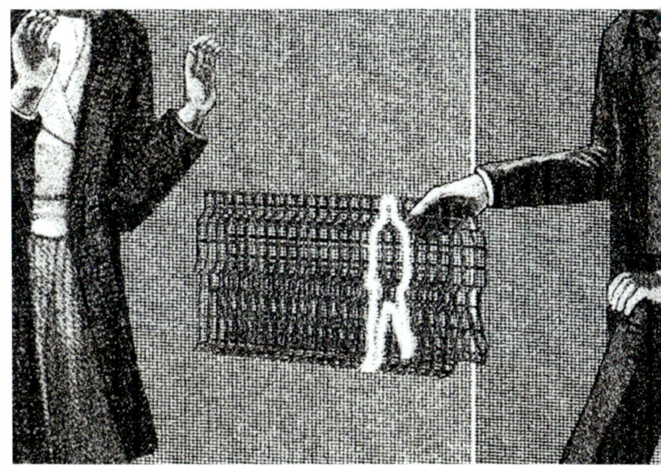

System Aesthetics

Powering everything from voice recognition to self-driving cars and the new ways of finance, A.I. algorithms are the invisible force that increasingly shapes our lives. As individuals and society, we need new visual metaphors to help us decide how much influence we want to give to these intangible systems. The works in this series are part of an extensive research project by FIELD, exploring the most relevant machine learning algorithms in code-based illustrations.

The field of Artificial intelligence has seen a major acceleration in recent years, especially in the specialisation of machine learning algorithms, controlled by large corporations with access to huge amounts of personal user data and computing power.

These algorithms develop behind proprietary shields and outside of public scrutiny, making a grassroots understanding or the emergence of independent alternatives nearly impossible. Often, the decision-making of neural networks is obscure even to the humans who developed and trained them, making A.I. a veritable "black box."

As visual artists, we find it important to understand and discuss these fundamental forces that change our society. We have started a deeper exploration of the less accessible information that is out there, such as scientific papers and open source code publications, to develop an understanding of these algorithms' inner workings, and translate it into visual metaphors that can contribute to a public debate.

Created by FIELD
Concept + Artistic Direction: Marcus Wendt
Design + Animation: Phillip Peters, Julien Bauzin, Paul Brenner, Dan Hoopert, Xander Marritt, Arnaud Peron
Creative Code: Jonas Otto
Project Management: Alice Shaughnessy
Head of Production: Alessandro Pula
Sound + Music: Kuedo

FIELD.IO (DE). As a creative studio specialised in art + technology, we create powerful new formats of visual communication. Together with selected brands and cultural institutions, we work as artists, designers and consultants across strategy and branding, moving image, and immersive experiences. Artist statement Reflecting on how our world is changing through technology, our works blend physical and digital, connecting audio-visual experiences with sculpture, photography and film.

Website

https://www.field.io/

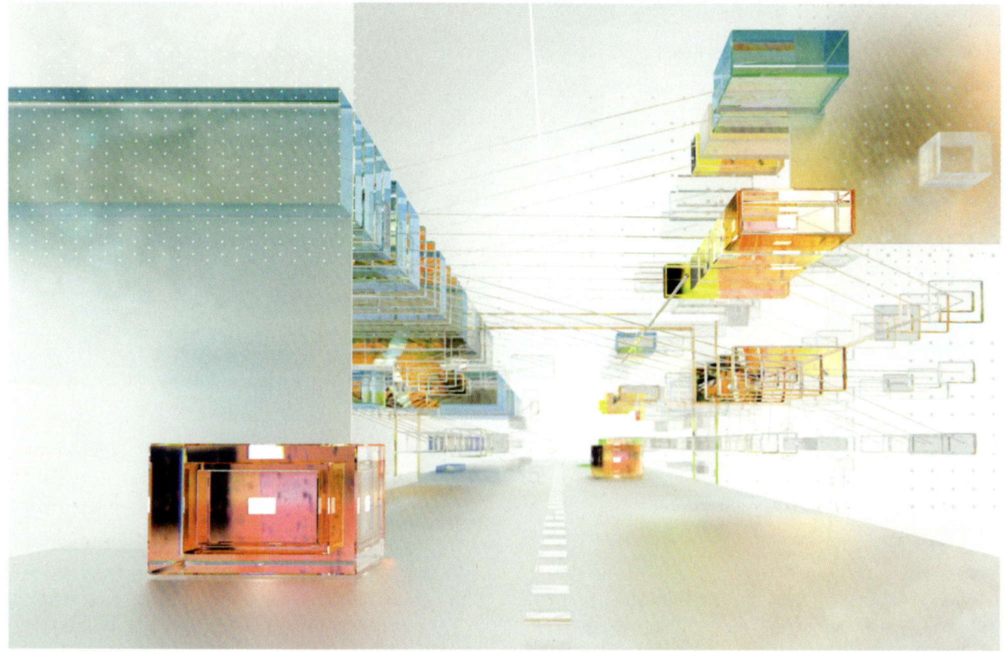

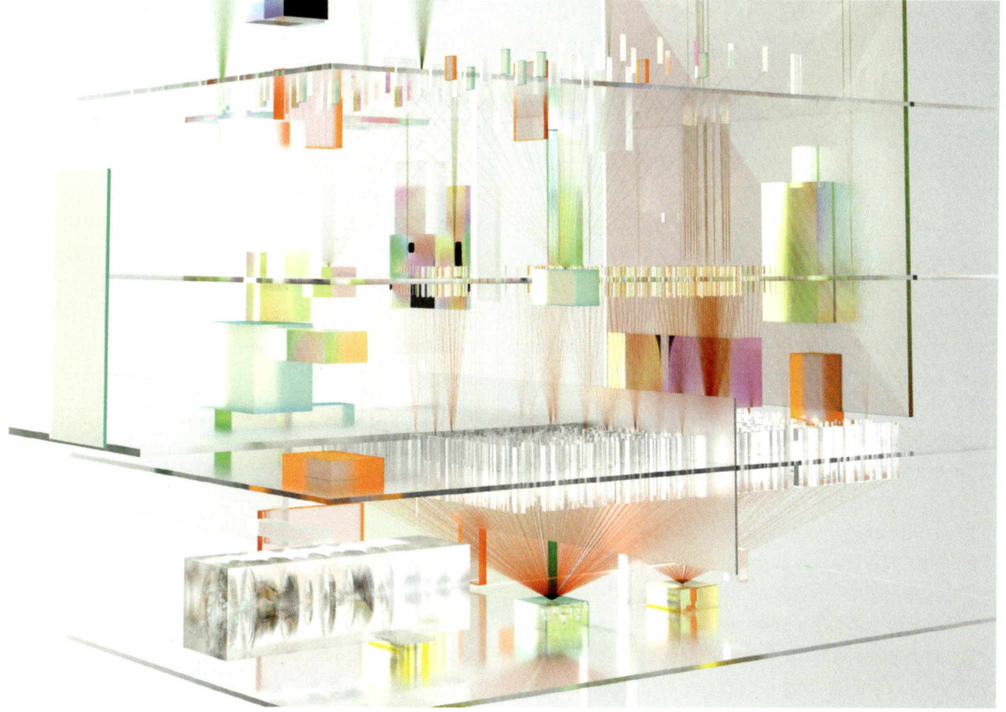

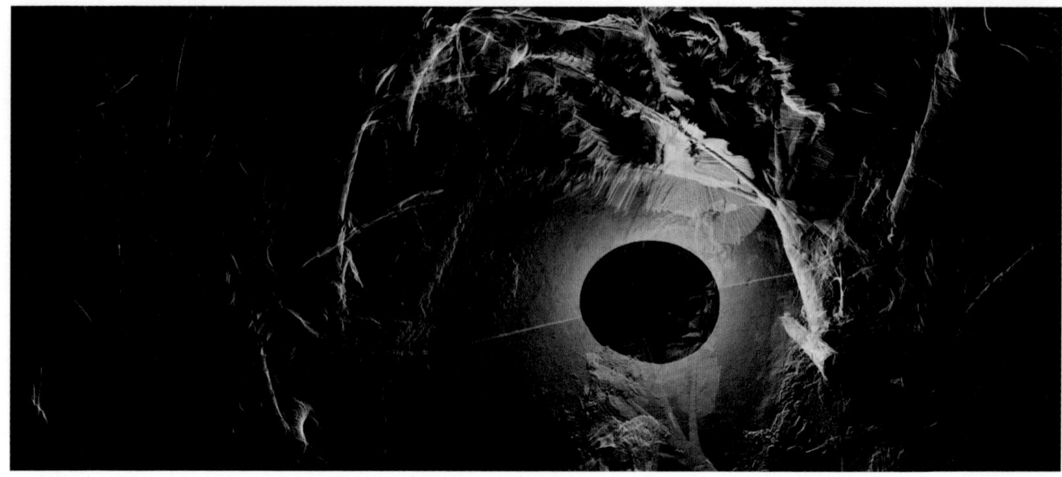

Mathilde Lavenne (FR) | 2018

TROPICS

TROPICS draws an orbit around a Mexican farm. Scattered voices seem to revive and disturb the memory of the place. Crossing the matter, the film attempts to stop time and men, and reveals the ghost of a lost paradise.

In the 19th century, a French community crossed the Atlantic to settle in Jicaltepec along the Rio Filobobos, in the Veracruz region of Mexico. These French families, who were mostly just farmers, were able to build large agricultural operations over generations despite the hostile tropical environment and climate. Since the Spanish conquest, Mexico has embodied a western mythological reverie: Amazons guiding the Conquerors in their quest for a new land, but also, the idealization of a new world filled with lush vegetation, the development of medicine through the use of new plants, and the evangelical ambition of a better world. If part of the European fantasy made sense of the first contact with the New World, it also destroyed a great deal of "primal" knowledge by merging with the pre-Columbian peoples. Taking the form of a 3D archaeological expedition, *TROPICS* draws an orbit around these territories from which arise scattered voices expressing their secret stories and their relations with the ghosts of past time. Confronting a conception of the world with advanced technology ironically creates a visual matter akin to constellations of information—reminiscent of our connection to the cosmos, but also of a certain mathematical essence common to each and every thing. At the pace of a pulsating sound resonating within a space without end or gravity, the film attempts to stop time and men, and reveals the ghost of a lost paradise.

In January 2017, I went to explore this tropical area in order to meet these families and their natural environment. I was confronted with the region's colonial past, strongly rooted in the exploitation of land and the development of a strong and ubiquitous agriculture, based on the western model imported by these families. While exploring the area, I was struck by the people's will to convey a pre-Columbian past, which was literally asking to rise out of the ground.

Every year during the rainy season, the Rio Filobobos that surrounds the area violently floods the lands and villages. For years, it has carted mundane objects of the pre- Columbian period from the mountain and regional territory: pottery, painted statuettes, and other artifacts and objects of worship that the inhabitants collect and keep in their homes. These ancestral remembrances literally wash up on the banks, and sometimes kneeling to the ground is enough to pick something up: fragments and other snippets of time past. Knowing the rules of the cosmos in order to find one's place in the world was at the heart of Amerindian wisdom—and this form wisdom was inseparable from the knowledge of agriculture such as the laws of nature, lunar calendars, seasonal cults ....

The film speaks of this memory, of a moment frozen

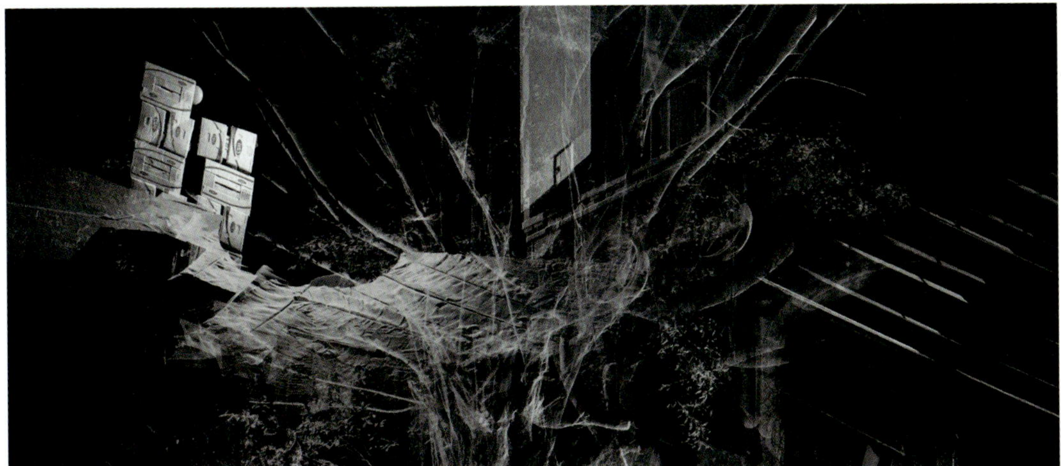

in time at the heart of Mexico, of a tropical microcosm that takes us through a form of archaeoastronomy.

Mathilde has long been interested in the anthropological dimension of the societies that she encounters through her work, but also in their relationship to the myths and cosmogony at the root of some of their beliefs.

Working from digital data, she uses a FARO scanner, a tool used in architecture to scan buildings. She installs this device on various sites and follows certain routes on the map, some of which she has tracked by foot to produce these stratified imyges, likened to "a kind of phantom map of the chosen site." Then, from the myriad of points thus obtained, she renders a three-dimensional landscape. Thanks to this process, Mathilde has obtained a superimposition of layers that gives her progression along these paths lined with banana trees the appearance of a voyage through appearances, in the most literal sense. Nature looks like a laminate of finely meshed films that connect different surfaces of reality, which are not necessarily related to one another in our ordinary experiences. The black and white shots could give the impression that the images were taken at night with infrared goggles except that here, the reversal of values and the greenish tone that characterize such images are precisely absent. The images give us the feeling of penetrating the structure of matter and reaching what usually remains invisible. With this work, we aren't invited to discover a landscape that we don't know but the very strangeness of the world of which it is only one element.

Direction, Edition and VFX: Mathilde Lavenne
Voices: Javier Grapin Cabrera, Sergio Eduardo Graillet Contreras, Martha Lilia Proal Bordonave, Margarita Lemus Pesqueda
Apparitions: Manuel Eusebio Rodriguez, Martin Bello Mendez, Maribel Mendez Vaca, Rosalia Mendez Delon, Carmen Perez, Jaquelin Ramos Mendez, Blanca Romero Mendez
Sound composition: Léonore Mercier
Sound design: Majordome
Sound Coordination at the Fresnoy: Blandine Tourneux
Sound mixing: Christian Cartier
Production: Elsa Klughertz / Jonas Films
Production assistant: Fanny Béguély / Jonas Films
Executive production: Carlos Couturier / Fundacion Casa Proal
Production coordinator: Michel Blancsubé
Graphic design: Lucie Baratte

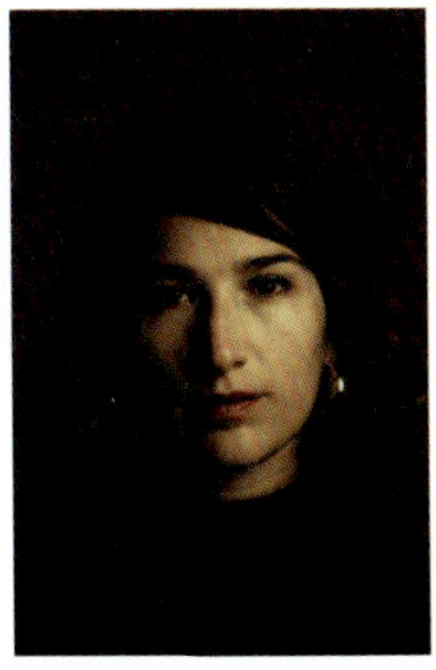

Mathilde Lavenne (FR), born in 1982, began focusing her artistic approach on emerging technologies and digital tools by writing short films and creating interactive installations in 2011. She received the SCAM's Pierre Schaeffer Prize in 2014 and the Contemporary Talents Prize from the François Schneider Foundation in 2015. She graduated from Le Fresnoy – Studio national des arts contemporains, with honors. Her short film *Focus on Infinity*, shot in Norway, was selected in many festivals such as Tampere Film Festival in Finland, Shnit International Shortfilmfestival in Switzerland or International Short Film Week in Regensburg. Her work was shown in France at the Palais de Tokyo, in Italy at the Villa Medici, at MADATAC in Spain. In 2018, she is selected to continue her researches for a year at Casa de Velázquez, Academy of France in Madrid.

Website

https://www.mathildelavenne.com/

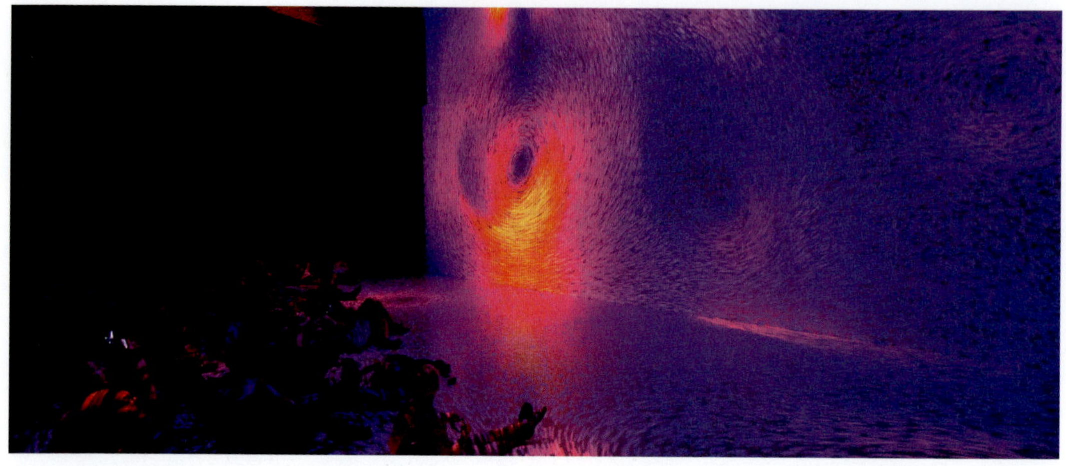

Turbulence

Turbulence is an ongoing series of immersive experiences created for large-scale, high-resolution media environments that embosom the viewer in digital flow of particles.

It's a set of visual experiments on particles simulated in different virtual environments. We turn the flat screen into a 3D virtual container where particles are set in motion using artificially simulated physical phenomena like wind or Coriolis force. We re-interpret data-sets acquired from other fields of interest to drive the simulations. We examine this technique as a way of visualizing data and we are seeking for more layers of visual correspondences between used data and results. The 3-part work screened at Ars Electronica Festival was created exclusively for Deep Space 8K.

Credits: MELT
Animation: Kuba Matyka & Kamila Staszczyszyn / MELT
Music: Urbanski

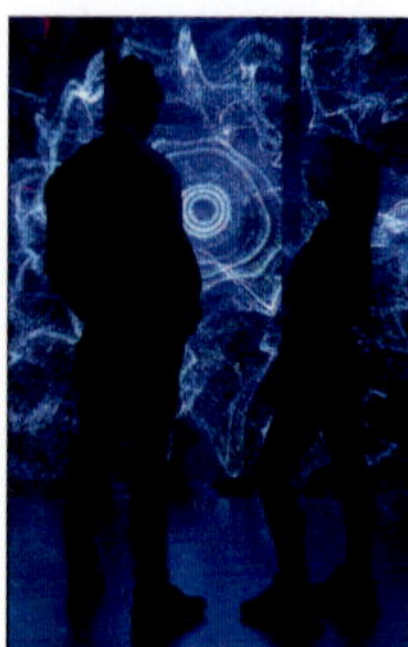

MELT (PL) is an award-winning studio creating unique experiences in every scale and form. Blurring the line between the real and virtual worlds, their works push media beyond limits to engage and astonish the audience. Their projects range from virtual & augmented reality worlds of adventures to massive scale multimedia spectacles and intimate interactive installations.

The studio is led by the duo of creative directors Kuba Matyka & Kamila Staszczyszyn, who were both honored in the New Europe 100–Financial Times's list of the most innovative change-makers in Europe in 2016.

Selected Awards

4x KTR (Design / Craft / Communication)

IAB MIXX EUROPE + 6x IAB MIXX POLAND

Adweek's Grand Arc & Best use of VR

4x Adobe Design Achievement Award

4x PGDA Polish Graphic Design Award

F5 "The Best of Polska"

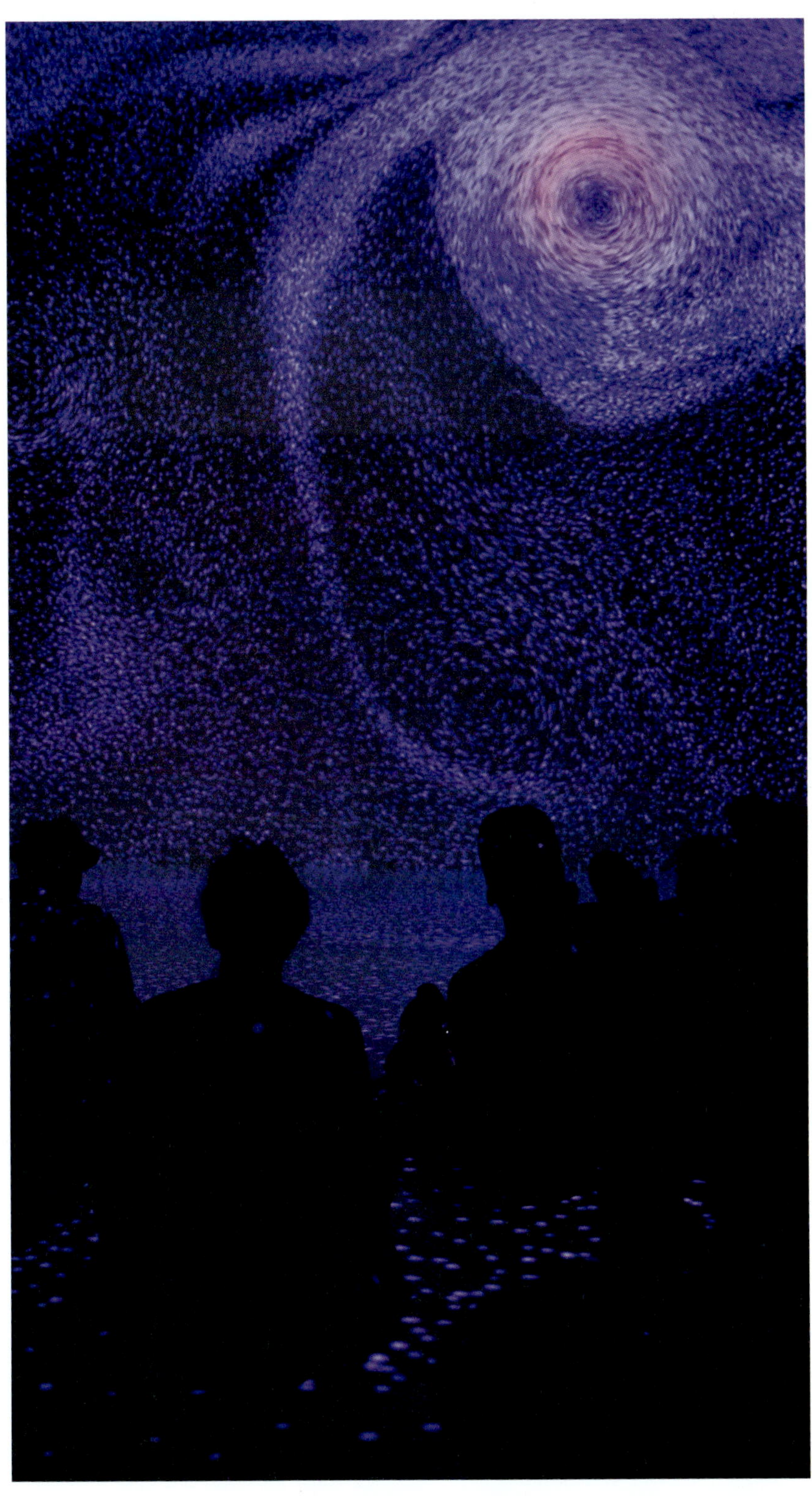

Turbulence

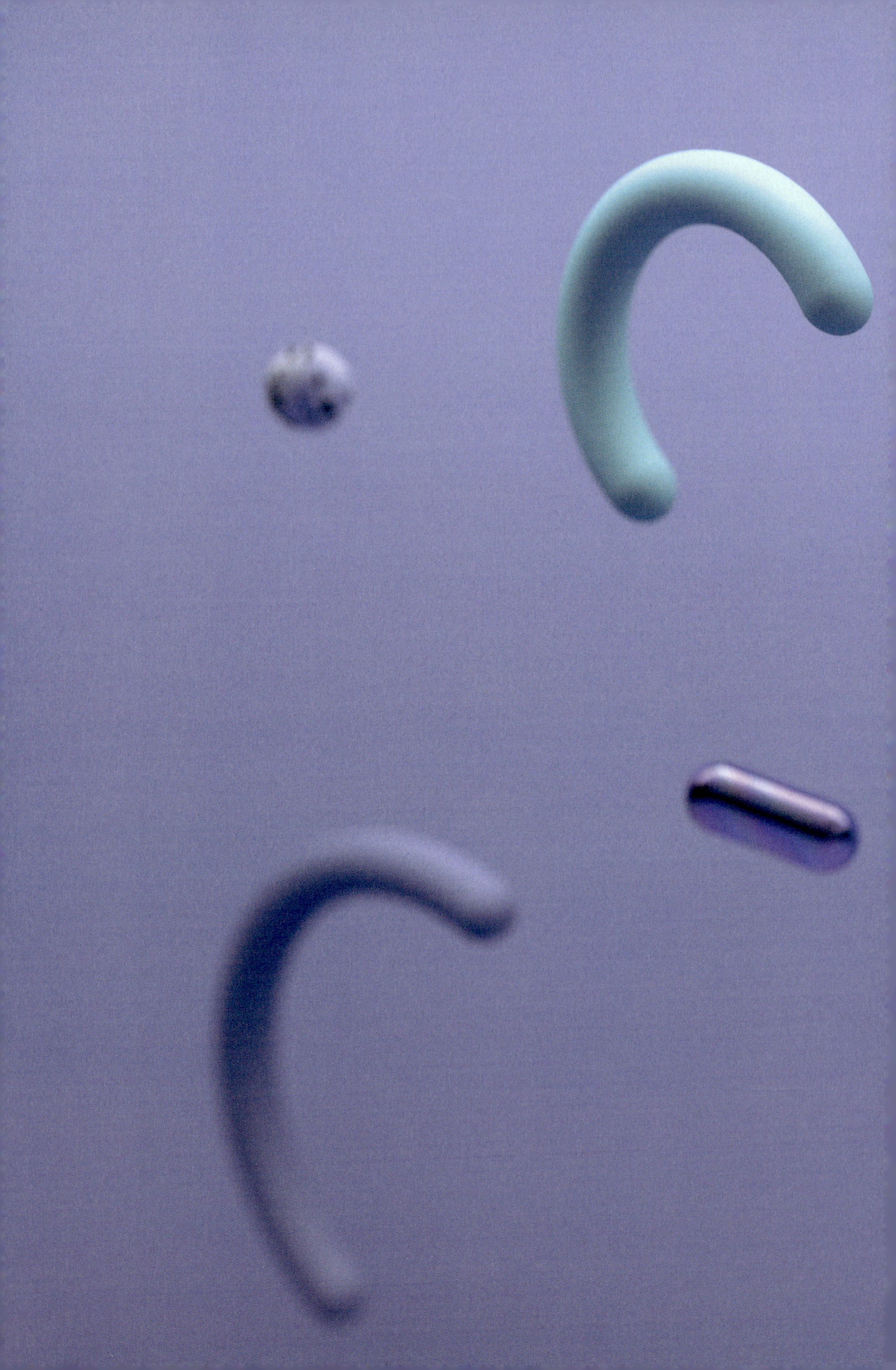

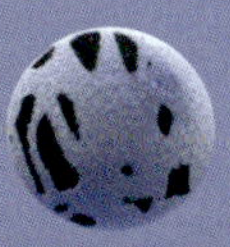

Contributors

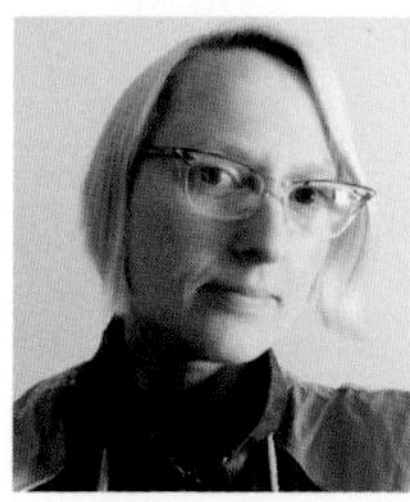

Abigail Addison, co-directs Animate Projects, a UK-based arts agency that champions creative animation practice, and produces ambitious inter-disciplinary projects, such as Silent Signal, with a range of partners. As a freelance producer she works with cultural organisations and individual artists on developing, producing and exhibiting experimental moving image projects. Abigail is a Trustee of film and photography charity Four Corners, and an advisor to Underwire Festival.

Diana Arellano obtained her BSc. and MSc. in Computer Sciences from the University Simon Bolivar (Venezuela), and her PhD from the University of the Balearic Islands (Spain) in 2012. Her main field of research was Affec-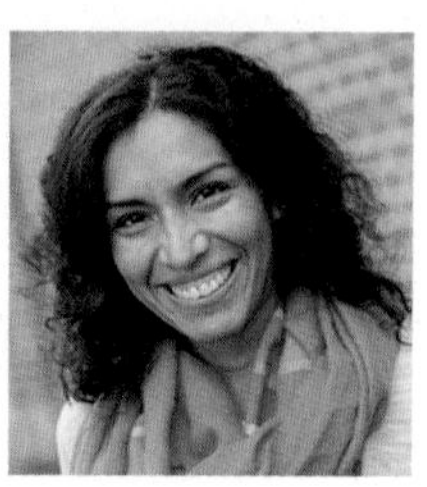 tive Computing, which she combined in later years with Machine Learning. During her time as Research Associate at the Filmakademie Baden-Württemberg (Germany), she was one of the coordinators of a German-funded project (SARA) focused on the generation of stylized character animations to study how autistic kids perceive emotions in other people's faces (2013–15). In her latest project on High-Performance Computing (2017), she researched on Machine Learning for Motion Synthesis in Animation. Currently, Diana works as Software Developer and Team Leader in the Pipeline Department at Mackevision Medien Design, in Stuttgart, Germany, a world-wide leading company in 3D car visualization and VFX.
Diana is also a long-time volunteer for ACM SIGGRAPH, where she started in 2007 as Student Volunteer for the SIGGRAPH conference. In 2012 she became member of the ACM SIGGRAPH International Resources Committee (IRC), becoming Chair of this committee in 2016. During her time in IRC she co-organized the events focused on the Latin America and Europe communities, as well as the popular panel "Women in CG". Diana is currently serving as ACM SIGGRAPH External Relations Chair, as well as member of the newly created ACM SIGGRAPH Diversity & Inclusion Committe.

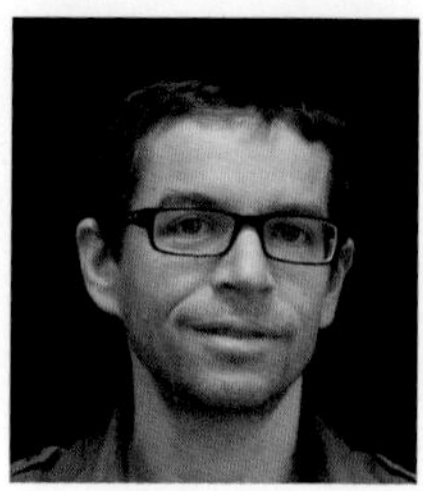

Reinhold Bidner studied at FH Salzburg, at Duncan of Jordanstone College of Art & Design (UK) and he finished his studies in Berlin. Until 2006 he was key researcher at Ars Electronica Futurelab Linz for time-based media. Since 2007 he is a freelancer in animation & media art, either as an individual or as a member of the art collective gold extra. He received various prizes, grants and residencies for his artistic work, and exhibits nationally and internationally since 2001. Currently Reinhold lives in Vienna & Salzburg and teaches at Art University Linz.

Franziska Bruckner, media scholar and Head of the Research Group Media Creation at St. Poelten University of Applied Sciences; curator and organizer of the international symposium series Ani-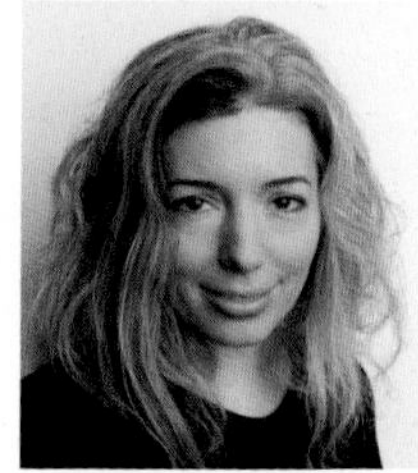 mafest Scanner. Co-coordinator of the working group Animation of the German Society for Media Studies and a member of the Executive Board of ASIFA Austria. She studied painting and animated film at the University for Applied Arts Vienna and Theater, Film, and Media Studies at the University of Vienna, where she worked as a University Assistant from 2009 to 2013 and earned her doctorate in 2017. She was a lecturer at Vienna University, the Eberhard Karls University Tübingen, and the University of Applied Sciences Upper Austria, Campus Hagenberg among others. Her research focuses on the history of animation in German-speaking countries, hybrids of animation and live-action films, animation in virtual and augmented environments, and the connection between art and film.

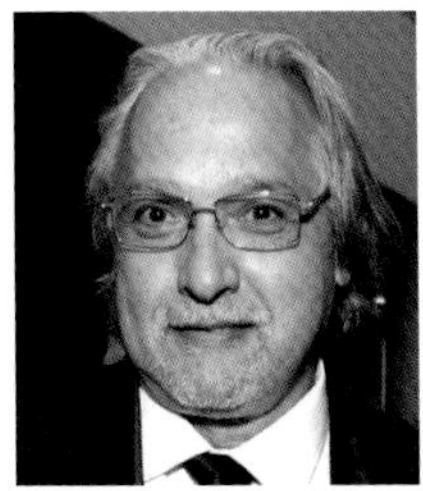

Mark Chavez, an award winning artist, has developed systems and techniques for animation in many different media including laser light (LaserMedia, 1980), television, games (Acclaim Entertainment, 1993) and feature films, that allowed him to work as an artist, supervisor and director. Recruited by DreamWorks SKG (1995), he worked on visual effects for a number of their fully animated films. At Rhythm and Hues Studios (2002) he worked on visual effects for numerous award winning live-action films. Recruited to join NTU/ADM (2005) as founding faculty, he has taught and mentored numerous students who have gone on to become award winning entrepreneurs. He was granted major funding from the National Research Foundation / Media Development Authority (2008) for research, the capstone of which is an award winning film, [Vengeance+Vengeance]. His exploration of Transmedia is the animated short film "The Adventures of Barty and the Pirate" and an accompanying mobile game "Barty Run".

Ina Conradi is an award-winning new media artist. Ina has exhibited and screened her works extensively: 2015 Currents New Media Festival, Paramount Studios, Hollywood, 2015 FMX Conference, Asia Animation Forum PISAF 2014, 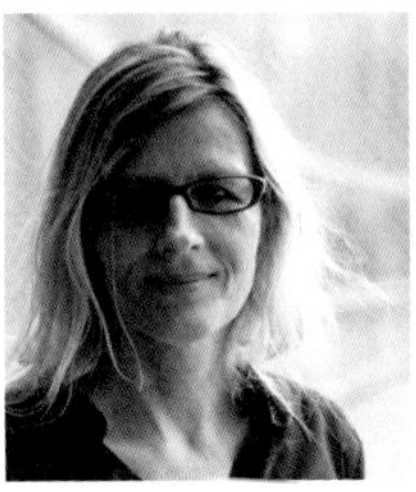 Korea, The International 3D festival Liège, Belgium, 3D Beyond Festival ZKM, Ars Electronica Festival, Siggraph Asia, the 67th Edinburgh International Film Festival. Ina holds Master's of Fine Art from UCLA. She is Associate Professor at the Nanyang Technological University Singapore where in 2015 she has been presented Koh Boon Hwee Scholars Award and Nanyang Education Award.

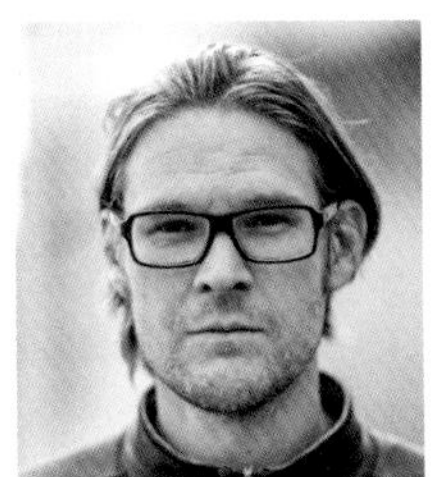

Juergen Hagler is an academic researcher and curator working at the interface of animation, game and media art. He studied art education, experimental visual design and cultural studies at the University for Art and Design in Linz, Austria. Currently, he is a Professor for Computer Animation and Media Studies in the Digital Media department at the Hagenberg Campus of the University of Applied Sciences Upper Austria. He has been involved in the activities of Ars Electronica since 1997 in a series of different functions. Since 2017 he is the director of the Ars Electronica Animation Festival.

Max Hattler is an artist and academic who works with abstract animation, video installation and audiovisual performance. He holds a master's degree from the Royal College of Art and a Doctorate in Fine Art from the University 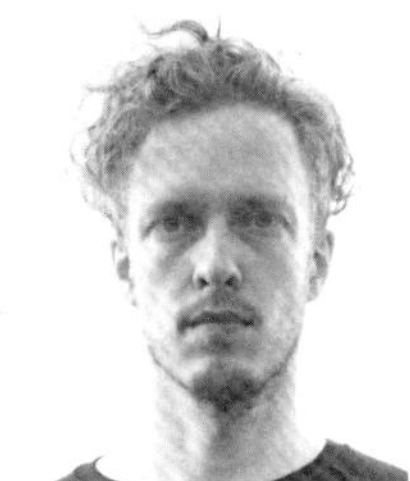 of East London. Max has lectured at CalArts, USC, Goldsmiths, KASK and many more. His work has been shown at festivals and institutions such as Resonate, Ars Electronica, ZKM Center for Art and Media, MOCA Taipei and Beijing Minsheng Museum. Awards include Supernova, Cannes Lions, Bradford Animation Festival and several Visual Music Awards. Max has performed live around the world including at Playgrounds Festival, Re-New Copenhagen, Expo Milan, Seoul Museum of Art and the European Media Art Festival. He lives in Hong Kong where he is an Assistant Professor at School of Creative Media, City University of Hong Kong. Max's current research focuses on synaesthetic experience and visual music, the narrative potential of abstract animation, and expanded artistic approaches to binocular vision.

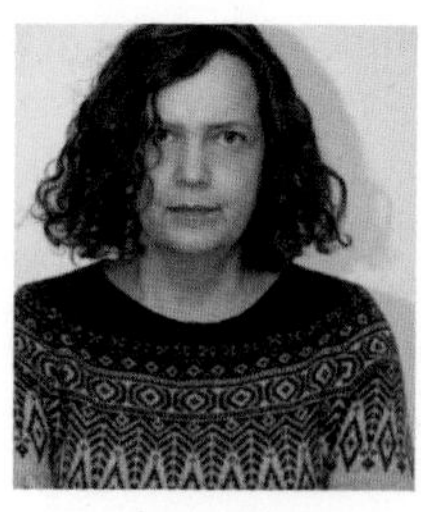

Birgitta Hosea is an artist and practice-based researcher who explores post-animation, performativity and hauntology through video installation, animated performance art and experimental drawing. She is Reader in Moving Image at the Animation Research Centre, University for the Creative Arts and Visiting Professor at the University of Chengdu. With a solo exhibition currently showing at the Hanmi Gallery in Seoul, other recent exhibitions include the Venice Biennale, the Karachi Biennale and Chengdu Museum of Contemporary Art.

Markos Kay is a visual artist, director and lecturer with a focus in art & science, digital abstraction and computational art. He is best known for his video art experiment aDiato-mea (2008), exhibited at Ernst Haeckel's Phyletic Museum,

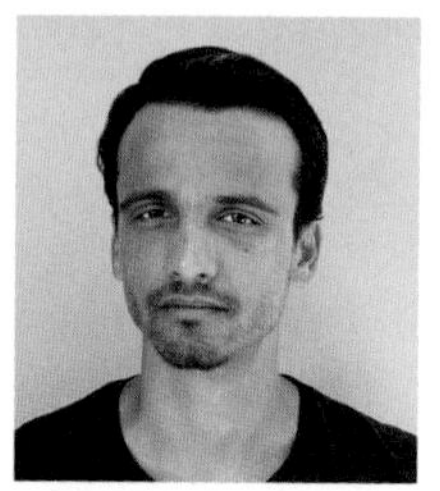

the conceptual visualisation The Flow (2011) and Quantum Fluctuations (2016), a visual interpretation of particle collisions. His work can be described as an ongoing investigation of the relationship between the digital and the physical through the use of computationally generative methods. The resulting experiments explore the emergence and complexity of nature and the digital sublime. His art and design practice ranges from screen-based media, to projection and print and has been featured worldwide in museums, exhibitions, film festivals and art publications

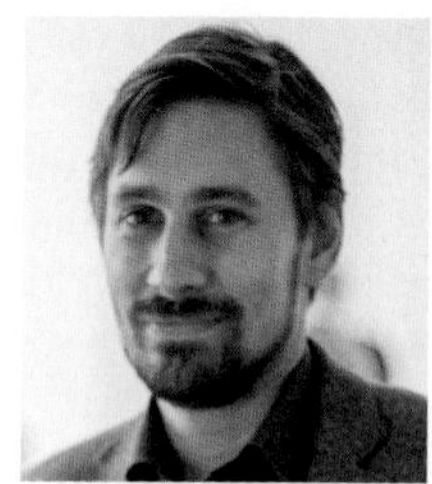

Michael Lankes is working as a professor at the Digital Media department of the Upper Austrian University of Applied Sciences focusing on the topics game art & design as well as usability & interaction design. His expertise ranges from serious games in the health domain to playful interactions supported by nonverbal communication channels. He is an active member in the games community in the context of HCI by organizing conferences. Lankes also gathered experience as a 3D artist and illustrator. Michael Lankes was involved in projects at the ICT&S Center Salzburg – PLUS – (now Center for HCI), the Ars Electronica Futurelab and at Sony.

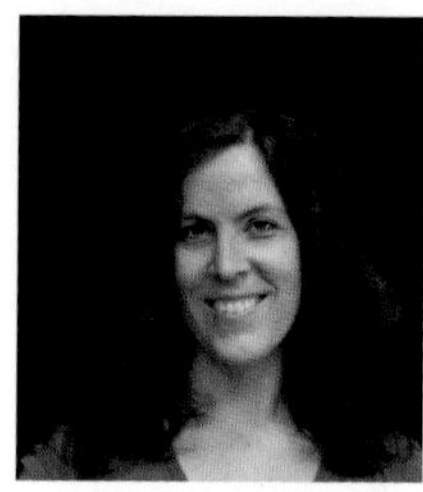

Sonja Prlić works as a media artist, director and dramaturge. She also is a senior scientist at University Mozarteum Salzburg. She is one of the founders of the artist group gold extra, with whom she realizes projects between theatre, media art and games. Her interest lies in the development of new forms for artistic games. She studied literature and dramaturgy and holds a PhD in science and arts. Her PhD on the topic of political art games has been awarded the Austrian Award of Excellence.

Stephan Schwingeler, born 1979, is professor for Media Studies at HAWK University of Applied Sciences and Arts. His first book deals with the topic of space in video games and is one of the first art historical publications in the field of

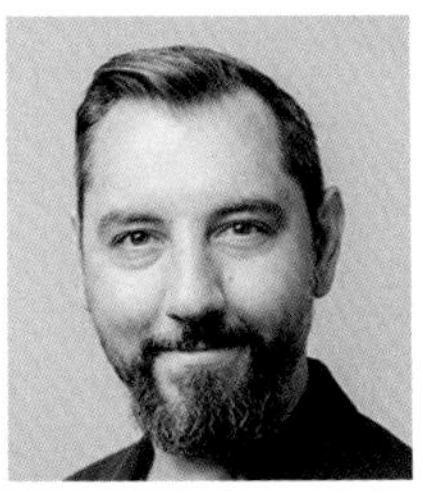

Game Studies. His Ph.D. thesis and second book examines the practices and strategies of Game Art and artistic video game modification from the perspective of art history and media theory. In the last couple of years he was also Professor for Game Design at mAHS Stuttgart and was responsible for running the GameLab at the Karlsruhe University of Arts and Design. Among other exhibitions and events he was responsible as a curator for the exhibition "ZKM_Gameplay" at the internationally renowned ZKM | Center for Art and Media in Karlsruhe. His exhibition "Global Games" presents videogames as political media. Based on "Global Games" the Goethe-Institut, in cooperation with ZKM, is currently touring worldwide through over 40 countries across the globe. Other curated exhibitions include "New Gameplay" at (Nam June Paik Art Center, South Korea), "Digital Games" (Ludwigforum, Aachen, Germany).

Indonesian-born **Anezka Sebek** has taught full time at Parsons in the MFA in Design and Technology program since 1999. She designs curricula in the BFA/MFA new media technologies such as virtual interaction (head-mounted

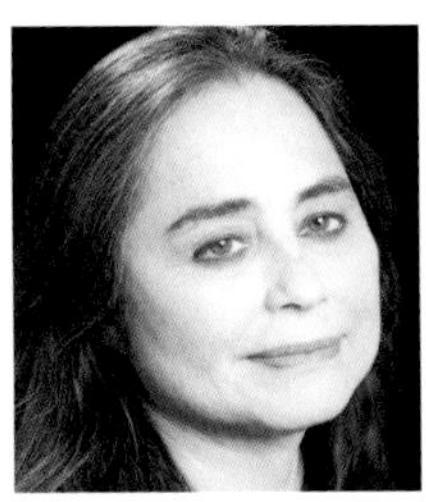

and projected) as well as teaching in the BFA/MFA in Design and Technology studio and thesis courses. Before turning to teaching, her extensive career in the film industry included projects for television, advertising, documentaries and feature films. She was best known as a visual effects and computer animation producer for technologically complex projects that combined live-action with digital effects. She has written, produced, and directed music videos, narrative shorts, and documentaries. Ms. Sebek served on juries for ACM Siggraph Electronic and Animation Theater (2003/04) and Ars Electronica (2008/09/11/13). She now furthers her study of the human condition at The New School for Social Research. Her Ph. D. dissertation

(2015) fieldwork looks at homeless women and children and the lack of educational and social mobility in post-industrial United States.

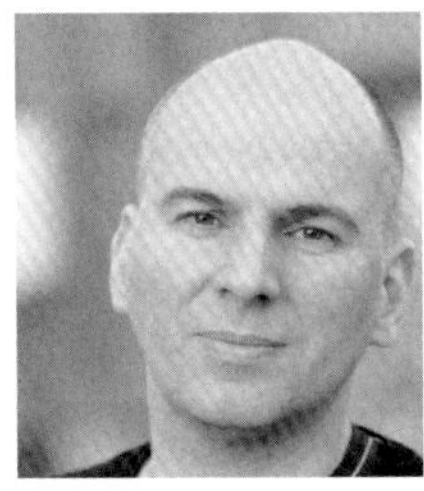

Ulrich Wegenast, born 1966 in Stuttgart. Master in History and History of Art at Stuttgart University (MA), postgraduate studies in Culture and Media Management (Arts Administration) at Hanns Eisler School of Music, Berlin. Since 2012 honorary professor at the School of Film & Television "Konrad Wolf" Potsdam-Babelsberg. 1987: founding member of Wand 5 and Stuttgart Filmwinter – Festival for Expanded Media, a festival for experimental film and media art. In 2001 development of the conference "media-space" He was member of the Wand 5-board until 2006. From 1993–2005 programme curator for the Stuttgart International Festival of Animated Film. In 2005 he became the artistic director of the Stuttgart Festival of Animated Film. In 2002 he developed the experimental film section for the Munich Filmfest. Curatorial work and jury work for the Goethe Institute and various other institutions and festivals around the world. From 2003 to 2004 he worked as a consultant for the Frankfurt Schirn Kunsthalle and 2005 for the documenta jubilee exhibition. 2005–13 member of the advisory board of the Goethe Institute (Film, TV, Radio), 2007–13 member of the jury of the German Short Film Award. From 2004–11 he was teaching Film/Media Art, Media Theory and Alternative Distribution at the Karlsruhe School of Design, Stuttgart State Art Academy and Merz Akademie in Stuttgart. Since 2005 he's head of the media department of the Baden-Wuerttemberg Free Art Academy. He has published a 6-part DVD edition on German animated film in cooperation with Absolut Medien, Berlin, and Goethe Institut, Munich which received the Willi Haas Award for best DVD-edition on German speaking film in 2012.

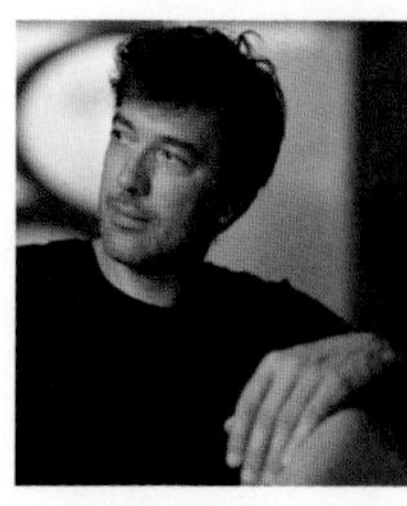

Virgil Widrich, born 1967 in Salzburg, works on numerous multimedia and film productions. He is one of the founders and managing directors of the multimedia company *checkpointmedia GmbH*, university professor of *Art & Science* at the University of Applied Arts Vienna and owner and managing director of *Virgil Widrich Film- und Multimediaproduktions GmbH*. His first feature film is Heller als der Mond (Brighter than the Moon). His short film Copy Shop won thirty-seven international awards and was nominated for the Oscar. Fast Film premiered in Cannes 2003 and won thirty-six awards until today. His most recent feature film is *Night of a 1000 Hours* (2016). In 2018 he directed his first music video, *Nena & Dave Stewart: Be my Rebel*. Virgil Widrich lives in Vienna.

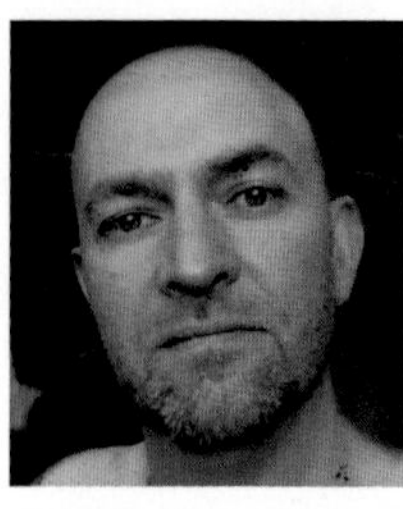

Alexander Wilhelm studied Industrial and Interaction Design at the UFG Linz and the ZHDK, Zurich. With his company "The Visioneers" he worked for clients like Audi and BMW for more then a decade in the field of interaction-design and visualisation. 2011 he became a professor for design and animation at the University of Applied Sciences Upper Austria, Hagenberg Campus. He also teaches at the UFG Linz 3D-Animation, Visualisation and 3D-Design.

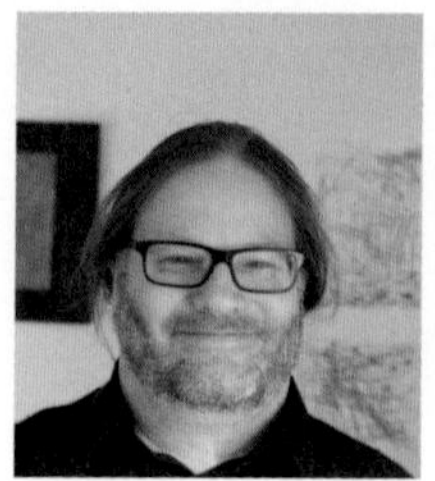

Karl Zechenter is an artist, director and curator living in Salzburg. He studied literature and political sciences at the University of Salzburg and is a founding member of the artist group gold extra focusing on interdisciplinary and media art works. Projects have been displayed by Nam Jun Paik Center, ZKM Karlsruhe, Games for Change, New York, and commissioned by the Humboldt Forum Berlin. He is co-leader in a basic artistic research project, teaches at the Graphics Department of University of Arts Mozarteum Salzburg and is head of the lobby group of all Salzburg art venues (DV).

Expanded Animation

ORGANIZERS

University of Applied Sciences
Elmar Glaubauf, Jeremiah Diephuis, Juergen Hagler, Michael Lankes, Christoph Schaufler, Patrick Proier, Alexander Wilhelm

Ars Electronica
Martin Honzik, Andrea Kohut, Veronika Liebl, Emiko Ogawa, Christina Radner, Gerfried Stocker

TRAILER

2018
Martina Stiftinger, Resonate

2017
Elmar Glaubauf, Victoria Wolfersberger

2016
Johannes Poell

2015
Joachim Dieplinger, Clemens Gaisbauer

2014
Johannes Poell, Markus König

TEAM

2018
Victoria Absmann, Martin Dorfer, Lisa Gierlinger, Santiago Hager, Fabian Kainz, Theresa Kammerhofer, Raphaela Klein, Andreas Köttl, Christoph Lendenfeld, Franziska Marinovic, Yvonne Marneth, Marleigh Pach, Matthias Patscheider, Max Penzinger, Nicole Rathmayr, Julian Salhofer, Astrid Wöhrer, Alessa Wolfram

2017
Victoria Absmann, Benedikt Blumenschein, Michael Brandt, Daniel Dietrich, Martin Dorfer, Marie Dvorzak, Florian Friedrich, Lisa Gierlinger, Kevin Gusztaf, Markus Hadinger, Michael Hammerer, Viktor Holzweber, Jasmina Huynh, Michael Klammer, Moritz Kubesch, Christoph Lendenfeld, Jacqueline Lowe. Lisa Mittermair, Raphaela Obermair, Paola Otero, Matthias Patscheider, Veronika Penz, Raffaela Pichler, Doris Rastinger, Julian Salhofer, Tobias Sichmann, Eric Thalhammer, Sarah Thiery, Kyra von Baeckmann

2016
Friedrich Bachinger, Benedikt Blumenschein, Martin Dorfer, Friedrich Florian, Florian Friedrich, Michael Hammerer, Daniel Hölbling, Verena Holzer, Sabrina Kainz, Alexander Köpplmayr, Daniel Lanner, Daniel Lanner, Christoph Lendenfeld, Veronika Penz, Philip Sonnleitner, Stefanie Zeilinger

2015
Friedrich Bachinger, Joachim Dieplinger, Clemens Gaisbauer, Lukas Holzer, Verena Holzer, Michael Loithaler, Monika Minichberger, Karin Pirklbauer, Isabella Samhaber, Teresa Timelthaler, Jan Winterauer, Stefanie Zeilinger

2014
Friedrich Bachinger, Georg Froschauer, Markus König, Thomas Manoila, Bermd Marbach, Katharina Maslowski, Johannes Poell, Manuela Salfer, Isabella Samhaber, Bernd Schmid, Lisa Thurnhofer, Teresa Timelthaler, Patrick Wagesreiter, Anne Zwiener

2013
Peter Affenzeller, Joachim Dieplinger, Clemens Gaisbauer, Philipp Gratzer, Christopher Lindner, Marc Muehlberger, Kristin Mueller, Hannah Oberherber, Manuel Preuss, Patrick Wagesreiter, Andreas Widder, Michaela Wiesinger

SPEAKERS

2013
Memo Akten (TR), Suzanne Buchan (CH/UK), Joe Gerhard (GB), John Gerrard (IR), Ruth Jarman (GB), Joreg (AT/DE), Friedrich Kirschner (DE), Quayola (IT), Karin Wehn (DE), Virgil Widrich (AT), Benjamin Wiederkehr (CH)

2014
Franziska Bruckner (AT), Csaba Letay (DE), Paolo Pedercini (IT), Fabian Pross (DE), Mario von Rickenbach (CH), Robert Seidel (DE), Tom Weber (DE), Ulrich Wegenast (DE)

2015
Sebastian Buerkner (DE/GB), Mark Chavez (US), Ina Conradi (SG/US), Pascal Floerks (DE), Devine Lu Linvega (CA), Erick Oh (KR), Johannes Poell (AT), Anezka Sebek (ID/US), Romain Tardy (FR), Alex Verhaest (BE)

2016
Abigail Addison (GB), Diana Arellano (DE/ES), Reinhold Bidner (AT), Manuel Casasola Merkle (DE), Erwin Feyersinger (AT/DE), Mihai Grecu (RO), Yuya Hanai (JP), Jonas Hansen (DE), Markos R. Kay (GB), Boris Labbé (FR), Marie Liis Rebane (EE), Johannes Friedrich Schiehsl (AT), Moritz Schwind (DE), Matthias Winkelmann (DE)

2017
Marieke Blaauw (NL), Nikita Diakur (DE/RU), Pablo Barquien (ES), Anna Diaz (ES), Max Hattler (DE/HK), Sabine Hirtes (DE), Cedric Kiefer (DE), Lev Manovich (US), Rafael Vangelis Mayrhofer (AT/GB), David OReilly (IE), Stephan Schwingeler (DE), Stefan Srb (AT), Martina Stiftinger (AT/GB), Eliot Woods (GB), Jonathan Yomayuza (US)

2018
Felix Bohatsch (AT), Vera-Maria Glahn (DE), Gerhard Funk (AT), Chunnung (Maggie) Guo (CN), Volker Helzle (DE), Birgitta Hosea (GB), Rainer Kohlberger (AT), Boris Labbé (FR), Leonhard Lass (AT), Mathilde Lavenne (FR), Kuba Matyka (PL), Henrik Mauler (DE), Sophie Mobbs (GB), James Paterson (CA), Hannes Rall (DE), Alex Verhaest (BE)

Expanded Animation received support from:

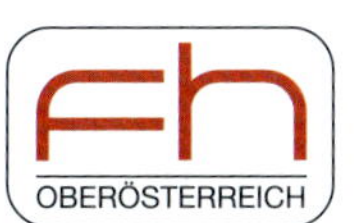 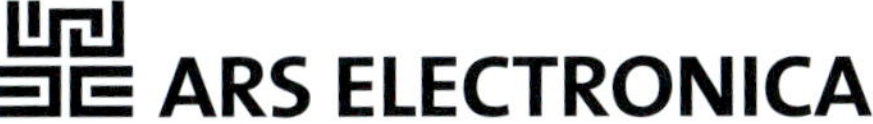

Supported by:

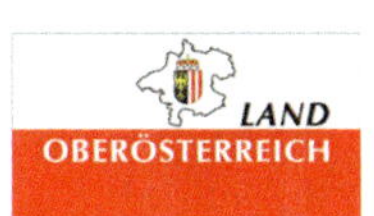 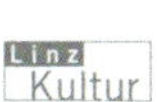 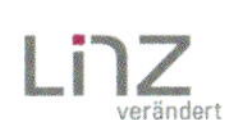

Symposium sponsored by:

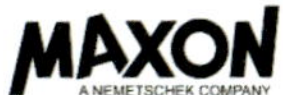 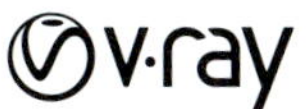 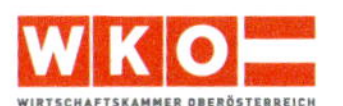 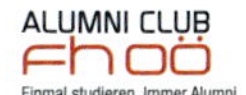

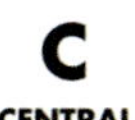 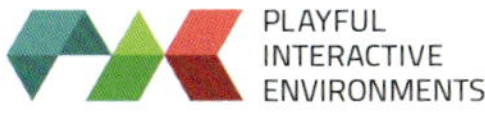 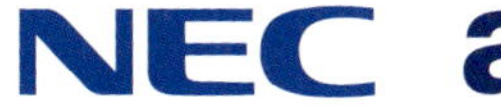 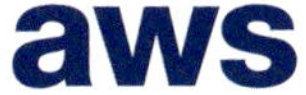